THE **HEYDAY** OF
MALCOLM MARGOLIN

THE HEYDAY OF
MALCOLM MARGOLIN

The DAMN GOOD Times

OF A FIERCELY INDEPENDENT PUBLISHER

Kim Bancroft

Heyday, Berkeley, California

The author and the publisher would like to thank Rina Margolin and Paul
Bancroft III for reading drafts of the manuscript and offering such good advice.

"Young Apple Tree, December" from *They Can't Take That Away from Me* by
Gail Mazur, © 2001 by The University of Chicago. Reprinted by permission of
the University of Chicago Press.

"The First Elegy," translation © 1982 by Stephen Mitchell; from *Selected Poetry
of Rainer Maria Rilke* by Rainer Maria Rilke, translated by Stephen Mitchell.
Used by permission of Random House, an imprint and division of Random
House LLC. All rights reserved.

Library of Congress Cataloging-in-Publication Data
Bancroft, Kim.
    The Heyday of Malcolm Margolin : the damn good times of a fiercely
independent publisher / Kim Bancroft.
        pages cm
    ISBN 978-1-59714-287-8 (pbk.)
    1. Heyday Books. 2. Margolin, Malcolm. 3. Publishers and publishing—
California—Berkeley. I. Title.
    Z473.H55B36 2014
    070.509794'67—dc23   2014008423

Cover Art: Yariki/shutterstock.com
Cover Design: Diane Lee
Interior Design/Typesetting: Leigh McLellan Design
Printed in Canada by Friesens

Orders, inquiries, and correspondence should be addressed to:
    Heyday
    P.O. Box 9145, Berkeley, CA 94709
    (510) 549-3564, Fax (510) 549-1889
    www.heydaybooks.com

10 9 8 7 6 5 4 3 2 1

CONTENTS

Malcolm musing at Kim Bancroft's cabin (PHOTO BY KIM BANCROFT)

PREFACE

"It's a habit of mine, a habit of mind, that I tell stories."
—MALCOLM MARGOLIN

WHAT MALCOLM MARGOLIN has created at Heyday has, by now, been recognized as a vital cultural institution for all of California, with Malcolm himself honored with a commendation from the chairman of the National Endowment for the Humanities. He initiated Heyday Books in 1974 to publish his book *The East Bay Out*. In 1978 the Heyday Books imprint served for Malcolm's now oft-reprinted *The Ohlone Way*. Since then, Heyday has flourished and transformed many times over. Now a nonprofit organization simply called "Heyday," Malcolm's company publishes twenty-five books a year focused on California's literature, history, natural history, and cultural studies, along with a significant journal of California Indian writing, *News from Native California*.

In the process of working on this book, I was deeply moved to learn about the many significant contributions that Heyday and its associates have made to California's arts, sciences, humanities, and communities. Truth be told, I started out just wanting a good excuse to hang out with Malcolm and listen to his stories.

I've known Malcolm since 1996, when his daughter, Sadie, was in my English class at Merritt College in Oakland. One day Sadie told me that her father wanted to speak to me about all those marks I was putting on her essays. No, she conveyed, he didn't want to complain about my grading; he wanted to hire me as an editor if I was interested. In our meeting, Malcolm said that he liked how I prodded a writer in the margins, asking good questions to develop the piece. He put me to work helping Darryl "Babe" Wilson on what would become Babe's memoir, *The Morning the Sun Went Down*, and so began a lasting friendship between Babe and me.

Though I eventually returned to a focus on teaching, I finally decided to leave classrooms behind, after nearly thirty years, in favor of writing and editing manuscripts, especially memoirs. When I encountered Malcolm again in October of 2011, I asked, "When are you writing *your* memoir?"

"Oh, I've written a few stories down about my childhood and family that I wanted my kids to have," he told me. But the time he might spend writing about himself typically yielded to a never-ending stream of pressing commitments and gratifying events competing for his attention.

"Let me record you telling stories, then," I suggested. After all, I thought, what can be more fun than getting this whimsical and perceptive raconteur to open his knapsack full of tales? And, perhaps as a great-great-granddaughter of a historian, archivist, and collector of oral histories himself, Hubert Howe Bancroft, it's in my blood to preserve the life experience of an important person in our state's history.

Malcolm agreed to let me record his stories. Thus we began, as he said, "staggering around" in his reminiscences and ruminations. Anyone who knows Malcolm can imagine why a book about him and Heyday would be delightful, but the uninitiated will also be intrigued by this truly unusual character, the company he keeps, and the company he has created.

Over the course of a year and a half, I conducted twenty-two interviews with Malcolm alone, and forty-eight interviews with Malcolm's family and friends, and with Heyday staff, board members, and authors. Everyone was generous in their praise of both Heyday and Malcolm. This book, then, represents only a fraction of hundreds of pages of transcripts, pared down to focus on the life of Malcolm and the work of Heyday. I've inevitably had to leave out many stories of those who contributed to or benefited from Heyday, including many of Malcolm's stories about his prolific throng of important friendships and unusual encounters.

This book aims to highlight the many wonderful people who have been part of Heyday's history, from Malcolm's family (his wife, Rina, and their three children), to the writers who bring in their ideas and see them blossom into books, to the employees who help make those books come to life, to the friends and associates who contribute to Heyday's cultural offshoots and its nonprofit board. Proud of the multitudes who have helped Heyday succeed over the years, Malcolm sought to insure that as many of *their* voices as possible were integral to this history.

I myself was inspired while listening to those whose work has wrought beautiful books and meaningful organizations. The voices here reveal how a business can be developed and persist in which employees feel their own power and purpose in collaborating with one another on an equal footing, a business founded on *doing right* by others. The interviews also demonstrate the courage and humility of a man who has stepped outside what would be the comfort zone for many of us in order to travel into other cultures and communities and make deep connections there. I came to admire the creativity and tenacity not only of Heyday's founder but also of those who write or work for Heyday, for *News from Native California*, for the various Heyday-associated organizations, and for the board of Heyday itself.

Malcolm speaks in the book of seeing his role in publishing as one of bridge building, reaching out and taking risks to build connection across communities, to take risks with the books he brings into print. Like those I interviewed, I learned from Malcolm about having a more generous attitude about life and human foibles, as he so generously laughs at his own. His oldest companion at work, Jeannine Gendar, a Heyday editor for over twenty years, said of Malcolm, "I remember that he used to joke when something went wrong and say, 'Well, it's all *my* fault.' But in reality, he *was* always willing to let the buck travel to him and stop there, which was a very fine thing."

Malcolm's willingness to take a risk included this project, which required a great deal of faith and trust on both our parts as we engaged in exchanging stories. During the first year of our work on the book, I was undergoing dramatic changes in my life, including moving to a cabin in California's northern woods, where I was starting my life over as an editor and writer. Malcolm visited me in the redwoods on an evening following a cold and cloudy day, so our interview that night took place by candlelight in my solar-disempowered abode and by the fire of my woodstove, with

Malcolm sharing his stories and listening to my own. Malcolm once said of listening to stories, "I love being warmed by other people's fires." Wherever he goes, he listens deeply and compassionately, sometimes sharing a story that provides both comic relief and insight—and builds connections.

Some of that compassion that Malcolm conveyed in our interviews is lost in the written excerpts here. There were many times when his voice broke and he barely contained his tears as he spoke about heartbreaking moments in his life and those of his friends: the remembered affection of a long-lost uncle; the pain of enduring his baby's dire illness; the hardships a Native elder felt in retrieving precious artifacts stolen for a museum in Russia; Malcolm's joy in officiating at the marriage of an employee.

Also lost in the written excerpts is the raucous laughter emanating from our conversations, not to mention the many times laughter from Heyday staff floated from the back rooms and onto the recordings. Several times, I recorded Malcolm asking me, "Are you aware of the laughter? I love it!"

Yet Malcolm's love for what he does and for the people in his life comes through on every page, as does the love returned. Malcolm's delight in others' pleasure and success is another form of his infectious generosity. "I love to see people prosper. I love it when the best comes out in somebody. I just think that's so beautiful."

This Heyday book has, to some extent, taken the form of what Malcolm called "island hopping." Among the islands presented here, some ecological consistencies are clear: the presence of a man who is as serious as he is irreverent, as private as he is open, as strong a leader as he is anti-authoritarian. On more than one occasion, humble Malcolm growled about the contradictions inherent in creating a book about his life and his own successes, the process as uncomfortable as it was revealing. But with our English degrees embedded in us, we could each recite to the other Whitman's reminder: "Do I contradict myself? Very well then, I contradict myself. I contain multitudes." And Malcolm certainly does.

ACKNOWLEDGMENTS

I THANK SADIE MARGOLIN COSTELLO for coming into my life—and bringing her father with her. Deep gratitude to Malcolm for letting me warm myself at the hearth of his stories and encouraging me to collect those of Heyday. Pete Bancroft merits thanks for helping us think through an earlier version of the book. Thanks to Rina Margolin for sharing her family stories, photos, and editing expertise. To our editor Gayle Wattawa, thank you for your kind and wise guidance as Malcolm and I wrestled all these stories onto the pages ahead. And thanks to Jeannine Gendar, Diane Lee, Ashley Ingram, and Leigh McLellan for their hard work in creating yet another beautiful Heyday book.

CHAPTER 1

MALCOLM, FROM EAST TO WEST

"There are so many stories from those early years!
It was so rich." —MALCOLM MARGOLIN

HOW DID A Jewish kid growing up in Boston in the 1940s end up immersed in the natural history and Native lifeways of California by the 1970s? Here Malcolm Margolin recounts stories of his family, youth, education, early work, and the eventual travels that brought him and his wife to California.

GROWING UP IN DORCHESTER

I was born on October 27, 1940, in Boston. I was once young, and I still like being young.

My father, Max, was born in the United States, just barely so. My mother, Rose, claimed to have been born in Russia, but I think she was actually born in Lithuania. She may have been putting on airs, or maybe that part of Lithuania had been part of Russia. She and her parents spoke only a Russishe Yiddish, rather than a Litvak Yiddish. I was always so amazed at my grandparents who had lived for fifty years in the United States and couldn't speak English. Now I find myself living for fifty years in the computer age and barely knowing how to use computers. I think I know now what they were doing: they lived in a daydreamy world, nested in their own truth. They were humble, religious people who lived in their own minds.

My brother, Bill, was born in 1946. Even though we were six years apart, we were close as kids. I remember him following me around. We played a lot together. I was lonely as a kid, so he was a friend. I helped him learn to play chess, and we played together. He stayed closer to home over

Malcolm's parents, Max and Rose, on their wedding day
(MARGOLIN FAMILY COLLECTION)

the years than I did, from attending the synagogue to working at the local settlement house in Boston.

The first home I remember was an apartment house in Dorchester where the four of us lived, at 82 American Legion Highway, opposite Franklin Park, near Blue Hill Avenue, which was called Jew Hill Avenue. It was an almost entirely Jewish neighborhood—only one non-Jewish family lived there. I thought the whole world was Jewish. That was a big part of my upbringing, and it's still a huge part of my identity. I've left the belief structure behind, but something remains in the tonality, in how I

Malcolm's maternal grandparents, Rebecca and Samuel
(MARGOLIN FAMILY COLLECTION)

feel about myself, something to do with that older memory of living in that neighborhood.

The apartment house that we lived in had four floors, with four apartments per floor. There was a coal-burning furnace down below and a kind of slummy backyard. I remember my mother and me looking out the back window into this yard. People ask me how I got into natural history, especially how somebody from a neighborhood like this got into natural history. It started with a Yiddish natural history. We had two kinds of birds: *faigels* and *faigelehs*. The big birds—pigeons—were the *faigels* and the little birds—

the sparrows—were the *faigelehs*. My mother would see the little birds going *boorvis*, "barefoot," in the snow, and their little feet would be cold! My mother worried about their little feet being cold, so she'd make them a *shissel*, a saucepan, of milk and hot Jewish bread. She'd heat up the bread and throw it out the window into the backyard. It would hit the snow, but because it was hot, it would burrow down into the snow. The little birds would peer down into the hole at this hot bread, steaming away in a well of snow, that they couldn't get to!

On the one hand, the whole thing was ridiculous, but it was so filled with love. You wouldn't get this knowledge from other natural histories, that birds and we are the same creatures, that they love good Jewish bread, that they shouldn't go barefoot in the snow.

I have early memories from the years during and after the war. It was so long ago that there were people alive who remembered the Civil War: veterans of the Grand Army of the Republic, Civil War spinsters, blacks who had been born into slavery. That old world was still present.

Back then, milk was delivered in a horse-drawn cart. We were a superior family because we had Hood's milk, as opposed to people who had Whiting's milk. Hood's milk tasted so much better. I just couldn't understand how people could drink that Whiting's stuff! The milkman had these metal racks in which he'd place the bottles, and you could hear the bottles clinking against the metal racks as the milk was delivered to your house.

During the war we had a Victory garden. Here's this bunch of urban Jews with absolutely no idea how to plant anything, but we were very patriotic, so we had a Victory garden. My job was to gather the horseshit because we knew that horseshit was good for the soil. I'd go down American Legion Highway with my shovel and pail after all the horse-drawn carts that had passed, and I'd bring the horseshit back to Frieda Sands, who would stick it on the soil in our building's garden. I'm not sure if anything ever grew.

Frieda was my mother's best friend. They'd known each other from the age of three and came from the Old Country together. Frieda had married Sam Sandofsky, who'd changed his name to Sam Sands. Sam Sandofsky—this was true wealth! Now you're going to be so impressed you're going to fall off your seat. Brace yourself! He was a fur cleaner. People's wealth was in their fur coats, and Sam cleaned the fur coats and put them in storage. He had warehouses full of fur coats. He'd earned this great trust with the old Russian wealth.

Frieda's mother lived in the apartment next to ours. We called her *Bubbe*, Grandma. Bubbe Hurwitz was one of the few people who came down through the back door which led into the kitchen. She'd come into the kitchen, sit at the table, and have a *shtikel*, a little piece, of herring and some *shvartz brot*, black bread, or a bialy or challah or some *bulke* or something like that. There she'd sit and sip tea.

Sometimes there'd be a knock on the back door. You'd open up to find a gaunt figure from the concentration camps. This guy had one eye that'd been blown out and a wad of cotton in its place. And he had the tattoo. He used to sell pencils. We'd always buy a pencil even if we didn't need pencils; it was your duty to buy pencils from this person.

Bruchas, prayers, were said over everything: prayers over the first food of the day, the first time you saw a child that day, the first sunset, or the first sunrise. There were hundreds of prayers. My friend Steve Sanfield reminded me of one in particular for when you saw somebody crippled or in great pain or wounded by life. It was translated, "Blessed art thou, Lord our God, King of the Universe, who delights in variety."

My grandparents kept kosher, but we didn't—not entirely. We wouldn't eat pork or shellfish, or mix meat and milk, or anything like that. We had four sets of dishes because you had to have four sets of dishes, but it wasn't as strict in our home as it should have been. My parents reveled in their cheating on keeping kosher. They reveled in being modern, yet they weren't modern people in the least. My father became much more modern as time went on.

CHILDHOOD HEROES

My father's father died when he was two years old. His original name was Bauer or Blauer, something like that, which should have been my name. But my father's mother, Bessie, remarried to a guy named Velvel Margolin, a tailor. Velvel and Bessie then had three more sons, my father's half-brothers. These were my heroic uncles: Milty, Jack, and Sammy.

I was fascinated by them all. As a young man, Sammy had a motorcycle and a girlfriend named Edith with long blond hair. Every fall, they'd get on that motorcycle and stop by on their way to Florida, with the girlfriend's hair waving in the wind. It was so romantic, so wonderful!

Sam married Edith, but very young he got multiple sclerosis. Edith had opened a little yarn shop. Sam would sit in the bare back room of the shop in a wheelchair. I'd sit beside him, and we'd listen to the baseball game together.

Jack was my hero. He was a boxer. When I was a kid, Jack gave me my favorite book of all time: Bill Stern's *Favorite Boxing Stories*. They were all the same story with different names, always a heroic quest. A baby was born that weighed only one ounce. Everybody thought the baby was going to die because the baby couldn't eat anything. It was bitten by a rat. The baby had a lousy childhood; the mother was poor. But this baby had spirit! This baby had vision! This baby grew up to be *Jack Dempsey*. The name changed, but the story was always the same, a story I never tired of. It was the Horatio Alger story, the Abraham Lincoln story, the story of somebody making it from poor origins.

My fondest memory of Jack was that he would babysit for me. He was muscular, strong. The fact that I was Jack's nephew gave me free passage anywhere I went because Jack was a *fighter*. He was charismatic and handsome. When Jack would babysit for me, we'd go up to Franklin Park opposite the house and take walks. Jack would take me to a mound there in the park. It must have been a bunker of some kind. There was a groove in the mound and a door at the end of it. Jack would grab me under his arms, and we'd jump over that ditch. I always imagined that behind that door lived a witch who emerged from the center of the world. I even saw the door open once, and this witch looked out at me. But I was in Jack's arms, jumping over this chasm—I was safe. We'd do it so often. It became a metaphor in later years: I felt that when I died, if I had been bad, I'd be dropped into that ditch, and the witch would get me, but if I was good, I'd sail over in my uncle Jack's arms.

Later on, Uncle Jack had a messy divorce from his wife; then he married somebody we didn't know, and he was alienated from the family. Her family owned a junkyard, and Jack worked there. Eventually, he got a stroke, so he was crippled. Nobody ever saw him, and he finally died.

I always thought about how that memory was locked in me, the extent to which we all have memories that are our own private memories and that become the last witness of something. Jumping over the ditch was so damn wonderful! I always thought that it was so wonderful to me but probably didn't mean anything to Jack.

Many years later, for my parents' fifty-fifth wedding anniversary, I returned to Boston for their party. I knew everybody except for a strange, crude woman sitting there, smoking cigarettes. I approached her and asked who she was. It was Jack's new wife, Debbie. She said she'd really wanted to meet me, that Jack used to tell her a story about us jumping over a ditch.

Milt was also a good guy. For a while he was an overcoat salesman; then he went from job to job. I always thought he worked in stolen goods. There was something both charming and shifty about him. It was a great sin in my childhood to buy retail. You had to know somebody in the business, and Milt always knew somebody in the business. To actually go into a store and buy something was a mark of being inconsequential. There were various crimes: being a fussy eater was a great crime; not having "card sense" and buying retail were great crimes.

So those were my father's brothers, great men. But I modeled myself after my father. Whenever I hear my voice on the radio or someone records my voice, I'm always amazed that it's my father's voice.

I remember once I was with Mahatma Gandhi's grandson Ramchandra Gandhi. He was talking about how difficult it was to have the name Gandhi and be Mahatma Gandhi's grandson, because people expected so much of him. Then he said to me, "But you wouldn't understand that."

I said, "No, I understand perfectly. I was Max Margolin's son! I understand exactly what it means." I had this sense of my father as a huge, great person. I don't think others considered him that way, but I certainly did.

I think that when my father was young, he was shy, but he grew out of it. He was a good storyteller, and he ended up being a very good businessman. He worked at the Boston and Taunton Transportation Company, which was run by this old guy named Louie Sagansky. My mother had worked there, too, which is how they met. They had eight trucks that went from Boston to Providence, Taunton, Fall River, and New Bedford.

Louie Sagansky was one of the great men of my life. Louie would arrive in the morning and smoke cigars. Then his buddies would come in, and they'd go to the ball game. They had an alcoholic mechanic named Happy, so none of the trucks ever worked. But still Louie went out; he'd go to the ball game and bring the manager of Thom McAn shoes to the ball game, things like that. My mother used to tell this story: During the Depression, everyone was earning so little money. They were all scrimping, barely hanging onto their jobs. But Louie comes in and pulls up the cuff of his pants, and he asks, "Guess how much these socks cost?"

They looked and said, "How much?"

And he said, "Ten dollars."

They were all amazed they worked for someone with ten-dollar socks. It redounded to Louie's glory that he had ten-dollar socks.

His brother was Doc Sagansky, a gangster and a bookie, well known in Boston at the time. The trucking company always had these bookies and other people hanging around. It was this old Damon Runyon world of people just hanging around. Such characters! I remember one of the bookies, Benny Abrams, but they called him Benny the Camel. He was this big towering guy, about six feet, ten inches tall and four hundred pounds. He had a bald head with two tumorous lumps on it, so he was called Benny the Camel because he looked like a two-humped camel. One day he comes in and he says, "I've changed my name to Benny Ford."

My father says, "Why did you do that?"

He says, "I thought I was too conspicuous."

I just thought that was so funny.

One time I went to see my father at work. Louie had been stood up. He said to me, "Kid, you want to go to the ball game?"

I replied, "Go to the ball game?"

"Yeah," he said.

Go to the ball game with Louie! Louie had a big Cadillac. I got into the Cadillac with the great man himself. We take off. He was just *speeding* down the streets of Boston. It was a time when you *could* speed down the streets of Boston. If a cop stopped you, you'd slip the cop five or ten bucks and get out of it. So Louie was speeding. He looked down at me and said, "You're scared, kid, aren't you?"

I said, "N-n-n-n-no!"

He said, "Yeah, I can see that you're scared. But let me tell you something: with so many nuts on the road, the faster you get off, the safer you are."

We got to the ball game, and he bought me a non-kosher hot dog. There was little Malcolm sitting with Louie Sagansky! We sat there like friends, like comrades.

Finally, the Red Sox came out onto the field, and running onto left field was Ted Williams, *the* Ted Williams I'd heard on the radio, the *real* Ted Williams. Not a picture of Ted Williams, or an account of Ted Williams. I couldn't take my eyes off him for the whole nine innings that he played. Every move that he made was just so beautiful.

Years later I was in the Temple of Tirupati in Andhra Pradesh, India, pushing through the narrow underground corridors of the temple with my daughter and a couple of my friends. For four hours we were in this crowd heading toward the inner sanctum. People were chanting, "Govinda," and pushing each other. It was the stuffy, claustrophobic bowels of the temple.

Suddenly you came to the inner sanctum, with a horseshoe aisle and the divinity Balaji at the far end. People just stopped and looked, and they seemed transformed in the looking. They gave their *prasad*, the offering to the god. Then the priest would come and take the offering and prod people to move them along. Quickly we'd be pushed out.

Outside, all the *prasads*, all the food, the offerings, had turned into slush on the ground. It was smelly, and you were ankle-deep in filth. Everybody walked around in a daze, as if transformed. I asked my friend Sheshadri, "What was that all about?"

He said it was the *darshan,* the exchange of a glance between a god and a human being. People come for that *darshan,* for the viewing and for that exchange of glances, the exchange of power. He said, "I don't think there's anything like it in the West."

I said, "Oh, yes, I once had a *darshan* with Ted Williams."

My father was Louie Sagansky's heir apparent. He had risen to general manager of the Boston and Taunton Transportation Company. When Louie died, my father was supposed to have been left at least a share of the company in his will. Maybe Louie had told him this; I'm not sure what happened. But instead of leaving it to my father, Louie left it to his son, Albert Sagansky, and to his son-in-law, Lenny Lewin, which I can understand.

Lenny had gone to Harvard Business School. Lenny Lewin immediately fired Happy. Every year Louie would go down to the Mack truck dealer, lay some cash on the table, and buy a truck, but Lenny stopped paying cash for trucks. He did it on credit and used the money to extend the trucking rights to other places. My father was convinced that the whole place would go broke, because the trick was that you take people to the ball game. That was how you did business; you run it on personality; you run it on who you know. He left what he saw as a sinking ship, surprised and perplexed to his dying day that Albert Sagansky and Lenny Lewin turned the Boston and Taunton Transportation Company into a major enterprise.

So then my father and his friend Henry Kantzer became freight brokers for containerized shipping. They got into it early and made a fair amount of money. He'd rent the whole container, then he'd sell space in it to people who had less than container-load quantities. He made out handsomely. I mean we weren't rich rich, the way rich people are rich, but for that world we became prosperous.

We'd go to the beach in the summertime, to Nantasket, a place called the Court, which had a horseshoe-like arrangement of twelve little apartments around the edge. People sat around the middle on lawn chairs. It was so damn crowded, but people loved to live in these crowded conditions. Every night, the men would play poker and the women would play casino or canasta or mah-jongg. Mah-jongg was always a mystery to me. I loved the sound of the tiles, the three bam, four whack, or whatever it was.

Malcolm, early bicycle enthusiast, age three, 1943
(COURTESY OF BILL MARGOLIN)

And the laughter! Every night there would be barbecues and laughter. I still remember all those families. I could tell you who lived in each of those apartments over the years, because people came back to the same place. Those summers were a good break from the city.

Running off Blue Hill Avenue in Dorchester was Woodrow Avenue, with three little *shtetl*-like synagogues for the orthodox. One synagogue wouldn't speak to the other. My mother's brother-in-law Sam was president of the Woodrow Avenue *shul*. I remember once years later when one of Sam's daughters, Elsie, came over when my mother was in her nineties to do a family tree. I thought it was going to be the most boring thing in the world, about this family of dull people I'd been dragged to visit and hang out with on Sundays. But when my mother went through our family tree, it was full of people who died, kids who died, the influenza epidemic, people who had been widowed, separated, and remarried. It was so filled with pain and tragedy.

When Elsie left, my mother looked at me and said, "This should probably die with me in my grave, but when Sam married my sister Ida, we found out he had left a family behind in Russia, and we ended up having to annul that marriage. I don't know whether the kids know it or not."

No wonder they were all so crazy! The amount of pain they floated over was so great.

Then there was the other world newly forming. I remember when we went over to my cousin Edith's house once, and she had made Jell-o. We looked at this most amazing thing—canned fruit floating in Jell-o! It was the most beautiful thing I'd ever seen in my whole life, a work of art.

What was especially beautiful was that she'd gotten the recipe from a *magazine*. These things called magazines provided an entrée into the whole of modern life. The house was always filled with magazines: *Life, Collier's, Look, Saturday Evening Post*. The magazines had wonderful pictures in them, like from *National Geographic*, so you could have this other life.

My father loved to read. He went to Boston Latin School, and then to Harvard for one year. He got a scholarship, but he had to drop out because of the Depression. He got a job that was beneath him, but he also loved what he did. He was very smart. When I was a kid, I felt that he knew everything.

My father was also tremendously critical. His own father died when he was young, so I'm not sure he knew how to be a father. He wasn't mean or anything. He was attentive. But I had a feeling of never being able to do anything right, never being good enough, never being as good as him. I think this feeling is common among kids.

I have a story of looking for my father's praise and not getting it. I created a character, this other person in my class named Stephen. I'd come home at night and tell my father all the wonderful things that Stephen had done, which were actually things that *I* had done. But I would tell him that Stephen had done them. He would praise Stephen and wanted to know why I couldn't be more like Stephen. Yet if I told him that *I* did it, he'd be critical. There's something in that fantasy, of seeing yourself reflected in others, that I find very easy and very satisfying. It's a psychological positioning.

Max Margolin with Malcolm and Bill (MARGOLIN FAMILY COLLECTION)

I still do it, attributing some of my best ideas to others and rejoicing in the praise they receive.

My mother, on the other hand, was very loving. She was a good person, smart and savvy, and she took care of many people. She graduated from high school, never went to college, but she was a bookkeeper. She loved having something called "good fun," which meant a good party or playing cards with her friends. She was a wonderful card player. She loved being crafty. She was a decent cook. At first she worked around the house, but in later years she worked with my father. In the early years they worked together for the Boston and Taunton Transportation Company, the trucking company. In later years she worked for him when he became a freight consolidator. They were close.

She was much more old-country than my father was. My mother was very fearful. You were forever hearing, "Don't worry your mother." A favorite story of mine about her was that when the Russians sent up a Sputnik with a dog in it, she refused to go out and hang clothes because she was afraid the dog would fall out of the sky and hit her. When I was a kid, it struck me as a reasonable fear. Only years later did I realize this was nuts, completely crazy.

We were always on the verge of making her feel bad about something. If you were five minutes late, she'd already decided that you'd been killed. Then when you'd come home, five minutes late, there'd be hysteria, this sense that you'd hurt somebody tremendously. I once realized that it wouldn't matter if I was five minutes or five days late because the reaction would be the same, so I may as well just stay out. I remember one day I had done something terrible. I forget what it was, but I realized that if I went home and told them about it, instead of having *one* problem, I'd have two problems. So I may as well just have one problem and deal with it myself. I responded to her fearfulness like people with a strict religious upbringing: once you break the strictures, you may as well just go all the way. There was no in-between. So I ended up climbing mountains, riding motorcycles, and taking all kinds of risks.

Despite those problems with my parents, I have a sense of having been born with lots of advantages, which is probably true of my generation. Our parents' generation worked their way from immigrant status through the Depression and beyond. They made their own life, their own place in the world, while I was already born with a leg up. I was probably reminded of it all the time. I always felt that sitting around the table was my mother, my father, me, my brother, *and* the Depression, and the Old Country, just as present as anyone else. The Old Country was very mysterious; it was not spoken about. The Depression was.

The Old Country was also the West End of Boston, where my mother and her family first arrived in the United States. It was a place of nostalgia. My brother ended up there working at the West End House, which was a settlement house, a kind of youth organization, including a summer camp. My brother went to that summer camp, later became a counselor there, and then head counselor. Eventually he ran the camp and the West End House, so he stayed in that old world, in a way.

Rose Margolin with Bill and Malcolm (MARGOLIN FAMILY COLLECTION)

I was eager to get away from that world. I needed years to disentangle myself from it. I'm still not totally disentangled. I was not a happy kid—morose, daydreamy, out of it, shy. I'm not sure what that shyness was: a vulnerability, an egocentric sense of self-importance, not wanting to be intruded upon, feeling inadequate. It's a combination of things. But it was pronounced and lasted right through college. As a matter of fact, it's lasted right through old age!

I'm not sure what that unhappiness was about, either. I was well taken care of. It wasn't as if I were abused, or as if any of these things were gross acts of negligence. So I'm not sure where that unhappiness came from, but it was certainly there.

I sensed that there was a trajectory from the immigrant generation of my grandparents to the generation of my parents, who made it but were never fully integrated into the culture. Then came my generation. What I was supposed to be doing, what I was bred for, was a split-level house in a suburb, with two children, a good Jewish wife, and a high income. My father wanted me to go to MIT and study engineering, then go to Harvard Business School and learn how to use it, and finally become a multimillionaire.

It's not that I didn't want to do that. I was just too muddled, as if a cloud were hanging over me. I enveloped myself in a self-induced state of day-dreaminess. I read a lot. I was episodically lucid. Every so often something would come through that I would understand. I just had tremendous confusion as to what I would be in life, who I would become, what interested me.

I think my parents were ultimately proud of me, or at least proud that I had kids. The true religion of Jews is grandchild worship, so I gave them grandchildren to worship. I don't think they ever quite approved of what I was doing. That may be wrong, my own imagination. I'm not sure what they thought. I never asked them. We weren't that close. I'm always surprised when my kids confide in me, and they're honest with me. My parents were people you kept secrets from. There was forever the business of approval, disapproval, restriction, things you just didn't ask. It was a house in which a lot went unspoken. Whether they were dark secrets of infidelities or betrayals, I don't know. I had a sense of growing up with secrets and ghosts in the world.

For example, there was Frieda Sands, my mother's best friend. She was the princess, beautiful, dynamic, the center of attention. She wrote poetry. Everybody envied her: she had the most wonderful husband, Sam, who worshipped her and made money in the fur business. They were wealthy. She had the most wonderful children. She was the queen bee of her world.

BILL MARGOLIN

Malcolm's brother Bill wrote up a few memories for Malcolm's seventieth birthday party—one of them is shared here.

Malcolm with brother Bill
(MARGOLIN FAMILY COLLECTION)

SOMETIMES YOU HAD to wonder about Malcolm's thought process. When he was about twelve or thirteen, my mother sent him to the store to get a loaf of bread. He walked to Dedham, perhaps six miles away, rather than to the nearby grocery store, located a couple of blocks from our house, where he usually went. While Malcolm, lost in thought, enjoyed a leisurely walk to complete this vital mission, the minutes and indeed the hours ticked by, and our poor worried mother ended up calling the police. As she was giving the sympathetic officers a description of her missing son, lo and behold, he appeared on the scene. The irony was that he had bought a white bread loaf as opposed to the pumpernickel she had asked for, but she did not complain. However, she did ascertain his destination before sending him on future missions.

My mother lived in her glory. My mother's identity, to some extent, was to be Frieda's best friend. But Sam ended up getting hypertension and a heart attack. The fur business started to decline. The kids didn't make out as well as everybody thought they would. So her life began to fall apart. Finally, Sam died and Frieda ended up in an old age home.

On a visit home once I asked my mother, "How's Frieda?"

She said, "I don't know."

"What do you mean you don't know?"

She said, "I can't talk to her."

I asked, "Why not?'

My mother insisted, "I don't want to say." I probed, and finally she told me, "Every time I talk to her, something bad happens. She's giving me the evil eye."

I grew up with that evil eye. It was the constant refrain. Whenever you praised somebody, the accompanying Yiddish expression, kenahorah—"no evil eye"— had to be said in order not to call attention to someone's good fortune. My mother felt that Frieda couldn't stand her good fortune, that my mother was living comfortably at home. It was that Old World just underneath the surface of life. These old-world superstitions, old-world ghosts and forces were running things.

Another mystery: When I was growing up, my mother always said she was born in Russia. Then when my brother went into the army, he needed security clearance, so they wanted my mother's immigration papers. It turned out she was not born in Russia but in Lithuania. The real secret that she was ashamed of was that she was ten years older than she'd said she was. What happened to those ten years? I have absolutely no idea. What happened in the Old Country? I have no idea.

These were things you didn't ask, things you could only daydream about. You didn't ask because you shouldn't know, because you didn't want to know. Things were left behind in the Old Country; people were left behind in the Old Country.

And then there's the Old Country of your youth, what's been left behind that you let go of.

EDUCATING MALCOLM

Early on, I remember a love of books. The one book in particular that I remember was the old Pinocchio, pre-Disney. I had that read to me again and again. My mother used to talk about how when somebody mispronounced or missed a word, I'd say, "You didn't tell it right," and I'd supply the word. I still remember the line "What's done cannot be undone." Somehow, reading that book, our own world was transformed into a wonderful, magical world, with the bad boy and fairy godmothers and great tragedies! So I loved *Pinocchio*.

An early revelation to me was *Make Way for Ducklings* because that was the first book I read that had something to do with the Boston that I knew. I remember being so intrigued that *Make Way for Ducklings* had Boston Gardens in it and Charles Street, the Charles River, the islands, and the swan boats. I'd never realized that books could have a meaning, could be about things that you knew. I thought that books were places you went away to.

I don't remember being taught to read, though I remember being taught to play chess and playing with my babysitter. Arthur Rabinowitz was his name. I surprised the hell out of him one day by beating him, too. Chess was important in my childhood. To be a good chess player, a good card player, was very important. My cousin Leonard ended up being a rabbi in Santa Fe; he was known as the tap-dancing rabbi. He was the chess *and* bridge champion of several states. I remember this character named Doc Kramer, a chiropodist, who fixed people's bunions and corns. Everybody had bunions and corns and went to Doc Kramer. Doc Kramer and my cousin Leonard would walk along the street and play mental chess. One of them would say, "Pawn to King 4," and the other would say, "Pawn to King 4." Then "Knight to King's Bishop 3," and the other replied, "Knight to Queen's Bishop 3" or "Bishop to Bishop 4." That's the Giuoco Piano opening in chess. They would play a full game of chess in their heads without out a chessboard.

I still play chess. In fact, I used to play with my friend Jeff Lustig almost every Monday for years. We'd go out for lunch, have a glass of wine, and play chess. It's a wonderful, indirect way of getting to know someone intimately. It's a parallel universe. You know somebody's raw thoughts. You know what they do when they're cornered, if they're defensive or aggressive. You know how they respond to crisis.

Do I remember being taught anything else when I was a kid? In kindergarten, I had a teacher named Miss Muldoon. I had an amazing crush on Miss Muldoon. I couldn't take my eyes off Miss Muldoon. She was the most beautiful person in the entire universe: graceful, thin, and shapely;

she wore nice clothes and smelled good. I adored Miss Muldoon. I still remember the last day of kindergarten, when I was going to be kicked out of Miss Muldoon's class and have to go into the dreaded Mrs. Rosenfield's first grade class. Into our kindergarten walks this young guy with a bouquet of flowers. Miss Muldoon looked at him in a way she never looked at me. My heart was broken! I realized I had lost Miss Muldoon forever. I mourned the whole summer for Miss Muldoon. She must be ninety if she's still alive, but I still mourn the young, forever unattainable Miss Muldoon.

I was very clumsy as a kid, very out of it. One of my memories is how I ached to be named the milk monitor or the eraser monitor or the ink monitor in the first grade. We had ink then! We had inkwells. You had to pour ink into the inkwells and write with nib-pens, which for a clumsy kid meant every day was a disaster and a reprimand. Every piece of paper had blotches on it. My handwriting was never very good. I ached for some kind of recognition, but at the same time, I was snarly. I denied its importance. I made a virtue of being out of it. I became defined as rebellious, but I was just out of it.

Square dancing was a first-order mystery to me. Everybody seemed to know what to do: they came in, grabbed their partners' arms, do-si-doed, hooked up, obeyed the calls. But I would wander around in the middle of it, completely lost! It became a metaphor later on.

One time Mrs. Rosenfield in the first grade gave me an important errand: Somebody had lost a mitten. I was to go around to all the classes and ask whose mitten it was. This was my great opportunity to go onto the second floor of the school, where I'd never been. The bigger kids were on the second floor! So I brought this mitten up to the second floor of the school.

I come to a door, I knock, and a voice commands me to come in. God almighty, they were the third graders! They were the *big* kids, with a teacher I didn't know. The teacher says, "What do you want?"

"Mrs. Rosenfield sent me up here to see if somebody lost a mitten."

She says, "Can you ask the class?"

So I said, "Did anybody lose a mitten?"

Someone snickers. She says, "I guess nobody here lost a mitten."

I went out into the corridor. I was so amazed again to be on the second floor. It was a whole new world up there, all these new things on the walls.

I came to a door. I knock at the door, and a voice says, "Come in!" It's the same teacher! "What do you want?"

"I want to know if anyone lost a mitten."

She said, "You know, you've already been here." Everybody laughed at me.

I went out and looked at the door to be sure I'd remember it, and then I wandered around the corridor some more. I finally come to a whole other different door, and I knock. A distant voice says to come in. I open the door. It's the back door to the same class! She sent me back down to my classroom since I'd failed in my mission.

So Mrs. Rosenfield had to send somebody else out in my place. I was never chosen again.

I suspect I was a hateful kid—gloomy, grumpy, mopey, uncoordinated. I was terrible at ball games, just horrible. I covered it all up by being hostile. I don't think I was a very good kid. I certainly didn't think so at the time. I was lonely. I lived in a daydream. I'd stare out the window a whole lot. I was pretty good at school because I was smart. Being good at school was effortless, so I didn't value it much.

I remember days that were so long! They went on forever and ever. You'd sit there and look at the clock and at this fly buzzing, the chalk on the blackboard, something boring going on. It's five minutes of one. Another hour would pass, and now it's three minutes of one. Another hour passes, and it's two minutes of one!

I was continually losing stuff. My mother was once so mad at me because she bought me a new navy pea jacket and I came back from school with a pea jacket that was not new. Somebody else had the new navy pea jacket. But they all looked the same to me. I had no concept that I'd just changed jackets. My mother was shocked because it was not only ragged and dirty, but it was three sizes too small. But to me it was still a pea jacket.

What I *did* love to do was to explore after school. I loved to walk home different ways, to look into different neighborhoods. A plot of undeveloped land called "the Jungle" lay between where we lived, at 82 American Legion

Highway, and the Robert Treat Paine School, where I went to school. It was a little woodland right in the middle of Dorchester. I loved to explore there.

Another thing I loved was stories. One teacher in the fifth grade, Mrs. Hurley, used to read us stories, whole books. I remember *Heidi* in particular. And at one point I loved math. I found geometry the most fascinating subject in the world. I also liked word problems: if somebody drives a tank truck halfway to someplace, and the tank truck is half full, then three chickens cross the road, and missionaries have to get across the stream, how many miles did the chicken go before the tank truck reached its goal? Those kinds of problems I was really good at.

I wasn't interested in anything else. I was terrible at the arts and music. I thought history was uninteresting, but I could easily remember and master facts. So school was a place for mastery rather than anything inherently interesting.

At the end of the sixth grade, there was only one public college preparatory high school, Boston Latin, one for boys and one for girls. It was difficult to get accepted there; you had to take a test to get in. They admitted something like twelve hundred students. I got in. At the first assembly, you sit in this big hall with the names of illustrious graduates all around—Benjamin Franklin, Cotton Mather, all the old Puritans, right through to the present. Anybody that had lived in Boston and had succeeded had gone to Boston Latin. The headmaster gets up before the twelve hundred students assembled for their first day of school. Everybody remembers his speech, which went something like this: "Look at the boy to the right of you. Look at the boy to the left of you. Look at the boy in front of you and the boy in back of you. Six years from now only one of you will graduate. Which one will it be?"

Sure enough, during the course of the year, when each report card would come out, you'd return to school the next day and find three empty seats. What happened to Murphy? Students just disappeared!

Boston Latin provided some intellectual challenge, but it felt senseless as well. A story emblematic of that education was that in Class Four, which was the ninth grade, we read Caesar's *Gallic Wars* in Latin. You sit there cowering behind your book, hoping you aren't going to be called on.

You have all these strategies for making yourself small, for disappearing, looking out the window, avoiding eye contact, anything not to be called on. Mr. Miller looks over the class, and finally his eyes light on Marty Savitz. "Mr. Savitz, recite!"

Savitz gets up. The passage was, "Caesar ran and threw darts in all directions." That's the translation of it. "To run" is a reflexive verb, *currere se*; you "run yourself." So Savitz reads, "Caesar ran in all directions and threw darts at himself."

There was a long pause, and Miller says, "Mr. Savitz, do you want to try that passage again, please?"

So Savitz goes more slowly now, "Caesar ran in all directions and threw darts at himself."

Miller asks, "Does that make any sense to you?"

Savitz goes, "No, sir."

"Did it ever occur to you that it should make sense?"

What a revelation for all of us! Nobody ever thought that this stuff was *supposed* to make sense. Nothing made sense at that time. You just learned rules, you did work, and you prepared yourself for some dismal thing called "the future."

I thought it was all a fraud, a game, nothing sincere about it at all. You just learned stuff to get good grades. But a couple of teachers were great, really inspiring. Skippy Sheehan made English come alive, and Dobbins made math into something wonderful. Sleepy Sam Nemzoff made history interesting. He was called Sleepy Sam because he had narcolepsy. He would nod off in the middle of class. The class would just disrupt into chaos. But when he was on, he was captivating with a good story, summing things up in a dramatic, beautiful way.

I was captain of the Latin School Chess Team. I had a sense of camaraderie with some of the other students, some deep friendships there. I think you have your deepest friendships at that age. Friends mean more to you in those years than they do at any other time of your life. You're breaking away from home. There's a sense of shared destiny.

We had moved to West Roxbury by this time, but my friends all came from Dorchester, from the old neighborhood. Sherm Rosen and I would play hooky; we'd go to Revere Beach, terrified that we'd be caught. Hugh McNulty, the class genius, and I were good friends. A group of people a year ahead of me were part of what was called the Mirsky group, named after Mark Mirsky, a charismatic character. He was into acting, literature. His father had been a minor politician in Dorchester. The Mirsky group was a bunch of intellectuals that all went to Harvard together. I was part of that group, but also part of another group. Moonman Levinson was a wonderful friend. I keep wondering what happened to Moony. He was so gawky! There was Doc Gretsky and Red Cohen, who was different from Froggy Cohen. Everyone had nicknames. A whole lot of that time was spent shooting pool or bowling.

Dating was just terribly awkward. I used to meet somebody named Ruth at the Boston Public Library. That library is still embedded in my mind when I think of libraries: You climb those big steps with that big "Boston Public Library" written there, the stone lions on either side. You go up to the second floor, with all the marble, into the Reading Room with the big reading tables and the Tiffany lamps. We'd be doing homework. You'd go up to the counter. A real adult in a dress or a necktie would come and call you "Sir" and ask what you were doing. They'd offer to bring you books and help you. It was something about the magnificence of the library that let you know that if you were into a life of learning, the culture respected it so much that it was providing this temple, this place of beauty and opulence for you, with fine art and fancy people, with infinite layers of potential there for what you could get in life. But I was also going there to see if I could get Ruth.

On the way to the temple of learning I'd pass another great temple. Boston Latin School was in the Back Bay, on Louis Pasteur Avenue. You could walk down Massachusetts Avenue on the way to the library and you'd pass several landmarks—like the Fine Arts Museum, which was an inspiration. Then at the corner of Huntington and Mass. Avenue was a little communist bookstore. Back in the fifties you'd get these little blue books, the Haldeman-Julius books, a series that came out of Kansas. They were little five-cent blue books. Hundreds of them came out, with titles something like *The Thoughts of Marx* and *The Thoughts of Engels*, *The Short Stories of Guy de Maupassant* and *How to Play Bridge*. It was the whole world of knowledge spread out before you, and it only cost a nickel. So I'd go there.

Nearby was the Boston Opera House. One of my great memories is when I saw a protest around preservation. They were going to tear down the opera house and put in a parking garage. All these high-class women were out there with signs: "Save the opera house!" One day when I arrive, the women are there with their signs, and the crane is up with the wrecking ball. The wrecking ball goes out, and it swings. It hits the side of the opera house and tings! Again it swings and tings. The crane moves again, and the ball crunches. The building starts to crumble. Everybody starts to cry.

I thought it was the most beautiful thing I'd seen in my whole life. Utterly wonderful. I both was horrified by it and found it magnificent, a grand moment, to witness that destruction. A character—Destructive Desmond, I think—in a W. H. Auden story would destroy irreplaceable objects. I always thought the world of Desmond. There was a part of me—there still *is* a part of me that can relate to that. I don't possess anything; I don't own much. Things just pass through my fingers. I'll preserve memories. I'll preserve culture. But I don't have possessions.

What else do I remember about high school? I was not good in school sports whatsoever. The worst of all was obligatory military drill in junior ROTC. In senior year of high school, you were automatically made into a second lieutenant, and you had to give orders to your platoon. We practiced giving orders. "Left, hup! Right, hup! Forward, march!"

I marched them all into a wall! They kept piling up against the wall. They'd look back to see if I was going to give them the order "About face!" But I just refused to give the order, so they kept piling up. I got dragged into the principal's office for that.

It was cold in Boston, so the obligatory PE was indoors a lot. Basketball was a nightmare, aggressive and fast; you'd get pushed around. You had to be alert, and you had to give a damn. My attitude was: "Here, you want the ball? Take it!" It was definitely not my style.

A group of us got into playing soccer because nobody would play soccer during the fifties, so we'd end up alone, out of it. That was the whole goal, just to be left alone, to kick a ball around and pretend you were doing something.

I'm not very astute in psychology or self-analysis, but what I do understand is that my being "out of it" in all these ways goes straight to the heart of my life back then. I'd buy books, I'd read. But I didn't care too much about most things. I was building up this protective cloud of confusion. I had a sense of living a muffled life. But I think within that darkness, within that muffledness, complexity develops. Out of it came a certain inner richness. There's also a sense that in that alienation you make your own world. You're not going to fit into anybody else's world, so you damn well better make your own world or be a misfit forever. I think that's what I've done, created a world around myself. It's a chrysalis, building a cocoon around yourself.

Every so often, though, I'd be inspired by a teacher. Every so often, somebody would say something that moved me. That was true with the incident that turned me into a writer. It was very memorable. I did not particularly enjoy writing at all, but during my senior year in Harvard, I majored in English literature, the default option if you didn't know what else to major in. For senior year at Harvard, you were given a tutor in a course called "Tutorial" for credit. The goal of the tutor was to look over what you had done in English Lit and fill in the gaps. If you had never taken a course in Restoration literature, then you'd read some Congreve, something like that, to fill in where you were weak. Where I had been weak was in early American literature.

So that fall they gave me as a tutor this woman, Joanne Holland, a Ph.D. candidate. She was not terribly much older than I was. She'd recently been married. She had a little office in the Radcliffe Quadrangle. We'd meet there once a week in the late afternoon and discuss things. We sat in that little overstuffed room throughout that fall, the discussion ranging from Melville to Fitzgerald, Thoreau to Wallace Stevens. The days got shorter and shorter, it would get dark earlier and earlier, but we wouldn't put on the light. We had the most wonderful conversations, long, honest, intimate. If there was silence, we were comfortable with that. The emotional vibration in the room was palpable, thick with the affection in one another's company. We were never lovers, but those hours spent together were utterly beautiful.

One day she said, "Listen, I was just told that I have to assign you a paper. So you're going to have to write a paper."

I said okay, and I did what I always did, which was to go back and do nothing until the night before it was due. Then at nine o'clock at night I'd sit in front of a typewriter, whack out five pages until three o'clock in the morning, and turn it in. This was called a paper.

So I gave it to her. Then I came back the next week. There was obviously something wrong. I said, "Is everything okay?"

She said, "That paper—it's good. I'm supposed to grade you on it, and I'll give you a good grade because I have to give you a grade. But I was expecting something beautiful."

I remember being enraged! She'd crossed a line. I fumed and finally said, "Okay, if you want something beautiful, why don't we just rip it up, and I'll give you something beautiful."

I went back and over the next week, I wrote a love letter. It was disguised as a paper on Huckleberry Finn's father, but that's what it was—a beautiful piece of writing. I had never been motivated by classes or grades, by anything else, but somehow writing directly to a person like that, I could do it. I understood *that*. It was the first time I ever realized what I could do with writing, what a powerful experience writing could be, for me and for somebody else.

The difference was that I was writing right *into* somebody. I was not just putting words out on a table; I was pretty good at words. But here I was writing right *to* somebody. There had to be that emotional connection that would get stuff flowing. That was the main point for me. I think a lot of what I write is a love letter.

It was like opening a door and finding a new room in my life, in my head, finding a new voice, some other Malcolm that I never knew existed. I found a Malcolm that wasn't playing the game; that's what it was. I knew I could play the game and get good grades, but this was something else. This was how to say something that moves and thrills, inspires and pleases and melts, melts the boundaries. It was probably the *one* educational experience I had.

My feeling from my own background is that you don't learn anything in school. If you want to change society, you look for other ways of teaching people things. You look for "conversionary" experiences. Look at how missionaries converted villages. You don't look at how things are done in school, because it's a failed enterprise. It's not true for all kids or my kids, but it's true for many.

What's amazing to me now is that I hated school, it was dreadful, yet I came out of it having learned stuff, having the capacity to think and understand and analyze. Maybe something in my daydreaminess, the cocooning, that muffled quality, allowed me to preserve information, to filter only what I wanted to hear.

I know I was around greatness at Boston Latin, in literature studies at Harvard, in various places. Even if I didn't partake in it, I was around it. It probably seeped into me in ways that I wasn't as resistant to as I thought.

RITES OF PASSAGE: THE BAR MITZVAH

Of course, I had a Bar Mitzvah. They sent me to Hebrew school, and I hated it, the smell of the place, the people, the whole thing. I resented having to go after school when I should be able to read and play and be free. To go to yet another school and learn a strange alphabet and these stupid stories—I did not like it in the least. The consequence was that I was a bad student, and they kicked me out.

So they had to get some defrocked rabbi named Mr. Karinow, who came to tutor me on the Haftorah, the part of the Torah you're supposed to read for the Bar Mitzvah. Mine was the Haftorah of Noah, supposedly the longest Haftorah in the whole canon of Haftorahs. The rabbi would come into the neighborhood, and I'd try to hide. He used to yell, "Malcolm! Malcolm!" But that didn't get me to come. So he used my Hebrew name, "Maier Laib! Maier Laib!" I was so embarrassed by this that I'd finally come out of the bushes where I was hiding. My mother was mad at me that I wouldn't be home; I'd claim to have forgotten.

I was the most unwilling student. It was passive resistance: not being there, not being involved or engaged. It was something you just had to get through for the sake of family, for the sake of others. I felt absolutely no personal engagement in it whatsoever.

Then on the day of the Bar Mitzvah, I go to the orthodox synagogue, the Woodrow Avenue *shul* where my grandparents went, one of these little wooden *shtetl*-like *shuls* from the Old Country. I still remember the smell and the color of it. I remember walking into that wooden world, the first three rows of people in gabardine, all men in front, the women off in the back. All these old bearded guys up in the front, speaking Yiddish. Most of them didn't speak any English. The rabbi was Rabbi Simches.

So I start reciting. The funny thing is that I can still remember the whole damn thing. *"Baruch ata Adonai…"* Once I start it, I can run through it all.

Suddenly, this alarm went through the congregation. Mr. Karinow had taught me the wrong Haftorah for the day! Then they gave me the right Haftorah, but since I'd flunked out of Hebrew school, I couldn't read it. So they had to have someone else read it. They still let me run through the wrong one, as an act of charity.

I think everybody was so pissed off at me in general that this debacle was just part of the ordinary—one more thing along the way. The whole thing was senseless to me. It's hard to explain how something can be so emotionally touching and so senseless at the same time. I felt at the time that it was part of the overall muddle of life. As I said, I was in this protective fog. I just went through the steps. The fact that it was the wrong Haftorah was only a minor part of the greater senselessness of the whole situation. There were bigger things that were senseless.

Because my father didn't trust me to write an appropriate speech, I gave a speech that he wrote for me in which I thanked everybody and pronounced devotion to the way of Abraham. I dimly remember my father showing me how to tie a tie, some moment of affection or connection in there. I can remember the tone of it, but I can't remember the content. I don't remember much about the party after.

They made a picture of me sitting on a chair with a *tallis* and a *yarmulke*. It was a black-and-white photo that was hand-colored. My parents had it

Malcolm's Bar Mitzvah portrait
(COURTESY OF BILL MARGOLIN)

framed, and it hung in the house as part of a conspiracy to embarrass me. It represented their determination that I be somebody that I wasn't. They could sit me in a chair looking respectable, take a black-and-white photo of me, capture a moment when I was singing the wrong Haftorah, and paint it up. There it hung in the living room for everybody to see. While I went my own way, the picture stayed the same. They gave me rosy red cheeks. I looked so healthy! I don't remember what they did with the perpetual smirk.

I don't want to give the impression that the experience was particularly painful. I want to get the right tone: I knew I didn't want to be there, but it was not an act of complete rebellion, either. It was going along with the obligation of it, giving the minimal. I just fundamentally didn't give a damn. I've always been that way. If it's something I don't care about, the amount of effort it takes to get me to do something I don't want to do is so spectacular that people just end up doing it themselves. But if I *want* to do something, there's no way of stopping me.

By this time we had moved to West Roxbury. A *shul* opened up in West Roxbury, but I never went there. My brother did. He was much more engaged and involved than I was. I think I hardly stepped foot into a *shul* again except for a friend's wedding or funeral. This was not a big part of my life. I haven't thought about this in—forever! None of my kids got bar mitzvahed, not as an act of hostility, but it would have been false. I didn't believe in God.

PARAGON PARK

Paragon Park was an amusement park in Nantasket, a kind of wonderland with rides and bright lights. We'd go there a couple of times a year. By the time I started to work there, it was run-down and seedy. I helped manage a hot dog–pizza stand for this guy named George Shankar. His nickname was Arkie, back when everybody had nicknames.

Arkie was a professor of political science at Pace University. He'd been divorced a couple of times and had alimony payments, so he opened up this hot dog–pizza stand as a summer job. I remember him hanging out in his professorial guise. He'd ask provocative questions, like "What is the nature of man? Are we acquisitive? Are we hostile? Are we cooperative? Here's what the different philosophers have to say." At the same time, he was fun to be around. He was completely irresponsible.

I worked twelve hours a day, seven days a week, except when it rained and they closed the park. I got to stay late at night. We'd play cards and gamble in the back room with the other guys that worked on the different amusements. For somebody that felt he was leading a sheltered life, it provided a sense of a raw world. Here were all these tattooed characters walking around. I remember the Simmons brothers, Lester and Simmy, two characters from Brockton, Massachusetts, that cleaned up afterwards. They had one wife between them, and they all slept in one bed. They were mentally retarded in some way. They'd work in the summertime, and then when it got cold, Lester and Simmy would go to the downtown area of Brockton and take off their clothes. They'd get thrown into jail for six months, where they could live inside and be fed. The town would let them out again in the spring so they could work at Paragon Park.

We were under the roller coaster, right opposite the stage where the acts were, so everyone would always come in for coffee, and I'd get to know them. I loved the various acts. There were two different lion tamers. One was Prince El Kigordo, this big black guy who used to get all dressed up in spangled uniforms and get into the middle of the lion cage.

The other guy, George Keller, had been a professor of fine arts in Pennsylvania. All his life, he wanted to be a lion tamer, so he finally gave up a life of teaching to do what he always wanted to do. He ended up with lions and tigers, pumas and leopards, about seven different cats. He had them in small cages hooked up like railroad cars, separate from one another. For his act he had a big round cage in the middle, and he'd get all of these different big cats together.

His wife accompanied him. She was somebody who had married a college professor, and here she was at this low-class carnival. She'd sit there with her cigarette holder, drinking a cup of coffee, dressed up as if she were going to the opera, complaining like hell about how miserable her life was and how she hated all of this. Then the third person with them was a big rough guy who had a gun. He was the guard on the outside.

One year I looked over the schedule to see who was coming. I saw the professor wasn't coming, so I asked what happened. Someone tells me, "He got eaten by his lions! He got killed." The next year, I see his act is back. "What happened?" I asked. "We don't know, but we booked it 'cause it's back on the list."

When they arrived, the big rough guy who'd had the gun was now dressed up as the lion tamer. The wife now had the gun, and she was on the outside. It was the most amazing thing.

All these marvelous acrobats showed up, whole acrobat families. One little Jewish guy, Solomon, would get dressed up in a little bathing suit, and up he went into a high tower. You could barely see him at the top. He'd jump into a little pan of water at the bottom—he'd call it a *shissel*. He'd land in the *shissel.* Then another guy, the Great Zucchini, used to crawl into a cannon and get shot out of it.

One wonderful time, Prince El Kigordo showed up for Fourth of July weekend and found the floorboards on the stage rotten. He wasn't going to bring his lions in there. He was afraid; this was not going to work. So he packed up his lions and left on Fourth of July weekend. The posters all over Nantasket and Boston said, "Come to Paragon Park, see Prince El Kigordo and his lions!" Only one act was available in all of New England on such short notice for the Fourth of July: Will Hill and His Trained Pigs. Everybody's gathered to see the big lions, and out comes this guy with a stalk of hay, in bib overalls, with a couple of trained pigs. What an uproar!

Working there gave me a wonderful perspective, and I'm grateful for it, not so much for what I learned about other people, but that I found myself being able to fit into that world so easily. I felt really comfortable in the carnival. It's not that I felt I belonged, because I never felt as if I belonged anywhere. A lot of these people were very sad, the sadness of clowns, of entertainers. They were people with a shtick but were not necessarily fully developed. They had some kind of weird skill: They could juggle swords, eat fire, or swing on trapezes. Maybe they got into show business for the glamour of it all, dressed up in glitter as if they were great stars. But they ended up in this seedy urban amusement park. I understood something about it, but I'm not sure what.

I worked there for five summers, and I'd open it up for weekends during the fall and spring. There was always a sense that as ridiculous as this world was, this *was* the real world, and that the world that I was from, my home life and school, was not a real world.

A SUMMER IN THE WEST

Then there was the summer of Walter Pitts in 1962. Back in college, I had a friend from Boston Latin School, Frank Axelrod, who'd gone to MIT while I went to Harvard. He was a year ahead of me. Frank was working in the lab of Jerry Lettvin, who was the social center of MIT. Jerry was a cognitive scientist; he did bioengineering and communications physiology. It was the luckiest thing that ever happened to Frank. Through Jerry, we met people like Norbert Wiener, the father of cybernetics, and other phenomenal people, including Walter Pitts.

I've never met anybody like Walter. Anyone who met Walter was absolutely knocked out by his intelligence. He had a photographic memory, and whatever went in then connected to everything else he ever knew. Walter had been the youngest person—still a teenager—working on the Manhattan Project. He was an applied mathematician. He developed a famous formula in mathematics called the McCulloch-Pitts theorem.

Walter was about age forty, while Frank and I were in our early twenties. Walter was always looking for mountain-climbing companions. When you get to be forty, everybody else gets hooked in with family and business, things like that. So when we were in college, during the school year, we'd end up going hiking with Walter to the White Mountains. It was my first experience of camping, hiking, going out into the wilderness.

Walter was a genius. When he got bored once, he learned ancient Nahuatl, and his translations of Nahuatl were later published. He got bored another time and learned ancient Greek, and his translations of Greek poets are still around. MIT gave him a stipend just to be there, with no duties, just so people could talk to him. Jerry Lettvin sheltered him and kept him alive in this kind of unique position, without responsibility, where people would come to him.

Walter became a good friend. I'd go up to see him in King's Tavern, where he'd always sit with a couple glasses of beer. He would be reading British history. He knew everything. I remember I took a course once in medieval travelogues just because I wanted to learn something that Walter didn't know anything about. I came back to visit Walter, and he said, "What are you taking this year?" When I told him "Medieval Travelogues," he said, "Oh, you must be reading Mandeville." He ended up quoting Mandeville, word for word, in something I had just read the previous day, but he knew it better than I did, and he'd read it twenty years before.

One day I was at Paragon Park, early in the summer of '62, when Walter and Frank came to visit. They wanted to go mountain climbing out west, and they needed somebody to come with them. Would I come? I said, "This is it." This was an opportunity. So I just quit!

We traveled for a couple of months. We climbed in the Wind River Range and the Tetons in Wyoming and up Mount Baker in Washington. We had a wonderful trip up Mount Olympus and the Olympic Peninsula, the Columbia Icefield, the Athabasca Glacier around Banff. It was high adventure with someone of great genius. He knew every plant. I remember we were up in the Wind River Range, and some guy approached us with a flower in his hand. He said it was a particular kind of mariposa lily. "I've been looking for this flower for my whole life. I've finally found it!" We all congratulated him. When he left, Walter said that it was not the flower the guy thought it was, just a variation of some other flower. He knew everything.

We had an old GMC truck, a Carryall. When it broke down, Walter would fix it. He was utterly awesome. But he was also peculiarly forgetful. We would rope up on a glacier for safety, two together. We'd pick up a fourth guy for one of these glacier climbs so that each of us could have someone to rope up with. When you're climbing glaciers, you get to the crevasse, you put your ice ax in, you belay the other person to jump the crevasse, then that person gets in and puts their ice ax in, holds the rope, and the other person jumps, so if you fall in, you have somebody set to grab you.

But one time when I was roped up with Walter, he jumped and just kept going! He'd forgotten about me, as if I didn't exist. I scrambled over the crevasse and came up yelling, "Walter, for Christ's sake!" He looked at me as if I were the strangest person he'd ever seen.

It was a wonderful summer that set me on a course of wilderness life, a course of mountain climbing. It gave me an identity that I hadn't had. It gave me a sense of adventure and travel. It was a great gift that Walter and Frank gave me.

I think I've been building a life not around larger ideals or ideas but around episodes. What I loved about that trip was how it was punctuated by acts of heroism and accomplishment. It wasn't as if we set out to have a great journey that would have a preordained coherence to it. When we arrived at a place, there was a mountain to climb.

TRANSITIONS IN COLLEGE AND BEYOND

College was one long Bar Mitzvah, tolerating what I had to tolerate. I was attracted to interesting people. I hung around an all-night coffee shop, the Hayes-Bickford. I remember one guy who went by several names: Julio Dumas, Jacques de Talleyrand. He was flamboyant, theatrical, brilliant, a wonderful raconteur, and a wonderful fraud. He was always the grandson of somebody or the nephew of somebody; it changed from week to week. People would buy him coffee and listen to his stories of derring-do, of great people he'd met, the larger world he traveled in.

I played a bunch of chess with various people, and I had a few deep friendships. But time passed. I think I was unhappy and lonely a lot of the time.

I started college in 1958, but I didn't finish until '64. I dropped out a couple of times. Once I lived in New York for nine months, just doing odd jobs. I lived, read, brooded, thought. My father was a freight broker, and the next time I dropped out, in the winter of 1963, I went off to work in Puerto Rico with the company he was part of.

I loved it there. I learned enough Spanish to get along. I had wonderful friends, the Cuétara brothers, José and Frank Cuétara. They had old farms and horses; we'd go off into the country. There was also an urban district that had cheap bars. There was gambling, swimming, snorkeling, beaches. It was a place so far away from home, a warm place, with such a different, sexy culture compared to Boston.

What pleased me most were the people, the beauty of the landscape, the exotic vegetation. José had these horses, and we'd go riding. I actually hate horses; I'm scared of them, but we'd go riding out in the backcountry over these paths. We'd go out at night into the forests and find these sleazy bars. I'd wander all over on my own, into small towns, sometimes sleep in the sugar cane fields at night. I had a lovely sense of swimming in the sea of a different culture.

Looking back, it seems that my whole college period was a time of *not* going forward but of recovering from a disease I didn't know I had.

Malcolm, freshman year (1958) at Harvard's Hollis Hall (COURTESY OF BILL MARGOLIN)

During my college years, I was in the cocoon more than I was getting wings. It was letting time pass, slowly acquiring social skills. I was finding out that the first act of independence was to withdraw, that I could define myself by not partaking. If you can define yourself by *not* partaking, then you can later define yourself by partaking. I could finally get away with being who I was.

My parents were highly displeased each time I dropped out. My father proclaimed that it was the most bitter pill he ever had to swallow. It was like that Bar Mitzvah picture, an image they had of me that no longer fit, but they were going to maintain that image no matter what.

A part of me wished I *could* be that image, wished I could please, wished people would be proud of me. If this were a therapy session, I'd probably focus on my father. I spoke like him, with his voice; I imitated him. I worshipped him! But he was overly critical. I felt like I could never come up to his standard. Consequently, I just didn't try. And rather than break myself trying to be the person that he wanted me to be and *I* wanted me to be, I just lapsed into a kind of escapism into other worlds, giving those other worlds more value.

One day some people were discussing something here I don't usually discuss, which is totem animals. Someone asked, "What is your totem animal and why? What quality do you have of that animal?" People were talking about lions and jaguars and all kinds of great animals. The only image that came to mind for me was when I was camping on the Olympic Peninsula, along the Elwha River for a month. A herd of elk crossed every morning. The bulls would come and bellow and lead the way across the river, then stand at the other side to keep guard. The does and fawns would then come, and finally the rear guard would come. I loved watching the stately procession.

This was the animal that came to mind, the bull elk. It's taking care of your herd. I think I picked that up from my father also.

Malcolm hiking in the Caribbean, 1966 (MARGOLIN FAMILY COLLECTION)

HEADING WEST

My wife, Rina, and I met at Harvard. She was a clinical psychology major at Radcliffe. After graduating from Harvard in 1964, I went back to Puerto Rico until 1966. She joined me, and we were quietly married there by a justice of the peace.

Then from 1966 to February of 1968, we lived in the Lower East Side of New York. In New York, she was working for someone doing psychological research. She was earning the money while I was writing stories that never got published, along with a few articles. A character named Ralph Ginzburg had started *Eros* and *Fact*, very controversial, edgy magazines in the sixties. I wrote a couple of articles for *fact:*. But I wasn't too serious about writing. I played chess a lot in Tompkins Square Park with old Russians. I didn't really have a plan for writing or for anything at that point.

I checked into an insane asylum for two and a half weeks for an experiment on LSD. The asylum was in Norwich, Connecticut, and the experiment was run by a guy named Walter Houston Clark, a professor of religious psychology. He wrote several books on psychedelics and the religious experience. I was part of this experimental group he had, where we were taking acid for two straight weeks, every day. It was terrifying—not all good trips. Rina claimed I was changed completely by it. She said I came back another person. Softer. Like I'd been put through the wash.

There were six of us, but one guy escaped. He was stoned. Later on, he looked me up when I was in New York. I said to him, "Jesus, what the hell happened to you?" This was such a sixties story! He got on a train to go home, and the train was passing through New London, Connecticut. A whole bunch of sailors in uniform got on the train. He was positive they were out to get him, that anyone in a uniform was out to get him. He was sitting next to a young woman, and so he laid his head in this woman's lap and started to cry. She was patting him on the head and said it would be okay. How beautiful and bizarre!

It *was* life-changing.

Clark wrote about the experiment in several articles, and he gave me a code name, something like Duncan Cohen. He wrote about why God gives atheists like me religious experiences, and why he, in all his life a true believer, had never had a religious experience.

I was totally out of my mind, but it was that oneness with everything. I still have that. The other night I was talking with about twenty people who were here discussing the Pacific Flyway of migrating birds. We were talking about doing a book and museum exhibit on ducks and geese. We were discussing what it felt like to watch the snow geese lift off, what it feels like to be part of a flock. I know exactly what it is, when that emotion sweeps through people, when we're connected to other people and animals. I have no trouble with that kind of empathy or connection. I know exactly what those ducks and geese are feeling, when one moves and others move with them. I don't know if that's religious or not, but I'm assuming that that's what he was talking about.

It's kind of funny. On the one hand, I have absolutely no patience with ESP or New Age stuff. On the other hand, I walk in that world. And I have neither need nor desire to reconcile that contradiction. But I assume there's something else going on, that there's a *lot* going on.

The reason I decided to do the experiment was that the opportunity appeared on the horizon. I don't mean to make it into a big mystery; things just come along, and I go to them. But it's like sailing on the open sea without a deep keel: it's a little dangerous. Still, it's a way of being that allows me to get involved with Indians one minute, with academics another minute, with librarians or Hmong poets another minute—it's just getting into other people's worlds.

The bad thing about taking up these kinds of opportunities and not having any plan is that you drift. But then the good thing about it is you drift! You're not sure where the tides will take you. There's a kind of temperamental proclivity to say yes. It opens doors to rooms that are sometimes hard to be in. Given what I did at various times, I could never run for political office.

Rina and I went out west in the summer of 1967 for three weeks when she had a vacation. We rented a car and drove out, camping along the way. We had a Rand McNally guide to campsites as we were driving across the United States, and we read about a place called "Yo-Semite" with tons of campsites, so we headed into "Yo-Semite" and found a campsite. We had air mattresses, so for three days we floated down the Merced River. At night we'd pack the air mattresses back to the campsite. We did that for three straight days; it was so damn beautiful, I could have done it forever!

Then one day we went to Yosemite Lodge for supplies, and there was a *San Francisco Chronicle* newspaper which had the headline "LSD Causes Birth Defects." We just sat by the side of the river, crying our eyes out, because we could never have kids.

We eventually made it to San Francisco, and it was the Summer of Love. People were so lovely here! We found such a wonderful sense of openness.

Then in 1968 we drove west again, this time giving up our New York apartment and ostensibly looking for a place to settle. I say "ostensibly" because in truth I was pretending. We were talking about having kids, and Rina didn't want to have kids in New York City. She said it wasn't the place to raise kids. I believed that the city was *the* place to live. This is where a true human being lives, New York City! But there was this business of having kids. So I thought I'd indulge her in the search. We would travel around the country and find no place better to have kids than New York City. I wouldn't like any other place, and we'd move back.

We'd been living on East 10th Street near Avenue A, on the fourth floor of a six-story walk-up. Opposite us was the studio of a guy named Al Jensen, a well-known painter. He became a dear friend. He was married to a woman named Regina who had been known as de Kooning's mistress, but I think she had to stand in line. Al had all of the great artists over to visit with him. This was the place to be in the 1960s.

Al painted little colored squares. He'd sometimes put numbers on the squares. I remember one day I was visiting him when he was painting these little squares. Henry Luce had come by and bought one of Al's paintings for $75,000.

That got my attention, and I summoned up the courage to ask, "Hey, Al, what's it all about? What the hell are you doing?"

He said, "Well, I was born of Danish parents in Guatemala, and I was suckled by Mayan women." Then he went off, talking about the Mayan calendar and numbers, stars and universes and predictions. By the time he finished the third sentence, two things became clear: I hadn't understood a word he'd said, and I was having a mystical experience. I just *lived* the flow of his words that I didn't understand.

He was in his seventies or eighties. He had two little kids with Regina, who was much younger. She so worshipped him that she just wanted to have kids with him. She thought that even if these kids didn't get to know their father through teenagehood, just to have been touched by someone like that was the greatest gift she could give to her kids.

When it was time for us to leave New York, Al pulled me aside and said, "Don't do it, Malcolm." He said, "If you stay in New York, you'll be great. If you go somewhere else, you're going to be a big fish in a small pond. Stay here. You have to be in New York because it pushes you. You suffer in New York because it challenges you. You'll be one of the best writers in the world. If you go somewhere else, it'll be too easy for you."

I always thought about that. In New York I might have gotten a much greater reputation; perhaps I might have been world-famous. But I also thought about how shallow greatness is in New York—how it depends on reputation. What *this* place, what Heyday has allowed me to do is to create a real community, to be really useful, to create a home for certain people and certain ideas.

So we came out west in early '68. I bought a VW bus for three hundred dollars in Queens. We sold everything we had. I built a bed in the back, and we just took whatever could fit under that bed, plus two bikes. We had some curtains, and that was it!

We had the most wonderful time driving down through Florida, across to New Orleans in time for Mardi Gras, and then a beautiful time going through Texas. It seemed like several years crossing Texas, it's so big! In fact, the whole United States is big. We finally reached Big Bend National Park—so beautiful, so lovely. God, that was a wonderful year. After Big Bend, we crossed the desert, the first time I'd seen the desert with the cactus blooming.

We finally arrived in California. One of the memories I have of California was a beach where we met Dan Carr. We were at a campsite where a family was camped next to us. They had an old Cadillac jalopy. The top had been cut off, and a shantytown had been built on top of it. There was this big guy, his wife, four kids, and a huge dog. They were coming back from Mexico. This huge dog named Yogi was tethered to a tiny canvas camping stool, a flimsy little thing. Yogi would get up and give a little tug on the leash. He'd look disconsolate and sit down again. I went up to Dan and I said, "Hey, that dog of yours is the best metaphor I've ever seen."

Dan said, "Let's talk." So we sat down and had one of those most amazing conversations that you have in your lifetime. He was a shipbuilder who built beautiful wooden boats up in British Columbia; he lived on the Sechelt Peninsula. His wife, named Sue, was a Sioux Indian and the most lovely, *sad* woman. She had a sadness to her that was not unhappiness but the sadness of a cloudy day. Such a real condition of the world. You felt there was a wisdom to it, a beauty. They had four kids. The oldest was Joyden. When you build a ship, the first plank you put in is called the joyden. And there was Haida, Kit, and Shawnee.

Dan was like a survivalist. He refused to pay taxes or send his kids to school. They educated their kids at home. He'd logged the Sitka spruce out of his backyard and built his own house. He had an Alaskan mill and would make boats out of the spruce and sell them for cash in order to pay no taxes. They grew their own food. Dan was an amazing character.

I remember we had this conversation there by the beach. He asked what we were doing there. I talked about having kids and maybe moving to California, looking for a place to live. He said, "You know, I have four of the most beautiful kids in the world."

I replied, "I think that's clear."

"And I love these kids as deeply as a man can love his children."

I said, "I'm sure you do."

"But," he said, "you know what?"

I asked, "What?"

"I don't think it's worth it."

We became good friends. I'd go up to Canada and build boats with him. Years later, I was off in Texas to create the first-ever Wildflower Conference in Dallas. I came back to a voicemail message: Dan Carr was at the San Francisco Yacht Club and needed me. So I went there to meet with him.

He was in trouble. The school district wanted to get his kids. The government wanted to get his money. Everybody was after him. They closed him down. He took his last boat with the family on it, and he was going to sail around the world. The sea was the only place he could be free.

So I helped him sail the boat down to Mexico. The kids would sail the boat by day, and Dan and I took it at night. We'd have these long conversations all night. One night I asked him, "Remember when we first met and we talked about kids, you said you loved them as much as a father could, but it wasn't worth it?"

He said, "That sounds like something I would say."

I asked, "What do you think now?"

There was a long pause. With all night at the helm together, we had so much time. You could say something and wait half an hour for a reply. I waited for the longest time. Finally he said, "I don't think it's worth it, but that's all there is."

Another thing that I remember on that trip with Rina is that, driving up the coast, we got as far as Monterey and we ran out of money. I had about twenty dollars left. The car needed work, and we limped into the VW dealer. We needed a special part, a vacuum advance, but it cost thirty dollars and all I had was twenty. So I said, "I'll be back." I went into downtown Monterey, found a pawnshop, and pawned the camera for thirty dollars. On the way back, I'm passing Cannery Row and see an old alcoholic hanging around. He tells me he's an old friend of John Steinbeck's.

I say, "No kidding."

He says, "Yep. Steinbeck and Doc Ricketts, they used to meet right here."

"Really?" I ask.

He says, "Yeah, buy us a bottle of wine, and I'll tell you about it."

So I took some of that money, and I bought a cheap bottle of wine. We sat there drinking wine, watching the sun go down, and telling lies. I realized it was total fabrication, but such a wonderful fabrication that I wondered whether I'd ever be so happy again.

We lived in a Big Sur campground for a couple of months and hiked everywhere every day. We learned about the plants and lived off wild foods.

We read Euell Gibbons's book *Stalking the Wild Asparagus*. The taboo against eating food out of the woods was strong for me; I was positive I was going to die. The first wild food I ate was a piece of watercress. You could identify it by the pictures and the description. So we learned to forage and eat foods out of the forest.

After Monterey, we headed further north. We camped on the Elwha River on the Olympic Peninsula and hiked through the Olympics during the summer. For the winter, we went into Seattle, where I drove a cab. I was the world's worst cabbie. Other cab drivers would come back to the barn with stories of people who threw hundred-dollar bills down, rich dope dealers, or people rushing to the airport, slapping down money. But wherever *I* went, old ladies whose husbands had just died would find me; they didn't have any money, but they needed to get to the funeral parlor. And I couldn't take their money. I was totally hopeless.

I did some writing up there. All the time, we had a typewriter in the back of the VW. So I did some writing about forests and forestry. I had left being a cabbie to plant trees on logged-over land. Rina and I were part of a tree-planting crew. It was only for a couple of months. It was rigorous work. I had a big auger that ran on a chainsaw motor. You just drill and move, drill and move. Rina was planting trees behind me. It was hard physical work. We were living in the camps. This experience set off a realization that this practice was not good, cutting down varied forests and then planting the one kind of tree. I wrote for *Science Digest*, for *National Parks* magazine, and for *The Nation* magazine. My editor at *The Nation* was Carey McWilliams. But I didn't realize his greatness until years later.

Later we went up to Vancouver, stayed with Dan Carr, and helped him build a boat. Then came the most wonderful experience, in the summer of '69. We left the car with Dan and hitchhiked to the ferry terminal. We took the ferry to Nanaimo on Vancouver Island and then hitchhiked from Nanaimo to Port Alberni. Then there was a hundred-mile dirt road to two Indian villages, Tofino and Ucluelet, and a place called Long Beach. By Ucluelet was a beach called Wreck Bay where we built a shelter out of driftwood, along with about thirty other families there. It was strictly for

Malcolm reading in the woods, 1967 (MARGOLIN FAMILY COLLECTION)

the summer because in the spring the tides would bring in the driftwood, and a shantytown would arise. Then in the fall the tides would rush back in and take the driftwood away, washing the whole thing clean.

We ended up building our shelter near a couple named Zoe and Klagen who had two kids, Bjorn and Gooseberry. Zoe was the guy; Klagen was the girl. I'm sure they had real names like Sally and Joseph or something. They helped us build our shelter. Zoe was the quietest guy in the world. We'd spend the time fishing.

Everything was so far away that strangers rarely appeared on this beach. One day this guy named Stuart shows up. Apparently Stuart had just dropped out of college. With two days to graduate, he decided he didn't want whatever degree he was going to get. Instead, he wanted to be a doctor. So Stuart set up shop and put up a sign saying "DOCTOR." With only thirty families living there, everyone knew each other, yet he put up this sign. He'd sit around waiting. About two weeks later, there came another sign: "NURSES WANTED."

One day a couple of guys were fishing for ling cod off the rocks, and one of the guys cut himself pretty badly with the gaff, this barbed spear. I said, "Let's go to Stuart's; I bet he has some stuff to sew it up." We go over to Stuart, but Stuart faints! We had to revive him.

A river flowed into Wreck Bay, and a guy who lived upriver was named Mr. Billing; it was very clear that he was to be called "Mr. Billing." He lived up there in a little house away from the beach. During the winter, Mr. Billing would go down to the ocean, and as the waters came churning up, he would pan gold. He'd take the silt and the dirt onto his blanket and wash it off, and gold flecks would be left. He kept dreaming that someday, a big vein would be found out there, and he was going to get that big vein. Every month he'd go to the post office in the little village of Long Beach and get one piece of mail, a travel magazine. He would look for articles on Acapulco because his dream was to go to Acapulco.

Mr. Billing had a two-way radio. One night when Rina and I were visiting him, we heard news that a storm was coming. He said, "I think the beach is going to be washed away tonight." Rina headed back and found the sandflies already jumping on the roof and the water coming up high. She got the sleeping bags and everything else out onto a bluff above. When I arrived, I saw it all go.

I was so happy that this paradise was going to end and I didn't have to put up with it anymore. It was the same thing in the Caribbean a couple years earlier. We'd camped on St. John, went fishing and diving. It was wonderful, but I could hardly wait to escape to the Lower East Side of New York. Paradise was so oppressive, so boring! I've often thought that you want a world that reflects yourself. If your self is not paradisiacal, if your self is incomplete in some ways, yet everything around you is beautiful, then you can't really feel at home in that world. That's why people become alcoholics. That would have happened to me. You need a world that reflects the range of your person.

So then we came down from Canada in the fall of 1969. We stopped again in Portland. We ended up doing some counseling for a while. Then we left and spent the winter in Monte Rio on the Russian River, and the spring on Eddy Street in San Francisco's Tenderloin.

Malcolm, 1967 (MARGOLIN FAMILY COLLECTION)

Still, we had one final fling in Mexico. We took that VW, and I had about five hundred bucks in my pocket. We had a wonderful trip to Mexico. Rina was now four months pregnant. The VW kept breaking down, but I had the VW repair book, *How to Keep Your Volkswagen Alive: A Manual of Step by Step Procedures for the Compleat Idiot,* so I kept putting the bus back together again.

We hit Mazatlán at Carnival time. A big party was going on in the streets. People were selling *cascarones*, eggshells with confetti in them, throwing them at each other, drinking and laughing. I got into the big celebration. It's one of my clearest memories in a life of episodic lucidity. The next morning, we were having breakfast at a restaurant that opened up on the avenue leading to the plaza. I was sitting there, having coffee, looking out on this avenue, watching all these people walking toward the plaza. There were people loaded down with things, women with their arms out, a kid on each arm, and a kid on each kid's arm. People with flowers, people pushing carts, selling things, with wonderful displays, rounds of cantaloupe and watermelon on sticks like lollipops. Huichol Indians in their *huipils*, those elaborately embroidered blouses. I remember one guy with neckties.

He had something that looked like a crucifix, and hung over it were these neckties. Some of it was spooky—and wonderful.

I remember watching all this parade of people moving down the streets, and for the first time in my life I was so *proud* to be a human being. I felt, "These are my people! It's not my culture, but this *is* my species." It was so beautiful, such a flow.

Then we spent some time in Mexico City. That pride of being human filled me that whole time we were in Mexico. I felt it keenly at the anthropology museum and again in Chapultepec Park. I just loved Mexico. I felt so at home in Mexico.

We spent several months there. We lived in a deserted tortilla factory for a month in a little town called Santa Cruz near San Blas. You know when you move into a new town and the people you first meet tend to be the marginal ones? Opposite the tortilla factory—god, I haven't thought about this stuff in years!—in a strange shell of a building, somebody had created a boxing school. All the young men would come during the day to learn boxing. They thought if they were lucky, they would make it to Tijuana, maybe to the big time. There was just no way out of these towns, but maybe if you were ambitious and strong—people have these dreams, like being an NBA player.

Only one electrical line came into the town, right to the grocery store next to us, which had a loudspeaker. Every so often the loudspeaker would go on. "Mrs. González is slaughtering her pig today. People that want *chuletas* and skins can see Mrs. González; she had a fat and wonderful pig." Then there would be a pause, and some blaring music would come on, with the third grade kids singing happy birthday to Mrs. Rodríguez, the teacher.

This spooky guy kept wanting me to walk out into the woods with him. He seemed a little scary. He was so insistent about showing me something. Finally, we were about to leave town. I figured I may as well do it, even if I'd probably get killed. But what he wanted to show me was a place in the woods that was *silent*. In these jungly woods, it was absolutely silent. When the moon shone, the palm trees were silvery, like metal, and why was that? That's what he wanted to show me.

I love it when people show me things. It's one of the rewards of being a publisher; you get introduced to other people's worlds.

I remember coming back through El Paso and crossing the border, suddenly finding myself in the United States again and feeling so horrified by the number of cops, the multiple-lane freeways, the violence of the place. I realized that I had learned something I would never forget. Then, several months later, I realized that I'd probably forgotten most of it. It's something that has to be lived; it's not something that can be remembered.

Those were all wonderful years, those years of Puerto Rico, the Virgin Islands, travels, freedom.

When we arrived back in Berkeley, we decided to live here. We chose Berkeley largely because I had college friends in Berkeley. On an earlier trip I had visited David Nawi, a friend from Harvard, who lived here. I remember walking up into the hills after being someplace on Telegraph Avenue, walking up into Tilden Park, and seeing deer and hawks. I thought it was kind of nice. I thought the view was okay, and the privilege of walking up into the hills was okay, too. This was not grandeur, like the Rockies, the Sierra, Pike's Peak, or the Olympic Peninsula. But Berkeley was a place to settle in for a while, a place of convenience. It had a library, places you could walk out to. I figured we would stay for a few months and probably keep wandering.

My friend Jeff Lustig said it best, quoting another friend, Chitra Divakaruni, an East Indian writer. Chitra said once, "In America you fall in love and then get married. In India, you get married, and then you fall in love." I didn't fall in love with Berkeley right away.

THE BIRTH OF HEYDAY

*"Publishing just appeared on the horizon; it was just something
to do. Things just come along, and I go to it."*

—MALCOLM MARGOLIN

THE PENDING ARRIVAL of Malcolm and Rina's first son, Reuben Heyday Margolin, in 1970 led them to settle down in Berkeley. Their daughter, Sadie Cash Margolin, arrived in 1974. From late 1970 to 1972, Malcolm worked as a groundsman at the East Bay Regional Parks, doing everything from cleaning up picnic areas and building trails to leading nature walks.

This work inspired him to write two books, *The Earth Manual: How to Work on Wild Land Without Taming It* (Houghton Mifflin, 1975) and *The East Bay Out: A Personal Guide to the East Bay Regional Parks* (Heyday, 1974). Malcolm's decision to publish *The East Bay Out* himself, from doing the typesetting to design and layout, led him to form his company, Heyday Books, in 1974.

Malcolm recounted the founding of the family and the publishing company, both endeavors imbued with joy, imagination, and humor.

REUBEN JOINS THE FAMILY

By June 1970 we'd found a little place near the corner of Bancroft Way and Acton in Berkeley, a small apartment that we paid $90 a month for. It had one room, a tiny alcove, and a kitchen. The alcove was like a closet. I painted the trim orange and the walls white. We put a crib in there, and we waited for Reuben to come.

I had a series of odd, temporary jobs, minimum wage, which involved doing anything, like handyman work. I worked for Easter Seal for a while, driving patients around. We probably lived on a couple hundred bucks a month, but you could get by.

I remember one morning Rina woke me up and said, "You don't have to go to work today."

I said, "How come?"

"Because the baby's coming."

It was June 19, 1970. We drove across the bridge to UC San Francisco because they had an inexpensive birth center there, and I could be present. We'd been doing Lamaze classes together, all that stuff.

When Reuben was born, his umbilical cord was wrapped around his neck, so he was blue because he couldn't breathe. When they unwrapped the umbilical cord, this beautiful coloration came through him, a beautiful glow like a sunrise. I remember looking at his little hand, and it was *my* hand, but freshly shaped and perfectly formed. I was so stunned that somebody had *my* hands.

For years I'd meet people who said that during those first weeks of Reuben's life, I was absolutely transformed, and I transformed everybody around me by talking about the beauty of this birth. I was just walking on air.

Then we brought him home. It was a thorough love affair, the real thing. I didn't know where I began and where he ended. There was a sense of conspiracy, a sense of intimacy—the utter fascination with each other.

One anecdote from around that time was when we had just moved into a house. We never had money, so we didn't have much furniture. I felt that every home needed a round oak table. What you needed to form a family was a round oak table. So I went down to MacBeath's Hardwood and got five slabs of Appalachian white oak. They were about three inches thick, hard, old-growth wood, the strongest, hardest wood that anybody could imagine. I took a course at Berkeley High in woodworking so that I could use their equipment. I spent weeks cutting that wood to size, planing it and joining it, trimming the sides and putting it together, drilling holes, clamping and gluing. Then I made a big circle. Scored the circle, used a jigsaw to cut out the circle, used a router to smooth the edges. I built a pedestal and sanded the whole thing down with increasingly fine

Malcolm holding baby Reuben, 1970 (MARGOLIN FAMILY COLLECTION)

sandings. I got a special grade of finish so that it would retain the color of the oak, not turn dark brown but keep that blond color it had. The thing was absolutely gorgeous.

I brought it home. It sat there, and I hated the goddamn thing! I just absolutely hated it. I told Rina, "Sell it for fifteen dollars." I didn't want to see the thing again. I'm not certain what that anger was about, but that table represented someplace that I just didn't want to go. I tried it out, and I just didn't want to go there. There was something phony about it. I was trying to get status through buying or making something. It wasn't me.

Later on, I underwent a series of explosive changes. By this time we had moved through several houses. This theme is recurring, oddly enough. We were living in a house on Edith Street, a beautiful house in a lovely neighborhood, paying $120 a month. It had a huge floor upstairs with a fireplace, a finished basement that you could use for your hobbies, for woodworking and stuff, a garage, and a big backyard with a fruit tree. It even had beehives. It was the loveliest place you could imagine.

I came home one day, and I'd decided that people shouldn't live in houses. So I moved us out to a campground in Chabot Regional Park that hadn't been built yet. We lived in a tent! By this time Reuben was about two years old. I don't quite remember what Rina said. I think it was kind of lonely out there for her. I was working during the day, and I'd leave her and Reuben and come back at night.

I remember what impelled it, the exact moment when I decided we had to move. By then I'd been working at the East Bay Regional Park District. I was on a levee in a place called Shadow Cliffs. Old Alameda Creek flowed past the levee. On one side of the levee was a wild area with a river and some people on a handmade raft floating down the river; it looked so gorgeous. On the other side was this manicured recreation area, a world of people in little chairs with picnic baskets, umbrellas, suntan lotion, a snack bar, and everything else. I just hated that world of artificiality.

To this day I cannot go into a store like a Macy's. I have ten minutes when I can tolerate a Macy's before I go crazy. There's something in the manipulation of it, in the Muzak, in the fact that it's all geared to sell me stuff. It blunts hostility. It's meant to blunt your zest. Some kind of rebellion in me comes out. I haven't thought about this much. It's the same reason that I never got a real job. It's not that I don't want to fit in. I'm a tremendously social animal.

Anyhow, after about four or five months of living in a tent, I put my tail between my legs, and we moved back to a lousy place in Berkeley. I think that whole episode of moving to the tent happened for the same reason I escaped the Caribbean, the same reason I was glad when Wreck Bay crashed, the same reason I threw the table out. I'm not sure what it's all about. Part of it was deeply felt, part of it was probably theatrical, performing for myself, as well as for others. I think we do that.

We must have moved to about eleven places in Berkeley—I once counted them all—in the first years of Reuben's life. We'd find a good place, but the landlord would evict us because the landlord wanted to move in, or it was a terrible place, but we'd take it 'cause we needed a place and then we'd move out as quickly as we could. At least we had hardly anything to move.

I was a hugely devoted father. I took Reuben everywhere and played with him. Rina and I took him on hikes. Rina would take art classes, and I'd hang out with him. We'd climb trees and walk on logs, go out into the woods, go to the airports and watch airplanes take off. We'd daydream about having a farm together. We'd build things together.

We had a closet in one place. He'd close his eyes, and I'd take him into the closet and hold him. I told him he'd have to keep his eyes shut because the spaceship was about to take off, and the radiation on the planets wasn't good for little kids' eyes. Then the spaceship would blast off, and we'd go through the air; we'd walk around on planets. I'd describe the planets that we walked on. Then I'd bring him back, and he could open his eyes again because it was now safe.

Probably the big event was that Reuben got very sick when he was a year old. We didn't know what it was. He couldn't digest any food. He was losing weight; he was in terrible physical shape. I remember one week we went to eight different doctors. Nobody could figure it out. We had him tested for cystic fibrosis, celiac disease, all kinds of terrible things.

One night he was up crying, and I had him in my arms. I was walking back and forth. I remember he got through to me where nobody else had gotten through. It just got down to some dogged loyalty, that I was going to see this kid through, without question, without hold, without ego. I was going to get through this goddamn thing, whatever it took.

Someone had recommended this doctor, Louis Meyers, a pediatrician on Telegraph Avenue. His office was like a waiting room in India. Tons of people were in there, along with his horrible receptionist. Every so often she would raise her head from the reception area and, in this imperious, nasal voice, would say, "Doctor will see you now." It came to our turn, and she said, "Doctor will see you now." She was such a horrible person; I would have left, but there was nowhere else to go.

We sat in the consulting room, and this little man came in with a kind of elfish look to him. He looked at Reuben, stopped, and said, "Oh! You have a *real* problem!"

We said, "Yeah."

He asked, "What's been happening? How long has it been going on?" We explained. Then he did the most beautiful thing that a human being could do: he opened the door and said, "I do not want to be disturbed, no matter what happens." He shut the door. Then he just stared at Reuben, the way an artist stares at a model. Observed him. Every so often he touched him, looked at him, really got the feel for it all. Every so often he asked a question. Time passed.

During Reuben's illness, we'd been keeping tabs on what he'd been eating, how he'd been behaving. The doctor then asked us to keep detailed charts. It seemed that some foods were better for him and others worse. He advised a very simple diet. Reuben thrived on that diet and ended up getting better. It seemed like it was multiple allergies. For a long time he stayed allergic to wheat and milk.

That experience influenced me a lot. There's always been a close bond between Reuben and me. The hold is still there. He was a good kid, with a sense of adventurousness to him. He was forever pushing his limits, climbing as high as he could climb, doing whatever he could do.

When Reuben was about four years old, we took him to Brennan's to buy him his favorite food, which was a corned beef sandwich. We said, "Reuben, you're going to have a baby brother or baby sister. We don't know which it is yet. We've had a wonderful family of three, and now we're going to have a wonderful family of four."

To jump ahead a moment, when Sadie was about six years old, we brought Reuben and Sadie over to Brennan's, we bought them their favorite foods, and we said, "There's something we want to tell you. You're going to have a baby brother or a baby sister; we don't know which it is. But we're going to be a wonderful family of five." And Jake was born.

Then when Jake was about two years old, all of a sudden I felt like hofbrau food. I said, "Let's go to Brennan's." All three kids shouted, "No!" in turn.

More recently, Reuben gave us a call. He said, "Let's have dinner at Brennan's." I knew exactly what he and Amber had to tell us. So sweet!

I have another memory from when Reuben was a baby. We were living on Berkeley Way then, in a little house. It was beautiful. It had a couple of bedrooms and a backyard with a fruit tree. Just lovely. The rent was $95 a month. When we moved in, it was owned by a male schoolteacher in Lafayette who'd bought four or five of these little houses together. BART

Malcolm mid-story with Reuben (MARGOLIN FAMILY COLLECTION)

was just being built. People knew that as soon as BART came in, this would be prime real estate, and some developers would tear it all down and build condominiums.

One neighbor was a woman named Susie, a member of the White Panther Party, a white woman's equivalent of the Black Panthers. We went around and downzoned the neighborhood so you couldn't build a birdhouse there over two feet tall. The owner was so infuriated that he could not build his condominium that he decided to sell all these places. He offered me this house for thirty-six thousand dollars. I remember the deep satisfaction with which I called him a capitalist pig! But I would have loved to have had that house. That was probably our one chance at ever owning a house.

WORKING AT THE EAST BAY REGIONAL PARKS

Somewhere in Reuben's first year of life, I went to work for the East Bay Regional Parks. I got hired by a guy named Gary Pickering, who later changed his name to Guido Pickering.

I worked at Redwood Regional Park. I remember my first day; I got there early, all eager to please. They sent me out with this old guy from Arkansas, Clyde Oden. It got to be eight o'clock, and he walked over and punched his time card and then explained, "You go over to the key box, and you get the key to a truck. Then you walk over to the truck, but you don't just get into the truck. You look around the truck. You look to see that the tires are okay; you look to see that there's nothin' under the truck. Then you pop the hood and check the motor oil. Then you check the transmission fluid. Then you get into the truck. You warm up the truck. Then you back the truck up to the shed to get the tools into the truck."

I said, "Geez, the shed is only ten feet away. We could just grab the tools."

He said, "Nope. You never bring tools to a truck. You bring the truck to the tools. So then you get the tools into the truck. You get to the job site. But you don't go straight to the job site. You go check the park out to make sure everything is okay. *Then* you get to the job site, and you unload the tools. Then it's coffee break time. So you load the tools back in, and you go to find a place for coffee."

I remember it was the longest day of my life. I didn't know they made days that long.

Clyde Oden had been there since the Civilian Conservation Corps days, the Works Progress Administration days. He loved to make stone walls, and he was a master at it. He was good at one other thing, water dowsing. I don't even believe in this stuff, but at the park, they had these big fields with irrigation pipes in them. They'd let the fields grow during the winter; then during the spring they'd mow them down, and you'd have to find the sprinkler heads. But nobody could ever find the sprinkler heads because they'd been grown over. Clyde would come with a dowsing rod and walk across the meadow. He'd find out where the pipes were and the sprinkler heads. He showed me how to water dowse. Sure enough, you walk along, and you feel the thing dip in. But I still don't believe in it!

Another thing about Clyde lives in my memory. We were broke one year, and when I told Clyde, he said, "If you're broke, there's an easy way to get rich."

I said, "What's that?"

He said, "Well, your wife is going to have another baby. Put money in the baby's name. If it's a girl, call her 'Penny,' and if it's a boy, call him 'Buck.'" So that's how my daughter became Sadie Cash. I'm still broke! But there was a kind of playfulness involved, a willingness to play along: "What would I do if I *did* believe in that stuff?"

When I first joined the crew, it was all male. Greg Phillips was the supervisor of Redwood and Chabot Parks. Jack Miller, a former cowboy, was the foreman of Chabot. Guido Pickering, an artist, was the foreman of Redwood. He'd graduated from the San Francisco Art Institute. He hired me and his friend Percy Millet, a black guy that had also graduated from the Art Institute, and this guy named Ralph Warner. The younger generation were all college-educated hippies and artists. The older generation were often old alcoholics.

I loved going out into the parks. We were doing some really good physical work, digging fence-post holes, building trails, and the like. Then I took over from a guy named Dave Hupp. Dave's mother was Lucy Hupp, a famous gardener in the Orinda area, with her husband, Jim. Dave Hupp was into environmental education. He created an environmental program for kids who would come in and do work. When Dave left, I took over the program.

We ended up doing wildlife habitat restoration with the kids. I was doing it as a groundsman—that's what my position was—not as a naturalist. That position wasn't wired into the place yet; it was just done on the side. But I loved it, leading around kids, like the Boy Scouts, on nature walks, doing land restoration, telling stories.

A loquacious naturalist named Josh Barkin was working for the East Bay Regional Park District at that time, out at Tilden. Josh Barkin fundamentally sat under a tree, and people would come listen to him. He was a puppeteer.

He wasn't a real naturalist, but he told wonderful stories. Everybody loved Josh. Tim Gordon and Ron Russo were also working as naturalists, but they were of my generation. They actually knew something about natural history. You'd go out there and magical things would happen. The Park District ended up building an environmental center, having people with the right degrees, and developing programs. But somehow that magic of meeting the Old Man of the Woods was gone: meeting somebody who could tell you beautiful stories that break your heart. That wasn't there anymore.

I learned a lot from Jim Roof, who was head of the Tilden Botanical Garden, a great man and a well-known botanist. I remember I'd drive along in a truck with Jim. He'd see a barren roadcut and stop the truck. He'd reach into the glove compartment, pull out a seed bag, and say, *"Eriogonum fasciculatum!"* Then he'd throw the seeds out there! Next year, you'd come to that spot again and find the whole thing alive with buckwheat. He came before that generation of botanists that were polite and nice and knew their computers. He was of a generation that had an earthy love of plants.

I really liked it out there. By then my parents were back in my life, and I took them out to the parks with me once. I gave them a ride in a dump truck because I thought they would really like that. They didn't like it one bit! I went along the trails, but they were much too narrow for the dump truck. My mother couldn't figure out what I did over there anyway. Then she finally decided that what people do when they work in the woods is that when the trees fall down, they put them up again.

Now we had children, and my parents came to visit every now and then. I remember one great incident. Part of Reuben being so sick when he was young meant he had earaches all the time, and he couldn't hear very well. As a result, he couldn't speak very well. My parents came to visit. They were just made for grandchild worship. "Max, look how beautiful he is! Max, how smart he is!" Everything he did they lauded. "He breathes in and out, Max, look. Isn't he wonderful?"

My father had brought a present, a very symbolic present, a big metallic elephant that was a coin bank. It had a saddle on the back and a slot. The trunk had a groove in it where you'd put the coin. You'd crank the tail, and then the trunk lifted up and dropped the coin into the slot on the elephant's back.

My father brought this gift out and unwrapped it. A toy that involves money: this was a big thing! He reaches into his pocket. He pulls out not a nickel, not a dime, but a quarter! He puts the quarter in the slot and tells Reuben to crank the tail. Reuben cranks it, and the thing flips the coin over. But instead of going into the slot, the coin goes down the elephant's back and rolls down under the couch.

At this point, Reuben articulates the first clear thing he's said in their entire visit, which is, "The fucking thing doesn't work!" I remember my mother stopped, looked, and said, "Max, so smart at his age—what he knows!" I mean, they were going to see the good in it no matter what.

With Reuben, there was always the danger that he was going to say the wrong thing. One time I was driving back east with Reuben, Rina, and Sadie, who was just a little baby. We headed back in this little tiny VW Fastback. I figured we'd stop and visit Geoff Stanford in Dallas.

To back up a little, I'd met Stanford when I was setting up the Texas Wildflower Conference that I helped create in Dallas. They decided I was some kind of environmental genius, that I knew how to organize things. I'd published a book by that time called *The Earth Manual* about how to restore wild land, which came out of my East Bay Regional Parks experience.

So the group flies me out to the Dallas airport and drives me to the house of this guy Geoffrey Stanford, who had been a British surgeon. He was tremendously wealthy. His wife, Dawn, was from British royalty of some sort on her father's side, and her father had been a consul in Monterrey when she was growing up. The two of them had tons of money and a house on a square-mile of land outside Dallas.

They'd have these parties and invite all the ruling class: the mayor; the head of the chamber of commerce; Dave Fox, a major developer. Big tables were set up. A maid would bring in food. The tables were arranged by status: the head table, the side table, the end table. Other displays of status were evident. As you were leaving, Geoffrey would stop and say, "Malcolm, don't leave just yet. I had a wonderful cheese flown in from England that I think you're going to really enjoy. Stay around for another half-hour. There are some things that I want to tell you about." He just played the part so beautifully.

So back on our way to visit Stanford, the whole time I'm telling Reuben, "Just don't say 'fuck'! These are very important people to me. You don't say those kinds of things in nice company. Just don't say 'fuck.'"

So we get there, and we're sitting at the table. The maid brings the food. And the first thing out of his mouth is, "Jesus, all the plates are the same!" He'd never sat at a table where all the plates matched. He thought that was the most amazing thing that he'd ever seen.

THE EARTH MANUAL: HOW TO WORK ON WILD LAND WITHOUT TAMING IT

The East Bay Regional Park District refused to rehire me at the end of 1972 because I refused to wear a uniform. Up until then we didn't have to wear one, but now they wanted us to wear uniforms. I argued against uniforms. "This is part of a militarization of the parks," I said, "and what we do *not* want is a militarization of the parks. What we *want* is something that grows out of the soil, out of the trees, that people can relate to. We want an egalitarian world. What you're trying to do is put in people with police authority, and that's why you want the uniforms. I won't wear a uniform."

So I didn't! And I didn't have a job. I was utterly delighted, utterly pleased to get out of there, because I could see that it was a trap. The work was easy, the pay was good. I could see becoming addicted to it. Something about it was too comfortable. There would come the limitations of predictability and comfort. I still remember the regular paycheck. That was the last time in my life when I had a regular paycheck—except for the last couple of years here.

The other thing that happened around then is that I turned thirty. I'd actually turned thirty in 1970, but it took three years, until 1973, until I could really do it. I mean, I had to work on turning thirty.

By 1973, I had all this information about working with kids on wild land. I went to this guy John Dewitt who ran Save the Redwoods League.

I said, "This is what I'm doing at Redwood Park. I'd like some money to write a book about how to work with kids on wild land."

He said, "See Huey Johnson."

Huey Johnson was the first employee of the Nature Conservancy west of the Mississippi. He later founded the Trust for Public Land. He was Jerry Brown's Secretary for Resources. He now runs something called the Resource Renewal Institute. He's tremendous. Stewart Brand called him a "thug for the environment." At the time, he was connected to Point Foundation, which had grown out of the *Whole Earth Catalog*. I told him that I wanted to write a book, so he had me visit him at the Nature Conservancy, which consisted of Huey and a couple of other guys. He had a swing hanging from the ceiling. You'd sit in the swing, swing around, and talk to Huey.

Huey asked, "How long is it going to take you?"

I said, "Five months."

He asked, "How much do you need?"

I said, "I could probably live on about…four hundred a month, so two thousand ought to do it."

He replied, "Okay, I'll give you a check for two thousand dollars."

He gave me the check, just like that. I'd lied through my teeth because we were living on much less than four hundred bucks a month. I was going to make a killing! I ended up writing the book in about four months. I thought, "This is easy."

I rented a little studio in back of Dan and Judy Phillips's place on Deakin Street. They were both writers. I'd work every day. It was during the Watergate era. I'd work for several hours in the morning, then go off to the Buttercup Café on College Avenue, get the newspaper, and read about Watergate. Then I'd go back and work.

I had been writing before Reuben was born and continued after. Some of it only got published later, when we were in Berkeley. Some of that writing really only provided a toehold in a world of fantasy for me, the fantasy that I could support the family by writing. I needed an identity. But it did ultimately happen, that I *could* support them with my writing for a while.

I remember that I really took some time to study and learn the craft of writing. I'd study authors and their writing. I'd read something, and if

EXCERPTS FROM *THE EARTH MANUAL:*
HOW TO WORK ON WILD LAND WITHOUT TAMING IT

FROM THE CHAPTER "WILDLIFE"

PLANTING FOOD FOR wildlife is a delightful switch. For ages wild animals have been used to feed humans; now you have the chance to feed them instead.

Let's examine the yearly food cycle of, say, a deer. In the late spring and throughout the summer, there is plenty of green grass, weeds, wildflowers, berries, and fruit. "Livin' is easy," as the song about summertime goes.

In the fall, grains and many seeds ripen, but the big event is the nut harvest. Acorns, beechnuts, hickories, hazelnuts—all fantastically nutritious—are readily available until the first snows.

In the winter, deer paw through the snow after acorns and eat whatever tough greens they can find (especially wintergreen). By the end of winter, however, they are reduced to eating buds and twigs. They seem to go about it with all the gusto of a starving man eating his boots.

If you want to increase your wildlife population significantly, early spring is the season when you should concentrate your planting efforts.

WORKING WITH KIDS

By and large, I had the most fun with school kids. In dealing with schools, be sure you get volunteers, not conscripts. Before I learned this lesson thoroughly, I often found myself facing thirty-six hostile teenagers who had

I came upon a good passage, I'd copy it out. I'd tape it up on the wall and write a letter to it as to why the writing was so good. I'd look at the way the passage was shaped. I'd see, perhaps, that it had a big statement in it, narrowed down to a smaller statement, and then it would pop out to a larger statement again. I'd notice the way something would be hit from different senses, the way it would be set up for something and then the rug would be pulled out from under you. I'd look at the structure of things, the vocabulary. I just studied the way other writers actually wrote. Then I was using all that in the writing that I was doing.

just slunk out of a school bus. In the immortal words of one teacher, I was expected to "put these damn kids to work and teach them something about the ecology." But no one ever told me how. Then one day, as I found myself looking into thirty-six smirks, I did exactly what any other gentle, basically sane naturalist would have done in such a situation. I turned my back and ran away.

"C'mon," I yelled. "The ecology lecture is this way." And I took off like a madman—up slopes and down slopes, across meadows and through forests. Most of the kids followed me close behind, tripping, rolling, stumbling, shouting, and—best of all—laughing. We left the teachers far behind. We splashed through the stream and drank water from a fresh brook. We ate miner's lettuce underneath a big oak tree. We talked and joked, and when we got back to the bus I asked the kids, "Did you learn anything about the ecology?"

"Yeah," said one kid. "It's fun." Since that day, whenever I found myself with a group of conscripts, I did my best to have fun and left the productive work for another day.

There's something important I'd like to add about the spirit of recruiting. It has to be honest. The temptation to exaggerate is enormous. I've worked with groups that were promised ecstasy, enlightenment, and The Salvation of Mother Earth. We had a rather disappointing time. On the other hand, groups who were told frankly, "We'll walk around a bit, look at how plants grow and how water flows, do a couple of hours' work, get to know each other, and maybe we'll really hit it off"—these groups tended to enjoy themselves much more. To the extent that we represent the beginnings of a new consciousness, unless we're honest, we've lost it all, right at the start.

I got the money from *Whole Earth Catalog*, and out of that grew something called Word Wheel Books. This guy Wally had been head of the East Asia Foundation or something like that. Wally was now the head of Word Wheel Books, and their model was to make copublishing arrangements with other back-east publishers. All the *Whole Earth Catalog* people—Sally Raspberry, Michael Phillips, who wrote *The Seven Laws of Money*, other New Age types—would have their meetings at the Erotic Art Museum or at similar "in" places. They were just so damned hip, it really hurt. Poor Wally! I remember that his wife was distraught. Here they lived in this big house in Hillside, and he had joined this "cult." Wally was not earning any money. His newfound friends were forever talking about how, if you follow your bliss, money will come. Then Word Wheel Books published *The Seven Laws of Money*. But Wally never benefited from that strategy, and his friends didn't help him much.

Word Wheel Books kept trying to figure out how to get a copublishing arrangement for my book. Around this time the major publishers in New York and Boston began to notice the tremendous success of the *Whole Earth Catalog*, *How to Keep Your Volkswagen Alive: A Manual of Step-by-Step Procedures for the Compleat Idiot*, and other such books that were self-published or were created by start-up presses in the West. Sensing something new was happening here, the established eastern publishers grew nervous and excited, and a steady parade of editors and agents began showing up in the Bay Area for what they must have thought would be a new Gold Rush. Among them were Ernest Scott and his wife, Anita, who founded San Francisco Book Company, which would be closely associated with Houghton Mifflin. As Word Wheel seemed to get stuck in the mud, they turned *The Earth Manual* over to Ernest, and much to my surprise I found myself with a ten-thousand-dollar advance against royalties and a Houghton Mifflin contract.

Back then, this was a spectacular amount of money. So in '73 I sold the book to Houghton Mifflin, and I had money in my pocket. The book didn't actually come out until 1975 because they had to publish during a specific season. *The Earth Manual* never did as well as anybody thought it should do. It became a cult item. But that's the story of books.

THE EAST BAY OUT: A PERSONAL GUIDE TO THE EAST BAY REGIONAL PARKS

With that chunk of money from *The Earth Manual* in my pocket and no job, I decided to write a book about the East Bay parks that year, which turned into *The East Bay Out*, based on what I'd learned about the trails while working for the Park District. While I was working on the book, it was a year of hiking the hills, thinking, and taking notes. Just being in love with the world.

With *The East Bay Out*, I didn't try too hard to get it published, but I did try. I sent it off to Ten Speed Press, and they thought it was too regional. The poetry publishers thought it was too much like a guidebook, and the guidebook publishers, like Wilderness Press, thought it was too much like poetry. Few people had ever done a regional guidebook before; there wasn't much like it out there.

I already had in my mind this model of the *Whole Earth Catalog*, which Stewart had done himself. It was a journal that combined articles about new do-it-yourself technologies with older traditions for those going "back to the land," a classic of the time. I got together with Hal Hershey, who had designed the first *Whole Earth Catalog*. He taught me how to design books. Rina did the drawings of the maps. A member of her women's group, Nancy Curry, did some illustrations. A wonderful calligrapher, Barbara Bash, now a well-known author of children's books, did some calligraphy.

I had such joy in doing my own book, writing it, designing it, typesetting it—and a pride that I was able to do things myself. I'd thought of myself as kind of a clumsy kid who lived in a daydream. This whole business of having practical capacity was such a surprise to me. It was so rewarding that I could actually typeset and design and do things like that.

I remember working on *The East Bay Out* on the light table. I'd put the page number on the righthand side of the page, then I'd put it on the lefthand side of the page, then I'd center it, put it up above and then down below. I'd think about which decision best exemplified the beauty of the work, as if it really mattered, as if anybody was ever going to notice. But there was something in making those decisions, in doing something real, that was very energizing and fulfilling, very self-gratifying. I liked the person that I was becoming through these activities.

And I didn't like the person that I was otherwise—rebellious, surly, covering up inadequacies with belligerence. I liked the person who was part of this creative force, moving something out into the world, creating

Malcolm, Reuben, and Sadie with publishing paraphernalia (HEYDAY ARCHIVES)

something through love and respect, giving it off to the world—I really liked that.

So we put out this book called *The East Bay Out* in 1974. It was a celebration of being alive, a celebration of the beauty of the parks. That book was a walking party, a gift.

I remember that we were living on a corner of Berkeley Way and Sacramento Street on the second floor. With the money I had left, I could have seven thousand copies of the book printed. So I did, with a list price of $2.95. The truck pulls up to the house, and the driver asks where Heyday Books is.

I say, "You've found it."

He says, "Where's the loading dock?"

I realized it was going to cost me twenty dollars to enlist his help. We loaded the books down onto the sidewalk. For the rest of the afternoon, I walked the books up the stairs, put them under Reuben's bed, stacked them against the walls, everywhere.

I was proud that I had published a book. I loved the design of it. I loved working with my hands, putting it together, the physicality of it all. But then came this horrible understanding that the books were going to stay under Reuben's bed unless I did something.

So I loaded some boxes into the VW bus, and I drove around. My first stop was to see Fred Cody at Cody's Books. I brought in a book. Fred looked at it, read some passages aloud to some people, looked at me lovingly, and put his arm around me. He thought it was wonderful. He took twenty-four copies. He asked if I needed money. I said, "Of course!" He went upstairs and said to his wife, Pat, "Write him a check for this." Pat wrote me out a check. He put up the books next to the cash register. I said, "My god, this publishing is much better than I ever thought!"

Back at that time, Berkeley was just *filled* with small publishers. Alta had Shameless Hussy Press. John Oliver Simon had Aldebaran Books. Don Cushman had Cloud Marauder. George Mattingly had Blue Wind. Bob and Eileen Callahan had Turtle Island. Betsy Davids had Rebis Press. Pat Dienstfrey had Kelsey Street Press. Phil Wood was just starting Ten Speed. Ralph Warner was just starting Nolo. Jerry Ratch had a press called Sombre Reptiles. Ishmael Reed had I. Reed Books.

And Berkeley was full of bookstores. You'd go down Telegraph to Cody's and Moe's; then you'd go to the Sather Gate Book Shop and to Hunault's, Lucas Books, Books Unlimited (the co-op bookstore). Then you could go down Solano Avenue to Sand Dollar, Ben Franklin's, and Holmes in Oakland. Hink's Department Store had a book section. It was this thriving world. Tom Wrubel opened the first Nature Company on College Avenue in 1974, and mine was the first reading that he had, for *The East Bay Out*, long before the Nature Company grew and grew and eventually collapsed.

And then all the distributors: Book People, LS Distributors, Cal West Distributors, Milligan's—a whole world of distributors. There were all these small presses, these books getting out into the world, all this ferment, this beauty around.

LAWRENCE DISTASI

LARRY IS BOTH an old friend of Malcolm's from those early Berkeley days and author of *Una Storia Segreta: The Secret History of Italian American Evacuation and Internment during World War II*, published by Heyday in 2001. He describes how their early friendship revolved around writing.

*Malcolm with his
boxes of books*
(HEYDAY ARCHIVES)

I've known Malcolm since 1972. I'd been working at Harcourt Brace in San Francisco as an editor and quit to become a writer. I was living on Deakin Street in Berkeley. Another friend further down Deakin Street, named Dan Phillips, was also an aspiring writer. And in Dan's backyard was a little cabin that Malcolm was renting as his office.

We had several writer friends who decided to have a writers' group once a week. Dan brought Malcolm along, of course. We didn't do what many writers' groups do, such as bring work and critique and all that. We just wanted to get together, shoot the bull every week, and encourage each other.

Malcolm was working on *The East Bay Out*. I remember taking a field trip with him one day to Point Pinole. I marveled at his ability and knowledge about plant life. He'd bend over and talk about this particular flower or that plant, or how this place used to be. That was really fun for me. I knew absolutely nothing about the East Bay parks, and he knew quite a bit.

With respect to Malcolm's publishing, he decided early on that he was going to produce *The East Bay Out* himself. I just marveled that he had the chutzpah to do that, because I certainly wouldn't have. I remember this specifically: he had made himself a light box of just four panels of wood, a piece of clear plastic on top, and a lightbulb inside for looking at his manuscript pages. That was his attitude: "This ain't shit! Anybody can do this. I can do this." He had that kind of confidence.

I saw this in a famous episode with my VW bus. Malcolm had one, too. I needed a valve job or something on the bus, and I told him, "Jesus, I'm going to have to spend a lot of money on this damn bus."

He said, "Just bring it over. I've done some work on mine." He had the "idiot's" repair manual. Again, he said, "This ain't shit. Anybody can do this!" Well—not quite that easily.

We were working in his backyard when he was living on the corner of Sacramento and Hearst. We took the engine out, and when we did, my heart sank. I thought, "Oh, Jesus, how are we going to get this back in?" But we did it! We took the valve casing over to a machinist, got the valves ground, put them back in, and somehow managed to get the engine back in the bus. I had a lot of moments of doubt, but Malcolm never admitted there was ever a problem. He just said, "No problem. We can do this; it's easy." And it worked.

That's my impression of Malcolm. It fits with the tenor of the times, too, when everybody was enamored of the idea that we could all do it ourselves. We could build, fix, repair, publish—we could do anything we wanted to, and we could do it ourselves, rather than going through the established people who are specialists.

MALCOLM ON FRED CODY, HIS BOOKSTORE, AND THE INKSLINGERS FAIR

CODY'S BOOKS WAS the most amazing center of things. Sections of it were so highly developed. People would hang around and attend readings. It was much more of a cultural center than a bookstore. Fred was bigger than life. He named it Cody's, and he was Cody, as opposed to

EXCERPTS FROM *THE EAST BAY OUT:*
A PERSONAL GUIDE TO THE EAST BAY REGIONAL PARKS

FROM THE INTRODUCTION

IT HAS BEEN primarily through the 60,000 acres of East Bay Regional Park District land—over ninety square miles altogether—that I have come to appreciate the beauty and history of the East Bay. I visit the bayshore parks each fall to observe the grand migration of geese and ducks, long lines of them pouring down the Pacific Flyway from Alaska, Canada, and even Siberia. I hike through the snow that powders the highest peaks each winter, and I watch the greening of the grasses and rebirth of hundreds of creeks, brooks, and rills in the meadows below. I wander along ridgetops where fossil clamshells remind me, gently but insistently, that there existed worlds of beauty and complexity here long before ours, and that there will be many such worlds long after ours is gone. Each spring I witness the burst of leaf-buds on the trees, the explosion of wildflowers on the meadows, and the return of songbirds from Central America—predictable, I suppose, but always coming as such a surprise that every year I hear myself saying, "I have never seen a spring as lovely as this."

FROM THE CHAPTER ON COYOTE HILLS PARK
(1988 EDITION)

In the spring of 1769 Gaspar de Portolá led the first land expedition from Mexico into California. The small band of sixty-three men trudged along the ocean coast, climbing endless numbers of hills and struggling across countless steep-banked creeks. On November 1st, three and a half months after they

Heyday and Malcolm. This was his baby, even though his wife, Pat, was maybe the brains behind it all.

As I got to know Fred, I'd come in once a week, and we'd have coffee. You could come in at times that were just chaotic, the place mobbed with people. It'd be noon, so everybody on staff had taken off for lunch except one poor person at the cash register and one person at the information counter. A chaos of students and people were milling around. You'd walk left San Diego Bay, they were exhausted, hungry, confused, and fighting among themselves.

The next day Portolá dispatched a party of soldiers into the hills to hunt for deer. I picture them now, reaching the summit. Here they stopped, astounded. Spread out before them was the San Francisco Bay in all its beauty. *"Un inmenso brazo de mar,"* they called it—an immense arm of the sea.

I think of that moment, the Bay as it must have been. Hundreds of square miles of saltwater marshland, drained and fed by an intricate nerve system of channels, shimmered in the afternoon sun. Herds of pronghorn antelope and tule elk grazed on the grassy plains of the shoreline. Strings of ducks and geese flew through the air, forerunners of the huge flocks that would soon arrive to darken the sky with their numbers. And everywhere the soldiers looked, columns of smoke spiraled into the air from the Indian villages below.

Near the mouth of Alameda Creek was an Indian village that probably consisted of a dozen or so dome-shaped tule houses. Surely the people of that village—an Ohlone group who spoke a language called Chochenyo and who called themselves the Tuibun—had no idea that they were being watched on November 2, 1769. I imagine that the village would have been largely deserted that day. Most of the people would have been camping in the oak groves further inland, preparing for the acorn harvest. Only a few older people would have been left behind. Perhaps the smoke seen by the soldiers that day was spiraling out of sweathouses along the edge of Alameda Creek, where a few of the older men might have withdrawn, in part to keep warm, in part to repair the sacred feather capes and headdresses for the winter ceremonies that would follow the acorn harvest.

through swarms of people to a door leading to a low-ceilinged back room. Fred would be there, standing at a table, unpacking boxes of books, avoiding the whole mess.

I'd come in, and he'd say, "Malcolm! Look what just came in. Look what Knopf just published! Look at this book. Let me read you a passage from it." All life would stop. He'd read a passage from this book. We'd dwell on the beauty of this passage. And then we'd go out for coffee.

For months and months, we'd go out for coffee and make plans for this or for that, for publishing together or for starting organizations. We'd make plans about conferences. It was so much fun making plans. One day I mentioned to him, "Fred, we just keep getting together and making plans, but we don't do anything."

He looks at me with total contempt and says, "Malcolm, can you imagine someone with so little imagination that they *do* everything they plan?"

One thing that Fred and I actually pulled off was the Inkslingers Fair in 1977. We dragged a whole bunch of people into it: Don Cushman at the Print Center; Lou Laub, who was a bookseller; Ernest Landauer, a poet; and Ann Flanagan, a typesetter.

The idea for the Inkslingers was to capture what was happening just then in publishing, something so vibrant, so fresh and new. It was the flowering of the small press movement. The idea was that we'd get people together and have a big party and a wonderful event in which we'd display all of these things. We'd get together with the best people to plan it and have the most marvelous meetings.

We got a small amount of grant money and some space at what was then the Adult School on Carleton and Grove (Martin Luther King Jr.). At the fair, we had 120 demonstrators: people making paper, people making foundry type. We had calligraphers, poets, printers with their presses. People would make up poems, and someone would write it in calligraphy on the paper that was being made, or typeset it and print out little books right there.

It was an amazing fair, with this dynamic sense of creativity. For years I'd meet people whose lives had been turned around by it, just by the vibrancy of doing these books and arts. You didn't need a big industrial process or a major publisher to do a book. You could just go in there, create something, and have great fun. The whole thing was so lively.

So Fred and I created that organization, the first time I co-created an organization. Fred was wonderful at getting people together. He was also totally mercurial. A week before the fair, the ad hoc committee of organizers got into an argument about something. Finally, Fred stops and says, "Maybe we should call the whole thing off." I was utterly amazed that somebody could be that limber, to have such presence of mind to shut the whole thing down. We already had so many commitments. And he was ready to call it off!

Fred was such fun to be with. There was a bigness to him, a big booming voice. He was totally frank, as funny as hell. We'd go out to lunch with various people, like Studs Terkel, who'd come to read their books. Reading there was always a thrill. And the people he collected who worked there were also amazing. They've gone on to be major industrialists or professors or cultural figures who got their start at Cody's.

Everybody loved Fred. I'd go to book or library conventions with Fred, and it was like walking into church with the Pope. Everybody would gather around him. Fred knew everybody. People would come from all over the world to see Fred. Things began at Cody's. People met each other at Cody's. It's where I met Chick Callenbach, where I met so many people.

Fred would come over to the house when we had Heyday there. We'd make lunch for him. He and Bob Callahan were lunchtime regulars. We'd sit around and make more plans and think about more things.

I really wanted the kids to be around Fred. I remember once I got a canoe, and Fred and I took Reuben out in the canoe. We went to Hog Island in Tomales Bay and spent the night over there, just to hear Fred tell stories—not that Reuben would ever remember any of these stories, but just to know how a great person conducts himself. To know that bigness of mind, that ease of concept. He was so grand to be around, intolerant of smallness. He had absolutely no use for anybody with small ideas.

Fred was one of these people that made you want to be your best around him. The stakes were high because of his intense enjoyment of good-quality material, of great thoughts. You'd throw things on the table as a gambit for conversation; maybe you'd bat it around a little bit, and it wouldn't work. Then you'd throw something else out, and that wouldn't work. Finally, you throw something on the table, and you both jump. Then the two of us would be in there scrambling away, raising the stakes until the conversation got bigger and better. There was a wonderful gamesmanship that he had.

Fred had lung cancer at the end. He was a smoker. I was one of two people outside his family that he would ever see, me and Pat Holt, who wrote for the *San Francisco Chronicle* for a long time and later for *Publishers Weekly*. He was withering away. Fred's wife had a sense that you were never supposed to talk about death. Everything was going to be okay. She was not a New Age person, but she had this feeling that attitude is everything. So it was expected that he was going to beat this thing, and he was going to be cured.

One day I was sitting there with Fred when he was in bed. We'd always gotten into these wonderful arguments, playful arguments. We'd both roar, just for the sake of enjoying arguing. So we're arguing about something. Finally, he stops and says, "Goddamn it, here I am on my death bed, croaking, and you're contradicting me." The forbidden had finally been said. The two of us just laughed and laughed.

He was so great, Fred. He furthered others. There were acts that he would do for writers that were so charitable and so magnificent. Fred was a role model in many ways, as close to a role model as I've had—he and my father and Louie Sagansky. Fred had a sense of how to run a business in a personal way. It never got beyond who you knew. The way I run Heyday is based on who I know. And that's how Fred ran his life and his business. That was his power, a personal magnetism.

THE INKSLINGERS FAIR AND BEYOND, AS TOLD BY **DON CUSHMAN**

A FELLOW WRITER AND comrade in the world of "slinging ink," Don Cushman played an integral role by starting the West Coast Print Center in order to make printing more accessible to everyday people and encourage the publishing of texts that regular publishers would not touch. Here he recounts the days when Berkeley was bustling with publishing companies, bookstores, and print shops, and how he joined with Malcolm to create the Inkslingers Fair.

In 1976 I started something called the West Coast Print Center. It was funded by the National Endowment for the Arts for the purpose of printing, but it turned into typesetting, design, and other small press functions.

There's a larger story; that was the height of the small press movement. Many small publishers, of which I was one, had sprung up. In the seventies, Richard Nixon actually started doubling the budget for the NEA every year because he thought it would glorify him. In 1976 the Bicentennial was happening, and then when Reagan took over, the budget was decimated and stayed that way ever since.

But at the time, I received more money from the Literature Panel of the NEA than anyone else. It coincided with this explosion of small press publishers, of which Malcolm started off in another branch. He'd had trouble with large publishing companies, dealing with Houghton Mifflin, I believe, and decided to publish his next work himself, and that turned into Heyday. So he really comes out of both traditions: the small press movement and a do-it-yourself mentality. *The East Bay Out* was successful, and then that provided the seed for what he's done since.

I myself was an English major at UC Berkeley. While I was going to Cal, I'd help out in my father's machine shop, repairing equipment, so I was always interested in mechanical stuff. George Hitchcock was on the board of directors of a national organization called the Coordinating Council of Literary Magazines, which was giving us all money to do our literary thing. They started the idea of having regional print centers. So I got ten thousand dollars to start one in Berkeley.

Then there was the NEA Literature Panel, run by this really great guy, Leonard Randolph. Looking ahead to 1976, they suddenly had money to do stuff. So they decided to put a bunch of money in the Print Center. I went from a budget of about ten thousand dollars to eighty thousand.

Not long after that got going, a bunch of complete maniacs decided to do something called the Inkslingers Fair, which was going to be a promotion of both the small press publishers and the publishing process. I got involved in that. It was Malcolm, Fred Cody, the one who owned Cody's Books, me, and several other people. We'd all meet once a week and decide how to have this event, which became named the Inkslingers Fair. Every time we started making real progress, either Malcolm or Fred would say, "Oh, no, no. Wait a minute! This is getting too organized!" Then we'd go back to zero. As soon as any progress showed up, Malcolm would sabotage it, and then something interesting came out of it later on.

So up until a few weeks before the fair was going to start, literally nothing had been done. Nothing had been solidified. We *did* have a venue, and people committed to it. Amazingly, miraculously, it all came together. I don't know how! The actual fair was in 1977 at the Berkeley Adult School. I dragged a printing press over. We had printing exhibitions, and people did printmaking and paper marbling, letterpress printing. Small presses had booths. It was an amazing event.

I became really good friends with both Malcolm and Fred after that. They're both just incredible presences. Expansive. The two of them embody Berkeley in a lot of ways. Fred was a bookseller but also helped start the Berkeley Free Clinic. He was an old lefty. He came here for the beginning of the U.N. He had that Scottish Presbyterian way about him.

Malcolm is all over the place: Jewish, Indian. Years after he published *The East Bay Out*, he started *News from Native California*. I printed the first four or five issues of that. I also printed the first edition of *Humphrey the Wayward Whale*, and a few other mad projects. So we just continued to do projects together after the Inkslingers Fair. He also became part of the Print Center in different ways.

The Print Center was this amazing organization that we had going. With the funding from the NEA, it was available for anyone to come in and use. We trained a lot of the early small publishers. It was completely insane! I did that for thirteen years, as long as the funding lasted, and as long as my mind held up. We thought it was going to be the beginning of something huge in national printing and publishing, but the NEA funding dried up. They got scared because of Republican opposition to the various and sundry things the NEA was doing. The conservatives saw progressive art as bad. Like Erica Jong's book *Fear of Flying*: she got an NEA fellowship, and everyone went crazy about the sexual matter in it funded by the government. If they had looked into even half of what we did, they'd have been even more freaked out. We did a lot of early gay stuff because no one else would. One press did stuff no one would touch, but we believed in First Amendment rights. A lot of people who had never published anything came to us, so this was their chance.

Malcolm and I used to have lunch together about once a week for many years, and we talked about how to survive all the time. He'd be using the Midwest printers, going from one to another when he'd reached his credit line. I was getting grants, but then the government wouldn't vote on the budget for another six months. We were always helping each other figure out how to keep afloat.

It was just Malcolm's stubborn commitment to that form of publishing that's allowed him to keep going. I also think Malcolm has truly enjoyed the fray.

MALCOLM: HEYDAY EXPANDS

So I FOUND myself in this thriving world of books and people that were publishing. When *The East Bay Out* got published, I went through those seven thousand copies in no time flat.

I recently heard a conversation with Tom Winnett at Wilderness Press when they had their thirty-fifth anniversary. People had said to Tom how brilliant and wonderful he was, how prescient. "Hey, listen," he says, "you're giving me a lot of credit. I was a lonely, goofy guy. I liked to go hiking; I did a book about hiking in the Sierra. How was I to know that the year that I'd do that book, all America would want to go hiking?"

During those days, it was the backpack and hiking revolution. So *The East Bay Out* was also popular at The Ski Hut and the Wilderness Co-op, all these backpacking stores that were springing up. It was also the beginning of a movement in natural history and ecology. We forget how recent this kind of consciousness is.

It's funny. I listen to myself talk about giving up houses and throwing out tables, starting a publishing company. There's a kind of lurching decisive quality about it. But it was all kind of…luminosities in the fog.

The question comes up often: What is Heyday Books all about? I describe it—it could be the description of my life—as the story of the rabbi who was asked, "Why is it that when I ask you a question, you answer with a story?"

He says, "Because I'm a terrible archer. If I were a better archer, I'd draw the bow, I'd shoot the arrow to the target, and you'd get your answer. But I'm such a bad archer that I shoot the arrow into the air, and wherever it lands, I draw a target around the arrow. That's the story."

Without a system, you have these individual islands of decision, of luminosity, of accomplishment. Afterwards, you put them together and try to make a description out of them. I just kind of get into something. That's not entirely true, but I get into something and just do it, and all these particular acts get done.

As for the name "Heyday," I needed a name for a publishing company, and I'd already named Reuben "Reuben Heyday Margolin" because that's just what hippies did. We liked "Reuben" because it had that old Jewish sense to it, and "Heyday" because it had a sense of celebration, of wonderment, like in our years of traveling together. Then we named Sadie "Sadie Cash." When it came time to name a publishing company, I couldn't think of a name.

Rina said, "Well, you're so good at naming kids, why don't you just name a publishing company with the same creativity with which you name your kids?"

So I said, "We'll call it Cash Books," but that didn't sound right. So we decided to call it Heyday Books. I think it was a placeholder. It was not meant to last. I thought that I'd publish a book, and I'd go on and do other things. I never thought I'd be a *publisher*. But then I published another book and another book. Before you know it, hundreds of books and forty years have passed.

It didn't take that long to sell all the copies of *East Bay Out*. We had to move by that time. We rented the house next to the writer Dorothy Bryant, on Stuart Street. One of the wonderful stories about Reuben the artist happened at that house at 1928 Stuart Street. We come home one night, and the door is wide open. The place has been burglarized. All the drawers are pulled open, and things have been dumped out; the place was a wreck. Reuben and Sadie are there, and Reuben says, "What happened? What happened?"

I say, "Hey, listen, some bad people came in and stole things. But it's okay. We'll clean up and get new stuff. Don't worry about it."

He says, "What do you mean, they stole stuff?"

"Well, they broke open the door, came in, and they stole things. I think they stole my camera and binoculars."

He says, "They stole things!" He runs through the living room and through the kitchen. I had a study in the back where I had a dragon of his made out of plywood. It had cotton batting pasted onto it and coils of toilet paper rolls for ears. It'd been painted gaudy colors. He came back, and he said, "Phew! They didn't take the dragon!"

So I said, "We're lucky!"

He thought for a minute and said, "Why *didn't* they?"

THE ARRIVAL OF SADIE CASH MARGOLIN

It was at that house we'd rented from Dorothy Bryant on Stuart Street that Sadie was born, on September 30, 1974, the year that *The East Bay Out* was published. One of my fondest memories of it all is that Sadie was born at home. Home birth had something to do, at the time, with self-sufficiency. It was part of what Heyday was about, part of what I was about. I wasn't going to work for the East Bay Regional Park District anymore. I wasn't going to live in a house. I wasn't going to work for anybody. It was all just part of becoming totally difficult.

At the same time we were so totally broke! I remember once we were down to one lightbulb. We used to move the lightbulb from one room to another because we couldn't buy another one. We bought odd parts of animals at nineteen cents a pound. We'd get the stuff that people would throw away. We'd get food from the back of supermarkets, saying that we had a rabbit to feed and we needed vegetable scraps. I even returned to collecting foods in the wild.

Fixing my own VW was a revelation. Probably the most influential book I read was *How to Keep Your Volkswagen Alive: A Manual of Step-by-Step Procedures for the Compleat Idiot,* because it helped me. I think that's the reason I started Heyday. It was also a self-published book, about something that people did themselves. That VW book convinced me I could pull the motor out of the car and fix it. I could crack the case and take out the rods, the pistons and bearings, I could put the whole damn thing together again, and it would run. That was far more valuable than any literary book I ever read.

Part of it was the era, a whole self-sufficiency movement, to master the craft of woodworking or car repair. There was the *Whole Earth Catalog*. People went off into the woods. Self-sufficiency was in the air, just like natural history was in the air, or Indians. It's not as if I invented these things. They were around, and I responded to them.

Part of that self-sufficiency was having our kid at home. But we had her with a midwife *and* a doctor, a guy by the name of Michael Witte who had a practice in Berkeley. It was in the bedroom; it was an ordinary and dramatic birth.

I was so stunned the baby was a girl. We'd had no idea whether it would be a girl or a boy, though we'd settled on only a girl's name. I think I'd been expecting a boy. Rationally, I knew it was a toss-up, but I'd never had girls in the family. I'd just had a brother. The thought that I would be the father to a girl! That was something I didn't know how to do. It was just a miracle, having this girl.

Reuben, meanwhile, who was four, was off in the other room with his best friend's mother, who was taking care of him. When the proper time came, we called Reuben in to see his new baby. I don't know where he got them, but he was wearing a cowboy hat and a gun. He comes in, looking all suspicious and surly. I say, "Reuben, Reuben, it's a girl!"

Reuben looks, and his first words are "I hate girls!" That defined the Reuben-Sadie relationship for the next several years.

Sadie was a joy. From the earliest days, Sadie was glued to the outside world. She was always sociable, with this great curiosity about things, responsive to other people, to what was going on. She had a most wonderful capacity to charm, to imitate. She'd go along with people, go with the flow of things. Reuben had my capacity to always be *outside* things, hearing some other song. He didn't necessarily join in the rhythms of whatever was around him. But Sadie liked people.

We chose Sadie as a name for the same reason we chose Reuben and Jacob as names, as a tribute to an older generation of Jews. The people I grew up with had names like Sadie and Sophie and Bessie. It was an older generation's name, now out of fashion. It wasn't that I wanted to bring the

Malcolm, Sadie, and boxes of books (MARGOLIN FAMILY COLLECTION)

culture back, but there was a *feeling* that I wanted to bring back. The Yiddish word for it is *hamish*. A *hamish maidel: hamish* means beautiful and lovely in a homey way, domestic. We really liked that about the name, and the playfulness to it. People were no longer called Sadie. I also loved the meter of it, Sadie Cash Margolin: the way the vowels and consonants played together, the way the whole thing sounded. It just seemed to slip into some groove that was very satisfying

One anecdote sums Sadie up for me. Rina, a few other people, and I were at Tule Lake, watching birds. We were passing around one pair of binoculars between us. You'd look out and see this raft of ducks and geese—just spectacular. Someone would look through the binoculars and go, "Wow!" Then someone else would look through them and go, "Wow!" When you

Sadie, Jake, and Malcolm at a Heyday party (MARGOLIN FAMILY COLLECTION)

passed the binoculars to Sadie, she'd also look through them and go, "Wow!" I was wondering what she was seeing because the lenses were so far apart, and she was just a little kid and couldn't quite get the binoculars up to her face right.

So the next time it came to me, I said, "Wow!" Then I put the lens caps on and gave it to her. Sadie looked and said, "Oh, wow!" It wasn't that she was looking at the birds; she was responding to the people around her. She had joined in on the ritual. That's what Sadie would do, join in and play on *your* playground. I always wanted to play on *my* playground. Sadie would play on other people's playgrounds.

When Sadie was in the first grade, the whole family was on a vacation. I remember she was learning how to spell words at the time. Sadie and I were off in a meadow, picking blueberries. She had this little daydreamy look on her face. I looked at her and asked, "What are you thinking?"

She said with special, emphatic pronunciation of the initial letter sounds, "I'm thinking that I'm **S**adie, and I'm a **s**tream, and **R**euben and **R**ina are **r**ivers, and **J**akie's a **d**rop of water, and **M**alcolm is the **m**eadow we're all flowing through." It's the most beautiful thing anybody's ever said to me.

Sadie was funny. There was a kind of sweetness and gentleness to her, but also a rebellion. When she was older, she was sick one day and asked me to write a note for her, excusing her absence. So I wrote, "Please excuse

Sadie for being absent yesterday. She was sick." And I signed it, "Malcolm Margolin."

She went off to school. That morning I'm at work, and I get a call from the principal: "Your daughter's forged your signature."

I say, "What do you mean?"

She says, "Well, we have this note that says she was sick yesterday, but it's a forged signature."

"No," I say, "I wrote that note; my handwriting is lousy, but I wrote it."

After a long pause, the principal replied, "It's funny; the signature doesn't match the signature on the other notes we've gotten."

It was always with such pride that I'd go down there and have to bail my kids out. I loved this rebelliousness in them.

Sadie was playful, so into her friends. I remember once coming home to tell the family that someone had offered to let us live in the lighthouse on one of those islands off the Richmond coast. Reuben was thrilled that we'd be living in a lighthouse. I don't know where little girls get this, but Sadie balled up her fists, stuck her fists on her hips, and said, "No!" I was going to take her away from her friends, take her away from her world. She was going to have to spend her time with her stupid family on a goddamn island. She lived for her friends, for her friendships, for her linkage with other people.

In the summer of 1980, we were again living on Berkeley Way, the second house we'd had on that street, and Heyday was still in a home office. Those were all good years, working out of the house. By the time the late seventies rolled around, I'd be working in the morning. I'd make my morning trip out to the post office and pick up my mail, hope to find something good. I'd have a cup of coffee at Peet's, come back home, and work. Then I or Rina and I would make lunch for people. I loved to cook. I'd make curried carrots. Fred Cody and Bob Callahan and various other friends would come by. We'd sit around and talk, then go back to work.

I just adored Bob Callahan. He started Turtle Island Press. He was an Irishman from back east, Connecticut. He was part of that generation just removed from the Old World. We shared that same sense of immigrant amusement and adventurism toward this country, that sense of exploration, living by your wits.

Bob Callahan, c. 1978.
(HEYDAY ARCHIVES)

Let me think of some Callahan stories. When he came to California, he hooked into people like Carl Sauer, the cultural geographer, and the linguist and writer Jaime de Angulo. Bob lived in Jaime's house and published Jaime's Indian stories. Callahan wanted to publish a new voice for California, yet his books were very formal. They were beautifully designed and well typeset. He brought out a lot of material by Zora Neale Hurston, Ed Sanders, and Robert Creeley. He had a vigorous mind, a keen literary mind.

Callahan loved to talk. If I can have a moment of reverse boasting: he was one of the few people I've met that could outtalk me, who could tell a better story! You could listen to him ramble on for days and days. A stream of stories would come out with such volubility and disorder. He was overweight and slovenly. He loved to drink. He was a volcano of disorder.

I used to give an annual lecture to the Friends of the River, and in return they'd give me some rafts and guides to take me and my friends down the river. So over the years I got several of my friends together for this. One year I got Callahan on. Everybody is there paddling away; they're trim in their bathing suits. Callahan is dressed in a jacket and a white shirt, shoes and pants. He's sitting at the end, and he's talking the *whole* time, telling stories. One of the things I remember him saying is, "This is fun, but you could really get in trouble if you hit those rocks!"

Bob had the finest mind that anybody could ever have. We'd hang out together, go to bars and Irish pubs. We'd spend St. Patrick's Day together. We went to underground comic conventions together. We hung out with Warren Hinckle and Hunter Thompson and people like that over in the city, and Ray Flynn, the mayor of Boston at the time. We'd go out and find the most amazing people.

I got him on my first board of directors because of his friendship. People in the office hated him. He was so disorderly and rude. He hit on everybody. The amount of roadkill in his life was extraordinary, and yet there was a hardiness to him. When you were around him, you felt alive. You felt your brain come alive. He was well read, so thoughtful about things.

At one point he started *Callahan's Irish Quarterly*, which ran for several issues. Then he needed money, so he added to his *Quarterly* an award for the Irishman of the Year. He'd name some banker the Irishman of the Year. The banker would buy tables for all of his friends, and they'd have a big dinner, and we'd all toast the awardee.

The whole world was an immigrant scam, yet he had a true love of beauty. He did beautiful books. Those Turtle Island Books were beautiful books.

Wires would cross. His finances and his health were a wreck. He died young. He had emphysema from smoking, but I think a stroke got him. He

Malcolm river rafting (MARGOLIN FAMILY COLLECTION)

moved back in with his ex-wife. She took good care of him during his later years. At the end of it, she said to me, "Where does it all go? All that humor, all that breath, all that sweetness, all that smartness, all that language, all those stories. Where does it all go? It couldn't have just disappeared."

There but for the grace of God.

Having such friends stopping by the house made it probably one of my favorite venues for Heyday. The kids were crawling around. People would come over and buy books. Those were good years. I finally had to get the business out of the house, though. It was a bit of a strain because the places got smaller as we had more kids and more books and more friends. But they were good years.

RINA MARGOLIN

I N ITS LONG ago beginnings, Heyday was just Malcolm doing most everything, with only me helping, providing feedback, proofing, and making maps. We were working out of a small Berkeley apartment (one of the very many we lived in over the years), and we were perpetually broke. I remember not having enough lightbulbs to go around and marveling at the large light table, fluorescently lit, that Mal made for my oversize maps. Such an improvement over the tiny box he'd made for his page layouts! And I certainly remember picking up the printer's proofs for *The Ohlone Way* at a general delivery near some campground and opening up to "Sioux" misspelled on the very first page. Oops. We laughed and fixed it.

Ever since I discovered I could read, I've loved books and images; in college I got comfortable with writing, too. So after having been totally involved, more or less by necessity, in Mal's earliest projects, I was very happy to remain tangentially involved for many more years, including several years handling subscriptions for *News from Native California*. It was always very important to both of us that Mal's books be the best we could manage, and I enjoyed that process. But the best for me was the extraordinary and moving material that came my way to edit or proofread, thirty or so books spread over as many years. I'm thinking now, for instance, about the chapter on praying in d'Azevedo's *Straight with the Medicine* (1978) that starts, "How can an Indian pray like a white man? The white man gets his prayers out of books.... He don't even have to think about it. He just says it and it is supposed to do him some good...."

Or the unbounded joy of John Muir's little mongrel at making it across an icy crevasse (*Stickeen*, 1981), or the tenderness of Karen Bender's story "Eternal Love" (in Gilbar's *L.A. Shorts*, 1999): "Married couples, she told her retarded daughter, learned to be married slowly, in separate rooms...." Or Inada's haunting internment camp reminiscences in *Only What We Could Carry* (2000), which I could well relate to, having grown up in wartime Germany and later its Displaced Persons camps before being allowed at the age of ten into the United States. Which may be why Roberto Durán's searing antiwar poem "Super Freak" got to me so, though it did not make the final cut into Heide's *Under the Fifth Sun* (2002): how often we numb ourselves to others' pain!

Our three kids, Reuben born in 1970, Sadie in 1974, and Jake in 1980, have accompanied Mal much more than I did to his many events. Later, two of them also worked for Heyday, Reuben as an editor and Sadie as a book-keeper. (Jake always lived too far away to corral.) As Malcolm published more books and put together a professional staff, I turned to raising our children, volunteering (and sometimes working) in other capacities, and exploring a variety of interests. I now tutor a little but mainly help out with our grandchildren (we've been blessed with four), so while I still sometimes provide feedback, meet an author, or attend an event, these days I generally hear of Heyday's challenges and accomplishments well after the fact.

I was not surprised years ago when Mal became the writer he'd wanted to be, but I was taken aback when he almost immediately turned his attention to publishing. Nor have I ever anticipated the varied and significant connections that he has long delighted in forging. So while I'm certainly gratified that what I helped nurture so many years ago has flourished, I'm as much in awe as everyone else of the breadth and quality of Heyday's publications and of its centrality and vigor as a cultural institution.

Before we had kids and found ourselves settling down in Berkeley and turning into our adult selves, Mal and I were able to spend many years taking turns working, camping and hiking—drifting really—to Puerto Rico

*Malcolm
and Rina
Margolin*
(MARGOLIN
FAMILY
COLLECTION)

and the Virgin Islands, to New York City, up the West Coast from Mexico to Canada and back again. We thought we'd stop briefly in Berkeley for the birth of our first child. We followed our hearts then, and our hearts have been our compass ever since. At the same time, we always supported each other's choices. (We tried to do the same for our kids; in any case, we must have modeled it, as they also seem to have followed their hearts in life.)

For myself, I've been very grateful to Mal for the chance he's given me not only to be useful to him but to volunteer and work in other capacities. I worked for earthquake safety in the public schools, hosted a folksinging group for years, kept a family performing arts camp going, relearned my native Russian and German (to communicate with a long-lost relative), made quilts and collages, discovered ESL tutoring, and, as I mentioned, have become a hands-on grandma. In turn I've wholeheartedly supported Malcolm's many passions and certainly his total commitment to Heyday. And while we still travel together, Mal has traveled much more widely than I, from taking each of the kids in their teens to other countries to, more recently, visiting Indians in Baja on his own. But we all still hike regularly together and still tend to celebrate holidays and birthdays with walks and picnics.

Looking back, it's been an amazing fifty years together and forty years of Heyday. Mal once came across a poem by Gail Mazur that I've always loved. It speaks to my hopes for our lives and work as well:

YOUNG APPLE TREE, DECEMBER

What you want for it you'd want
for a child: that she take hold;
that her roots find home in stony

winter soil; that she take seasons
in stride, seasons that shape and
reshape her; that like a dancer's,

her limbs grow pliant, graceful,
and surprising; that she know,
in her branchings, to seek balance;

that she know when to flower, when
to wait for the returns; that she turn
to a giving sun; that she know

fruit as it ripens; that what's lost
to her will be replaced; that early
summer afternoons, a full blossoming

tree, she cast lacy shadows; that change
not frighten her, rather that change
meet her embrace; that remembering

her small history, she find her place
in an orchard; that she be her own
orchard; that she outlast you;

that she prepare for the hungry world
(the fallen world, the loony world)
something shapely, useful, new, delicious.

THE CALL TO NATIVE CALIFORNIA

"I've always felt like an outsider. This was a place where I really was an outsider, so I didn't have to feel bad about it because this is who I was. Here it wasn't awkward in the least." —MALCOLM MARGOLIN

IN EARLIER CHAPTERS about his youth, Malcolm tells stories of haphazardly seizing opportunities to travel, write, and work, with an organizing principle he describes as "episodic lucidity." In the same seemingly random way, Malcolm's work in the East Bay Regional Park District led him to learn about the hidden Ohlone Indian history in the larger San Francisco–Monterey coastal area. His further study inspired the writing and publishing of his book *The Ohlone Way (1978)*.

In the process, Malcolm developed extraordinarily rich friendships in Native Californian communities. Malcolm's growing appreciation of Indian cultures is reflected in many of the books and the journal, *News from Native California*, that Heyday has published, as well as the multiple organizations Malcolm has helped found and support. This chapter focuses on two books on California Indians that Malcolm wrote or edited and the web of valued connections he has built with the Indian community over time.

ON WRITING *THE OHLONE WAY*: *INDIAN LIFE IN THE SAN FRANCISCO—MONTEREY BAY AREA*

I published *The East Bay Out* in 1974, and then I was looking for a quick book to write, design, typeset, and publish. This whole business of doing things myself was just so wonderful.

Without much forethought, I decided to do a book about Indian life in the Bay Area. When I had been working for the East Bay Regional Park District, I gave nature walks. I didn't know anything about nature; I knew less about Indians. But lack of knowledge never stopped me. Also, the only books about the local Ohlone Indians were a couple of dismal accounts written by archaeologists, illustrated with photos and drawings of bones.

I thought it would be an easy topic because they were seemingly "simple" people who lived, from what I understood, under oak trees. An acorn would drop down, and they would cook it up. It *seemed* there wasn't much to their lives. And I admired something in this imagined simplicity, in this direct living, in what I mistakenly saw as a lack of complexity.

Active interest in Indians thrived all around me. Every hippie had an Edward Curtis sepia print of Native Americans on the wall. We were all very much affected by books like *Black Elk Speaks* and, while it now embarrasses me to admit, the fantasies of Carlos Castaneda.

Other things were happening at the time that also stimulated interest in Indians. Out of the political turbulence of the sixties came the militant American Indian Movement, AIM, which was founded in 1968. The Indian occupation of Alcatraz from 1969 to 1971 was especially significant, as were the siege of Wounded Knee in 1973 and other actions throughout the country. Up until then, many Indians had to muffle their Indian identities to protect themselves from racism, the contempt of others, and internalized shame. Now there were proud Indians, standing up and being strong.

I didn't take part in the Alcatraz occupation, but like everyone else in the Bay Area, I followed it through the newspapers and especially on KPFA, the Bay Area's Pacifica station. Whites rallied to support the Indians. People on their yachts were bringing food in. Big-name lawyers got involved. There were occupiers like Richard Oakes and Ed Castillo, who were spectacularly handsome. We saw a new image of Indians, not in the old mold—sad, broken down, defeated—but as rebels, as heroes in movie-star ways. They were on the radio and television. An Indian world that had previously been absent or subterranean was suddenly on the main screen.

This rise of Indians into the American consciousness came at the same time as Vietnam and the earlier explosion of racial segregation into public awareness. They were all bringing about a deep questioning of American institutions and values, our sense of ourselves as the home of the brave and the land of the free, as saviors of the world from fascism, as models of justice, democracy, and economic opportunity for all. We suddenly saw ourselves as colonizers, as a racist nation.

So part of my own development had to do with plugging into the broader cultural support for Indian rights and a generational shift in values.

Going back to *The Ohlone* Way, I had all that interest in Indian life, and at first I thought I knew something from having done a little reading and from talking about Ohlone life when I gave ecology tours in the parks, so I thought it would be an easy book. I gave myself three months to research it and three months to write it. I'd been so successful in writing *The Earth Manual* in four months that I thought this was plenty of time. But I got into it and discovered that there was much more to it than I'd thought.

At that time, nobody had ever done anything like this, a comprehensive look at a people in California. The information was scattered all over the place. I read diaries, archaeological reports, anthropological surveys, old newspapers, and county histories. I went into archives, caught a mention here, a mention there. It was the days long before computers. Photocopiers were still fairly new. So I'd read something and copy it out.

In 1975 or so, I rented a study on Dwight Way, underneath an apartment house, next to the laundry room. I'd go through the laundry room into this dark little study. There I'd read and type. I had a whole bunch of big envelopes that I'd label. I'd read something about how the basket weavers would collect sedge roots, size them, and weave them into baskets. Then I'd copy it down several times, put one into an envelope about gathering, another into an envelope about basket weaving, and another marked "plants." I'd end up copying these items over and over on all these scraps of paper. When I emptied an envelope to review the contents, it was almost like a kitty litter box.

The envelopes began to build up. This is when we were really poor. The project just kept getting longer and longer the more I got into it. If somebody had told me that the whole thing would take three years, I never would have started it.

Then there was the business of *really* understanding something, understanding it afresh. I was so ignorant about Indian life that when I began it,

I didn't realize there were still Indians in California. I thought it was going to be all library research.

Somewhere along the line, I met Vera Mae and David Fredrickson; someone introduced me to them. Vera Mae was an anthropologist raised in Minnesota. She was loud, literary, outspoken, and she drank a lot. We took to each other immediately. She passed away in 2011. I like what I wrote about her in *News* when she passed:

> I think of her as pure energy, exploding volcanically to the wonderment, embarrassment, amusement, and consternation of all around her. She was a force of nature—a hurricane, a tornado, a thunderstorm, an earthquake. She was also a nourishing rain, bringing abundance into the world, hosting parties that never seemed to end, generous to friends and family, a catalyst, a den mother, a true friend.

Her husband, David Fredrickson, was an archaeologist. Dave was one of the people who revolutionized the relationship between Indians and archaeologists. He worked closely with Indians. He listened to them. We lost David recently, too, in 2012, and for his obit in *News*, I included part of a 1988 speech that he gave at the Society for California Archaeology when he was accepting an award. It says a lot about Dave's ethics. He said, "The people come first....The artifacts are only insignificant remains. The people, their ideas, their actions, their concerns about life, *these* are what we, as archaeologists, should be studying." And I added to David's words, "If some archaeologists are indeed putting people first, it's in no small measure due to David and his influence."

He was a quiet, lovely, decent man, a folksinger, a poet. I fondly remember listening to him singing cowboy songs as he played his guitar. He made me homesick for a life on the lonesome prairie I never knew except through David's singing—he was remarkable. He knew the early bohemians and poets, like Robert Duncan and Jack Spicer; he was part of that group. But he was also a methodical man: he kept lists for everything, including all the people that had ever entered the house.

Vera Mae and Dave ran the world by having parties; I met everyone at their home on Milvia and Parker in Berkeley, a place I describe as "where the psychically wounded came for repair, where poets and folksingers came for inspiration, where young archaeologists came to meet their elders and be initiated into their calling, and where a thousand ideas and projects were born." When I was writing the book, I first visited Vera Mae and Dave thinking that they'd give me advice. But it was really all the people I met through them that mattered.

I'm not sure, but I think it was through them that I met Phil Galvan. Phil was an Ohlone Indian from the Mission San José in Fremont. He was the caretaker of a nearby convent there. He was a Mission Indian from the old times. It's odd, but the Mission Indians often maintained their identity better than those outside the missions. The dominant society had no place for an Indian; you disappeared. In the mission you were degraded, but at least you could still be an Indian.

Phil had a lot of knowledge, a good sense of what the old ways were like. But what really knocked me out was not just what he knew, but *how* he knew, the way he carried his knowledge, his attitude and his bearing. We could be in the same place at the same time, but it seemed as if we were in different worlds.

I remember, for example, sitting with him on his porch, talking. We were both looking out across a meadow to a grove of trees. Suddenly he said, "That's the fourth time that hawk has flown into the tree that way; I'll bet it has a nest there." Not only had it never occurred to me that there was a nest in the tree, but in truth I had never even noticed the hawk. In fact, I'm not even sure I noticed the tree.

Phil, like so many other Ohlone people I met, utterly amazed me. The cultural loss was profound—language, traditional skills, systems of belief, customs. But through all those years of cultural assault and attempted annihilation, they still held on to a way of relating, of being—a tone, a pacing, a reservoir of emotion that are just not part of our world. I did the library research, I scoured the literature, but that inner world that I glimpsed served as a tuning fork that gave tone to everything I wrote.

When it came to writing a chapter, I'd fast for a day or half a day. Then I'd empty the relevant envelopes and pore over the contents, sorting through the scraps of paper, categorizing them, clustering them, and ultimately taping them to the wall. If I was writing about deer hunting, I'd take pictures of deer and maybe pictures of bows and arrows and put them up on the wall, too. I'd walk around the room, looking at the scraps of paper and making sure that what I was seeing was embedded in both my imagination and my intelligence. When there was a note about how a hunter stalked the deer, I would stop everything and try to picture it. Was the hunter bent over at the waist? Did he approach the deer directly, or did he angle up to it? If I couldn't imagine it, I would ask others—modern deer hunters, for example, about what they thought.

Often there was a kind of crazy intermediary step before I'd scroll a sheet of paper into the typewriter. I'd get a big pad of newsprint, and I'd put some statement at the center of the page. Then I'd write free-form, random thoughts and impressions around it, amplifying it, contradicting it, playing with it, saying whatever came into my mind to see if I could stretch the statement, make it limber, give it life or at least dimension. If I was feeling uptight, feeling the "criticizer" looking over my shoulder and telling me that I didn't know anything and didn't have the necessary skills, nagging me the way the criticizer will, I'd write in deliberately large and sloppy letters just to insult the criticizer, let it know that it wasn't welcome at this stage of creativity, tell it in no uncertain terms to shut up and get out of my life.

Then, when I was loose and worked up, I'd sit down at the typewriter and peck away. I'd generally go through several drafts. Finally, when I thought I was finished, I'd put the chapter in the "done" pile and go home. That night, though, I'd stay up thinking about it and feel I'd cheated. We were so broke, and I needed to get the book out, but I also needed to get it *right*. So I'd go back the next day, pull it out of the "done" pile, and work on it some more.

There was a low lintel on the doorway. Whenever I was *really* finished, I'd know because I'd whack my head against the lintel: I'd grown two inches taller when it was really done.

FROM *THE OHLONE WAY*

THE DEER HUNTER

HUNTING, ESPECIALLY DEER hunting, was among the most important things in a man's life. The hunter pursued and killed deer without pity, but never without reverence. Deer were spiritually powerful animals in a world in which animals were still gods, and deer hunting was an undertaking surrounded at every step with dignity, forethought, and ritual....

The hunt itself is a splendid sight. The hunter, often with a companion or two, his body painted, his bow and arrows properly treated, lean, hungry, alert, connected with the dream-world, his mind secure that he has followed all the proper rituals, approaches a herd of grazing deer. He wears a deer-head mask, and perhaps an amulet hangs from his neck. He moves toward the grazing grounds slowly, almost diffidently—in many ways more like a suitor than a potential conqueror.

As soon as he sees a herd he crouches low and begins to move like a deer. ("He played the pantomime to such perfection," noted a French sea captain who witnessed one such hunt, "that all our own hunters would have fired at him at thirty paces had they not been prevented.")...

What is the hunter thinking about as he moves closer to the herd of deer? There is an intriguing suggestion by J. Alden Mason, an anthropologist who studied the Salinans, just to the south of the Ohlones. Writes Mason: "The hunter always chewed tobacco assiduously while approaching the game, as this tended to make it drunk and less wary."

Chewing the strong native tobacco undoubtedly affected the hunter's mind; but why, by altering his own consciousness, should the hunter think he was making the deer "drunk and less wary"? To understand this—to understand the subtle ways in which the hunter felt that his mind was linked to the mind of a prey whose nature and intelligence were not very different from his own—is to glimpse some of the drama and spiritual complexity of deer hunting as it was practiced by the Indians of California.

The typesetting and the design I did myself. My friend Christopher Weills was doing some publishing. He had a Compugraphic typesetting machine, so I rented time on it, setting my own type. Rina did the proof-reading. In doing it all again, I found satisfaction, completion, control. But it wasn't the same thrill or challenge as with *The East Bay Out*.

I felt that the text had settled into itself, that I had really good writing in there and good images, and that I'd captured something. I had complete confidence in the book, the confidence you can only have when you're igno-rant, when you don't know anything. If I did it now, I'd redo the illustrations and the text with a much greater sense of detail, finesse, and subtlety. It's something I could do much better now.

On the other hand, I could never write this book again. I know too much to make any generalizations. When I first got into it, the Kroeber paradigm was dominant, an assumption of a moment of purity before the whites came, that early Indian civilizations were followed by decay through to the present. In fact, there's been an evolution to the present with many changes. I would now see the past through the eyes of the people that I know today. The illustrations would be illustrations of people that I know now, more than reimagined people. I would do them with a softer touch.

Hey, listen, I've learned something in thirty-five years! I've evolved.

RECEPTION OF *THE OHLONE WAY*

When *The Ohlone Way* came out, I felt really good about it. Some aspects of that book are now more taken for granted, but back then they were acts of courage, edgy, like talking about the acceptance of gays or showing nudity. In a sense, the book was very much of its era, of the seventies and the concerns of that time, even as some of the politics in the book are still relevant to this day. I recently put together a special supplement for *News from Native California* on Indian leadership, interviewing several contem-porary tribal chairs and cultural leaders. I was amazed at how many of the older traditional patterns and attitudes persist to this day in the Indian community—like how the leaders have power without aggression, a way of being that isn't competitive yet is effective. Perhaps I was even more amazed at how much we all have to learn from them.

I enjoy speaking and storytelling, so when *The Ohlone Way* came out, it was an excuse to perform. I was at all kinds of events and gatherings, bookstore readings, camps. I never said no to anything. If three people were gathering in Turlock at 7:30 in the morning for a Kiwanis Club breakfast and they needed a speaker, I was there. You just never say no. So I was out speaking all the time. That's probably been as important as the writing, this public presence. The number of people that sit down and actually read a book and get something from it is rather limited, but the number of people influenced by hearing something, by radio interviews, by what they see on TV, that's bigger.

There's a statement, I forget who said it, to the effect that you write a book and publish it, then you go out into the world to give readings and interviews, and if you're lucky, you discover *why* you've written it. A book isn't just a finished, dead product. It's alive, shaped by the interactions of those who read it and by the growing awareness of the author about what it means. That was true for me.

KQED, the local PBS station, wanted to interview me at Coyote Hills Park, where the East Bay Regional Park District had a reconstructed Indian village. The folks running the program were going to interview me about Indian life, but I suggested they interview Indians, too. So I invited up some folks I knew. It was a weekday morning, and this parade of eight cars showed up, with old men, old women, and young kids. I watched them approach. The way they were walking, the way they related to each other, it was all part of an ancient way of being.

The naturalist, Norm Kidder, was trying to show how to start a fire using a "hearth stick" that had this little recess in it. It looks like a regular stick, but you twirl another stick in that recess to heat the tinder and get the flames going.

The Indians are looking on. One laughs and says, "Oh, I thought you rub like this," showing across, not down. Another jokes, "Hey, I have a Zippo; that might work better!" You could see that they were embarrassed that this white guy had the technology, and they no longer did; how awkward it was for everyone to see that they had lost so much. But they had the capacity to pull a whole family together on a weekday for an event about their culture. And they had this way that the young related to the elders, an underlying structure. It was a whole way of life missing in the white world.

I've always been self-conscious about being a white guy writing about Indians. One time I was asked to speak at a conference about Indian life in the Bay Area. In the front row sat these big surly guys from AIM, the American Indian Movement, their arms crossed and hostility written all over them. At the end of my talk, one of them raises his hand and asks, "Why are *you* writing about our people, telling our story? Why don't you write about your own people?"

Why, indeed? I admitted that they had a valid point and suggested we have a cup of coffee together and talk about it.

We talked for a couple of hours as I tried to make the point that it was essential for white people to grapple with Indian history and appreciate Indian ways. If I was getting it wrong, I'd genuinely appreciate being corrected. There were painful truths and beautiful truths and so much to puzzle over and wonder about. I was doing my best.

The conversation continued. The substance of it was certainly important, but I forget what was said. I do remember that the more we talked, the more we liked each other, the more I enjoyed being in their presence, and I think the more they enjoyed me. I don't remember whether at the end we thoroughly agreed. I do know that we left as friends. And the question they asked still challenges me.

Overall, I have gotten very little criticism and lots of support from the Indian community. I don't know if it's that I got it right or that people were so puzzled by what in the world I was doing in their kitchen that they were stunned into silence. Maybe some of both. I was gratified—actually, utterly relieved—that the book received such a warm welcome from the Indian community. That response was more than desirable for me. It was essential.

I was also delighted that *The Ohlone Way* was praised by the academic world. Robert Heizer, perhaps the most noted anthropologist in California, read it a few months before he died and said it was the best portrait of a California Indian group he'd ever read. The *American Anthropologist* gave it a great review. It's been assigned at dozens of colleges and universities. I was so pleased by this. I expected to be savaged. They all loved it! Some academics said that *this* is what they hoped to do when they got into anthropology, but they got sidetracked into little problems and small studies, or they felt that if they did anything this speculative, they'd be clobbered. They had to have footnotes. They feared criticism. But as somebody outside the circle, I was able to do something that those better situated couldn't do.

I'm surprised and gratified at the influence that the book has had, the number of people I meet who tell me that their lives were affected by it, who've gone on to do their own research, how it's changed their thinking, what it's meant for the Indian community. It came at a time when many Indians were eager to learn more about their past, to recapture what had been stolen from them. Perhaps people felt validation. It used to be that if you said you were an Ohlone Indian, it didn't mean anything to anyone. "A what kind of Indian?" The original people of the Bay Area had become invisible, the memory of them lost; the existence of a popular book and an author who was eager to make it public gave them recognition and even standing.

My wonderful friend Ray Marquez was a garbage collector in Watsonville, and like quite a few other people there, he was Ohlone Indian, but he was also part Mexican, so he called himself a Mexican because to identify himself as an Indian was painful. Then, along came the protest at Alcatraz and various other actions, and a wider cultural interest in the Indians, especially with the ecology movement. All of a sudden it became bearable in his own eyes to be an Indian.

Ray went to his mother and said, "What do we know about our background? How do we get back to the old knowledge?"

She said, "Well, the last person that knew anything was your uncle, and he's dead. There's only one way that I know to go about it. You fast for a few days. You climb that mountain. When you get to the top, you'll look around for the old village site. You'll know it when you see it. What you do is you sit there, dig up some earth, and hold it in your hands. You close your eyes, and the old world will come back to you. This is what I've heard."

So Ray, a garbageman, fasted for four days. He climbed to the top of the mountain—I'm not sure which. Ray looked around and found what he realized was the old village site. He sat down, dug up some earth, held onto the earth, and closed his eyes.

Then he had a vision. In the vision, he was back at the bottom of the mountain looking up at the top, where he could see the outlines of an old village. He was going to walk up to that village in his vision. As he was walking up to the village, suddenly these other Indians came down and attacked him. They beat him, whipped him, scarred him. He was trying to get through, but he couldn't get to the top.

Finally, Ray just dropped the earth in his hands and came back into the rational world.

He returned to his mother and asked, "What happened?"

She said, "You know who those people were?'

He said, "No."

She said, "Those are our ancestors. To get to that old world, you have to go through two hundred years of pain. Nobody's been able to do it."

What she told him was that the past is lost; pay attention to the present. He opened up a little self-help community center in Watsonville, something for alcohol abuse, for job training, for pregnancy counseling. So he paid attention to the living. It was the best he could do.

To some extent, I provided some connection to that old world.

Today when I go around to Indian conferences, I talk to activists in their early thirties who remember growing up with *The Ohlone Way*. The book ended up selling more than a hundred thousand copies over the years. It's become an essential part of courses. It's been wonderfully stolen from. It's been dismembered, parts of it appearing in different places, in course packets and other places. Some people have written me letters about how alienated they had been from their backgrounds, how little they knew, and how this book provided them with a body of information, a sensibility, respect. That's gratifying.

Malcolm with Darryl Babe Wilson (HEYDAY ARCHIVES)

DARRYL WILSON (1939–2014)

D ARRYL (BABE) WILSON was from the Achumawe and Atsugewi tribes, part of the Pit River Nation, from northern California. He was a writer for *News from Native California* and the author of a memoir, *The Morning the Sun Went Down* (Heyday,1998). Here he shared some of his reactions to *The Ohlone Way*.

The Ohlone Way is alive: the descriptions of nature, the ocean, the wind, the sun—of life. When I was reading *The Ohlone Way*, I could imagine how the people came down to the ocean through the redwood forest. I could feel myself going through the forest with my ancient people, heading for the mussels growing on the rocks. There were big, big mussel feeds for six or eight months out of the year. A lot of that book refers to those older experiences. It was a pretty close description of what the old people told me about the redwood country, long before I knew there was a redwood or what it looked like.

I wrote a thank-you letter to Malcolm that was published in *News from Native California* to express the impact that his publishing effort has had on the Native community, a positive explosion that came out of the seed that was planted with that book.

PETER NABOKOV

A PROFESSOR OF WORLD ARTS and Cultures and American Indian Studies at the University of California, Los Angeles, Peter Nabokov has been a longtime friend of Malcolm's, as well as a contributor to *News from Native California*. His book *Native American Testimony* (1991) provided an important collection of Native voices responding to the European invasion. Peter describes meeting Malcolm and shares his perspective on the contributions of *The Ohlone Way* to the field of Native American studies.

I just loved the guy as soon as I met him. Here was an interesting man with old-fashioned, hippie values, a make-it-with-whatever-you-got attitude, and a funky old VW who came to California to learn. It was clear that we shared a number of things, including a background as easterners; his was steeped in Boston culture, though I think of him as an East Village denizen. We also shared discovering the wonders of the Native American world. Shortly after meeting him, I met his family, his wife and kids, and I saw how his little vest-pocket, closet-in-the-wall publishing operation was going.

Like most of us who were studying American Indians in the 1950s and '60s, I had already become curious about what was, until then, the least known of the cultural regions, California. What Malcolm was learning about had been dropped by American anthropology. Lévi-Strauss came to visit Berkeley's Department of Anthropology when I was there, and he chastised them roundly for dropping California Indians. Well, the ball was picked up by Malcolm Margolin in a huge, huge way.

That initial book, *The Ohlone Way*, displayed Malcolm's wonderful talent as a clear, unpretentious writer, his sense for the almost practical mechanics of Indian life: how people fed themselves, their tool inventory, their range of techniques to wrest a living from the land, their spiritual life, their social organization. Then he imagined their world. Malcolm also had the natural history background, which most anthropologists don't have, and that was of inestimable value in bringing to life this most wondrous, magical, and—to use a word that he often uses—*capacious* of natural landscapes, rich in all variety of foodstuffs. He describes so well the fresh water, salt water, the marshes, the acorn, the botanical and biological wonderment of north-central California. He brought it all to life in *The Ohlone Way*, which is still in print.

MALCOLM: ON WRITING *THE WAY WE LIVED: CALIFORNIA INDIAN REMINISCENCES, STORIES, AND SONGS*

THE WAY WE LIVED [1981] began with what was left on the cutting-room floor from *The Ohlone Way*. I'd done all of this research and had many stories and fragments of poems left over, pieces that I liked, not just from the Ohlone but from all over California. I also wanted to do something that was entirely in an Indian voice, a corrective to *The Ohlone Way*, which had been *my* interpretation of Indian life. Now I wanted it in people's own voices. That may have come from urgings of others or from a sense of self-criticism, or maybe it was just the next step.

I ended up researching and reading more. When I started the book, I thought I already had a lot, but I spent a couple of years collecting more, researching, thinking, putting the pieces together.

I was also collecting a lot of California Indian photos. I went to the Field Museum in Chicago, the Heye Foundation in New York, the Smithsonian in Washington, the Peabody at Harvard, and the Milwaukee Public Museum. I had hundreds of photos, as well as copies from museum archives. I remember I once brought them down to the California Council for the Humanities and knocked out the folks there by laying down tons of photos and saying, "Hey, this is our heritage." So that's how I ended up putting the book together.

I revised it in later years to add a whole lot of new stuff. *The Way We Lived* started out with stuff that was about the past. In the second edition, the present becomes much more powerful. The balance begins to tip.

To the extent that I'm critical of it, I think now that I should have done a little more understanding and a little less explaining. My good friend Tim

Buckley, an anthropologist and Zen monk, made a wonderful distinction between *understanding* and *explaining*. In retrospect I see that when I started the book, I had the need to know, the need to be the guy that explains. What does this mean? What does that mean? Now I've evolved to the point of usually just telling stories about a topic, where the meaning is less clear or narrow than it used to be, not as articulated.

I'm still interested in the indigenous past. I would love to do a grand encyclopedia of California Indian life. I'd love to commission people to do paintings to recreate that life before the coming of the Europeans, the way we did with *A State of Change: Forgotten Landscapes of California* by Laura Cunningham, something of that magnitude.

EXCERPTS FROM *THE WAY WE LIVED*

THREE LOVE SONGS

DESPITE THE AUSTERITY *of people in northwestern California, despite the prevalence of arranged marriages everywhere, and despite the many restrictions on sex, love still raged beneath the surface, as poignant, pressing, and irreducibly tender as it is throughout the world.*

I.
Before you go over the snow-mountain to the north,
Downhill toward the north,
Oh me, do look back at me

You who dwell below the snow-mountain,
Do look back at me.

—HARRY MARSH, WINTU

II.
When he walks about,
When he walks about,
Pushing the deer decoy back away from his face,
Right there in front of him
May I come gliding down and fall!

—HARRY MARSH, WINTU

(sidebar continued on the next page)

III.
The sleeping place
Which you and I hollowed out
Will remain always,
Will remain always,
Will remain always,
Will remain always.

—FANNY BROWN, WINTU

THE TRUTH WILL SET YOU FREE

The dreadful events of the recent past have left deep scars. Every person of Indian descent has been forced to deal not only with ongoing prejudice, but an inheritance of injury and humiliation that goes back many generations. It hasn't been easy. Do native people have any choice but to go through life absorbed in bitterness, feeling in their very bones the anger and shame of being a defeated and despised people? Is denial the only alternative to hatred of others and hatred of oneself—denial of the past, denial even of one's own Indian ancestry? Even in the bleakest of times there have always been other voices within the Indian community—wise voices, sad and truthful and proud—that counsel another way of coming to terms with the past.

ALL KINDS SHOULD know who they are and be proud of who they are.... Before, it was so bad to be an Indian that you were ashamed, or you had to be somebody else. Many of the people would say I'm Filipino, or I'm from Canada. I'm from the dark French or whatever. They'd be anything except Indian. At one time, being Indian was so bad, if you got an education, it didn't do any good anyway. They wouldn't hire you....You think anybody would go to a doctor? The banks wouldn't hire you. Nobody would hire you because you were an Indian. And so in our minds being Indian was so bad, and we didn't really know why. Why was it so bad to be an Indian? But it's because of what they did to us, and they portrayed us that we were the savages. We were this and we were that. And we thought maybe we were....

The truth will set you free. We can talk about the Holocaust. We can talk about all the things that happened other places, but you can't talk about what happened to the Indians. Our kids know it. We tell our kids. We all know it. And the hurt is still here. So how do you get rid of that hurt? The way to get rid of the hurt is to put it out. Let everybody know, and after a while it will become history....The truth will set you free. And our kids won't be so angry.

—VIVIEN HAILSTONE, YUROK/HUPA/KARUK

NOW I'LL SHOW YOU HOW TO DO IT

A continual agony that modern Indians have to face is the possibility that their culture may die—that in another twenty years, fifty years, or a hundred years their language will no longer be spoken, their beliefs will exist only in written texts, the complex knowledge and skills acquired over thousands of years will have disappeared from the earth. For those who grew up experiencing the richness of traditional culture, the threat of its demise is horrifying, painful, almost unendurable. In recent years the specter of cultural extinction has inspired many with a sense of urgency and personal responsibility to learn the old ways and to pass them on.

As I GREW older, we went to different conferences, and people were saying that the art of basketry was dying. And I couldn't believe that, because I had lived in a home that had all kinds of baskets. And my grandmother made baskets. My mother. And then finally it dawned on me that that would be possible if someone else didn't take over.

And one day I thought to myself—I said, "Well, I think I could do that. I think what Grandma is doing I could do." So I went home—asked my mother for materials. My materials she gave me. I whipped out a newborn carrier real fast. I mean, it was like a day. The next day I took it to my grandmother's. I said, "Grandma, look." And she looked at that. And I could see that she was really impressed...that I had taken the time to go and make one of these, but she said that it looks like it was made in Japan because I stitched different. And then she said, "Now I'll show you how to do it."

—BARBARA BILL, MONO/YOKUTS

PETER NABOKOV

IN MALCOLM'S ANTHOLOGY on California Indian life, *The Way We Lived*, the range of historical, cultural, and geographical topics was brought to life through the voices, which is also what I tried to do in *Native American Testimony*. His book is an object lesson in how to put together a good anthology. All of that speaks not only to the ability to stay in the office and write well, but also an ability to ferret through an incredible range of neglected material, a lot of it collected under the leadership of Alfred Kroeber for the twenty-five or thirty years when he reigned over California ethnography. Kroeber had collected all this stuff that was buried in unassuming monographs and studies. Malcolm went through it and found the beating heart in each of these neglected books: a woman saying this, or a man remembering his childhood. It was just terrific, a masterpiece.

DEEP HANGING OUT IN CALIFORNIA INDIAN COUNTRY

Malcolm is known for his now figurative Rolodex of diverse friendships and connections. He engages new friends and old by both listening intensely—his tall, lanky body leaning in toward you—and responding with the gift of a perfect story that sheds light or humor on the conversation.

Surely Malcolm has enjoyed some of his best and deepest experiences exchanging stories in Native California. Longtime staff member and Heyday author and now board member Patricia Wakida said it well:

> What Heyday does so brilliantly and uniquely is provide a place for the voices of California that wouldn't be available to the greater public without us. The most obvious example is the California Indian world. All the Indian publishing and events happen at Heyday because that's where Malcolm's heart and soul are. If you just ignored him, he'd ramble right off to Indian country, to some roundhouse, and he'd be hanging out there with his friends.

The roundhouse is at the center of many California Indian communities, so it is no surprise that Malcolm has created a Berkeley Roundhouse out of the cultural institution that Heyday has become. Here he shares stories of the many significant friendships that he has nurtured and that have nurtured him in his visits with Native Californians on and off rancherias and reservations throughout the state for decades.

MALCOLM

PEOPLE OFTEN WONDER how I've made this life for myself among California Indians. It was all such a revelation. It's like going down a rabbit hole and wondering why everyone isn't there.

Maybe there's a protean quality to me, how I shape myself around others' experiences. It seems related to not knowing who I was earlier in my youth.

And then I'm a good storyteller. When in trouble, tell a story!

Partly it's also that I'm not an academic. I don't have a Ph.D. or money from an institution, so I'm not using anyone's story to increase my power. The basket weaver that made that basket [pointing] came to visit with her cousin Judy Talaugon, a Chumash woman from the Santa Ynez Reservation. I knew Judy's folks, Joe and Marge; we're good friends. Judy's now sixty. She was talking about how it used to be that the white anthropologists would come in and they'd write something, then go away, and you'd never see them again. The whites would get publication and tenure. They were taking things away from the community and using them for their own advancement.

On my part, there hasn't been a whole lot of self-interest in these connections. I don't make any money out of it. The fact that I'm flat broke has meant a lot.

It doesn't seem very hard to be accepted, from my perspective. Other people tell me it's very difficult as an outsider to be accepted into the Indian community, that it's suspicious and hostile. I see it as vulnerable. It's been wounded.

I probably do more good than harm. I'm a good writer, and I think that I reflect people's values. They can see themselves. I accept people on their own terms, and respectfully so. If somebody's a Christian, I'll talk about their being a Christian Indian, about their being a church member. It's about accepting them for who they are, not comparing them to some standard—being a "pure" Indian or "impure" Indian. It's just seeing the miracle of who somebody has become.

I felt so at home in that world. I'm not sure why. I felt *useful* in that world. When *The Ohlone Way* came out in 1978, I had the sense from a lot of Indians that they appreciated that someone cares about what their way of life is like, that someone is trying to understand. I have something to offer, something to bring to the potluck. I can feature people; I can photograph them. I can write articles about them. I can reflect them back to themselves. I'm not exploiting them. As a publisher, I can support them by getting their voices heard.

Part of it is that I don't want to be an Indian. Although any belief and practice have ended, I'm clearly a Jew from Boston. I don't want to adopt anyone else's culture. I have my own culture. I'm not Indian, but I also don't feel that I'm part of the dominant culture, either. I've been outside of all worlds. I could understand what it means to be separate.

I'm not sure what the attraction is to the Indian community, but it's there. The attraction is there for me with other communities, too. I've worked closely with Japanese Americans, African Americans, Hmong, and others. I get that same feeling from them, the sense that I've been part of each community, that I'm valuable to people in it. That's the role of a publisher, furthering others, setting the stage for others to come and perform.

Clifford Geertz defined anthropology as "deep hanging out." That's what I've done, deep hanging out, but it hasn't been systematic. I was with some Indians recently at a get-together here. They were treating me like everybody's elder, saying that I've got this memory of the Indian community over the last thirty years from the people I've known. I remember once when a younger Indian met me, she was absolutely stunned that I was still alive. She thought that I was of Kroeber's generation, that I was one of the old-time anthropologists.

THERESA HARLAN

THERESA HARLAN (Jemez Pueblo and Santo Domingo Pueblo of New Mexico) is an independent curator and writer on contemporary Native American art. She was the administrator of the Traditional Folk Arts Program for the California Arts Council and reviewer for the Alliance for California Traditional Arts and the National Endowment for the Arts, Folk Arts Heritage Award. Theresa also sits on the Heyday board. She wrote the following piece as the curator for a traveling Heyday exhibition (2007–2010), "Sing Me Your Story, Dance Me Home: Art and Poetry from Native California."

In the late 1980s while working at the American Indian Contemporary Arts Gallery in San Francisco, I became acquainted with Malcolm Margolin. I still remember the way Malcolm established a relationship with the gallery. It was the year we had an exhibition of California Native artists that included Frank LaPena, Brian Tripp, Charley Burns, and Karen Noble. I watched this tall bearded man walk comfortably around the gallery chatting with artists and guests. Malcolm became a constant attendee at our events. He told us he thought our work was wonderful and wanted to know more about us as an organization.

Malcolm became a fast friend because he was genuine and did not make presumptions about Native Americans. Our exchange of information increased, and we discovered we shared a wide California Native network. Sometimes other persons from organizations and museums would approach the gallery, and their requests leaned towards a superficial, if not an exploitative, air. Malcolm did not ask anything of us, but simply offered his friendship and delightful style of storytelling. A mutual and informal partnership developed between those of us at the gallery and Malcolm and Heyday Books, a partnership that was organic and filled with creative discussion.

MALCOLM: STORIES FROM NATIVE CALIFORNIA

I LOVE PEOPLE'S STORIES—from Indians and others. I don't think about how people work in a mechanical way, but I'm continually asking people what they do and where they grew up, where they're from, what their goals are. That's part of the deep hanging out.

One thing about the old-time Indians: they're deeply funny. It says something when the people have been so defeated, yet they're so deeply funny. I remember a celebration of the first acorn crop of the year. Lanny

*Lanny Pinola, Strawberry
Festival at Kule Loklo,
Point Reyes, 1993.*
(PHOTO BY SILENE DIFILIPPI,
HEYDAY ARCHIVES)

Pinola, a Kashaya Pomo, gave me a little tray of paper containers, like for
ketchup. They were filled with acorn mush. He tells me, "Malcolm, can
you go give the elders some acorn?"

So I come around with this tray of acorn, and the elders are looking
with utter alarm and confusion. It turns out that Lanny's practical joke was
that the first acorn of the year is supposed to be given by a young virgin.

There were such characters out there, like Laura Somersal, a Wappo
woman I'd visit. Laura's nephew, Clint McKay, told me a wonderful story
about her. He was once going to collect abalone at Stewart's Point. She said,
"Oh, when you're at Stewart's Point, get me some of that good seaweed."

He said, "Okay." He went to Stewart's Point and got the abalone. He's
in his car, driving down the coast, and then he realizes, "I forgot Laura's seaweed!" So he stops at a beach, picks up some seaweed, and brings it back.

She cooks it up, tries it, and says, "Oh, nooo! *This* isn't from Stewart's
Point!" Her knowledge was so exact.

That older generation alive back then—people like Wallace Burrows,
David Risling, and Vivien Hailstone—they had been raised by people who
remembered California before the Gold Rush, people who had direct contact with that old world. They also had contact with such tremendous pain.
Out of that suffering can come humor. I'm sorry that humor has to be at

such a price, but there's a humor, a warmth. Out of the knowledge of deep defeat comes knowledge of the human race. Hanging around these people was so wonderful. Their resilience was so great.

I remember once I was hired by the State Indian Museum to help put together an exhibit on the Gold Rush and its effect on Indians. I called April Moore, who's Nisenan and grew up on the Auburn Rancheria. Her great-aunt was Lizzie Enos, who was raised by people that remembered California before the Gold Rush. April had gotten these stories from her Aunt Lizzie, and I'd heard some of them.

I called April, and I said, "I'd love to hear some of Lizzie's stories. Can we get together?"

She said, "Let's meet at the Placer County Courthouse."

I said, "What a hell of a place to meet."

She said, "I gave them some baskets. They have a little museum in the basement. They'll find us a meeting room."

So I went up to the Placer County Courthouse, and I met April down in the basement. She told me stories about the Gold Rush. One I found the most poignant of all. I remember when I was a kid, we'd go to downtown Boston, and you'd get dressed up to be shown off. You'd wear your best clothes. When *they* went downtown, the kids were made ugly, given rags and their faces were made dirty, because the parents were afraid that someone would kidnap the kids if they looked beautiful.

When we walked out, she said, "I bet you're wondering why I wanted to meet you at the Placer County Courthouse."

"Why?" I asked.

She pointed to the courthouse walls. "Look at that stonework. My grandfather built that. When you talk about Indians and the Gold Rush, be sure you include that."

It was a small show of this wonderful survival through all that pain. That need to be modern, to be contemporary. You're part of the world.

George Blake builds dugout canoes out of huge trees. A museum hired him, up in Hoopa Valley. He was busy gouging out the canoe with a chainsaw. The museum people came and said, "Wait a minute, wait a minute! We wanted you to do it the old way with an adze and fire and stuff."

He said, "Listen, if you pick up the canoe the old way, with a horse and carriage, I'll make it the old way."

It was a world in which voices were so much alive. I was up with Chuck Donahue, who also made dugout canoes, in the woods around Yurok country. This mourning dove starts cooing. He said, "Do you know the story of Mourning Dove?"

I said, "Yes, I do. *Orowi* in the Yurok language. But how do you tell it, Chuck? I'd love to hear the story."

So he told me the story about how in the old days, when the world was first made, animals were kinds of people. There was a gambling game, and Mourning Dove was a gambler. He was gambling and winning a variety of Indian treasures: black obsidian blades, a red woodpecker scalp, white deerskin, abalone. These treasures were all originally divinities that had turned themselves into treasures. He was surrounded by all these divinities, by all these beauties in the world.

Somebody came to him and said, "Mourning Dove, your grandfather is dying. You better hurry up and see him."

But Mourning Dove said, "No, hold on. I'm on a winning streak! A couple more games."

He kept gambling and won some more while his grandfather died. Then the transformation happened, and he became the bird Mourning Dove. You can still hear him, made to mourn for his grandfather for eternity, and in the flecks of feathers around his neck, you can still see the treasure that he won.

That story is not really about mourning; it's about doing your duty. The animals in the woods all had stories to tell you. You were living in a moral world, walking through a world filled with meaning.

The stories of these shattered nations! So many people have lost their language and culture and land. There's the story of L. Frank and the Hawaiian recognition. L. Frank is Tongva from the Los Angeles area. If you're Tongva from the Los Angeles area, you're totally screwed. Indians have a tough time anywhere, but when Los Angeles and freeways and this brutal culture are built on your tribal land, you don't have a hell of a lot there. Everything's been wiped out. Total disruption.

Somewhere in the midst of this total loss, the native people of Hawai'i decided they would give diplomatic recognition to other Indian groups. So they came to give diplomatic recognition to the Tongva. The ceremony was at UC Irvine. The Hawaiian nation came with ambassadors and gifts, protocols and treaties. This straggly bunch of Tongvas gets together with a matching set of ambassadors and treaties. There were speeches and an exchange of diplomatic papers with recognition of one another, and then songs, gifts, and vows of eternal alliance against enemies.

But for all the pomp and circumstance, it was the parking regulations that took up most of the time. UC Irvine had completely incomprehensible parking regulations. I don't remember the details, but it was something like this: Pink passes were good on alternate Thursdays, when you could park on the left side, on south-facing streets, but on alternate Wednesdays you'd get towed, whereas with the blue parking pass you could do something else entirely. It was puzzling, and everybody's sitting around discussing their parking passes.

Finally, L. Frank says, "Let's stop! Extinct people can park anywhere."

Jimi Castillo was one the Tongvas. The Hawaiians had a presentation of hula dancers. Jimi had led a rough life. He must have been a good brawler in his youth. Eventually, he became a prison chaplain.

Jimi was watching the hula dancers, all these beautiful young women. Then before one dance, a woman announced, "You'll notice a funny expression coming across our faces because we do this dance for our genitalia." They begin to dance, and you see this wonderful expression coming across their faces.

I look over at Jimi, and tears are coming down his face. He says, "How could they have hurt people like this?" He was talking about not only the Hawaiians but his own culture, too.

Then there's Bertha Norton, Aunt Bertha. Dugan Aguilar took that photo of her when she was 100 years old at the roundhouse at Grindstone Rancheria, not far from Willows in the Sacramento Valley. The roundhouse ceremonies there are the oldest continuing traditions in California. Wallace Burrows died there at the age of 104, and Oscar McDaniel died at the age of 98. They had been young men and learned the traditions from the people that knew the traditions from before the Gold Rush. They were already well advanced when they learned the rituals. They'd do the Big Head dance, called the *Hesi*, so dramatic and so beautiful!

I'm sitting there in the roundhouse while we're waiting. During the *Hesi*, they whistle the *Kuksus* in from the woods. The crowd comes into the roundhouse. The drummer has a floor drum and a big stick. He's banging on the floor drum, the singers are singing, the *Kuksus* come backing in through the door. A fire is casting the shadow of the Big Head masks on the rafters. They're dancing around. People are throwing beads and money, and women are waving their scarves, trying to contain the power. It's an enormously powerful dance.

I was talking to Bertha while we're waiting for the dance to begin. I asked her, "You've been here for a long time. What was it like in the old days? What are your earliest memories?"

She said, "Oh, when I was a little kid, we used to get on top of the roundhouse roof. They told us we couldn't do it, but we did it. From the roof, we look down the dirt road coming from Stonyford, and we see buckboards coming up the road, the dust rising up and the dogs running behind, all them Indians coming in for the ceremony. We look down the dirt road to Colusa, and more buckboards and more Indians are coming, the dogs running behind. We look up the road to Covelo to see more buckboards. They're all coming.

"They come and tether the horses over there, they feed them horses real good; gotta feed the horses real good. Then we all eat and come into the roundhouse and build the fire. The dancers and the singers get ready. They whistle the *Kuksus* in from the woods, the dancers begin, the floor drums are going.

"Suddenly, you hear this big noise. We all look out through the door of the roundhouse, and all them dogs are fighting!"

She says, "I haven't seen a good dogfight in years! Don't Indians have dogs anymore?"

Just so funny.

That roundhouse culture is amazing: you go into a roundhouse, and you feel like you've always been there. It's like going into the center of the world. Everything outside of them is just a daydream, a fleeting fancy. You get inside them, and it's contained: The light is always the same; the fire is always the same; the jokes are always the same; the dances are always the same.

People would remember these roundhouses. They were like Ivy League colleges where the great stories were told, where the great singers would be, where people like Pedro O'Connor would sing the old songs. One of my favorite stories is about this guy Bill Franklin, a sweet man. Bill grew up in Ione, up in the foothills of the Sierra, up toward Jackson. The Ione roundhouse was among the most famous and greatest of them all.

Bill was a dancer as a teenager in the Ione roundhouse in the thirties. The war came, and he went into the service. During that period of time, roundhouse culture collapsed in California. The older generation was dying while the younger men had gone to war or found jobs in the city, in the shipyards. Bill did what a lot of men did: he got a job in logging. He eventually built a house in Shingle Springs and raised a family.

It got to be the forties and then the fifties and the sixties. Bill suddenly realized the culture was gone, and it wouldn't come back easily. So he got his kids and Indian friends, and they went out and searched the roads for roadkill, deer and flickers and things like that. He remade the regalia. He built a rec room next to his house and brought the kids in to rehearse the dances and sing the songs. Then, in the late sixties, he got together with Glen Villa and Harold Burris and some others, and they decided to rebuild the roundhouse.

They rebuilt a beautiful structure at Chaw'se—Indian Grinding Rock State Park—in 1970. They wanted it on State Parks land because it would be protected and not owned by one tribe. That would get it out of tribal politics.

The roundhouse there is big, roomy. Every year they have a huge ceremony with the best dancers and the best singers. Late at night, you see people come in to do their ceremonies that they can't do anymore, to name kids and such.

The roundhouse lasted for twenty years, until 1990, when the roof collapsed. They then rebuilt the roof, and it lasted until 2012, when it fell in once more. I assume they'll rebuild it again.

I was there several years ago, talking to Dwight Dutschke, Harold Burris's grandson. We were talking about how the roundhouse had been built. I was wondering about the construction of it all. I was asking why there were four posts in a cribbing instead of a single center post. Why were they tied up the way they were? There was a back door. Did they have to do that for code purposes or was that how it was in the old days?

Finally, he looks at me and he says, "I know what you're getting at, Malcolm."

I say, "What's that?"

He says, "You're getting at the fact that we didn't build it too good."

I say, "No, Dwight! That's not at all what I'm getting at."

He says, "We didn't! We know construction. We know how to build things. We know that you don't put posts in the ground without creosote and drainage. There was nothing in the old rules that said we couldn't use creosote. But we didn't. We know that you don't tie the rafters with grapevine if you want the roof to last. We could have used metal; we could have used nails or struts. There was nothing in the old rules that said you couldn't do that. But there was another old rule we had to follow."

I said, "What's that?"

He said, "We have to build a roundhouse so that it falls apart every twenty years. That way every generation learns how to rebuild it. If you want to keep a roundhouse alive, you build it one way. If you want to keep the knowledge and the culture alive, you do it another way."

The last time I was up at Ione, my good friend Brian Bibby and Glen Villa's grandson Conner asked, "Do you want to take a ride over to Ione? We'll show you around."

So we went out to Ione. They showed me where the roundhouse used to be, and where the cemetery was, and the gate Conner had built with his father. They showed me the baby-smashing rock where the pioneers had smashed babies' heads. They showed me where the yerba buena plant grows strongest and the footprints where the great animals had walked the world. They showed me the viewpoint where you could see Mount Diablo across the whole Central Valley. They showed me all these different things. It was this wonderful naming of things, senseless in a way, no plot to it, just the preservation of fact, the accumulation of memory, this investment in the land, so fragmented, so deeply felt, such sadness and such beauty!

I once brought Bun Lucas up to the foothills. He was an old Pomo man from Kashaya. He wanted to see what he called "other Indian round-houses." I went with him and my son Jake, who was just a little kid. Bun may also have been keeping an eye out for grizzly bear skins. There used to be grizzly bear shamans up at Kashaya, which was about ten miles from the coast. Shamans could turn themselves into grizzly bears. In half an hour they could go to the coast and come back with shellfish and thus prove their power.

I asked Bun, "Are there still grizzly bear shamans?"

He said, "I don't think so. We don't need them anymore. We have cars."

We ended up one night in a campground, me, Jake, and Bun. I set up a tent. Jake and I had sleeping bags. Bun had a rat's nest of blankets. It looked like a garbage heap. He was also weighed down with amulets because he was in a strange country, and he was afraid of being spooked by bad spirits and stuff like that.

Into this campground comes this bunch of bicyclists. They're all trim and neat in their spandex, and they've got little tiny backpacks and little tents. Everything is neat and compact. They look over, and there's me, Jake, and this old Indian in a rat's nest. But Bun was very friendly, so he went over and looked at their bicycle tires. And he says, "I know something about those bicycle tires."

"What do you know?" they ask suspiciously.

He says, "When your car gets stuck, these tires are so strong that you can put a bicycle tire around one bumper to another, and you can tow a car." They're looking at him as if it's the most horrifying thing they'd ever heard.

There was one old Ohlone guy from the Fremont area. He talked about fishing and hunting and catching sea lions in the Mowry Slough during the Depression. He used to tie ropes around them and haul them through the streets of Fremont up to his house. He'd cook them up, and they'd eat them. Now he was afraid of being caught by the police or by the

Bun Lucas, Strawberry
Festival at Kule Loklo,
Point Reyes, 1993.
(PHOTO BY SILENE DIFILIPPI,
HEYDAY ARCHIVES)

game warden, so he was always looking for other places. One day he was hauling the sea lion along a part of the marsh that he'd never been to before, and the sea lion suddenly slipped into a groove. He hauled it effortlessly along that groove. He realized he'd found that place where his ancestors had been hauling sea lions for thousands of years. It now moved easily. It becomes a metaphor for reviving traditions and language.

I learned a lot from Frank Lobo, a Juaneño Indian from San Juan Capistrano. When we lived on Stuart Street the first time, we rented from Dorothy Bryant and her husband. They had an old house that they were going to destroy, but they needed someone to rent it for a few years until they saved up their money. Even though the rent was low, we didn't have enough, so we ended up sharing the house with Frank and his wife, Sue.

Frank was so knowledgeable. He was a dropout from the academic world. He couldn't get his act together to write his thesis, but he had the deepest kind of knowledge. There was something in his mannerisms, in his way of thinking, in his intonation, humor, and understanding that I really absorbed.

I remember I was reviewing a book somebody wrote, and I said something like, "The facts are all correct, but the book lies in a deep way." The lie had to do with the tone and the mood of things. Getting the facts right is necessary, but it's not sufficient. What's harder to capture is the pacing, the tonality, the nuance, gesture, the posture that you have toward life. We don't always have the vocabulary for describing all that stuff, but that's what has to be captured and put forth.

Frank was responsible for much of that for me. I picked up a lot from Frank.

There's a story of somebody who went to see a Zen master. All of his life he wants to learn from the master. He finally approaches the master. After five minutes he comes back to his village, and he says he's learned everything he has to learn. They say, "What happened?"

He says, "I watched him tie his shoe."

I watched Frank repair his car, and that was all I had to know—the meticulousness.

At a recent Heyday event, I introduced to the audience Kathleen Smith, who is Dry Creek Pomo and Bodega Miwok. Even though I've known her for thirty years, when I think of her, I think of this picture that was taken when she was younger, Kathleen with her mom, Lucy Smith, and with Laura Somersal, and David Peri. What I said was that just sitting on a log with people like this for a half-hour, you can learn more than you can from four years at Cal.

David Peri was a very important friend for me, a Bodega Miwok guy who lived in Sebastopol. David had the most beautiful stories to tell. He had a sense of that old Indian world that was so rich and deep. He'd talk about these old stories he'd heard from the elders, like Essie Parrish, Mabel McKay, Laura Somersal, and Elsie Allen. He had a wonderful story that Elsie Allen told about the game of staves, a gambling game:

> This rich Indian woman comes to the village. She's so wealthy that she's driving a buckboard, and she's got a pleated white blouse, a jacket, and a valise. She starts playing this game, but she's losing and losing. She's lost the buckboard, the horse, and finally the dress. She's down to a bra and slip. They say, "What are you going to bet now?"
>
> She says, "I'll bet my husband."

All these other women are thinking, "If she's willing to bet her husband, he's probably not any good; we'd better not take it."

David's grandmother was Sarah Ballard, the last speaker of the Coast Miwok language. A linguist, Catherine Callaghan, would come over to interview this last speaker, to squeeze out the last drop of information that she could possibly get. David told the story about how one day his grandmother said, "There's a particular word that I'm thinking about, and this word is going through my mind, but I don't know what it means."

The linguist goes and looks it up in the dictionaries and the old vocabularies that people had written years ago. Catherine comes back, and she says, "I think it's the second person interrogative preterit of the verb 'to urinate.'"

Mrs. Ballard says, "Huh?"

She says, "I think it means, 'Did you pee?'"

Mrs. Ballard lights up. "Oh! Yes! That's it! I remember every night my grandmother would tuck me in, and that's what she'd ask."

Such amazing people I've known. There was my wonderful friend Alex Ramirez, an Ohlone guy. His grandfather Onésimo had a shack up above the town of Carmel, on the crossroads with Route 1 going into Carmel Valley. The anthropologists used to hang around there, since all the Indians coming up from Big Sur or down from the Santa Cruz area or in from the Salinas Valley would stop at Onésimo's shack because he grew marijuana. They'd all light up and share a joint. There the "anthros" could find these old-timers who spoke their languages.

We had a conference once in Monterey that Tim Thomas ran when he was working for the Maritime Museum. It was a conference on missions and Indians. Alex Ramirez was there, Doug Monroy, Gregg Castro, Ed Castillo, Linda Yamane, the ethnohistorian George Phillips, me, and some other people we knew.

The conference began with Monsignor Weber, who gave a speech on the sainthood of Junípero Serra. It was the stupidest speech I'd ever heard. I could have made a better case for sainthood than he did. He talked about three miracles that they needed to make Junípero Serra a saint, and they

Alex Ramirez, c. 2010.
(HEYDAY ARCHIVES)

had two miracles in the can. They thought the third miracle could be a cancer cure, but the church disallowed cancer cures, so nuns were pounding up Junípero Serra's bones and giving this mixture to people with lupus to cure them of lupus. We sat around, mouths open, horrified and amazed.

The conference went on so long that we got through our elevator speeches, and we actually had to think about what had been going on at the missions. What were those priests thinking as people were dying? What was the relationship between people? Why didn't people escape? Why wasn't there more armed revolt? We really tried to figure it out.

Finally, the last day of the conference was at the Serra house. When Alex Ramirez got his turn to speak, he said, "We began this conference talking about three miracles. I'm going to tell you about three real miracles. One miracle is that I walked through the front door of the Serra house. When I was a kid, we had to come through the back door. Another miracle is that I'm sitting here talking with all these people who have Ph.D.'s and who have written books, and I'm an Indian, and you're listening to me. That's a miracle."

"Now," he says, "those are small miracles. I'm going to tell you the big miracle. In 1923, they wanted to rebuild Mission Carmel. Everything we talked about, how the missionaries robbed us of land, robbed us of language, enslaved us—we knew all that. That was no secret. Everybody knows that. When they went to rebuild the mission, my grandfather Onésimo came and laid the cornerstone. Why did he do that? *That's* the miracle."

Maybe my hanging out in Indian country, all these connections, has to do with a sense of *witness*. I had a wonderful old friend, Ed Robbins. He knew the old writers of Chicago, Dreiser and Algren, and Hemingway and Fitzgerald from Paris. He was a friend of Woody Guthrie's. He was an old Commie, and like many other old Commies, he invested in real estate and ended up making a fortune. He lived in Berkeley. He'd come to the office, and we'd hang out and talk. He was such fun to be with, capacious, easy, full of life.

When he died, I was at his memorial service. He had a brother there, Mort, who was about fifteen years younger than Ed, so growing up, Mort never really knew Ed very well. But they got together later in life and had lunch every week. Mort and I were talking at the memorial service. He said that he always wondered about the fact that he had nothing in common with Ed. He wondered why in the world Ed wanted to have lunch with him. Then Mort said he finally began to feel that maybe it was something like this: "In life we have various people that we need. We need kin, we need partners, parents, friendships. We also need a witness, and I was his witness."

I feel that maybe one of my jobs in this Indian world is that of witness.

But this is to give some importance to the fact that I just really enjoy the hell out of it all! When Kathleen Smith came to the office to speak, she was talking about foods. I love the sound of her voice, the intonations, the Indian rhythms. You just move into this other world. Some people know more facts than she does, but *she* has the mood, the nuance, the tone, that intonation.

That may be where truth lies, not in the facts, not in the big themes, but in the tonalities, the rhythms. There's a kind of indirection to a lot of it. Indians don't always follow the rules that English teachers lay down, of being succinct and going directly to the point and being well organized. Their writing often drifts and winds around. Truths rise up mysteriously out of the middle of incoherence. You set the mood for facts that can rise up of their own accord.

My friend Julian Lang is so dedicated to his language, *in love* with the Karuk language. He came down to work at what was then the Lowie Museum and later the Hearst Museum. When he left there, we had a desk for him at Heyday for about a year, our Karuk Language Desk. He'd write for *News* and do his own work. He was such a delight to be with. We did talks together, once at Fort Mason in San Francisco, another time at the Huntington Library in Los Angeles. I just loved hanging around with him.

I love to hear Julian talk. William Bright, a linguist, talked about the Karuk language as especially sonorous and rich. There was something about the cadence of it, the elongated vowels. I thought that if you heard some-body talking in Karuk, this is how Cicero must have sounded in the Roman Senate—the most marvelous big volume, the luxurious sound of words, the musicality.

It's so wonderfully complex. California's a state with a hundred dif-ferent languages, five hundred different tribes, a complex history like this. That's my idea of paradise!

In doing *The Earth Manual* and *The East Bay Out* and *The Ohlone Way*, I felt that I was a fraud, that my knowledge was shallow, that I should know more than I did. I could talk a better game than I knew. Whether this is true or not, I'm not sure. I have that feeling much less now. I'm more comfort-able acknowledging what I don't know. I don't feel like a fraud. But I still feel like I articulate more than I really know.

I think of the wonderful story Franz Boas, the anthropologist, had about meeting a young Kwakiutl—or now the term would be Kwakwa-ka'waku—man on Vancouver Island who was kind of a doubter. He didn't believe in the old world or the old traditions. He wanted to be a modern person. In particular, he thought his village shaman was a complete fraud. He was a whistle-blower, I guess.

One day this young man saw the shaman heal somebody. In the healing process, you suck the disease out of them, and then you take this disease from your mouth and display it to the world, like a coyote hair or something like that. This person was watching the shaman closely when he was healing somebody. He spied the shaman insert something into his mouth and then later pull it out, claiming it was something he had sucked from the patient.

It was then that the young man realized that the shaman was a total fraud. He decided to expose the shaman to everybody. But he also realized he had no credibility unless he really understood shamanism.

So the young man apprenticed himself to the old shaman. He learned the tricks, and he learned the songs and gestures. He learned how you insert something and how you pull it out, how you display it and stuff like that. To his amazement, people got better. He became known as a great healer and as a great shaman. He was a leader among the Kwakiutl people.

Franz Boas finally said to this shaman, "But you're a fraud. You've become the fraud that you wanted to expose."

This shaman says, "Listen, I think maybe in the old days, people could do it right: they *could* suck the thing out. Nowadays we don't know how to do it, so we're just doing the best we can. But," he said, "maybe on the other part of the island, some people still know how to do it right."

Let me see if I can say this right. While people approach me as an expert on California Indian life, I'm so keenly and painfully aware of how much there is to know, how complex and nuanced and subtle that world is, and how superficial my knowledge. I tell good stories; I try to get it right. I do the best I can. But I hope that "on the other part of the island" there are people who really know this world with the depth and the fullness that it deserves. I'm proud of what I do, and at the same time I'm appalled at how inadequate it is. I keep learning, all the time learning, but the more I learn, the more I see how much more there is. What a tragedy. What a joy!

HEYDAY INTO NATIVE CALIFORNIA

"The individual stories about being on these Indian reservations, the people I've talked to and the things I've learned, are just so wondrous, the stories so great, so beautiful, that I tell them all the time. I build around them."

—MALCOLM MARGOLIN

WITH THE EMERGENCE of *The Ohlone Way* in 1978, shortly followed by *The Way We Lived* in 1981, Malcolm and Heyday rambled their way into supporting various organizations that have supported various communities and cultural interests of Native California. One of the most significant efforts is *News from Native California*. For over twenty-five years, this journal has provided thoughtful stories, essays, news, and calendar events, along with artwork, from across California. Heyday has also had a hand in supporting indigenous California basket weavers and those seeking to help Native languages survive. The Berkeley Roundhouse, based in Heyday, is the most recent development to help nurture the future of California Native cultures. Malcolm and Heyday friends share stories of these ventures here.

MALCOLM: THE FOUNDING OF *NEWS FROM NATIVE CALIFORNIA*

In 1987 I created *News from Native California* with my friend Vera Mae Fredrickson. Vera Mae worked for the Lowie Museum, now the Hearst Museum, at UC Berkeley, but then she got let go. I wondered, "What can we do with her?" I had to do something. I figured we could do a calendar of events. All these Indian things were going on, but you never heard about them. There was no way of hearing about them in the age before computers.

So Vera Mae and I decided to have a calendar of Indian events and send it out to people we knew. We went off to a Chinese restaurant and planned out the calendar on a paper napkin. I assumed some space would be left over, so I thought we could get Frank LaPena to write about art. Maybe Logan Slagle, a Cherokee lawyer, would write a legal column, and Victoria Patterson could write an education column. By the time we were through eating, I'd sketched out on the napkin what became *News from Native California*. The founding napkin has been long lost, and I've often wondered what was in the kung pao chicken, but that was the accidental creation of it, in the spirit of, "Let's *do* something!"

Once we realized we had something more than a calendar of events, we got David Peri involved. For the first years of *News*, I'd take the articles we were thinking of including to David's home in Sebastopol for discussion and approval. I was insecure about my capacities to understand Indian life and know what was authentic and what was phony, so the visits had an essential purpose.

But what really drew me were the stories he'd tell: about his Miwok upbringing along the shores of Bodega Bay; the traditions that were passed down; the nuances of the wonderful Coast Miwok language. Such funny, beautiful stories of that older generation, people like Essie Parrish and Laura Somersal. David appreciated them so deeply. He'd tell stories of deer hunting trips into the woods and excursions to the wetlands to gather basket root. He would bring out a recording to show me, or some rare and beautiful artifact. Then he would reminisce about complex conversations, whether they were in seminar rooms—he taught at Sonoma State—or in his anthropology fieldwork with Samuel Barrett or on a journey with Alfred Kroeber.

He was also the funniest guy. We'd go off drinking and have these long meals. He had the tone, the nuance of that older generation of Indians, the slowness, the wonderful humor. I could listen to him forever. David died in 2000, but not before having an enormous influence on many people's lives. His life was so charged with energy, chaos, and wit. He was a tremendous resource.

When he died, I said about him in *News*: "I remember once laughing at a story, which set his parrot off in gales of laughter, which made me laugh even harder and made the parrot hysterical, and finally I had to beg David to stop because my side was hurting so badly, I was afraid I'd injure myself if he continued."

So *News* got going. Vera Mae and David Fredrickson were crucial. Vera Mae collected the information for the calendar of events and wrote articles for the roundup of news. She handled the advertising, and both Fredricksons took care of recording subscriptions.

When we started doing *News*, some very old people were still around, born at the turn of the twentieth century or earlier. They had been raised by grandparents or great-aunts who themselves had been born before the coming of the whites and still remembered California from that time. You could feel that older world in the way they talked, in the way they moved, in the way they related not only to other people but to the world around them. These were people with such depth of knowledge, such humor, and such deep victory over defeat.

With *News* we set out to see what we could capture of that generation and that frame of mind. While we were in some modest way doing so, something completely unexpected came along and swept us off our feet—a major cultural revival. We came to deliver a eulogy to California Indian culture, and we ended up witnessing a rebirth. The process was immensely moving to witness.

DAVID PERI AS DR. COYOTE

David Peri had a semi-regular column in News from Native California *for years, "Ask Dr. Coyote." Here he answers a question about whether a non-Indian can participate in Indian ceremony:*

"INDIAN RELIGION" is not something you "participate in"; it's something you live, and you don't live it on special occasions, such as ceremonies. Ceremonies are not the religion. They are the accented expressions of complex understandings about the relationships between humans and those others living through their lives in a shared universe for which all have responsibility.

JEANNINE GENDAR

JEANNINE GENDAR IS the longest continual employee at Heyday, having started there in 1989. Editor extraordinaire, she worked on producing *News* from 1989 to 2000, in addition to editing books. Malcolm describes Jeannine as "a major presence at Heyday, calming and at the same time inspiring." Here Jeannine discusses her role with and perspectives on *News from Native California*.

In 1987 Malcolm, with Vera Mae Fredrickson and David Peri, had started *News from Native California* as a calendar of events. Of course, being a Malcolm project, it quickly grew to more than that. People loved it because at the time there was a dearth of information about California Indians. *News* was quickly becoming an organ for the statewide community of people that could make use of the information.

But the magazine was in trouble because there was no money to do it, no time, no personnel. Lee Davis was with the California Indian Project at the then Lowie Museum. Lee schemed to get a party together at Randy Milliken's house in Oakland; Randy has since become a scholar of the mission records. He knows more than anybody about Mission Indian genealogy in California. Lee invited various people: Bun Lucas, a Pomo man who had some pretty deep knowledge about Pomo tradition and doctoring; Bev Ortiz, who was a Ph.D. candidate at Cal at that time and had also worked for the East Bay Parks for years; and Kathleen Smith, Dry Creek Pomo and Bodega Miwok and a really good cook, among other things. She's a very good writer and visual artist, too. I was also invited. At the time I was the assistant to the head of the California Native American Heritage Commission in Sacramento.

Lee's idea was to bring together this assortment of people that could help Malcolm do something about *News;* also, the meeting was designed to be a sort of healing thing for Malcolm. There was a blessing. Kathleen made chicken soup with matzo balls. I think Lee believed Malcolm needed help. He was probably just fine, but he seemed distressed about keeping *News* together, so that was some of the motivation, and to create a good ambiance for the whole endeavor.

Another aspect of the scheme was to connect Malcolm and me, because at that time I was not part of that community. After that meeting, I started volunteering for *News*, helping with editing and design. A couple of years later, Malcolm and I both scratched our heads and thought maybe I should come to work for Malcolm. So we made that happen.

I had a really good run working on *News from Native California*. I think the magazine was terrific during a lot of those years. The issues looked good and had many really wonderful articles in them. Malcolm did a great job connecting with people who offered funding for a million different little special issues and projects, everything from poetry to a special issue on birds in Native California. I think we even had a whole special section on cordage, and one with California Indian Legal Services (CILS), including a history of fishing disputes in northwestern California along with other kinds of legal issues that CILS had been working on.

In July 2012 at the Oakland Museum we celebrated twenty-five years of *News from Native California*. Linda Yamane (Rumsien Ohlone) presented a basket to the museum, and then everyone came over to a party at Heyday. We got the most wonderful feedback that showed the value of *News* and Heyday over the years. Even just the presence at the event of certain people after all this time was gratifying. We've been a forum for underrepresented people. People *wanted* to be involved all across the state, including people who were not necessarily connected to each other. California Indians do not act as a single entity, but people have gotten to meet each other, in part because of events we did. That gave people a little bit more power or better resources for language learning and the cultivation of other traditions. The whole effort toward language revival and the basket weavers' gatherings, all the cultural revival endeavors going on: I think that we were making an underpinning for all of that to take place.

L. FRANK

ARTIST AND PHOTOGRAPHER L. Frank (Tongva, Acjachemem, and Raramuri) first met Malcolm at an Indian gathering at Indian Grinding Rock State Park (Chaw'se) in the Sierra foothills. She describes how they later connected at another gathering and then she began her work with *News*, contributing quirky Coyote drawings, among other work. L. Frank also muses on Malcolm's role in the Native community. Their friendship has clearly been a delight to them both.

I was in a huge meeting, and Malcolm was way across the room with Julian Lang. A month earlier I'd been on the phone with Julian, who told me, "I think you should do some drawings and write some words next to them."

He didn't know that I *had* done drawings with words next to them, but I said, "Okay."

I knew I was going to see Julian at this meeting, so when I got there, I gave him this big stack of line drawings that I wanted to show him. Julian was seated next to Malcolm across the room, and they were looking at my drawings. I kept hearing this loud laughter, "Ha, ha!" It was Malcolm laughing. He wasn't paying any attention to what was going on with the meeting. By now we've been at lots of conferences together. He's kind of like me, which is why we shouldn't sit next to each other.

Afterwards, on a break, Malcolm says to me, "I've been looking for something for the back covers of *News*, and these would be perfect." So then we communicated a lot more and became very good friends.

I never had any room for questions about how I should trust Malcolm. It's not my place, my culture, to question. I just had to wait and watch. If other Indians trust him, especially elders, then it's my job to do the same. If those people had been letting him in, then who am I to question? It wasn't even what people said but that they *allowed* him there and that he was integrated. It's just the effects of immersion.

But I will say that up north they thought Malcolm was a miner without his donkey. When Indians didn't know him, they'd say, "Who's that old miner?" They still laugh about that.

For me, Malcolm knows when to talk and when *not* to talk. He doesn't assert himself in a ceremony. He goes with the flow of the mood of a ceremony. And when he talks, at least to non-Natives when I've heard him talk, the things he talks about concern the landscape, the flora and fauna. That's just beautiful. Other than that, he's just a guy, no walking on water or on eggshells. He just doesn't misbehave, and if he does, it's the right way.

Coyote under a tree, by L. Frank : "An Acorn Is an Acorn Is an Acorn," from the Fall 1992 issue of News from Native California

One time Malcolm and I were asked to speak at a winery in Napa. They gave us each a hotel room. Malcolm came to the door to take me down to the banquet. I look through the peephole, and I'll be darned if he's not wearing a suit and a tie. I said, "Whoa!" I was flabbergasted. That merited some joking.

We go downstairs, and we're seated at a table with about six or eight people we don't know. To his right is an elderly woman, very stately, elegantly unfolding her napkin. As we sit down, she and Malcolm start talking. I realize who she is, one of the biggest landowners in the valley. I say, "I'd like to speak with you about your land."

She says, "Oh?"

Then Malcolm says, "They want it back."

Mostly when he and I are around each other, little stories are created. Our interaction is wonderfully absurd. It's been an exciting ride, a good ride. A lot of instruction. There aren't a lot of people you can look up to or work with that can inspire you. He's got the kind of mind I don't mind listening to. Malcolm appreciates if you come in with an idea that's not everyday.

And *News* reflects that. I look at what has happened in the community in relation to *News from Native California*, and it's very important. I don't know how to put this, but it has been a place to not be extinct.

Our very good friend Bev Ortiz was doing an interview for *News* at the first basket weavers' gathering. I didn't know anything about plants; I just had an inkling. But I came up to her and said, "I'd like you to interview me." I didn't care about my name being there. I didn't even care if I was going to be wrong about things, but I said, "I want my people to see their name in writing so they believe they exist." So, for many of us, it was a place to exist, to be. We're substantial.

Otherwise, I'm considered extinct if it weren't for places like *News* and Heyday. My personal goal with Heyday was making sure that my cousins and others were visible. It's worked out. My name got attached, even if they were little cartoons. Then grantors started talking to me. I started sitting on boards. It all came about through art and Native families and Heyday, and through those associations, through networking, other Natives were able to use my name to get grants to do what they needed to do for their families. But it all came out of having a place to be visible.

Another connection has been this conference I helped start at UC Berkeley called "Breath of Life: Silent No More." Leanne Hinton did the linguistics part. It's now become a national model. We needed to get some money, all the things you need to start: a fiscal receiver, help getting the word out, anything organizational. Malcolm and Heyday were right there at the very first. That's Heyday.

As a matter of fact, Heyday—not *News*—donated two hundred dollars to me to create another conference about linguists working with Natives. That conference was also the first of its kind. These linguists have done several papers—Native linguists, also. Malcolm donated two hundred dollars for food because it was a three-day event, and I had to feed people. He was behind that. I'm planning on more. He's helped from the beginning, and now.

Heyday is a necessary tool for our revitalization process. We couldn't have done it as quickly without Heyday. We'd be less connected. It would take longer to establish the connections. I think it's played a good role in the history of our people.

DARRYL BABE WILSON

ARRYL (BABE) WILSON (Achumawe and Atsugewi) was a regular contributor to *News* nearly from the beginning. Malcolm says of Darryl, "He was among my closest friends—poetic, emotional, deeply knowledgeable, our sage, storyteller, and philosopher." Darryl discussed how the magazine was initially received and how it has grown in popularity.

News has turned out to be such an artistic display of Native survival on the California frontier. At the beginning the magazine was cool, somebody's beautiful wild idea. The old grandmas of my life in the homeland would say, "Plant a garden before you go; till the soil, yes. But first plant a dream." *News from Native California* had that kind of origin. It came out of a dream, with its own velocity, its own destiny, its own purpose.

I think in the beginning, 90 percent of the Natives didn't trust it—if they knew about it—because there's such a wall built around the Native being that encourages doubt and instability to ferment. I was one of them at first. Throw it over there, don't want to read it. Just don't have trust. I don't think anybody ever dug around for authenticity at first. It was just an overall general distrust between Native people and the American establishment. History is so scrambled. Some of it is a total lie, no truth connected to it. And in many instances, history has been recorded by the invading body from Europe, so it's distant from any possible truth. So you hold it as suspect.

When I got to know Malcolm, I found he has always been overly generous. And fair, truthful, respectful. He asked me to write for *News*, so I did. I've written historical pieces, or about my people, about the grandmas that said to plant a dream before planting a seed, things like that. When I go to other people's land, everybody else has a point of view, too, so I write about what I see there. I was recently at Swinomish Lodge, and I wrote about the Swinomish experience from my point of view. When I go down to Chumash country, I write about them and the developments they're making in the landscape, and the cultural traditions they're reviving as they live beside the ocean. So I'm always expanding the horizon.

Here is an example of Darryl's writing for *News from Native California*, the introduction to his article "How the Great Canyon Was Made":

It was a summer before I kept track of time. In our decrepit automobile, we rattled into the driveway, a cloud of exhaust fumes, dust, and screaming excited children. A half-dozen ragged kids and an old black dog poured from the ancient vehicle. Confusion reigned supreme. Uncle Ramsey (after we became parents, his official title changed to "Grampa") was standing in the door of the comfortable, little pine-board home just east of McArthur. Aunt Lorena was in her immaculate kitchen making coffee....

They spoke in our language, *A-Juma-wi* and *Opore-gee*, and they used a very crude and stumbling English. The English words were strange. I preferred the "old language." As our lives moved into the world of the English-speakers, and our "old" language became less and less important and less and less used, something within the old people hesitated.

Although I hesitated (and possibly shuddered), I did not surrender. Somehow I simply had to capture the "old" ways. Unknown to me, that was my objective long ago. Often the old people would look at me as I huddled around my father's legs and they were talking while my sisters and brothers were screaming and racing through the land, "...that child is different. He is not the same as all the others." It is not true that I was different, it is that *my people are unique* and different from the waves of Europeans that flooded our land. At an early age I was attracted to this phenomenon. At 5-years-old, I could not know it, but it simply was a part of my destiny to record as much of the "old way" as possible....

Our natural place upon earth is east of Redding, California. Mt. Shasta and Mt. Lassen are what we identify as the western cornerstones of our land. This beautiful land holds the dreams and conflicts of my people. It also is the origin of many stories.... How the earth and nature were made is different from tribe to tribe.

There is a deep canyon just south and laying dead west of where Fall River and Pit River merge. It is several miles long and thousands of feet deep. Grampa Ramsey told us how that canyon was made, because if it was not made, the valleys clear back up the Pit River and into Dixie would be flooded.

Born one score and four moments after the assassination of Abraham Lincoln, white-haired and balding, built like a little bull with a twinkle in his clouding eyes and a gruff giggle riding on his mischievous sentences, Grampa Ramsey was our private connection to the ethereal.

(FROM *NEWS FROM NATIVE CALIFORNIA*, VOL. 5, NO. 3, MAY-JUNE-JULY 1991)

FRANK LAPENA

FRANK LAPENA (WINTU) is an artist and professor of Native American studies, retired from California State University Sacramento. He has contributed columns to *News* since the magazine's inception. He, too, counts decades of friendship with Malcolm.

News from Native California has given us a voice, so you get a grassroots perspective on issues. It's also been a way for people to talk about things that concern them, about an event that takes place or to acknowledge special people, like the elders who are carrying on the traditions and the songs. The people that write for *News* are involved in various levels of society or disciplines, but you get a more humanistic perspective about California Indian life. You see real human experience and a dimension of love.

In a way, the magazine has worked because Malcolm was outside of the culture, so it provides a neutral place. However, I remember one negative reaction, someone saying, "I don't know about those guys. What are *they* doing, talking about Indian stuff?"

I said, "Hold it now! They're talking about things that *we're* interested in, and they're giving us a platform to deal with it all, not only with the Indian community but with the outside community, too."

When people want to know about events, they sometimes call *News* since the folks there have their fingers in all the pots, and people are feeding information to them. But when outside people call and want to ask questions, the *News* folks might say, "Well, we have some contacts here, but we have to call and find out if we can pass along their number." So they're conscious of treating people respectfully. Like if they say, "We had this call, and these folks are working on doing a history; would you be willing to talk?" I might ask, "Well, who are they?" I find out and then say, "Okay."

I think that's important, the respect.

Malcolm describes Frank as "a cherished friend, guide, and mentor, from the first issue of *News* to the present," saying that "his art columns, which feature Native artists throughout California, derive much of their power not only from Frank's practice as an artist and from his years as a professor at Sacramento State, but also from his deep immersion in traditional dance, song, and ceremony." In 2004 Heyday published a book of Frank's reflections on traditional dance, called *Dream Songs and Ceremony*, from which the following excerpt is taken.

If I could capture the essence of dance it would be that we are all connected as one. There are no boundaries, there is no age, only eternal movement without end. There is a rhythm to our life cycles; each birth is part of the dance as are the memories of older dancers and the songs of past singers—there are no dances without songs. It is through the repetition of the song and the movements of the dance that the mind and spirit are engaged. To dance is to interpret the words or joy of the song.

In ceremony, dance follows the rhythm of seasons: of wind and calm, summer heat and winter cold, the moon waxing and waning, the heart beating-pulsing through one's body back onto past generations; of family members, friends, and lovers. Emotions of joy and sadness are all part of the rhythms and cycles of dance.

In order for a dance to be real, a fire is built to carry what we are doing to the above world. It is also why we circle the dance floor when entering a dance area; we are initiating and dedicating ourselves and the roundhouse, or dance area if we are dancing outside, to ceremony.

At a home dance, everybody recognizes who most of the dancers are, because they are related through marriage or are family members. But whenever dancers in regalia take the floor, they put aside their own identities

and become deer, bear, or another animal, or they become "stand-ins" for
the human race.   FROM *DREAM SONGS AND CEREMONY: REFLECTIONS ON*
TRADITIONAL CALIFORNIA INDIAN DANCE BY FRANK LAPENA (HEYDAY, 2004)

ALLOGAN SLAGLE (1951–2002)

A MAN FONDLY REMEMBERED by Malcolm and in the Native California community is Allogan Slagle, an activist Native lawyer and a writer for *News*. Malcolm's
description of him is followed by a piece written about Logan by Kenneth Lincoln.

MALCOLM

Another key person in the life of *News* and in my life was Allogan Slagle,
a Keetoowah Cherokee and a member of the Groundhog clan. He was
an attorney who specialized in federal acknowledgment, but whose interests, intelligence, devotion, and foibles were broad and legendary. From
the first issue of *News* until his death in 2002 Logan wrote a column called
"Groundhog Day," which he characterized as "a byline of warning barks,
with chirps of cautious optimism, from the news burrow to the grassroots."
With his column, he aimed to educate readers on a wide range of political
and legal issues.

WITH RESPECT: ALLOGAN SLAGLE
—KENNETH LINCOLN

He reminded me of the great white rabbit, Wakdjungkaga, a Winnebago
creator, divinely tricky and amicably randy—he was always a bit frumpy,
wearing cotton plaid shirts and baggy jeans before grunge was in, and
squeaky tennis shoes. He had a turned-in, tip-toey walk, as though he were
stepping on eggs or ice, and a wild bright alertness to edges and corners.
He made me think of a bird's quickness to spot danger, a mouse curiously
scurrying. Logan walked right out of *The Hobbit* with a shuffle and mutter
to himself, wrinkling his nose, squinting behind seriously thick glasses,
and looking down at the ground like Wordsworth's leech-gatherer. Only
this boy was an advanced high school student in my first freshman honors
class at the University of California, Los Angeles. He was my only student

ever to join the faculty at the University of California, Berkeley, our institutional archrival.

Logan had deep dark eyes behind coke-bottle lenses, thick black eyebrows, and curly cobalt hair that was always disheveled. There was no roughness about him, no calloused knuckles—he had an artist's hands, a doctor's touch. He moved with his knees bent like a slow-motion jogger, a slightly forward trip to his walk. All this made sense when he told me he had minus 1400 visual myopia and deteriorating retinas. Doctors said he would go blind by the age of twenty-five. There was no time to lose.

Logan drew on a fierce energy when needed. He was brilliant, eccentric, lovable, absolutely dedicated to human needs, and one of the truest voices of clarity and hilarity in the land. I miss him deep in my soul. This is a grief piece, a howl and ache, blues for a dear lost friend parted too soon. A bone in my throat, singing.

Logan was born August 31, 1951, in Shelby, North Carolina, close to Xualla or today's Qualla, the core of the Eastern Cherokee Nation. His lineage was runaway Cherokee in the Allegheny region, those most civilized of "real peoples" who chose not to remove to Oklahoma under Andrew Jackson's order but stayed home in the Great Smoky Mountains; they were the original tribal Refuseniks.

This man was functionally paranoid. He had things to worry about, from the Vietnam War to killer bees and earthquakes; shadows of holocausts of Indians and Jews and all other Others dispossessed in the world; rabies and mad cow disease, cancer and diabetes, smallpox and napalm. He was skittishly alert with the peripheral attention of survivors who know forced entrances and speedy exits. He told me early on that Buddhist monks could meditate at the brain frequency of paranoid schizophrenics, only they could go in and out of a trance at will. It was worth thinking about.

Logan worked tirelessly, seven days a week, for more than thirty years, often on little or no sleep. He had a near-photographic memory. He was obsessive about detail (the passion of the scientist, Nabokov said, the precision of the artist). Logan had a poet's originality, a lawyer's edge, a healer's compassion—an offbeat genius that I will never forget.

(FROM *NEWS FROM NATIVE CALIFORNIA*, VOLUME 16, NO. 3, SPRING 2003)

PETER NABOKOV

PETER NABOKOV DISCUSSES how he saw the impact of *News from Native California* in the Indian world.

Malcolm's two books on Native Californians garnered my wholehearted enthusiasm, excitement, respect. Then to top it off, he starts the magazine *News from Native California*, using his vast network with Indian people. I'd give my left arm to be part of and have access to Malcolm's network, but he's much more social and gregarious than I am. Increasingly he made *News* into a forum, the like of which does not exist elsewhere in the United States.

At the time there was *Akwesasne Notes*, a wonderful newspaper put out in northern New York State by some Iroquoian folks who were traditionals. They initially did some interesting things. It was a lot of scissor and paste in the days before computers, but they produced a real journal of record for the country's Indians. In San Francisco, the American Indian Historical Society, created by the dynamic duo of Rupert Costo and Jeannette Henry, had a strong militant position. They produced the *American Indian Historian* magazine, which I loved. All of that was spawned from the activism of the 1960s and pre-existed *News*.

Then Malcolm comes along and does something similar, but bases it more on the cultural stuff, with some political information, and with mostly Indian contributors. The journal also had a great layout. And then there's Malcolm doing his foreword; I always enjoy his prose because he's such a good, clear, unpretentious writer.

Malcolm understands the huge and dark historical echo chamber of California Indian history but is not hung up on revenge or retaliation as others might be. He's never been that way. But he's not afraid to speak truth to power. He's put terrific pieces in *News* about Indian removals and other difficult issues, yet he's always upbeat. He's inclusive rather than exclusive in terms of welcoming folks to come under the huge tent that he has pretty much single-handedly created—Heyday, *News*, then these subgroup passions, the Central Valley literature or the basket weavers or the nature-related material. He finds a great artist and nurtures a book about them.

He draws out the best from us. He champions the idiosyncratic folks who respond to his warmth and invitation. He's just an amazing cat!

JENNIFER BATES

JENNIFER BATES (ME-WUK), a basket weaver and advocate for traditional arts, discusses what *News from Native California* has meant to her.

For ten years I've coordinated the California Indian Market at the Black Oak Casino in Tuolumne, where I work. The first year, I had about fifteen artists. I started inviting Malcolm to bring all of his California books and magazines to sell at the market because Malcolm and what he's produced, including *News from Native California*, are so much a part of Native life for California that he just needs to be at Native functions! If Native California is this big puzzle, Heyday and Malcolm are each a different piece, and without them, you can't complete the puzzle. Every year he comes up, and if he couldn't, Jeannine or somebody else came up for him.

My mother, Dorothy Stanley, started getting *News* when it came out. When she passed on, I took all of her *News* magazines, and I continued the subscription. I knew young people who had to do reports, and I'd remember a really good article in *News* that they could read. I didn't know which issue it was, but I'd dig through until I found it and say, "Read this." So much information!

When I opened my gallery (Bear n' Coyote Gallery in Jamestown), I had *News* there for sale. I had my advertisements in *News* for my gallery. When I split up from the man I was with at the time, he took all my copies of *News*. I'm still going to try to get them back. They're valuable to me! Part of me says, "Oh, they're just magazines. No big deal." But they have so much information, and a lot of things are written about friends of mine and people who had passed on that I knew, including my mother. Malcolm gave me a copy of that specific one about my mother when I told him I didn't have it anymore.

The magazine's played a really good role in communication, which, in this incredibly large state, is amazing. From one tip to the other, you'll find *News* someplace. It's a good resource and window on what's happening throughout California. I always read the calendar of events because I do want to know. I always want to go to these events. Does time permit me to do that? No! But at least I know what's going on. "Did you hear that they're having a big time in such and such place?" It opens the door to all kinds of information.

Also, they always have a little bit about political issues. It's never been a real political magazine, but they touch on things that people need to know about, like sovereignty struggles or casinos. When they talk about all the cultural stuff, the big times or bringing back a dance, like the Spring Dance up north, the Condor Dance down south, it's good for people to know about the efforts to revive these traditions. The *News* reporters keep talking to the right people, the real people, about what they're doing in Native communities. That encourages others, especially young people to see, "There *are* people who do this ceremony" or whatever it is. The young people who read it can get inspired to do something. The magazine is an inspiration for the young and the old.

Introducing new books is also important, learning about new Native artists, be it music, writing, other arts. That's just awesome. When you think about how big California is, and how really small the Native community is in the whole state, *News* truly keeps us together and connected.

MALCOLM: FORMING THE SPOKES AND RUNNERS FOR BASKET WEAVERS

MALCOLM EXPLAINS THE beginnings of the California Indian Basketweavers Association and his connection to it, and then Jennifer Bates describes the organization's role in the Native community.

One of the great joys of my life has been hanging out with Indian basket weavers. Time slows down, laughter comes easily as you watch patient fingers transform a pile of what seem to be ordinary twigs and roots into objects of wondrous beauty. I've witnessed this transformation dozens of times, maybe even hundreds of times, and I'll never tire of it, never fully understand it, always be grateful that I've been allowed to see the beauty of the human spirit take physical form. Basketry, often referred to as the greatest artistic achievement of California Indians, is more than an art; it's a way of being in the world, a form of meditation, a job to be done, a joy to behold.

We've worked with the Basketweavers' annual conference from the planning stages to the present. One of my fondest memories is a gathering where I was talking with Julia Parker, a great weaver and teacher. It was in the early days. We were up on a reservation where the Basketweavers' conference was, and I'm looking out: there's Georgiana Trull, this aristocratic Yurok woman, and Aileen Figueroa, also Yurok, and Norma Turner from North Fork, and Vivien Hailstone. All these great old weavers were there. I look at Julia and say, "Isn't it wonderful how basketry has attracted the best people in the world?"

She says, "No, Malcolm, you don't understand. The baskets make us this way."

When I met Julia, she had jet-black hair, so black it was almost purple. She has piercing but sparkling eyes, like root beer. Strong! She's now in her eighties, but she's strong, vivacious, beautiful. She is Kashaya Pomo/ Coast Miwok, a member of the Federated Indians of Graton Rancheria. She married into the Yosemite Miwuk and learned many of their traditional skills.

We did a book on Julia's acorn processing, written by Bev Ortiz. I got a photographer, Raye Santos, to follow her and photograph the various steps. I'm in the office, and the phone rings. It's Raye Santos saying, "Malcolm, you're not going to believe this."

I said, "What?"

"Julia just dyed her hair blond and got a perm."

I said, "You're kidding! Put her on the phone." So I said, "Julia, what did you do?"

She said, "I didn't want to be one of them museum Indians. I'm a modern person, and I want everybody to know it."

"What should I do?" asked Raye.

"Photograph her hands," I said.

But it was black–and-white photos, so her hair turned out to look white.

Another impeccably gifted basket weaver was Mabel McKay, Marshall McKay's mother. She was fierce. Greg Sarris wrote a book about her, *Weaving the Dream,* in the Portraits of American Genius series that UC Press started. Mabel spoke Cache Creek (Southern) Patwin, Pomo, and English. She was, I think, the last speaker of the Cache Creek language. When she died, she wanted to be buried next to her friend Essie Parrish of the Kashaya reservation. I was up at the funeral there. It was a rainy, miserable day, cold and horrible. The funeral was a bit chaotic. Protestants and Mormons prayed, and then there were the old believers who prayed and keened. Old and new prayers were mixed together in something that seemed improvised and clumsy.

Frank LaPena was there, and he had a boom box. He turned on the boom box. It was Mabel singing her funeral song. She was the last person that could sing herself to the other world.

JENNIFER BATES

JENNIFER BATES (ME-WUK) and Malcolm have enjoyed a forty-year friendship that developed out of her mother's friendship with Malcolm. Jennifer played a significant role in founding the California Indian Basketweavers Association (CIBA).

I can't remember exactly when I met Malcolm; I just know he's gone through most of my life with me. My mother, Dorothy Stanley, knew Malcolm before I did. My mother and I used to go to the Festival of the Lake in Oakland and the Oakland Museum to demonstrate acorn cooking (*nupa*), so I probably met Malcolm one of those times. Malcolm and my mother got along really well. My mother passed away in 1990. In 1988 or '89, I opened up an art gallery for California Indian artists in Jamestown, in the Sierra foothills. Malcolm used to visit.

Sara Greensfelder, a cultural activist from Nevada City, put out a questionnaire to as many weavers as she knew. There weren't many of us, but the ones she did know included me, Julia Parker, Lucy Parker, Gladys McKinney,

Julie Tex, Kathy Wallace, and Kathy's aunt Vivien Hailstone. Sara asked questions like "If you're a weaver, from what tribe? Would you be interested in getting together with other weavers? What would you want to discuss?"

I answered her questionnaire. Sara took all this information from the weavers, and then she invited us to a gathering. She'd gotten some money from a grant to get us all together. We first met over in Pomo country, in Forestville, in 1991 with about fifty weavers or more. I think Malcolm was at that one. We were planning to meet out in the open, but it was raining, so the winery next door opened their warehouse to let us go inside with our chairs.

We had an amazing time. Pegg Mathewson was there and Bev Ortiz. You'd hear, "Oh my God, I didn't know there was another weaver in my area!" All these women talking about basketry opened my eyes to the issues happening up north with the Yurok and the Hupa and the Karuk people. For example, all the spraying going on there was leading to stillbirths and cancer and deformities. If you were picking material by the roadside, you didn't know if it was sprayed. When you pick your materials, it goes into your mouth to split it and clean it, so some women had blisters on their lips

Malcolm with sisters Kimberly Stevenot (left) and Jennifer Bates (HEYDAY ARCHIVES)

after picking willow because they didn't realize that it had just been sprayed. I never knew anything about all that.

We talked about how difficult it is gathering for our baskets sometimes, stories about people getting shot at because it was private property or getting arrested if we were on the side of the road picking material. All these issues popped up. It was so mind-blowing *and* mind-opening to everything going on around us, how we had been so quiet in our own little spaces. Now I realized, "All these people are doing the same thing I'm doing!" It was a wonderful time. That was the first unofficial gathering.

The second year when we got together, we had twice as many people. We asked, "Do you want to do an organization? Is this something that's important to you?"

They said, "Yes, let's go for it!"

So we did start an association, and we put a board together. A lot of us were sisters. My sister Kimberly came on board. Julie Tex and Gladys McKinney were sisters, and we had some sisters from up north. The third gathering, the official one when we became an organization, was held on the Me-wuk rancheria at Tuolumne in 1992, and again in 1993. We decided we'd do two gatherings in a row in the same place so people would be more familiar with where they were going. After that, we went up north, and then down south. We tried to hit all of the state.

I became the first chairperson for the association and was chair for thirteen or fourteen years.

One of my mentors was Julia Parker because she worked in Yosemite, where I was living at the time. When I started making baskets, the first one I made was terrible! I wasn't weaving the right way, but that's how you learn. "Nope, that's not right!" she'd say. It took a lot of time to learn to do it right. I remember a Mono woman was teaching me and my husband at the time, Craig Bates, how to collect and prepare redbud, which we use here for our baskets. So we went out and got a bunch of redbud and split it up. We were all happy. We took back our homework and said, "Look, here's our redbud."

She looked at it and said, "No good!" And she threw it to the side!

I said, "What do you mean it's no good?"

Now I know: when you split redbud, it has a lot of little nodes, and you have to split them in half. You can't split around them. You have to twist that redbud to where it splits that node in half.

I thought, "She doesn't know what she's talking about!" I was only about eighteen at the time. So I just kept it and let it season. Later, I got it out to make my basket, soaked it, and cleaned it. Sure enough! Those nodes that you don't split can't get through your stitch. And if they *do* get through, it catches and splits, and the red comes off. I had to throw it all away and start over. That meant I had to wait until the following fall. It was a hard lesson to learn, but one of the best. From then on, I thought, "If anybody asks me or tells me anything, I'm going to listen. I'm not going to question it because I think I know everything at eighteen." I realized that this elder, who's made *hundreds* of baskets, knows what she's talking about. I put that story into my own teaching because if you don't really believe me, then you can learn on your own.

I knew Malcolm all the way through CIBA. When we did our CIBA gatherings, Malcolm and Frank LaPena were our announcers for our raffle every year, with me. I think I called them Mutt and Jeff. We always stayed in touch. Malcolm was always instrumental in giving us advice, or dropping a name of people to contact for grants, things like that.

While I was the chairperson, we were going through some rough times. Sara and I thought, "Let's get some people who really know about grants and how to work with nonprofits." We asked Malcolm and several others who we felt could help us. They came here to meet, and we picked their brains. Malcolm and the other folks we invited were very good at giving us encouragement and teaching us how to go about doing things. In that respect, he helped CIBA tremendously.

MALCOLM: SUPPORTING LANGUAGE REVITALIZATION EFFORTS

OF SO MANY issues that Malcolm and Heyday have provided help for in Native California, the preservation of threatened indigenous languages has been among the most crucial. Malcolm explains how he became involved in Native language revitalization.

MALCOLM UNDER A TREE

JENNIFER BATES

WHEN YOU READ some of Malcolm's writing and when he talks, even if he just says, "Look out the window there, and look at that oak tree," he's pointing out something that's interesting. He'll write about how he'll go find a quiet place under an oak tree and go to sleep. I've seen him actually lying there asleep under an oak tree. That's Malcolm, comfortable under an oak tree.

When I have the Indian Market here, I always invite him and a lot of other people I know, and everyone's talking to each other all day. Sometimes I'll wonder where Malcolm went. I'll go outside, and he's lying under an oak, sleeping. Amazing.

He does need to recharge because Malcolm is so well liked and respected that everyone loves to talk his ears off. And he's a very good listener. You have to listen to understand. We all listen, but we may be thinking, "I gotta get the laundry done and do the grocery shopping," while we're saying "umhmm" to the other person. Or you think, "I know where this is going and how I'm going to answer this." That's not listening. Malcolm listens to understand. There's a big difference. So if you have the gift of listening to understand, that's wonderful because you're gaining more knowledge and understanding. He gives 100 percent to that person so he can learn, and that's why he knows so much.

But that's why he needs to lie down under an oak tree, so tired from taking in everything that he does!

Malcolm under a tree, from Heyday's 30th anniversary card. (DRAWING BY ZAK NELSON)

After I started *News from Native California*, Marion Weber, who is Laurance Rockefeller's daughter, came by, and she wanted to start a foundation to support Indian culture. She gave $100,000 a year for it. It was the Native California Network, and it came with her friend Mary Bates Abbott, who would be the administrator of it. So I had the funds and an almost all-Indian board, with Frank LaPena, Carole Korb, Paul Apodaca, and various other Indians. Mary was the executive director. I was the one non-Indian on the board. We'd get together and give these small grants out.

Somewhere in the first year or two of getting *News* and the Native California Network going, I think I was the one who suggested we do a language conference to get together the last speakers of the California languages. We had a conference up in Marin, and we got all these people up from Southern California and Northern California. Mary Jones, the last speaker of the Konkow language was there. When I introduced her as Konkow, she corrected me. "You don't say, 'Kon-cow'! We're not cows! You say, 'Koyom'kawi.'" She was very precise about what to say. Here she was, the last person to speak her language, and she insisted that we get it right.

We must have had about thirty people there. We had this despair over the loss of language, just despair. Then came the question of what to do. There were educational models of trying to get the languages into the curriculum of schools. I don't have much belief in schools. They're a failed institution. People just don't learn that way. You teach them a couple of words, they'll take a test, and then they forget the words.

Leanne Hinton attended as a linguist, and she suggested a master-apprentice program. So from that conference the master-apprentice program started, called Advocates for Indigenous California Language Survival (AICLS). We've kept it going for years, both the conference, called Breath of Life, and the Advocates. I published their newsletter and helped them get grants. It's such a beautiful program.

Today when you go to any Indian conference, people often introduce themselves in their Native languages, languages rescued from the jaws of death or in some cases resurrected from the grave. It's so extraordinary to hear these languages again. It grew out of that master-apprentice program. Here you have these people getting together with their fragments of language, their wax cylinder tapes, their linguists. Finally, somebody is getting up and even just saying in their language, "My name is _____, and I'm speaking the Wukchumni language. Welcome to my land!" Everybody bursts into tears because it's so lovely, so dramatic.

We got Georgiana Trull involved. Several years ago there were still a dozen Yurok speakers. Georgiana Trull was, as far as I know, the only person alive that spoke "high Yurok," the aristocratic Yurok. Other people spoke common Yurok. We wanted to get her an apprentice, a Yurok apprentice, of course, but she wouldn't take anyone that wasn't from a "good" family. We finally found Carole Korb (she was later Carole Lewis), who grew up in a very good family. So we apprenticed Carole Korb to Georgiana Trull.

I saw Carol a few months later, and I asked, "How's it going?"

She said, "It's the most humiliating experience of my life."

I asked, "Why? What's happening?"

She said, "I've been studying now for two months, and I'm still learning how to count."

"What's the problem?" I asked.

Carol tells me, "Malcolm, there are eighteen different ways of counting in Yurok depending on what's being counted. After a lesson, Georgiana will ask me, 'How do you say "three tables"?' When I say something, Georgiana will reply, 'Oh, no! You can't say it that way! Bad things will happen if you say it that way.'"

There was Matt Vera, a Yowlumne speaker. He ended up studying with his mother. People would ask him, "Why do you study? Why are you learning this language? Nobody's going to speak it in a few years. There's nothing written in it. It's a useless language. You're the smartest person in the tribe. Why don't you get a degree in law or social work or something to help us out?"

Matt said, "The world was created in Yowlumne. As long as there are trees and birds, there will be a language of the Yowlumne because that was the language of creation."

I've been witnessing the old-timers who knew their world, and their language was crucial to it. Bun Lucas was among my favorites. Bun grew up in Kashaya and didn't speak any English until he was five or six. He was a sweet old man. He got a job in the UC Berkeley linguistics department, teaching their field methods course. He worked with Leanne Hinton. A field methods course teaches the student how to find someone with an obscure language and then, by talking to them, you can get a vocabulary and a grammar and a sound system. But it was also important how you deal with somebody socially to get all these things that you need.

The only place that Bun knew how to get to in Berkeley was my house. So he'd come about three hours early and sit in front of my house, reading the *National Enquirer*. By the time I got home, his head was full of crop circles, UFOs, and alien babies. It made as much sense as anything else. Then I'd drive him over to Cal, and he'd teach this class.

I remember one lesson. I forget what the word was, but it had a strong guttural in it. There were several different gutturals in Kashaya, coming from different parts of the throat. Bun said the word, but the students just couldn't get it right. They had their fingers on his Adam's apple, trying to figure out where the sound was coming from. Finally, they had it right. Then he'd say, "But that's not how my uncle used to say it." His uncle came from Rockpile, another little Indian community two miles away, and he had a different way of pronouncing it. When they finished that, he'd say, "That's not how my aunt pronounced it."

You end up seeing how these little communities were distinct, each so proud and invested in its distinctness. We live in a process of homogenization, where everything is becoming the same. This was a world of dispersion and diversity, of everything separate, everything splitting off. There was a different force involved in making and preserving that world.

Seven people from the Kashaya reservation went into the Second World War. For all seven of them, Essie Parrish, the medicine woman of Kashaya, sewed a magic handkerchief which had a shamanic symbol in it. She prayed and danced the power into that symbol so that it would protect the people in the war. Of the seven, six came back. One died. The one that died didn't have his handkerchief.

Bun talked about how, when he came back from the war, he was let out of the military back east and made his way home on a bus across the country. He went up to Cloverdale, and then he had the long walk up the Cloverdale–Stewart's Point Road, past places that they used to talk about where monsters lurked, where a monster lived on one leg; historic sites, massacre sites; places with sacred rocks. He walked past all that.

He finally got to Kashaya Reservation. There were two roundhouses, Essie's roundhouse and the old roundhouse. The old guys would sit around on a bench outside the roundhouse. If it was warm, you'd sit in the shade, and if it was cold, you'd sit facing the sun. They'd move around the round-house as the sun moved.

Bun arrived there, and they stopped talking. They looked at him and said in Kashaya Pomo, "Hello, Bun! You're back!"

He stood mute. He said he couldn't find his Kashaya. This was the lan-guage he was born with, yet he couldn't find it. He just didn't know where it was. He was crushed that he couldn't answer them, so he went back to his mother's house and stayed there. He said it was like a lid had been holding down his language, like he'd been protecting it. Finally, there was a hole in the lid, and the Kashaya came pouring out, and he found it again. I always thought about that as a metaphor for how things are protected in times of danger and how they come back in times of safety.

All that wonderful language work. You meet people who could just break your heart, so amazing.

I love the work that others did around the revival of bird songs in the Southern California desert. Bird songs are sung for four nights straight in the middle of winter, when the nights are the longest. They're linked verses that describe the wandering of divinities over the world, like Coyote and World Maker and First Man. They wander through the world looking for the right place for people to live. These songs recount their journeys across the landscape. The verses are sung, a gourd rattle shakes, and then someone does a dance. For four straight nights you follow their journey along.

A project was set up to give tape recorders to some of these old men so when they were wandering around, maybe doing their shopping, they'd suddenly remember one of the songs, and they could get them down. The songs were all linked, so if you remembered *one* of the songs, you'd probably remember several more in the chain. They'd run out of the super-market into the parking lot and sing these songs into the recorder. Since that time, there's been a major revival of ceremonies down there.

My friend Preston Arrow-weed, Quechan, studied acting under Jay Silverheels, the guy that first played Tonto. Preston Arrow-weed is exactly my age, born in October 1940. He grew up in a mud wattle house where they spoke only the Quechan and Kumeyaay languages. They made a trip to Fort Yuma to buy groceries only once a month, the only time he ever saw a white person. They'd buy him a soda. At five years old, he spoke no English, knew nothing about the outside world.

Then the government came in and sent Preston to school. The first thing that he found out in school was that there was so much food. He couldn't believe that you had all these meals with so much food. The next thing he discovered was that they had a play. Because he couldn't speak any English, Preston had to be the rain. He spread his hands out, he wriggled his fingers like raindrops, and all the kids rose up from the floor like flower blossoms. He thought it was the happiest moment of his life. So he got into acting.

Preston sang the bird songs. He always wondered why in the songs the divinities came down the Colorado River, but then at one point they went to the west, leaving the river, and then they continued south again for a few miles, finally rejoining the river. He always wondered why they made that detour. He was once out with some archaeologists, and they showed him that that was the old channel where the river had been. The song main-tained the memory of that old channel of the river, when the river had long since changed its course.

Another singer there was my wonderful, wonderful friend Ernie Siva, a Serrano singer. Once Ernie was singing this song, and I asked him the meaning of the song.

He said, "Well, if you want me to tell you what the words mean, I'll tell you what the words mean. But that's not what the *song* means. The meaning depends on where it is in the sequence of songs. What gives it meaning is who taught it to me. What gives it meaning is who I'm going to teach it to.

What gives it meaning is if we ever sung it at a funeral and whose funeral we sang it at. That's what gives the song meaning."

Linda Yamane, who's Ohlone, talked about listening to the wax cylinder recordings of her ancestors. She'd put her kid, Robbie, to sleep at night, and then she'd turn on these wax cylinder recordings with the scratches. She'd hear an old voice. She'd make out a word and then look in the old vocabularies to find out what that word meant. Then she'd have *that* word. She talked about the tremendous tension she felt in saying that word. She could finally bring it out. For the first time in seventy-five years, that word would be alive again. She was bringing the language back, giving the language life.

EXCERPTS FROM **LEANNE HINTON'**S *FLUTES OF FIRE*

EANNE HINTON HAS written a language column in *News* almost since its beginning. Some of these columns were collected, expanded, and published in the Heyday book *Flutes of Fire* (1994), and since then Heyday has published two more of her books. The following excerpts are taken from *Flutes of Fire*, together showing the range of her interests and knowledge. The first discusses Native languages in general as part of "the California Mosaic."

Even today, there are about fifty different California Indian languages still spoken, each with its own particular genius. There is so much to learn from all these different languages about the amazing choices humans have in organizing and talking about the world around them. There are so many ways to construct language itself, many ways to play with it or to use it to powerful effect. The elders who speak these languages have so much to tell us about the vocabulary of different kinds of knowledge and activities, about the worldviews expressed in the way utterances are put together, the infinite number of ways people have of constructing their lives. At a time when these languages (along with over half of the languages in the rest of the world!) are endangered, it is more important than ever to learn the lessons they can teach us.

The second excerpt exemplifies Leanne's more technical writing, in this case regarding "directional affixes," and illustrates the complexity of Native language communications.

To the English speaker, one of the most amazing aspects of the grammar of most California languages is how much can be said in a single word. Verbs, especially, through processes of affixation, are incredibly rich in meaning. Directional affixes are part of this complex verb structure in many languages. For example, in Yana, directionals are obligatory on verbs of motion. One cannot simply say that someone is "going" without saying which direction he or she is going in. So in Yahi (Ishi's language, a variety of Yana), there is a full set of suffixes that go on verbs of motion, one set for going in a cardinal direction, and another for coming *from* a cardinal direction. And these are also different from the independent words for the cardinal directions.

théndji	'west'
-pdji	'to the west, in the west'
-haucu	'from the west'

The third selection is a poem Leanne wrote to those studying and relearning languages for which there are no remaining living speakers. Leanne dedicated the poem to Cindi Alvitre, L. Frank, Ernestine DeSoto, and Linda Yamane.

TO THE LONELY HEARTS LANGUAGE CLUB

At night
when the work is done
and the children are in bed
and the roar of the freeway is quieted
and the house cools and darkens and sighs into stillness,

She holds in her hands the pages
on which rest spidery symbols
of sounds whispered by dying grandmothers
and written down by a crazed linguist, long dead too,
of words spoken for the final time generations ago
entombed now in perpetual silence,

the last sound waves decayed into carbon traces
in a paper monument to the passing of a language from this earth.

Called each night by a power beyond her understanding
She lifts a page into her circle of light
and begins a ceremony of resurrection.
The pencil scratchings that encase the grandmother's gifts
fall away and the words reawaken;
Her voice frees them one by one
and they fly into the night,
echoing into and out of corners.
The air vibrates with their saying.
The world resonates with their being.

MALCOLM: THE BERKELEY ROUNDHOUSE

A CROWNING ACHIEVEMENT FOR Heyday's contributions to Native California is the Berkeley Roundhouse, created in 2012: Malcolm's concept of an organization within Heyday that centralizes California Indian publishing and events. Lindsie Bear was the first to be hired to lead this organization. Malcolm explains how he conceived of what the Berkeley Roundhouse could be.

The roundhouse is a metaphor, of course, for being a community center. All of this writing and publishing is just an excuse to be engaged in the world, what I can do to get invited to places, to be active, to meet people, to be useful, to have fun, to explore places. We can do it through books, through a magazine, through events, through films. At the heart of it all is just wanting to be engaged, to move around, have people in my life, have a scene and a clubhouse. And I want to correct injustices, to have surprises and affection.

The specificity of a magazine or a book, the physicality of it, that's good, but it doesn't quite reflect for me the grand opera that I seem to be part of, the people, the places, the experiences. Ada Charles recently died. She was 103, born in 1909. She was the last person I know raised by people who remembered California before the coming of whites. She was the last link.

I've been so privileged to have known people like this, that I was alive at this particular time in history. It's not just the writing of books or the production of books or the events. It's the milieu, the spirit of it, the social aspects of it. It takes different shapes and forms. It takes the forms of text, of talk, of films. But there's a way of being, of thinking. I want to keep capturing all that.

The roundhouse was a communal enterprise. To build a roundhouse was a major public works project. You had to gather people around. People from different areas would come help dig out the part of the roundhouse that was in their place to sit. There were ritual ways of sitting in the roundhouse, corresponding to your relationship with the moieties and the clans of that area. So if your family and my family had mutual undertaking arrangements—I'd bury your dead and you'd bury mine—we would sit in particular places in the roundhouse.

So the roundhouse symbolized and reflected these relationships. And there was something about the way it holds the community together. There's a range of activities in there. So I use it as a metaphor.

I'm aware of the tremendous amount of wealth that Heyday has here, the tremendous amount of connection that we have here. It's so deep and there's nobody that has anything like it. We're creating a place for all that in the Berkeley Roundhouse. I want to create a place, so that when you walk into this place, the tone changes. There's something in the visual aspect of it, including the paintings on the wall. Lindsie, as she's editing News, has created a "sepia-free zone." It's to insure that we don't have overblown sentimentality. There's another tone in here.

Here's what I envision. We're also going to have courses, an artist in residence, a library, writings coming out of the roundhouse, meetings, the California Indian film series which we just jumped into, and other plans. Grant applications have gone out. We pretend that it's carefully defined, and there are deliverables and schedules. But it's not that well defined.

When I gave a talk for a book we did with the San Francisco Arts Commission at the California Historical Society, I started out by saying that we do about twenty to twenty-five books a year. When you're doing that many books, you have to have systems and schedules and budgets. We have all of those, and we spend a lot of time on them. If we were just doing tele-phone books or plumbing directories, that would be sufficient. But we're not. We're doing something else. And while you need these things, you need something else. You need passion and ferocity.

This place is a creative enterprise. It lives on risk, on not quite knowing what you're doing. It's not paint-by-number. If it becomes paint-by-number, the whole place just dies of rigor mortis. It's troublesome sometimes, with the finance committee, the board, and staff, but we have to make certain we retain the spontaneity to make quick decisions, to take risks. So the roundhouse still has a flexible structure: me, Lindsie, Frank LaPena, L. Frank, Jennifer, a circle of friends.

The roundhouse will change over time. When I introduce Lindsie as the person that's taken over California Indian publishing, people say to her, "You've got big shoes to fill." My statement to Lindsie is, "If you try to fill my shoes, they're not going to fit. Fill your own shoes!"

I just took a trip up to Kashaya with Lindsie, and Fort Ross. The story is so amazing. Metini was the Indian village at Fort Ross. When the Russians arrived, around 1812, they confronted Metini, then built their fort there and employed the Indians. Some of the women were either kidnapped or taken to marry. I think the fort was dismantled in 1836.

The Kashaya remained more isolated than many other Indian commu-nities. In this isolated world, the Kashaya remembered the Russians who had taken women off to Russia, along with various implements, dance regalia, a condor cape, and other stuff. Lindsie and I just met with this delegation that had been to St. Petersburg, in part to visit the missing implements and regalia. Also, Lester Pinola had heard all his life about a couple of great-great-aunts who were kidnapped and taken away. No one had ever sung for them. He wanted to go back to Russia to find out what happened to them so he could sing for them.

We ended up spending a couple of days up at Kashaya, taking their stories, seeing if we could raise some money for them to go back once more.

All these stories are related to the sense of the Indian elder. I've grown old enough to understand what being an elder means. It's been the most fragile and lovely thing, to have people's trust and affection. To go around and be treated well. It's just been wonderful.

LINDSIE BEAR

LINDSIE BEAR HAS been the director of the Berkeley Roundhouse program since 2012. Lindsie arrived at Heyday having grown up in Bishop, where the Bishop Paiute Tribe is headquartered. She also had spent years working in bookstores and in a major publishing house. When she was hired to take on the Native publishing program at Heyday, among other accolades that Malcolm used to describe Lindsie, he said, "She's so much fun"—true to one of Heyday's principal hiring qualifications.

Here is Lindsie's story of how she got to Heyday and her vision of her work ahead.

I met Malcolm at a Western History Conference in Oakland. I was there with UC Press, where I was working at the time. We were in the Book Hall with our booths, and up comes Malcolm. He looks around, smiles, and says, "What's *good?!* Find me something *really* good." In talking about what was good, one of my coworkers who had worked at Heyday, Kim Hogeland, introduced us.

I have a very beat-up copy of *East Bay Out* that I was given when I moved to the Bay Area. Before that, I lived in Bishop, California, where I grew up, and a little outside Santa Fe, and then I came to Oakland. So the idea that there was anything resembling wilderness here seemed pretty impossible to me. This was a big urban experiment for me. So *East Bay Out* was just great. It felt like it was possible to be connected to land that was hard to see, with all the concrete. I was used to grand, vast wildernesses. That book really helped me appreciate smaller and closer places.

Anyhow, we talked for about an hour about books, and that was it. Probably a year later, Kim, my same coworker, sent me the job description for the Berkeley Roundhouse. I immediately thought, "I'm in *no* way qualified to do that! That's a huge job. You need an elder to do that."

But there was a line at the bottom of the job description that said, "Must be as comfortable in a university as you are in a reservation." I remember being stunned by it because I had grown up in a reservation town and hung around a lot of reservations. I'm ethnically part Native, but it wasn't the same people of the reservation I grew up on. And I'd gone away to college at St. John's and got into university academic publishing, so for me these two worlds were wholly separated by a gigantic ideological wall I'd built between them. The university side is often not as valued in a rural setting, and knowing old Paiute fishing techniques was not really valued in the university setting. So that line in the job description made an impression on me. To have them both be given equal weight and value was startling.

I still said I probably wasn't interested, but I was curious about what they were doing, so I agreed to have lunch with Malcolm. By the end he had talked me into applying! I saw something grassroots and expansive, the sense of possibility, the creative freedom, the sense that it wasn't just one person in isolation doing this job. There were all these communities and activists and artists and linguists doing this work. It just needed someone to help pull it all together.

But what really grabbed me was that at the end of the conversation, Malcolm said something like "We won't be able to pay you as much as you make where you are, and it'll probably take more dedication than a normal job, but I promise you that you'll be happy!" It was such a definitive stance, so overpowering.

When I had some time, I went up to a fire lookout on Bear Basin Butte, right after all the rounds of interviews. I was up there in the middle of nowhere. I had decided again, "I don't know if I can do this. *They* might think I can. But that's a big job. And there are other exciting things to do."

It turns out you get cell reception at the top of mountains. My phone buzzed. It was a message from Malcolm! The call was a job offer in which he quoted Chaucer in Middle English. I love Chaucer! He defined the word *"Yeis,"* which is a Middle English term used in Chaucer that meant "Yes to the tenth power." This is a *big* "yes." He defined that and used it in a sentence: *"Yeis,* we would like you to come work with us."

It was unfathomable to me that anyone could say no to that. And I trusted his judgment. If he thought we could do it, we could do it. And who would not want to be part of a world where that's what a job offer looks like!

The town I grew up in, Bishop, is next to the Bishop Paiute Reservation, with a series of Paiute and Shoshone reservations all around there. As young people, you had friends you hung around with, but there was a real divide. There were some Hispanic folks, but mostly it was a white and Indian town, with much more overt racism than I see in other places. I'm dark-haired and olive-skinned enough that I could kind of pass either way. I'm ethnically part Indian, but I know very little about being Cherokee. I'm the perfect product of assimilation. I knew this growing up. I also knew that being part Cherokee did not make me "part" of the club. It made me even more of an outsider in the way that being close and still "other" is even more the "Other." It was just easier not to talk about it. So some friends or people knew, but it didn't "count." It certainly didn't make me any closer to Paiute.

But I was also raised in an Indian environment with Paiute culture, with traditional crafts and cooking, eating mutton and fry bread, pine nuts and fish. I had friends who could banter in Paiute, so I was around the language a lot and even learned a little bit. So I really have had that gift of being immersed in the day-to-day of Indian culture. And that was some preparation for the Roundhouse.

You don't just get a job here at Heyday; you get citizenship in a small, independent nation. Part of my job is acquisitions, talking to people and seeing manuscripts, deciding which ones we'd like to pursue, bringing those in. A big part of the job is running *News from Native California*. It's a quarterly magazine, and definitely a community effort, but it gets pulled together. There's the soliciting of articles, editing, layout, art direction, and marketing. I'd like a lot more people to get *News* because I think it's really good! There's also grant writing and events.

My vision for the Roundhouse is to preserve the porosity of the place. It's a very porous place: people can come in, have ideas, we can help them work it out. People call us for all kinds of things. They call looking for their uncle. They call because they want directions. Such a wide array of voices is represented here—by the books, by the magazine. So it's not a hard place to penetrate. It's not dense and solid. That to me is really important. It's not a publishing house in the sense that it's removed, above folks, an inaccessible media center. It's a place where people can come and go, where they can talk about things. We publish something or we don't, but sometimes it's the exchange of ideas on the way that creates something else.

There's a lot of room to mess up, a lot of forgiveness, a lot of ways to make mistakes without humiliation. The place has a forgiving nature, which I think is really important because it helps people open up, tell their stories, even if they aren't particularly eloquent in how they're doing it—but they feel heard. I think that's one of my goals. It's something unique here, and I want to preserve that.

Another goal I have is to hand my job off to someone who is a California Native. As far as I know, there haven't been a whole lot of Native folks in publishing. As industries go, it's really not one that's been very welcoming or interesting—whatever the reason is. I'd just like to give more Native kids an opportunity to do this if they want to. I'd love to be able to pass this off to someone who can say, "This is my home. These are my people. And I get to represent them." I'm starting an internship that's directed at Native youth. It depends on what the Native students want to do. It could be that they're interns for *News* and the Native books. But if you're a Native student and you're really interested in ecology and conservation, you could intern in the other areas. That's definitely on the plate.

I'd also like to represent a fuller range of the arts and expressions of California. We're planning a film festival. We're also putting together classes and presentations. We have some ideas about doing an art gallery in the space downstairs. We're working on writers' workshops. There are so many different media that people are working in, so we have to expand our capabilities of highlighting and promoting that. That would be a good, natural development with the way publishing is moving, as a multi-platform industry. It would be nice to have that with our Native stuff.

Since I started this job, I've been going to events every other weekend, something happening somewhere, traveling with Malcolm to his talks, conferences, salons. Malcolm and I have spent a lot of time on the road driving. It's been great! I can't imagine anybody who wouldn't want to go on a road trip with Malcolm. You don't need a car radio when you go with Malcolm. There's always something to talk about, some idea, a migration of birds that's coming in. He has an amazing stamina for people and feelings and conversations. He can start at dawn. I think our average arrival time getting back from trips is about midnight. We go all the way until the very last minute when we have to come back, so it's a lot of early mornings when you can see the world wake up, and late nights. That's a great time to talk in the car.

I've heard lots of great stories in the car with Malcolm. There was one about Malcolm hanging out with a Hupa friend, talking about all the Hupa words for clouds. The friend was asking, "What's the English word for when the clouds are almost touching?"

Malcolm goes, "We don't have a word for that."

The friend told him the Hupa word. "Well, what's the word for when one cloud is near another cloud, but they're moving past each other?"

Malcolm said, "Yeah, we don't have a specific word for that either."

We were driving, and it was cloudy, and Malcolm was pointing out the features, and telling me this story. It was so rich to think of what the world looked like with a taxonomy for clouds.

As interactions go, I enjoy following Malcolm around at these events. People come up to our table where we're selling books. They're old friends, and they go talk to Malcolm. They hang out. But people also come who need to tell him something. They either need to tell him what something meant to them, or they need to tell him something that's happened. I've seen him be a confessor figure. He's a safe place for people to come and get something off their chest, whatever it is. It's often really big and sincere. A lot of what I hear has been completely unsolicited stories about how *News* touched someone or changed them, like publishing someone's cousin's work right before they died and how much that meant. People cry openly to him, and he can just be there with them and take that in.

That's been really powerful to see, how lovely it is to have as a friend someone who is open and respected and respectful. I think people walk away feeling lighter. That's been really special. He seems to be able to just be there with them, and he also knows when it's time to ease the tension, crack a joke, never put walls up, but let people be that raw, and then let them off the hook. It often takes the interlocutor to say, "All right. You're going to be okay."

And then there are the things we're not supposed to see, how Malcolm helps people in ways that don't get publicized. No one knows, and he keeps it very much under wraps, as the decent thing to do, but when people thank him, you get how much he has probably helped a family when they really needed it. He has this quiet way about it. It's beautiful.

VINCENT MEDINA

V INCENT MEDINA (OHLONE) began his work in the Berkeley Roundhouse at Heyday in July 2013, to help with the expanding array of duties that Lindsie is taking over from Malcolm. Here Vincent explains what a good fit Heyday is for him, as he surely is for Heyday.

My role is the Roundhouse Outreach Coordinator. I work primarily for *News from Native California* to connect with my own community, the California Indian community, to bring them more representation, to bring in the California Indian voice, and to ask what they want in the magazine. Outreach includes going to lectures and conferences, bringing the voice of *News* with me. I also write, so I work on articles. I work on the calendar, too. So I'm working on a lot of different fronts.

I've already been down to Anaheim at the All Nations Conference for the California Indian Museum there, and I have a few other trips planned. It's nice because many people I see are my friends. It's already my community, people that I have a lot of love and respect for.

So far working at Heyday is great. I love it! Lindsie is perfect; she's awesome. Everybody here has been really great. There's a shared culture of a lot of people here in the beliefs and attitudes. I like that. I have a job doing exactly what I want to do, working on our culture, working in publishing, writing, telling my own story. It's everything I've wanted, so I'm looking forward to being here for a while.

I met Malcolm maybe about three years ago, but he has a very, very deep connection with people in my family. I know that when *The Ohlone Way* was coming out, my older cousin Philip Galvan was one of the main ones documenting a lot of that information. So there's a longstanding family connection.

The Ohlone Way has been criticized, but it served a time and a place. When there was so little out there, *The Ohlone Way* was at least one published book that discussed it. I remember being a kid in high school and reading that. It gave a place to turn when you often feel alone and isolated in your own area.

I personally have gotten close to Malcolm in the last three years. There was always something about Malcolm that I connected with, from the first time I met him. I'm not exactly sure what it is. Maybe his way of thinking, his philosophies, and his presence are all things that I relate to.

Heyday has always been omnipresent in my life and a big part of my own experience writing. I try to stay active in social media. That's one way that I believe that California Indian people can get their voice out and be heard, to have people tell their story in their own words versus through anthropologists and the like telling our stories on their behalf, which is what we've seen happen for such a long time.

About three or four years ago, I started a blog titled "Being Ohlone in the 21st Century." It's strictly about *contemporary* Ohlone issues because I grew up often seeing Ohlone people being mentioned or written about in a very unflattering and often embarrassing, minimalist way. We're painted as a hunter-gatherer people who were surviving off the earth. Then the Spanish came. The Ohlone people, from what I read, trickled out of the story. They were once here, they ate acorns, and they went away.

That's not the reality that I see at home in my family, and it doesn't match my own family's connection to this place. When I started doing research to see what was out there, I didn't find much. I *did* see my family and how strong they were. I saw how a group of people had some of the worst things happen to them: their land taken away and attempts to change their culture entirely. But somehow people kept their culture alive, their stories present, and their physical presence in this part of the world that they refused to leave.

That is what drives me to write, because I want people to know that we weren't merely hunters and gatherers that survived, but we had and have a complex system of religion, language, horticulture—of connecting to one piece of land that we were and are happy on. To me it's important to get that perspective, to show the vibrancy on the modern side of it. Over time, every culture adapts and changes. Every language picks new words. Every religion picks up new concepts. What I try to focus on is *living* Ohlone culture. We didn't just stop being here. We're still thriving. Maybe we don't dress the way that our ancestors dressed or eat the same foods, but our roots are the same, and the connections are the same.

I'm also on the board of directors for AICLS, the Advocates for Indigenous California Language Survival, so I do extensive work with Chochenyo, the Native language for this area. Heyday fosters an environment where cultural revitalization can be discussed and documented by Indian people themselves, versus anthropologists doing it. What gives me a lot of hope is the process of understanding traditional media, traditional boundaries, and then working within those boundaries to create new things.

I grew up in what we call today San Lorenzo, San Leandro. That's actually the village that my ancestors have been living in for thousands of years, called *Halkhis*, in the San Lorenzo–Castro Valley area. In the mission records we can go back and see these things. My great-great-great-great-grandmother was born in the exact same area as I was. So there is a very deep connection there.

My family never gave up their Indian identity. In fact, they very strongly advocated for their Indian identity, even when it wasn't popular to be Indian. I know a lot of people said they were Mexican or Filipino or other groups. But from my father's generation and my grandfather's generation, it was instilled that they were Indian, that we're Indian. They never gave that up.

What did happen is that a lot of the specifics went to sleep. I don't like to say that they died, because they didn't die. They were documented, but they either stopped being practiced for a purpose or they stopped being practiced because some people forgot them. So for a long time, for a couple generations, mostly what we had was the fact that we were Ohlone, the fact that we were Indian. If that's all we have, we're not going to give that up! That was preserved in our history, knowing where we come from, a connection to this place.

But the basketry, song, and dances *were* all continued. My father, for example, doesn't speak Chochenyo. My grandfather doesn't speak Chochenyo. But they understand the importance for it to come back now, for all the cultural practices to be brought back, like the songs, dances, religion, and language. It really wasn't that long ago that they were spoken and practiced, in the bigger picture of things.

One of the elders in our family, my cousin Philip Galvan, passed away in March; he was in his late eighties. He was born in the old village of Alisal, which is a post-mission village and rancheria over in what we call Sunol today. In the last few years of his life, Philip started to hear Chochenyo being spoken again. In the first two or three years of his life, he heard it spoken frequently in the old Indian village—the last fluent speakers passed away in the 1930s. When he heard it spoken again, I remember he said to me, "That's really something! I wish I could do that."

That he heard it the first three or four years of his life and then heard it come back in the last three or four years of his life shows a huge, important reversal, how things can be brought back in one lifetime. Imagine seeing songs go away and come back, and the dances now come back. That's just one lifetime. There's this correcting of the past. The process will take a long time, but it will happen for the right reasons. Imagine when I'm an old man what I may see come back, or when I have a family, what my kids will be able to see or hear.

CHAPTER 5

HEYDAY STRETCHES INTO NEW TERRITORY

"The role of publisher is the role of furthering others, setting the stage for others to come and perform. —MALCOLM MARGOLIN

THOUGH MALCOLM AND his family had settled down in Berkeley, his intellectual wanderings continued to grow and expand, as did the range of his publishing company, Heyday, like a basket that begins tightly coiled at the center and radiates out and out.

MALCOLM: JAKE ARRIVES AND HEYDAY TRANSFORMS

Jake—Jacob Orion—was born on September 29, 1980, a day before Sadie's sixth birthday. Later, Sadie got mad at Jake because he'd get his birthday party before she got hers. But Sadie always felt that Jake was *her* kid. What Rina was doing there was puzzling to Sadie; maybe it was to take care of a few things while Sadie took care of her child. Sadie was very caring and very possessive of Jake.

Jake was just the cutest little baby, adorable, a roly-poly, happy, content little kid. He was born in the hospital but with midwives at a birthing center. When Jake was born, the house seemed to be full.

One of my fondest memories of Jake was when he was very little, in a house where we lived on Berkeley Way. We had a treadle sewing machine with a fern placed on the sewing machine table. The cat was sitting on the table, looking out the window. The cat's tail was hanging down. I was sitting there reading. Jake comes in and doesn't know I'm there. He looks around, and then he goes and pulls the cat's tail. I realized he's one of us. It was just

Malcolm and Jake
(HEYDAY ARCHIVES)

this love of engagement. You don't just sit around. You don't like stasis. If nothing is happening, you make something happen.

That was the time of bringing lots of people into the house. One guy, John Stokes, came in and was playing the didgeridoo. I remember Jake sitting there, just staring. He stopped breathing for an hour while he was listening to the sound of the didgeridoo.

I remember another time, when someone gave us a live lobster. We put the lobster in the bottom of the refrigerator in the fruit compartment. Reuben was the only one who knew about it at first. When Sadie came in, he asked her to get him an apple. Sadie opened up the drawer, found this lobster in there, and screamed like hell. So then they both laid in wait for Jake. Jake came in and went to the fruit drawer as commanded. His hair literally stood on end. He didn't understand the word "lobster." He thought it was the *monster* in the refrigerator.

TRAVELS WITH KIDS

By the late seventies, I was traveling a lot, going to Indian big times or visiting friends. Sadie would come around with me to these various Indian events, more than the others did. Reuben was already older by the time I got into it, in the late seventies. Sadie was very young, so she'd come along.

We'd go off to Hoopa and hear the Hupa language spoken, see the World Renewal dances. We'd go up to the Yurok reservation and hear elders speak the wonderful Yurok language, and we'd go up to the Karuk and hear Julian Lang, Margaret Chase, Violet Super, Charlie Thom, and others speak the wonderful Karuk language. We'd go off to Achumawe country, to Miwuk country. We'd hear all these beautiful languages and attend these amazing ceremonies.

Sadie was probably six when we started. When we were recently reminiscing about it, she characterized it as 95 percent boredom and 5 percent complete heartbreak. I always thought that when she gets old, she'll probably be the last person alive who witnessed this abundance of languages across the state, this grand flow of sound and wide range of musicality. I thought it'd be so peculiar that it would be in the hands of a little white kid from Berkeley. Not that she would remember it all that well, but just to have *seen* it.

By the time Jake came along, in the early eighties, I was even more involved in Indian books and life. Jake, like Sadie, would come with me to Indian events all the time. Pat Cody, Fred Cody's widow, always used to repeat to me her favorite story about my travels with Jake. We were in Monterey for something. He was just a little kid. I bought him a cookie. He was eating the cookie, and I said, "Let me have a bite of that cookie."

He says, "No!"

I say, "What do you mean, 'No'?"

He insists, "No, it's my cookie."

I tell him, "Listen, man, I just bought you that cookie. I want a bite of your cookie."

Jake says, "Look around you. Look at how beautiful the world is! Think about something else besides the cookie."

That was being hoisted by your own petard!

I remember I once asked Sadie if she wanted to come camping in Los Padres with me, and she said, "Yeah!" I was kind of surprised since Sadie wasn't that much into camping. We got some camping stuff together, and off we went to Los Padres wilderness. When we get there, she looks around and tells me that she'd thought we were going to find "the lost parties."

Sadie was wonderfully companionable. She'd go with me to sell books. I still go out to Indian places, and people ask, "Whatever happened to that little girl of yours? That pretty little girl, whatever happened to her?"

It was important for me to travel around with the kids. My friend David Guy runs the Northern California Water Association, and we were doing some work up in the Sacramento Valley. He'd bring his kids along. One day he asked if I would mind letting one kid come with us when we were interviewing. The kid was into videoing. Could the kid actually video it?

On the one hand, it struck me as an interference, having this kid along. On the other hand, I knew *exactly* where David was coming from. Sadie and Jake always went with me. Your first duty in life is to give experience to your kids, to introduce them to the world, to help them broaden out. You have to see things through their eyes. And it shakes off the loneliness of just doing something yourself. Share it with somebody.

I liked myself in the role of Daddy. I played that role well. It was a good role. Plus the kids were fun to be with, a whole lot of fun.

REUBEN HEYDAY MARGOLIN

REUBEN MARGOLIN IS himself the father of two small children, daughter Neko Skye and son Micah Viento, with his partner, Amber Menzies. Reuben is also a talented sculptor with a mechanical bent. One of his large hanging sculptures gracefully moves like the wind in tules at the David Brower Center in Berkeley, California. Born in 1970, Reuben was a small child when *The East Bay Out* was published in 1974. He shared his early memories of life with his parents in the outdoors and in creative endeavors of all kinds.

My earliest impressions of Heyday have to do with nature. If you take a hike with my dad, he finds the world to be incredibly beautiful and mysterious.

Reuben with Malcolm (MARGOLIN FAMILY COLLECTION)

But even more importantly, he gets you to feel the same way. That attitude naturally just moved into his work, as well.

Hiking has always been part of the family. We'd go all over the place. Our family vacations included bicycle trips in Oregon. He was quite adventurous. We were always going out and doing things, camping, canoeing.

My father was very, very supportive. He always said that when I was little, if I was walking on a log, he'd let me walk on it and try to instill courage, and if I fell, not to make a big deal of it. At the same time as he always encouraged taking risks, he was quite tolerant of things not working out, projects that failed.

One of my favorite memories is when Malcolm would say, "You want to go to the moon?"

I'd go, "Yeah!" So he would bundle me up in his arms and put me in the closet with him; that would be our spaceship. He'd start making all this noise and rumbling. Then we would get out, and he'd talk about what the moon looked like, how Earth looked. It was wonderful! He also said that you can't open your eyes; only adults can open their eyes on the moon. We probably went to the moon ten times, and I never opened my eyes.

The earliest memory I have of the publishing company was the fact that all of our beds were pieces of plywood with boxes of books underneath them. I remember him having an office at home where he would go and type. He had a typewriter which he held onto for years. In fact, I have it today. He was always a storyteller, too. He told great stories that would entertain people and make them laugh and cry. It all pointed to what Heyday is now.

Both of my parents are extremely artistic in temperament. My mom does a lot of painting and collages, and she makes animals and dolls. She's very visual and gifted in what she does. My dad was also a bit of a tinkerer. He was always trying to fix the VW van, with big socket wrenches and all kinds of tools and remnants lying around. He also did some woodwork. It was ideal for a kid because there were tools around and someone interested in showing me what to do. I still have all of his tools, and I use them daily, both the mechanics' tools and the woodworking tools. I keep them sharp.

Both Mom and Dad were incredibly supportive of whatever path I happened to be on. There was a general sense that a rich life would be an artistic life, but there was not a lot of pressure to follow in his particular footsteps. I did actually work at Heyday Books for a little while in high school. I fixed the "pig," I think it was called, this typesetting-printing machine that had millions of cogs and gears and chains going back and forth, and various chemicals. It would pull the paper through, but it was always broken, so I was basically there trying to fix it the whole time, which was fun.

Heyday was clearly a very rewarding and engrossing job for my father. Heyday became an amazing community where he met a ton of people and made a lot of friends. My sister went around with him more often to various Indian dances, and she got to see a lot of California. He would always invite people over to dinner. He had Heyday Books, and we had the family; in some ways they were separate, two different animals, but a lot of close friends that he knew through Heyday also hung out with us as a family. Like Fred Cody was really close, and Vera Mae Fredrickson. I remember countless dinner parties with everyone sitting around, talking.

One time I was kind of bored; I was a kid. I was in the other room with this paper clip that I bent into a U and stuck into the wall socket. It made a big bang! Everybody came running. I remember trying to say that I had thrown the paper clip over my shoulder, and it *happened* to go into the socket. It made a lot of sense to me then!

My father's network of friends meant that I got introduced to tons of people. For instance, I got a job helping build magnetically shielded labs with Gary Scott, Leanne Hinton's husband, and that job allowed me a huge amount of freedom for exploration during the ten years following college. That came through friends of the family and Heyday. Then, when I went to study art in Italy, I first stayed with friends of the family. Through Lee Swenson and his wife, Vijaya, close friends of Malcolm and Heyday, I got introduced to an international collection of friends, including Dashrath Patel, and that sent me off to India. These are all absolutely amazing characters that I got to know through Heyday. I learned a lot from them, and they've made my life richer.

There's a saying that goes something like "It's hard to reach the sun in the shade of the tree where you sprouted." It's about what it's like having a parent who's well known. But for me, it's been an absolutely great thing. It opened the door to a huge, intellectual crowd that I'm lucky to have met.

It's also nice to have a little bit of my own recognition locally as an artist, to feel that I'm my own person, too, as a sculptor, but every once in a while, it's good to have help. Recently I needed a place to live for me and my family. I sent out an email to all of my friends, and then my dad sent out an email to all of his friends. I realized right away that his email list was about one hundred times bigger than mine! I thought, "Wow! This guy *does* know everybody!" Wherever I go, someone will say, "Oh, you're Malcolm's son." But that's good. I'm proud to be.

There might be a little bit of competition. We went on a family vacation recently to Yosemite. We all stayed in a vacation house that had a pool table. My father promptly beat me at pool. We've played tons of pool, and he always beats me. Then he brought out a chess set, and he beat me twice at chess. Then we went for a hike. He had woken up at five-thirty in the morning, yet my sister and I were basically running up after him along this trail that came to a beautiful waterfall. I was sore for the next couple of days. He's strong.

MALCOLM ON SHOOTING POOL

WHEN MY FAMILY moved to West Roxbury, I used to go back to the old neighborhood where all my friends were. At the center of Blue Hill Avenue was the G&G Delicatessen, where everybody would hang out—the politicians, the local businessmen, the bookies. Next to the G&G was an alley that led to Mickey's Pool Hall. Cigar smoke hung in the air. Mickey would be behind the counter. There were four tables of billiards, without the holes in them. These huge, wonderful guys would play three-cushion billiards, when the cue ball has to hit a ball, then hit three rails, and *then* hit another ball. The intelligence it takes, the skill! These huge guys with big bellies hanging over the table would make shot after shot. They were so good at it.

Then down the rest of the pool hall were the pocket tables, where the kids would be. We'd turn on records with rock and roll. We thought we were so hip. At the same time, sitting around on the benches were these old Jews in their gabardine and with their Yiddish newspapers, getting out of the cold. It was the men's world, the study halls of Poland. As hip as we were, there was still that feeling of being in that old world that you could never escape.

When Reuben was a young kid, I'd often take him over to the pool hall on University Avenue. For several years, we'd play straight pool for 100 points. It's a game of skill, very little luck, relying on positioning and stuff. When he was very young, I'd beat him 100-4, 100-6, 100-10. He was struggling, but he was getting better and better.

Finally, as he was getting older, we had one game where he had 99 points, and I had 96. He made a shot and called the 3-ball in the corner pocket. It clicked against another ball—which I overlooked—and then went into the corner pocket. I said, "Hey, you finally beat me!" It was the first game that he'd ever beat me.

He thought for a minute, reached in, and pulled the ball out. He said, "I want to beat you something awful, but not like that." So I ran the table and beat him another time.

Finally, I think it was on his eighteenth birthday, he beat me. I was so proud of him because I was shooting well. It wasn't a night when I was shooting badly. He's been absolutely spectacular ever since.

SADIE MARGOLIN COSTELLO

MALCOLM'S DAUGHTER, Sadie Cash Margolin Costello, Ph.D., was born in 1974, the same year *The East Bay Out* was born, and she was age four when *The Ohlone Way* came out, so her life has spanned that of Heyday. Sadie is an environmental and occupational epidemiologist at UC Berkeley, as well as the mother of two small children, Arden and Elsie, with her husband, Josh Costello, a theater director in Berkeley. Sadie's scientific work entails analyzing the impact of pollution on industrial workers. Sadie shared memories of growing up that included negotiating the infamous stacks of books at home, hiking with the family's very own naturalist guide, and traveling with Malcolm to Indian country.

One of my first memories was when we were living on Stuart Street in Berkeley, and Malcolm's office was in the house. You walked through a bathroom to a bedroom that had been converted into his office. The bathroom was unusable because the bathtub was filled with books, boxes of books. Actually, the whole bathroom was filled! The hallway back into his office was also filled with books, and his office itself. My parents' bed—they never had a proper bed frame—had a mattress on a board on top of boxes of books. I just remember lots and lots of boxes of books everywhere! Whole walls. Shipments would come in, and we'd have more stacks everywhere.

I remember my father working from home and the sound of the typewriter. I remember my mom was making maps, I'm not sure for what. She had a light table, and she'd work over the light table, tracing out these maps. I *really* wanted to help. When his office moved out of our home, it was a big shift.

Much of my early childhood was spent hiking around the hills and oak trees, maybe when Malcolm was writing *The Ohlone Way* and thinking about all these places. Now my kids are about the age I would have been at that time. I have whole flashbacks of "This is my life!" When our whole family recently went to Yosemite, the kids were playing around in rocky creeks that I seemed to remember. I hadn't been to Yosemite in a decade, a really long time. Taking my little daughter with her brown eyes and her blond hair and seeing her jumping over these rocks, I was thinking, "Oh, I've been on the other side of exactly this moment!"

My later memories, maybe ages ten to fourteen, are of the Indian reservations, taking drives out and going to powwows and festivals, camping out.
Sometimes Jake went along; I don't remember Reuben going. I remember
Malcolm interviewing people or just talking to them. Sometimes he was
selling books, and I'd help him at the tables. Sometimes he was just interviewing or getting to know the culture, or he'd been invited up by friends.
I don't remember getting a lot of context for going to some of the places or
what his role exactly was, just that this was going to be something special
and unusual, and we kids had a great chance to see it, so we should soak it
up, appreciate it, and be polite.

As a kid and an outsider, it was both awesome and boring. It was neat to
see a whole other culture, to witness and experience something new, exciting and different. It's also alienating because I didn't belong. Malcolm was
useful in the community, but I had no role. I just felt like an outsider kid. I
was rarely invited to hang out or play or join the other children who were
my age. I didn't feel unwanted, but the other kids my age had their life and
their thing—like the dances—that they were involved in. And what was I
doing there? I wasn't going to get it, which I totally understand. I don't think
I ever pushed it. I just remember watching them play and me standing to
the side. A couple of times an adult would bring their teenage kids over or
take me over to them. Everyone was fine. But they were part of a big family
experience and a tribal gathering, a history of getting together with people
they maybe didn't see all the time, or they were learning dances and passing on all these traditions. So for them it was an important experience that
they didn't necessarily want to share with some kid who had tagged along.

I do remember a really cute guy who was a lead dancer for one of
the bird dances! He was a few years older than me and really popular. I
have a few memories of a dance in Chaw'se that went *very* late into the
night, with dancing and fires, singing and more dancing. The dances are
amazingly elaborate. Another important one was out in Point Reyes at
the village near the Bear Valley Center, after a big effort to reconstruct the
roundhouse there. I remember a lot of dancing after that. The dancing was
simultaneously so heartbreaking and so boring. There's no building up, no
So You Think You Can Dance going on there, yet it all made sense with the

space, in a roundhouse, with people coming and going, and getting the huge headdresses into these small openings, all clearly rooted in time and history.

I remember meeting L. Frank in particular. She's wonderful. It was up at Chaw'se. Malcolm had a booth, and I was sitting there while he was wandering off for what seemed like hours on end, talking to people. L. Frank came up and sat in the shade next to me. She was so sweet and nice, just very welcoming and personable. A lot of the people I met on those trips were lovely and warm, but L. Frank definitely made an effort, or she was just interested in connecting with me, and I connected with her. She'd sit there for hours in the shade, talking to me while I was stuck at this table.

One time there was a jewelry stand where I saw a very elaborate silver ring that had a chain on it that attached to a bracelet. I thought it was gorgeous. L. Frank was nodding and said it was pretty, but she mentioned it was actually a slave bracelet, an ownership bracelet. I thought, "Oh, damn! That's a bummer, but it's still pretty, and I want it."

I remember seeing L. Frank when she got her face tattoos and thinking they were cool, striking. But she's so beautiful and striking anyway; they just made her even more so. I thought that the tattooing was an awesome dedication to a history and culture. A face tattoo is a very devoted statement. It was an eye-opener to me that people could have that kind of devotion to their culture.

Because here Malcolm was, heavily involved in a culture *not* his own and *not* passing on his own culture—or what would have been our own culture. Instead, he was watching and involved in helping this whole other culture. I think that was because he found a place or role; he found himself knowledgeable and useful. That reaction also seems pretty rooted in a lot of people who came out to California in that period, intentionally leaving behind a more traditional upbringing. Both my parents certainly did that. My mom was also starting fresh in some ways. I think they left behind both a lot of good and bad, some alienating things. From their perspective, they were doing us a favor. Maybe they were.

Probably most everything I know and think now is a result of all those experiences in Native California, what I came away with, like the complexity of trying to hold onto and value a culture in a time and place where it hasn't been valued for so many years, and at the same time, trying to be part of the world as it exists now. I remember going up to a Fourth of July celebration on a reservation and thinking, "Something about this seems a little odd!" It was a lovely celebration, the kids all dancing and happy, venison or salmon roasting over an open pit. *And* there were fireworks. It was a folding in of old and new, trying to keep some old traditions alive while trying not to be too isolated.

I think my experience is like that of people who travel a lot: they tend to have a perspective of Americans and American culture that seems a little more global, a little less Eurocentric. I find myself often having the same viewpoint of people who've grown up overseas. Of course, *my* "overseas" was here in California, visiting Indian country, places where you can imagine an alternative history to what we have now, perhaps even a history that should have been, that isn't. Those travels also made me reflect on what it meant to have been an American in that time and in those places.

Also, my mom's an immigrant, and my dad's parents were immigrants, so I've gained some understanding of the complexity of history, a non-black-and-white version. I often find myself feeling that I have a similar worldview to those who didn't grow up in the States, or whose parents didn't grow up in the States, or kids who had spent a lot of time traveling. I would sometimes be more knowledgeable than my classmates, based on all those experiences and exposure.

JAKE MARGOLIN

J ACOB ORION MARGOLIN was born in 1980. Malcolm's book *The Way We Lived* followed soon after, in 1981, so Jake's early years, like Sadie's, coincided with Malcolm's growing attachment to Native California. Jake is currently a performer and director. He tours frequently with the award-winning experimental theater company called the TEAM. With his husband, Nick Vaughan, Jake creates multimedia installation art. Jake's impressions of life with both of his parents speak to the importance of creating beauty in the world and feeling awe for startling performances.

Heyday was always completely present in my life because it was so present in my parents' life, and so we were very much a part of the Heyday worlds.

As a family we'd always go on hikes. On vacations and holidays or week-ends, we were always out hiking. We'd go up into the Berkeley Hills, where I think my father actually helped build some of those trails. He knew every-thing, it seemed. When we'd go on hikes, he'd tell us stories of the geology and the cultural history of the place. All of that is reflected in *The East Bay Out* and *The Ohlone Way*. So our family life was never separate from Heyday, even though the office was no longer in the house by the time I grew up.

I loved the office on University Avenue. I have such visceral memories of that building. I loved the smell of that elevator. I've just never smelled it anywhere else, the satisfying smell of the cleaning chemical they used, which was satisfying the way that the smell of gasoline at the pump is memorable and satisfying. Strangely, it's one of the strongest memories of my childhood, that elevator.

Also, the people who worked at Heyday were so great, as were the Heyday parties, including one at Angel Island for a picnic. Things were always happening. I remember being completely in love with a woman named Francine who worked there and hanging out with Francine on Angel Island.

Some of my earliest memories are going with my dad frequently to big times and powwows, conferences and book fairs, events on reservations all over the state, where we'd set up a table and sell books. I remember going to one big time when we stayed in the roundhouse all night where dances went on for hours. It was awesome. I remember watching, sometimes going in and out of sleep next to my dad while he was sitting next to a friend. The Big Head dancers came in with their huge headdresses. They'd slowly come around the circle, casting shadows on the walls, and the singers were singing all night long. I still remember the song that they would sing with the Big Head dancers. The song has gotten stuck in my head. I just loved that feeling of going to sleep at night with things going on.

The food was incredible, too. One time we went on a long drive to somewhere in Northern California that had a big Pacific salmon run. They had these fifty-yard-long pits, at least in my memory as a kid; they were huge, full of fire and stakes with salmon roasting on them. I was a pretty picky eater at the time and said I didn't want to eat any of it. My dad looked at me and said, "You damn well better eat this salmon, or I'm gonna kill you." I remember it being the most delicious thing I've ever eaten. We loved it.

We met some amazing elders who told wonderful stories. Often I'd just be sitting at the book table when my father would go off and talk to people. I'd man the table. So I grew up with people coming up and telling me how important the books and *News from Native California* were to them. It was cool to be part of that. Those travels were such a big part of my childhood.

I look back on all that and realize I was very lucky to get to participate. At the time, though, it just felt normal. It was just what you did with your dad: you go to big times and see ancient dances.

Maybe one lesson I got from growing up with all that was seeing how Heyday was an extension of my dad's life, how much he enjoyed what he was doing with his work. I think it taught us that we should do exactly what we want to do and try to make a living of it. The only way I thought I could really have disappointed my parents was if I wound up following a career that I didn't care about. The way that I knew to succeed in their eyes was by striking out on my own and trying to fulfill whatever it was that I saw as my function in the world.

I remember that after a year of college, I decided to drop out, and I was really nervous about telling my folks for some reason. But when I told my dad, he said, "Thank god. I thought you were going to be the only one of us to make it through college in four years." There wasn't any great point in doing anything by other people's rules.

My dad could have ended up teaching in a university or working for a historical society or something like that, but he did what he wanted to do, even if it was riskier. I didn't realize until I left California exactly what Heyday was, because when people would ask me what my dad did, I'd first explain that Heyday was a publishing company that did books by and about California Indians and California natural history. I then realized how Heyday had broadened so much because of my dad's interests, from all the interesting people he met, from poetry to Japanese history in California, and all the other varied things that Heyday does. It seems that Heyday has always published books that reflect Malcolm's interests at the time, and the people who he has become interested in.

As for my mom, what always sticks with me is what she said when I was a kid going off to camp or wherever: "Be good to your friends"— because they're all you've got. It was her motto to be good to the people around you, and ultimately things will work out. Having good friendships is what matters.

I'm sure Reuben talks about this, also, but my mom is a visual artist. I was never much of a writer, but I think artistically I've followed what my mother did. Watching my mom with her painting or her enjoyment of painters was a big influence.

I realized, too, as I've worked teaching kids and as my friends started having kids, that parents have to be real advocates for their kids in order for their children to be able to do certain things. My mother was always involved in our schools, in programs, helping out whenever I was involved in drama or music or art projects. At the time I didn't really appreciate how lucky I was to have a mom who advocated so much for me. But I think that one reason I'm involved in the arts is because of her commitment.

Also, my parents always looked at the world through a lens of *beauty*, whether it was in the relationships with the people they knew, or the gardening that my mother was doing, or the cards we'd make for each other. For both of my parents, their highest level of praise for something that someone said or for a story or an action was "Oh, that's *beautiful*." Beauty in a very broad sense. Beauty above all else: that was instilled in me and in all of us as the goal of life, to identify the beautiful things in the world and then be near them, gather them around you, appreciate them, and pass them on to others.

MALCOLM:
HEYDAY MAKES ITS FIRST MOVE, TO 2054 UNIVERSITY AVENUE

BY THE EARLY eighties I started having some people working with me. First, back at the house there was a work-study student or two, and then

The Margolin family in 1983 and several years later (PHOTOS BY HEATHER HAFLEIGH, MARGOLIN FAMILY COLLECTION)

Francine Hartman arrived in 1982. She was a UC Berkeley student who came from Scottsbluff, Nebraska. She'd been named Francine because her parents had a worship of France. She'd gone to France for a year to study abroad. She loved literature. Francine was skinny and hungry, hungry for experience, for life.

Hunger is good. It's what keeps us going. I'm hungry. Hunger for validation or for experience or love or something like that. It's *engagement*. I guess you can engage through hatred or anger, but that's not my idea of how to engage.

Anyhow, I was so pissed off at Cal, giving Francine these courses in criticism, this opaque, self-involved, incomprehensible stuff with Derrida in the New Criticism, stuff that was lacking juice, meaning, guts—without anything that nourishes the soul. She was so stressed about it, trying to understand it, as if this were the key to understanding life. I thought it was such a damn fraud, so horrible.

Francine began working with me in the house. I remember one of her first days there: I took Rina out to lunch. Then the cat started giving birth to kittens, but one of them wasn't doing very well, so Francine had to give it mouth-to-mouth resuscitation. She was afraid that we'd be mad at her because the kitten had died. She was very, very funny.

Finally, we faced a combination of too many kids, too many visitors, and too much of a domestic scene for me to keep the office at home anymore. Also, I felt like I couldn't ever get away from the business since I was working at home, so I was never fully at work or fully at rest. And in a sense Rina didn't have a home. It was public territory. People were coming in all the time. So I thought it would be a good thing to divide it up and get the business out of the house.

Another part of the move was some restlessness. This business of doing my own books had gone as far as it could go. Every book up to that point I had written, edited, typeset, and put out as part of Heyday Books. People were writing wonderful articles about this new wave of publishing, the do-it-yourself movement. I was into self-sufficiency. But that process had gone as far as it could, and it wasn't going to get any better. I just wanted to do something else.

So I ended up moving the office out to 2054 University Avenue, to a tiny office on the fourth floor of the Koerber Building. Francine went over with me to the new office. Heyday was growing an identity of its own by then. This was a big transition. Then came the realization, "How do you support this damn thing?" Now I had another rent and a salary and responsibilities like that.

So I started something called the Book Camel, the aim of which was to distribute books—ours and other people's—to nontraditional bookstores. I was already selling my own books, *The East Bay Out, The Ohlone Way*, and *The Way We Lived*. I'd also done *Stickeen*, a reprint of a John Muir book about his dog; we'd set that one, and so I did my own edition of it. I thought that since we were distributing these books to bookstores and other places, it would be just so easy to bring other people's books along, and it wouldn't be much extra work. We had a warehouse. We ended up getting this stream of books coming in. Francine, and later other people, would go around and sell books to wilderness supply shops and other places.

But it turned out to be the tail that wagged the dog. It was a total pain: a whole lot of work, a lot of accounting, a whole lot of drudgery—collecting money, bills and losses, shortages and damages. It became a business in itself. Accounting has never been my strong point, so I had no idea whether this thing was making money or taking money. All I knew was I hated it, yet we were tied into it.

Then I tried another business. It started with this woman, Kendall, who came to work for me. Her father was Walter Munk, a very well-known professor of oceanography at Scripps in San Diego. They lived next to Dr. Seuss and next to Sam Hinton, the folksinger, Leanne Hinton's father. The Munks lived on La Jolla Park Drive, overlooking the ocean. Walter had an amphitheater in his backyard. I remember talking to Walter's mother once; he had been born in Vienna. His mother was explaining to me about the family mansion in Vienna, how difficult it was to maintain a house like that with only four servants. I said, "I know what you mean."

Walter was a different breed of character, with the amphitheater and his tremendous wealth. But he gave us a gift—a piece of typesetting equipment that we could use. He thought it would be a great gift to Heyday.

It was a Compugraphic, the new style of typesetting system that came after the Linotype and other hot-metal type systems. Today we have computers, but bridging the two of them were these strange things that had rolls of film; the letters were cut like stencils out of these strips of film. They'd be put on drums inside a machine, and they'd whirl around. Lights would flash through them. Words would be registered on pieces of film, and you'd develop the film in darkrooms, then lay it out on galleys. So now we had this production going on at the University Avenue offices.

We soon took over some offices on another floor of the Koerber Building for the typesetting business. At the time several typesetters in Berkeley were serving the growing small press movement. In my mind the best of them was Archetype, run by my friend Rick Heide. They did careful but not overly fussy work for many of the upstart, radical, and environmental groups in the East Bay. Rick was an utterly decent fellow, struggling like all of us, and we invited him to share our space. He moved in, and we quickly developed a partnership, copublishing several books together. I think the idea was that he could typeset the books during the lulls when the machines were idle. He was a joy to work with. Years later he compiled material for two successful anthologies we did: *Under the Fifth Sun: Latino Literature from California* and *Illuminated Landscape: A Sierra Nevada Anthology.*

So we had the Book Camel for distribution, *and* we were doing the typesetting for other people's books. We typeset lots of books for people who were publishing their own work. Since I'd been publishing my own books, I felt a kind of ideological fervor about it: you didn't have to depend upon other people to publish your book. If you had something you wanted to say, you could do it yourself.

We were typesetting the books for this cast of amazing characters coming through, Eldridge Cleaver, Alice Walker, an old guy from China—for some strange people, for so many folks. We did books on dancers, on the stock market. Francine was doing a lot of the actual typesetting.

But once again it was a business, and a mean business. This was work for hire. You end up counting your time. People bring in corrections; you charge them for doing the corrections. You bill in minute intervals. It wasn't the kind of loose, open quality that I like. It was this never-ending mass of problems: typos, machine breakdowns, schedules. I didn't like the business.

FRANCINE HARTMAN

F RANCINE HARTMAN WAS one of the first employees of what was then Heyday Books. From her home now in Madison, Wisconsin, Francine recounted with great affection how she met Malcolm when she was an ingénue college student at UC Berkeley and the subsequent years of working by his side as Heyday moved from its early childhood into its early adolescence.

It's funny how clearly I remember the first time I met Malcolm, in 1981, now over thirty years ago, in the winter. I'd had a fractured education. I dropped in and out, went here and there, including school overseas for a year, but I finally ended up at Berkeley. After my first quarter, I was looking for a work-study job. I found a notice for what was called the Berkeley Creators, a nonprofit that served as Heyday's fiscal receiver. I had great office skills: photocopying, typing, and language. My father was a longtime printer. Although I didn't do it myself, I was familiar with the linotype machine and printing presses, so I thought I could figure out this publishing job.

When I answered the ad and talked to Malcolm, it quickly became clear that the Berkeley Creators was more of an umbrella, with just Heyday and some other people hiring work-study students. Anyway, I arranged an interview to meet this man. I was used to working in offices with establishment sort of people. Instead, I show up at a house, wondering if this is the right place. Malcolm opens the door. I wasn't alarmed, but he was definitely different. I walked into the kitchen, and he offered me a cup of coffee. We sat there and just chatted. We were talking about Kandinsky. I thought, I can do this, talk about something I don't really know about but that's interesting. I was a bit intimidated because he was very erudite. I still didn't get what kind of publishing this thing was—in his house, no less. But he seemed like a very interesting guy, tall, thin, with a giant beard, smile, and laugh. I felt comfortable with him.

So we're hanging out, talking. I keep wondering when we're going to have the interview. He still hadn't asked about my typing or other office-related experiences. Then it became clear it wasn't that type of inter-view, but just "Who are you? Can I work with you? Do you have a brain? Is this possible?"

What I was going to be doing was rudimentary typesetting at first. Malcolm showed me how. The actual first machine I worked on was some kind of newish seventies-era Linotype. The machines were clunky and can-tankerous, but I got used to them.

Malcolm, his friend Bob Callahan, and a couple other people had a time-share with this very basic typesetting machine. I remember we'd go in for two hours at a time. After I learned how to do the keyboarding, I'd just type away while Malcolm would sit and write and do whatever he was working on.

The first thing I worked on was keyboarding for *The Way We Lived*. I enjoyed it and found I was good at it. I was also learning a lot about indige-nous people in the process. I'd only lived in California for a year or two, so it was great to learn about California Indians. I felt so deeply the touching stories in *The Way We Lived*. They completely opened my eyes to a very dif-ferent population and history, learning about so many levels of attachment that people had to California. I saw what a big place it is, how many Indian groups there were. It was quite amazing to me, so different from anything I'd known.

After that, Malcolm showed me how to do a paste-up. "You can do it! You just do this and this and this." We proofread the galleys and circled in the corrections. We had a paste-up board, a waxer, and an X-Acto knife. The process seems odd now. I'm not really skilled as an artist, but it was somehow safe for me to learn about graphic design in that tactile way.

Meanwhile, my work with Malcolm included an association with Rina and the kids. Jake was about three or four months old when I started, cute as a button! I had no idea what a person would do with a baby. Reuben and Sadie were older. I could understand them. They could walk and talk. How to characterize my relationship? It wasn't really family, because I wasn't there all the time, but I was there often, and I was certainly very comfortable with all of them. The family made me so welcome. They were so warm, always inviting me to stay for dinner.

At the time I was living with my then-boyfriend, who was from a very different, corporate world, working at Chevron in Richmond. Our paths were diverging at that time. Being with Malcolm and Rina and the kids and learning all this stuff about books was so lovely and comforting.

We'd finished *The Way We Lived*, and Malcolm was shopping it around. He was doing all the marketing for it since I didn't really know anything about that, but I was learning. My association was really an apprenticeship for me. I don't think Malcolm's intention was to be a mentor or anything, but that is definitely what I received from my time at Heyday. I felt I had a facility for the work, but also Malcolm was amazingly generous, patient, and funny. My work there gave me a definition to hang onto: "This is who I am, what I do." That was important at a time when I was so worried about where my life was going and how to pay the bills.

I continued with Malcolm for the next year or so while I was finishing school. At that point, I was doing more office work, filling out orders, typing up correspondence. It was still just Malcolm back then. Rina did whatever she could, but the kids were young, so she was pretty busy. She drew maps and certainly weighed in on decisions.

One of the funniest things was when a litter of cats was born right next to my desk. It was the quintessential Berkeley experience. We worked in the office in their house on Berkeley Way, with a couple of tables set up and old funky Underwood typewriters. Malcolm, Rina, and Jake had all gone out for lunch, which was uncharacteristic. Rina said, "The mama cat is pacing around, so it's possible something will happen here." She pointed out a book on healthy cat care, possibly thinking I might need the information.

Well, yeah! The kittens were born right then. Suddenly I'm the cat midwife! But one of the kittens wasn't making it. The mama was not cleaning it after it was born. I picked up this tiny newborn kitten in one hand, and in the other hand searched the healthy cat book, trying to figure out how to resuscitate the cat. This was not in the job description! She didn't make it, and I felt so bad.

Around 1983, Malcolm got the space on University Avenue in a funky building with a temperamental elevator. It was thrilling for me because we had a real office downtown, and I lived only a couple of blocks away, so I could walk to work.

Happily, after I graduated, I started working full-time for Malcolm. I didn't have anything else to do, and I was very happy to do it. Quickly, I started wearing a lot of different hats. The phone would ring, and I'd say, "Yes, this is Heyday Books." So I was the office manager and the salesperson. It was a little bit nuts, but I got to go to work in my sneakers and overalls—that was awesome!

The whole experience was very deep for me, even though it was only about three years total. In addition to his amazing talent as a writer and his ability to become a self-taught anthropologist, Malcolm is very perceptive. He has a knack of pulling out hidden characteristics from people. I could tell that when we had other interns doing research or whatever. After a couple conversations he could figure out, "This person is exhibiting a particular ability." Malcolm was really a creative genius; he could talk a person into anything: "You can do this. You're going to be in charge of layout." For me, I thought, "Really? I have no idea about it. Sure. Okay." Yet it works out.

So my apprenticeship—even though he didn't intend it that way—worked out beautifully for me *with the exception* of a little interlude called the Book Camel. Oh, was that ever painful! The idea of the Book Camel was that Malcolm would purchase certain books about hiking, fishing, anything related to natural history in the Bay Area or greater California. I was in charge of peddling books. I drove around to bookstores and non-bookstores, bait and tackle shops, hunting stores, *whatever*, trying to convince people to buy books. But most people didn't want to buy them, and I was just miserable at selling. Malcolm said I could do it, and I tried, but I was so bad at it. I didn't believe in myself. I could probably do it today, but back then I was very hesitant. If I'd relied on commissions, I would have starved! I was way more comfortable at the desk or handling stuff at the office. I was not a born schmoozer.

By then Malcolm was working more with other people, printing their books; we were something like a vanity press. It was the result of a wonderful gift of a groovy machine, called a Compugraphic or something. It was an odd little machine, with a keyboard and a very small display screen that showed about a hundred characters at a time. You'd insert separate fonts into a wheel. Light would flash on it and the image of the character was burned onto a piece of film. Malcolm had a time-share to use a similar machine, while various people doing small press work were also using the apparatus.

Malcolm received this first machine as a gift from Walter Munk, a renowned oceanographer at Scripps, the father of Kendall Munk, who was one of the interns at Heyday. She invited all of us to her wedding. Her mother had designed an amphitheater at their house in La Jolla that they used for the wedding. I remember it was a wonderful evening in late December 1982. Rina, Malcolm, and the kids were there. Vivaldi music was playing; the couple is walking out. Jake was a little over two years old, and he had a cough. He coughed some and then said loudly, "I got big, bad cough!" Everybody around him was cracking up when we're supposed to be paying attention to the wedding, but he was so adorable. I was just in love with that boy.

Francine Hartman with the newest technology of the day (HEYDAY ARCHIVES)

Anyhow, Kendall convinced her father to invest a little in Heyday, so he had given Malcolm this machine. It was secondhand and very basic, but it worked great. We were able to do better book design, which Malcolm understood, and I was learning. Soon we started doing production for other people. Malcolm knew everybody who had ever written anything, and they all wanted to know him. For some clients, we could handle everything from design through printing and do everything for them, but we tried to keep it clear that it was not under the Heyday imprint. Malcolm could give them direction or whatever, but it was their book.

We did a number of small books, including a group of short stories we produced, *Thursday's Child,* from a writers' group that met weekly. Milt Wolff and Ed Robbin and other writers contributed to the book, and Ed was the editor. I loved working with these men. Milt was a veteran of the Abraham Lincoln Brigade. Ed wrote a novella called *Birth* that we produced for him. It was quite lovely for me working on those books because, by keyboarding them, of course, I got to read them. It became a kind of Zen exercise in typing away and reading and not really having to worry too much about keyboarding.

One man, Howard DeWitt, an instructor at Hayward, was writing a biography of Van Morrison called *The Mystic's Muse* (which came out in 1983). Howard was a real character. He knew a lot about popular music. He'd deliver his book one chapter at a time. That book helped launch me into my next career because as I was typing it, I'd find errors in his text, typos, whatever, and I thought, "You don't want to say *that;* you want to put it this way." So I'm copyediting on the fly! It was like midwifing the cat, learning on the job. That led me to a career as a copy editor and, eventually, as an actual editor.

Another person whose book we did was Grant Petersen. I typeset his first book, called *Roads to Ride.* He had this idea about doing guidebooks for bicycle excursions around the Bay Area, guides that would include maps and elevation descriptions and that would even tell you if the road was rough or paved. Grant had ridden his bike everywhere, a hardcore bicyclist and a really nice guy. Back then Grant didn't know squat about books. I didn't know much more, but Malcolm knew a lot, so between the three of us, we got this book going that Malcolm published. Sarah Levin did a lot of the layout and the illustrations for the maps because she could use a Rapidograph without shaking violently the way that I did. I think Malcolm did three editions of *Roads to Ride*.

At that point, around 1987, Malcolm was starting to do *News from Native California*. Heyday wasn't a tremendous moneymaker at the time, but it was growing. We hired different people to do fulfillment orders because *The Ohlone Way* just sold itself, which I'm sure it still does to this day. It's the most remarkable book that everybody who lives in California should be required to read. So other people were coming in to help out with office work or freelance paste-up for book design or cover design. Sarah was taking more advanced classes in graphic design. She was talented and knew a lot more than I did.

We also did a couple of poetry books. One person, I have to say, came in at the wrong time of day. It was late on a Friday afternoon, and I just wanted to get my work done and go home. But Malcolm said, "Join us; we're just going to have a meeting and talk about putting together a book."

I was trying to be nice, but I was just not in a great mood. We gave the man an estimate for his manuscript. Again, it wasn't going to be under a Heyday imprint, just printing for him. So I came up with an estimate for production. I'm noticing his satchel says, "Eldridge Cleaver." I thought, "Right. He must have gotten that from somewhere else"—you know, secondhand. No, it really was Eldridge Cleaver! So that was my brush with notoriety.

What more can I say about Malcolm except that everybody adored him. He was just so generous. Everybody around knew how talented he was, how dedicated to the work. Along with natural history in general, it was very important to him to educate people about California Native history without being maudlin or sentimental, helping maintain information about various aspects of Indian culture in California. I thought it was a higher goal than most people have in their life. Clearly, it was not just a business. Malcolm's enormous task was to educate people in a *loving* way. Not "I'm gonna hit you over the head with the terrible imperialism and extermination of Indians by the Europeans," which is the truth. He never came across as heavy-handed. His style was more to be loving and truthful.

Anyhow, after the Book Camel episode, I spent more time back in the office, meeting with clients, and that was all good, but finally I was tapped out. The business was revving up, and I'd been living pretty bare-bones for a long time, working really hard, and I was a very responsible employee. Malcolm was working really hard, too, but there was no money to spare. I was just tired of being broke. I was twenty-five or twenty-six and had been struggling financially forever. I knew I couldn't ask for more money 'cause I knew the accounts, and there just wasn't any more money.

We parted on very good terms. At my going-away party, he laughed, "Francine has sold out for a dental plan." It's true! I went to work for an upscale place in the city. I had to go to Macy's and buy some clothes to look like a grown-up. I was working for a political think tank, but I didn't know what I was getting into. My boyfriend at the time, who's now my husband of twenty-three years, asked, "Do you know what you're doing there?"

I said, "I don't care! Benefits, health plan, real money!" In fact, I got the job from somewhat inflating my résumé about working at Heyday, but I also got a tip from a good friend of Malcolm's, a printer's rep. He told me this organization was looking for someone. So I had Malcolm to thank for that, too.

It was sad to leave Heyday. Who knew that a work-study job would turn into an apprenticeship, a career, and a community for me? That's what Heyday was. How rare is that? He's an absolute creative genius, what he sees in people, how he pulls them in.

I later worked at the University of Wisconsin Publications Office for thirteen years as a senior editor. I realized after working there a while that the way I answered the phone and spoke to people was the way *Malcolm* would. Maybe 90 percent of the time when Malcolm answered the phone, he'd say, "Hey! How are you?" He'd greet people he knew on the phone with such warmth and interest. He made everyone feel like they had some-thing to say, and he was going to spend some time with them, whatever their dilemma was. It so impressed me, and very much unconsciously, I incorporated his style into my approach to my work. I couldn't always rise to his level, but he embedded in me that this is how you treat people. Everybody should be so lucky.

MALCOLM: THE STORY OF *HUMPHREY THE WAYWARD WHALE*

B ESIDES DOING OTHER people's books, we kept squeezing out our own books with the Heyday imprint. We did whatever came along: several bicycle guides to the Bay Area that were fairly successful, a couple more Indian books, some reprints. There were a variety of fumbling attempts at finding a tone and a subject.

Then in October 1985, when Reuben was fifteen, Humphrey the whale came into the bay. I was watching people stand around these newspaper kiosks in wonderment. This big drama struck me. Every day some detail was in the news. "What happened to Humphrey?" It was like Indian stories, with a big animal drama unfolding. Finally, they ended up bringing Humphrey out with Bernie Krause's whale sounds, leading it back out the bay. This big cheer erupted.

I thought, "This is an instant book."

So I went to Ernest (Chick) Callenbach, a writer friend, and to Carl Buell, who'd been illustrating some books for us, and I said, "Let's do an instant book on Humphrey the Wayward Whale." Chick and his wife, Christine Leefeldt, wrote the book in a couple of days. I edited it. Carl did some drawings. My friend Don Ellis at Creative Arts Press had printing presses down there. We got some paper, we worked the presses, and we set up the bindery with friends there. Then we just started printing this skinny little book. We priced it at about $4.95 a book. We got it out in three weeks from the time the whale left.

I had this old alcoholic sales rep at the time who had emphysema. He was taking books around to the bookstores. He'd wheeze up in his old car and open the trunk. We'd take out what was just coming off of the presses and load up his car, and he'd go around and distribute them. Every morning I came in, and the phone was ringing with people wanting to know where they could get this Humphrey book. We ended up selling *forty thousand* of them in a few weeks! The presses were breaking down; we kept printing them.

At the end, I found myself with a chunk of money. I got rid of that type-setting equipment, I got rid of the Book Camel, and I went off to Mexico with Reuben. I was so glad to be out from under all that stuff. It was just wonderful. It was so lucky! I mean we could have struggled along forever. If there's something about this episode that's important or fated or sym-bolic for me, it was seeing the beautiful animal story, seizing on that story, pulling it out, and getting rid of something ugly—the typesetting business and the distribution business.

But there was also in that story the orchestration of friends. It brought the best out of Chick and Christine and Carl. The sales rep almost came alive. It was a matter of teamwork, getting a crew together. It was going beyond the writing of the book, but the whole orchestration of the people, and the *fun* of it. It was so much fun!

Back at 2054 University, life in the Koerber Building was interesting. The *Madness Network News* set up its office there, as did the Network Against Psychiatric Abuse, a bunch of ex-mental patients against shock therapy. I discovered this guy Leonard Frank, who ran this organization and looked like me. People would come into the building who had just gotten out of the insane asylum or they'd just had electric shock treatment. They'd see me when my beard was still brown, and they'd say, "Leonard, I've come out to see you."

I'd say, "Listen, you want the Network Against Psychiatric Abuse. I'm not Leonard."

And they'd yell, "Don't fuck with me!"

Meanwhile, for years I'd walk down the street and people would stop me every couple of months, and they'd say, "Leonard, how are you?"

I'd say, "I'm not Leonard."

They'd go, "Oh god, you look exactly like Leonard," referring to yet *another* Leonard.

So one day, somebody said, "Leonard, what are you up to?"

I said, "Hey, who is this guy Leonard? I keep being stopped. Give me his name and phone number and let me get in touch with him." Turns out

"The Three Malcolms": Malcolm Margolin, Leonard Shapiro, Leonard Frank
(PHOTO BY HEATHER HAFLEIGH, HEYDAY ARCHIVES)

it was Leonard Shapiro. So I get the information, and I make the call. This voice answers, "Hello?"

I say, "Hey, listen, is this Leonard Shapiro?"

He says, "Yeah."

I said, "This is going to be the goofiest, stupidest phone call you've ever received, but my name is Malcolm Margolin."

He says with awe, "Malcolm!" He knew exactly who I was. So we got together.

Sometimes the three of us would meet, dress alike, and go out for lunch. Back then, we all wore denim jackets and blue jeans.

We used to have all these wonderful parties up at the office at the Koerber Building, and the kids would come. At one of these parties, I invited these two guys. It was the party with the "Three Malcolms." Everybody at the party was just knocked out; they couldn't believe that there were these two other characters in Berkeley, and we all looked alike. So at this party the kids are playing around, having fun. Finally, I come up to them, and I say, "What do you think?"

"Think about what?"

"About those two guys."

"What about them?"

"They look like me!"

They said, "No, they don't."

I just thought that was so wonderful.

DEVELOPMENTS AT HEYDAY

I loved to go to parties. That was also a big part of that time. There was always a party, an opening, a reception, a reading, something like that, with alcohol, people, life. I've built up this place on parties with people that I've met, that I've befriended. I went to a lot of parties!

But I was not only a publisher; I was also a writer. I had an entrée into these worlds as an intellectual, as a writer, as somebody who's made a contribution to history, to natural history, to the community of Indians, to ethnic stuff. So I came in not just as a publisher, not just as an interpreter, but as part of the fraternity, as part of that world. And I just loved to mix. I was equally at home with Indians on a reservation that had just gotten out of jail as with Nobel laureates and full professors. I don't think I changed my voice for any of them; I was just equally at home.

Meanwhile, I remember those days as being a steady turnover of people at work. Francine ultimately left. She went off to Wisconsin. I have a particularly vivid memory of how she caught her husband—how she strategized and "stalked" him. He was a nice guy. They're still married. They have a couple of kids. It's a successful marriage.

With this turnover of people, there was chaos. We were always so broke, so fiercely broke. We never had the right equipment. We could never pay people well. We were just always in an emergency, at the edge.

I was amazed the other day, looking at the book we did on glaciers. We're turning out gorgeous books. Despite whatever financial problems the place has had over all these years, there's a firewall between the financial problems and the work that gets done, which is pure and holy. It's the best of human effort, of creativity. It doesn't get infected by this other stuff that goes on. It's like something on an altar. If you lose that, you've lost everything. There's no purpose to the whole damn thing. That was always true.

Several big things happened over there on University Ave. Amy Hunter came to work for me and was around for maybe eight or nine years. She was great. She came in as sales manager. There was a sense of friendship and partnership that I had with her that was really great. I even officiated at Amy's wedding. I've officiated at various employees' weddings, which has always been very flattering.

Amy met her husband on a bicycle trip; she loved bicycling. She was from old New England *Mayflower* stock, real white people. She had an outdoor wedding in Marin somewhere. I remember we had a terrifying rehearsal: I was supposed to go pick up the bride's mother, put my arm like this, and walk down the aisle, then go pick up the bride's father and deposit him over here. It reminded me of square dancing, when I was always lost! And here I was supposed to lead all these people around.

For the ceremony I said that even though this wedding wasn't ordinary, it still worked in the deepest of traditions. In the old days, in ancient Greece and ancient Rome, they would send a cart pulled by bulls to the bride's house to get the bride. They had bands, with people making noise to let the gods know that the bride was going away. This tradition comes down to us today as a jalopy tied with tin cans and the soap and other garishness. At the end, Amy and her husband walk off to a tree, and behind the tree is a bicycle built for two, with tin cans, and off they drive. It was so beautiful, so beautiful.

As Heyday was growing, it basically defined itself around what I could do, what I was interested in. For example, I rode bicycles a lot at the time, and we did some bicycle guides. But it wasn't completely tied to my interests. The California definition also came about because that's where I could distribute. I never decided to focus only on California, but if someone brought me a book that needed national distribution, I just wouldn't do it because I didn't have the capacity to get it out and promote it. I couldn't do well with it. One of the things that motivates me is shame. I'd be ashamed to take somebody's work and not do well by it. It's not just pride to do it well; it's shame to do it badly.

Heyday also grew out of my reading and research and the people I met. I've had various strong friendships connected to writing and publishing.

Malcolm officiating at the wedding of Heyday editor Lisa K. Manwill and Peter Marietta (COURTESY OF JEANNINE GENDAR)

One is with Alan Rosenus, who's a writer and who had a small press of his own, Orion. My friendship with Alan was based on a mutual love of Joaquin Miller. We went to Joaquin Miller's house on the hundredth anniversary of Miller's death just to walk around and talk about him. Joaquin Miller triggered that friendship. We worked with Alan to publish *Life Amongst the Modocs*, and I wrote the introduction for the book.

I've always related to Joaquin Miller as a poet, as a cultural icon, as a theatrical person, as a liar and a showman, how he was pretending he was somebody else. I think very often you discover truth *not* by being yourself, but by presenting yourself as the person you would *like* to be and fitting into that image of something. I'm not sure the truth sets you free. The truth can imprison you. Imagination sets you free. I could relate to that freedom and openness in Joaquin Miller. He had that wondrous opening to *Life Amongst the Modocs:* "Lonely as God, white as a winter moon, Mount Shasta starts up sudden and solitary from the heart of the great black forests of Northern California." Such a grand sweep of rhetoric, open to the bigness of the world.

We also published Alan's book on General Vallejo. So few people are into that era of early California history with a sense of keen intellectual inquiry—that play with ideas, but outside the academic world.

204 THE HEYDAY OF MALCOLM MARGOLIN

We have dinner once every three months. It's an opportunity for a strong opening up of our lives to each other. Alan doesn't have much to do with the rest of Heyday, but he provides this one-to-one, deep friendship removed from the communal operation here, from all the people I know. This is the longest "stranger on a train" conversation in the entire world! In a way, it's like confession. There's something similar in his Jewish background to mine, something similar in our ages, in our interest in California. Going back to that story about Ed Robbins, whose brother said at Ed's funeral that we need a witness in our lives: in some ways, Alan is my witness. We check in on each other. We dip the dipstick in to see how much oil is there.

Steve Sanfield, poet, writer, and storyteller from Nevada City, is another such witness. Whenever we get together, a stranger might think that we are fighting as we unleash a fusillade of stories at each other, competitive in a way, a kind of story-slam. Over the years these shared stories have created a bridge between us of deep love, acceptance, and understanding.

I've always said Heyday moves like an amoeba. Some people have goals. They see something outside themselves, and they move toward that goal. I've never had that, never seen a goal. Heyday is kind of an emotional, globby thing. Every so often it puts a pseudopod out into the world. This pseudopod blindly reaches out, and if it finds nourishment the globby body oozes slowly into the pseudopod. If the pseudopod finds the new territory infertile, hostile, or simply unpleasant, the amoeba draws it back into its body for a while, eventually thrusting out in another direction.

Somehow or other, that's how Heyday advanced. I never got into the business of books all that much, studying how distribution works and stuff like that. It's not that I have contempt for it. The process hasn't been marked by clarity and intellectualization. No flip charts have been sacrificed. No diagrams have been drawn. It's just moved around. It never gets too far from an emotional core of wonder. Love. Fear. Egotism. Love of *beauty*—that's so present. An ongoing kindness toward people. I love to see people prosper. I love it when the best comes out in somebody. I just think that's so beautiful.

David Peri told a wonderful story about a dugout canoe maker. The guy was adzing out a canoe and tapping the side of it. At first David thought it was a nervous gesture of some sort, and then he realized it was deliberate. He said, "What are you doing?"

The canoe maker said, "I'm listening to the music that the boat makes."

The blueprint of the canoe locked in a song in the thin and the thick parts. You'd tap around until the boat sang the song that you wanted to hear. Isn't it just beautiful? That was David Peri; he was so filled with seeing the beauty of these things.

And the thought occurred to me: Could that be how to create books?

I don't remember when I particularly began thinking about publishing others' books, but I think I come at the publishing as a writer, so I'm much more involved in the writing. I loved being involved in the editorial process. I'm as creative in helping create books that other people are working on as I've been with my own books. I don't feel that I've given up the life of a writer to do this, either. I enjoy working with other people and creating projects. It's what a publisher does: you shape it. It's just a continuation. Someone comes in, and we help shape the book that he or she wants to write. Usually a publisher says "Yes" or "No." They see what comes in as good or bad. For me, we work on it as a writer would work on it. When an interesting book comes in, we help create something even better.

JEANNINE GENDAR

JEANNINE GENDAR WORKED for *News from Native California* as the managing editor from 1989 until 2000. Then from 2000 until the summer of 2011 she served as the editorial director at Heyday and then as an editor at Heyday. Jeannine offers perspective on Malcolm from a friendship that has aged winsomely with their twenty-year association.

In 1989 I had been working for the state of California for about twelve years or so. My last interlude with the state was as the assistant to Larry Myers, the head of the California Native American Heritage Commission. That was my first experience (other than personal) with California Indians. Larry chose me because he knew that I could write and do layout jobs for communications and other projects.

When I started that job, I went to the library for information. I think I found *The Way We Lived* and a copy of *The Ohlone Way*, too. There was a book about Indian trust land that had to do with Oklahoma. There was hardly anything about California Indians, but I read whatever I could get my hands on. Then, I went to one of the yearly California Indian Conferences, this one up at Humboldt State. There were all these wonderful people. They had traditionally cooked salmon on vertical skewers at Moonstone Beach. It was all so real. Malcolm was there, and that was the first time I met him.

I have a funny story about trying to meet Malcolm. When I was working for the Native American Heritage Commission, *News* first started coming out right then. The first issue I saw had a black-and-white cover photo of adorable little figurines that Bun Lucas had been carving. The magazine was just beautiful, with all this information, exactly what I'd been looking for. So I wanted to meet Malcolm.

I was going to the big time at Chaw'se, at Indian Grinding Rock State Park. One of the guys I was working with at the commission said I should look out for Malcolm, that I couldn't miss him because he had a long gray beard and wouldn't look like anybody else there. So I spent the day looking for people with long gray beards. Finally, I saw somebody. I went up to him and asked, "Are you Malcolm Margolin?"

He said, "No, but I wish I was!" I think it was Bill Toney, a craftsman up in Lake County. At last I did meet Malcolm. I got to know him better at various places over time. He was charming, playful, friendly, intelligent, and a really good storyteller. Malcolm tends to welcome people into his sphere.

As I mentioned before, I eventually got involved in *News from Native California* through our Indian connections and came to work at Heyday. It's really been a delight to be able to work together over the years. He's a little older than I am, but we both come from the same hippie ethos. We balance out the desire to do something really well with the need to keep things in an appropriately loose and in-the-present way of life, being compassionate, not necessarily toeing the mainstream line.

After ten years at *News* I started to feel some entropy, like I wasn't meeting new people. The process of keeping the magazine itself together was so involved that I wasn't getting out and meeting people, bringing fresh life into the magazine, and it needed fresh life.

Meanwhile, I had been doing some book editing for Heyday also, so I switched over to editing books. Malcolm then hired Margaret Dubin to be the managing editor for *News from Native California*.

Around that time, two people in a row who were editorial directors at Heyday went out on maternity leave and decided to be stay-at-home moms. So I fell into the position of editorial director. I didn't have a degree in English, but I was always stronger verbally than I was visually, although I was pretty strong visually. I had a degree in art with an emphasis on graphic design from San Diego State. My working life was all over the map, a lot of it verbally oriented. Coming to Heyday, I'd done a lot of careful work, but I hadn't ever done the rigorous editing called for in publishing. I learned a lot while I was working on *News*. Very early in that process I learned some important editing skills, like the need to balance keeping a person's true voice with keeping things editorially correct. By the time I was editing books, I was skilled, but I had much more to learn. I've learned so much in the ensuing years. And Heyday has learned so much in the ensuing years.

When I first started working on *News*, we were in the Koerber Building. Sarah Levin was doing design for the magazine. At first I was just volunteering, helping out with whatever needed doing, which was pretty much editorial. We still had waxers and other now archaic tools. Right about then, the personal computer became more common. The term "desktop publishing" was new and fresh and meant something wonderful. We had this dusty little room in the back of Heyday's offices in the Koerber Building where we put *News* together. We'd have a big rush at the end to get all the layout and design stuff done in time. We had almost no equipment. We'd run over to Canterbury Press, on the corner of University and Martin Luther King, and do all the last-minute scanning of photographs, try to throw it together.

In those days Malcolm was putting out only two or three books a year, so he was involved in *News* also, reading articles pretty closely, helping bring in new material, mining sources out in the world at large. Then we had the whole business aspect of it, too, which was on index cards at the time,

our database of subscribers. We were always trying to get more subscribers. The accounts included all the little galleries and stores that carried six
issues of *News* for people who'd come in and buy Indian crafts and goods in
obscure parts of California. I'm sure that it's all unchanged in some ways.

As time went on, we got our own gradually upgraded Macs so we could
do more ourselves. Sarah left, but she trained me to do some basic design,
so I started doing all that. I had a computer at home. It got so that I hardly
ever went to Heyday, only when there was an issue ready to print, and there
might be some last-minute tasks. Malcolm and I would trade pieces of paper
back and forth so we could see what was going into the magazine. I gradually assumed a little bit more responsibility for the content.

Then it got to the point that Malcolm had the long view, and he
was arranging for the special issues. He'd have suggestions and contacts.
Between the two of us, we'd make those contacts and get those articles.
Malcolm, of course, was always traveling around and talking to people, so
he'd have them send things in to the magazine.

We did a lot of visiting at annual events, like the California Indian
Basketweavers Association gatherings. In fact, we were there at the very
beginning of that. Also, the California Indian Conferences, the Society for
California Archeology conferences, the big times at Chaw'se and at Kule
Loklo, the Strawberry Festival at Kule Loklo—Malcolm always went to
that one. A million little events over the years. We'd be out there and pick
stuff up.

Meanwhile, Heyday and *News* were growing. In earlier jobs I was
trained to take responsibility, just take the ball and run with it, and that has
worked out really well here. I think I'm a person you can leave things with,
which Malcolm needed as the organization was growing. His managerial
style was loose! It's a given in an organization like Heyday that nobody will
ever have enough time to do everything he or she could be doing—or have
the money to do it. Malcolm needed to let go of the little stuff. I think he's
always kept an eye on content. But it seems that once he felt he could turn
a lot of things over, he was very comfortable doing that. There may be
some aspects of the process he doesn't let go of easily, but with everything
we've worked on, it's been pretty simple.

And if I or anyone was ever distressed about anything, Malcolm was there. If something went wrong, he'd joke with me—and I'm sure he does with others, too—"Well, it's all *my* fault." He was always willing to let the buck travel to him and stop there, which was a very fine attitude. One of the reasons we've been able to work well together is we've tended to completely avoid topics of blame. We just make things happen. That's at the heart of our working style. In other words, we both take plenty of responsibility and have the urge to do things well, but we tend not to point fingers.

For example, one time we were doing a special bird insert to *News*, sixteen pages with lots of beautiful paintings that involved birds by different California Indian artists. I don't remember why, but we had them overprinted. Maybe we were going to have them bound into a book or put in another magazine. Anyway, as a result, in addition to what actually got inserted in the magazines, we had boxes and boxes of extra copies of just the insert.

When you do books, you have to work in increments of 8 and 16 and 32 pages because of the way printing equipment works. I'm not real good at 3-D thinking, so I probably did the imposition wrong, or I got the trim size wrong, so it couldn't actually be reduced to the proportions that would go into the book that Malcolm had in mind—some horrible screw-up! I was just mortified. Here were all these copies of this thing that now had no home at all. It was horrible. You hate to waste paper.

Anyway, Malcolm just *laughed!* It was wonderful, such a relief to me. I still felt terrible, but he had this really wonderful response when I screwed up. It just seemed to tickle his funny bone.

Another great story happened when we were still up in the Koerber Building, around 1990. All of a sudden Malcolm got a lot of invitations for speaking engagements. It was the beginning of his becoming a major Bay Area, even statewide, raconteur. He's still very intense about those things, but at that time, it was pretty new. He'd be pensive for hours before the event, thinking about what he would say and doing a lot of research. He never had the sense that he already knew enough to give a talk.

So one day he was planning to give a talk in a few hours. We're looking out the back window of the Heyday offices in the Koerber Building, and he sees his car being towed away, probably from parking in the wrong place. I had my car that day, so I said, "I can give you a ride."

We were rushing to get him to BART so he could get to wherever he needed to be. We hurried to the elevator. I'm grabbing my keys out of my voluminous bag, and I drop my keys. Miraculously, they fall through the crack between the floor and the elevator door, all the way to the basement! The guy who was the superintendent in the building was this mysterious character that only manifested during full moons, so we had a hard time rousing him. The keys actually fell below the basement, so he had to use some kind of a magnetic picker-upper to get them.

Of course, by then Malcolm had gotten another ride to BART. It all turned out well in the end, but he laughed for a solid month over that. It was just great!

So his sense of humor goes back to what I was talking about before: there are some times when you just have to let go and be in the now. *That* was definitely one of those times.

PATRICIA WAKIDA

THE KOERBER BUILDING is remembered by many Heyday employees, past and present, for both the amazing views it provided on the top two floors and for its quirky facilities and fellow inmates. Patricia Wakida is a former employee of Heyday, as well as a Heyday author and board member.

The Koerber Building was the freakiest place, filled with weird characters, doors that were forever locked, and signs that said things like "The Time College," right out of a Berkeley sixties stereotype. All these custodial characters "helped" at the building, like Roscoe, who had gray shaggy mutton chops and long stringy hair. One guy walked around the halls wearing one of those ski masks covering his face. It was crazy scary. We called him the Ninja Guy. He was working for the building as a janitor, so he'd take the trash out, but he'd actually go through the trash.

A group for the mentally ill was in that building, but also the *Yoga Journal*—everybody! Upstairs was a woman who occasionally helped us with large bulk mailings; she wore huge flowered muumuu dresses and kept a parrot in her office. An older immigrant guy would try to sell you gold chains and watches in the lobby at a little table. He was a heavyset, Lebanese dude with a distinct accent. I guess he got someone to say he could sit in the very narrow lobby with a table to sell us stuff. It was such an old-country kind of thing. Everything in that building was just weird.

That said, the Koerber Building was a wonderful location with beautiful views through the tall windows of spectacular sunsets and storms raging, especially when we moved to the sixth floor and expanded.

Another thing that happened when we moved upstairs is that Malcolm purged the Heyday archives. He just went through his stuff one day and dumped it. The purging was a shock to us. "How was your weekend?"

"Oh, I just threw out all my shit."

I said, "Okay, but shouldn't you keep that and put it in the Bancroft Library or somewhere?"

Malcolm laughed and said, "Yeah, I think Kevin Starr is going to be really mad at me." He put up a *New Yorker* cartoon by his door for a long time, a picture of a stick-figure guy with a caption that said, "I got rid of all the excess in my life." It was funny. I think he just wanted to shed all the sentimental stuff, all the papers and history. He just didn't want it. He kind of bragged about the purging to everybody. He could watch the shock and the anger, then point to the cartoon.

MALCOLM: MORE KOERBER BUILDING MEMORIES

FOR YEARS, THE Koerber Building had been owned by this guy Richard Stancliff, an old hippie. It was all run-down. It had Roscoe, the maintenance man, who was a complete oddball, and Ninja Man, this guy who had a little office that he lived in. He paid a hundred dollars a month for this closet where he lived as his home. He'd wander the corridors at night. He had a beard and something around his head, like a shroud.

The first time I met him, I said, "Hi, how are you? My name is Malcolm."

He said, "Hello, how are you?" He couldn't speak much.

Then I met him again, and I said, "How are you doing?" but he couldn't respond. I met him a third time, and I said, "What's up?" He couldn't speak.

One day, he comes to me, and he says, "My mother just died."

I said, "Oh, I'm so sorry to hear it."

He said, "Yes, I had to tell you because you're the person I'm closest to."

The whole building was filled with strange people. It was my style.

The elevator kept breaking down. This incident was so ripe! Mary Jefferds was on the East Bay Regional Park District board of directors. She was a warrior for the environment, *warrior*! She fought everything. For years she fought the East Bay Regional Park District. Then when she got on the board, she still fought them. She wouldn't give up. When Heyday was still operating in the house, Mary Jefferds would come by. Jake as a little kid loved everybody, but for some reason, when he would see Mary Jefferds, his face would drop in horror and he'd shriek. You couldn't comfort him. I'd watch Mary come in the house, bracing herself for this rejection. So when we moved to the office, she said, "Thank god that I can now see you and I don't have to have this baby yelling at me."

Her first trip to the building, she went up in the elevator, and it got stuck for four hours.

The elevator was continually getting stuck, the heat wasn't working. It was run-down but low rent, and we had the whole top floor that we finally graduated to, with great views. I loved the place.

"IT WASN'T MAKING MONEY ANYHOW": HEYDAY BECOMES A NONPROFIT

"There is nothing that denial has not been able to get me through."

—MALCOLM MARGOLIN

OF HIS VARIED talents in developing Heyday, Malcolm readily admits that accounting was not one of them. Making beautiful books was his focus; "keeping the books" was not. Jeannine Gendar described Malcolm's management style as "loose," based on a "hippie ethos." This loose style has facilitated positive office relations at Heyday, vital in a business, but it can also contribute to making a business broke, "spectacularly" so in Malcolm's words.

Still, Malcolm has kept his publishing venture afloat when many bookstores and publishers have shut down altogether under the weight of social, technological, and economic changes affecting the book world. Why has Heyday persisted? In part, because of the significant publications and community activities that it helps produce. To insure that such cherished work continues, Heyday supporters transformed Heyday into a nonprofit organization committed to cultural creativity of all kinds, as Malcolm and friends explain.

MALCOLM: CLAPPERSTICK INSTITUTE

The place has always been broke in ways that are just utterly spectacular. If I were a different kind of person, I'd be alarmed. When my daughter, Sadie, came to work as our bookkeeper one year, she was shocked. She lifted the hood! None of the other kids had lifted the hood. She realized what a small motor it was, with few cylinders and most of them misfiring. In those days we kept our accounts on index cards in boxes. I remember she labeled one box "Big Scary Bills I Can't Deal With."

SADIE MARGOLIN COSTELLO

WHEN I WAS about twenty, I needed a job, and Malcolm brought me in to be the bookkeeper, but I had no idea how to balance a checkbook. It took me a while to wrap my head around the fundamental basics of what I was supposed to be doing. It was eye-opening to do the books. I remember going to his office one day and saying, terrified, "You raised us like this?!" There was no money! And tons of debts. It was a complete disaster. Huge checks would come in, and they were instantly soaked up by other things. Any ideas I had at the time of the stability you were supposed to have in order to raise a family were blown out of the water.

Heyday is basically a rogue, outlaw institution. People who are scrupulously obedient and follow rules don't create things like Heyday. Yet, as it's gotten bigger, it has to follow rules. It's the most interesting thing to watch evolve.

When it started, I simply owned Heyday—it was Heyday Books in the beginning—but it wasn't a corporate enterprise. I just filed the IRS Schedule C as the sole proprietor at the end of the year to show how much I made—or lost—each year. I finally decided to turn it into a nonprofit since it wasn't making money anyhow, and that would facilitate getting funds as an *official* nonprofit.

The process goes back to when we started *News from Native California* in particular, in 1987. John Kreidler over at the San Francisco Foundation said, "Why don't we give you some money to help with the magazine?" Of course I agreed! He gave us a couple thousand bucks, but he added, "You have to go through a fiscal receiver because you're not a nonprofit." So we went through Intersection for the Arts. The San Francisco Foundation would give them the grant; they'd deduct 10 percent for their service fee and give us the rest.

Then we started to get some other grants for the Indian stuff and for *News*. Intersection for the Arts was still serving as our fiscal receiver. I always thought of us as a commercial publisher selling books but needing a small subsidy to make things work. The more subsidies I got, the more books I did, and the more it allowed me to do books that were never going to make any money. We became more and more dependent on the foundations. We then started Friends of *News from Native California* to get support from individual donors. It got more and more complex.

Finally, I went to Tom Layton, who was head of the Wallace Alexander Gerbode Foundation. Tom Layton is like my Mycroft Holmes. When Sherlock would get into trouble, he'd go off to the club to consult with his brother, Mycroft. At crucial points in my life, I'd see Tom Layton.

So I went to Tom and said, "Hey, listen, we've got all this Indian stuff we're doing. We're getting grants and contributions, but we're running them through a fiscal receiver. It's just so complicated. More and more, the place is becoming a nonprofit, but I don't want to give up power to anybody." I'd been watching various friends who'd founded organizations, then turned them into nonprofits with a board of directors which eventually came in and fired the founders. I didn't want that to happen.

Tom said, "What you do is you keep control of Heyday and set up a separate 501(c)3 that will be like a Friends of Heyday. I'll give you a grant so you can go to the law firm of Silk, Adler, and Colvin." They're the big nonprofit-oriented lawyers. "With our grant, you can get the best legal advice in the world. Have them set you up as the *designator* of the board."

So off I went to Silk, Adler, and Colvin. They assigned me a wonderful attorney, Rosemary Fei, and we created something called Clapperstick Institute as a nonprofit arm of Heyday. That was in 1997. I was the board designator, meaning I could appoint board members and fire them at will. This approach was utterly perfect.

Then I got Bob Callahan, George Young, Lee Swenson, and Leanne Hinton to serve on the Clapperstick board, four close friends of mine, but they didn't know each other. I structured this thing so that nobody would have any power over me. It was interesting to figure out. The grant money would come into Clapperstick Institute, and then it would come over to Heyday. They were like a Friends of Heyday organization. I think Tom called it a "captive nonprofit."

Now I was head of both Clapperstick and Heyday, trying to keep track of the different funding and its uses. The head of Clapperstick would write letters to the head of Heyday: "Dear Malcolm," and sign them "Malcolm," in order to explain where the money was going, keeping a paper trail. It got ridiculous—I'm sitting there writing a letter to myself! I realized I was going to end up in jail.

And to be honest, I wasn't keeping good records. At the time, I'd hired Patricia Wakida to do the accounting. I thought she was utterly wonderful, but I neglected to ask whether she could add. She was so remarkably terrible at the accounting, it was epic. But there's a polymorphous creativity to Patricia, a tremendous engagement in life, a zest, a playfulness, an amazing fearlessness. How can you fire someone like that? She's such fun to be around! Eventually, I moved her into grant writing and development. Other executive directors create positions with job descriptions and look for people to fill them. I seem to find people and create jobs around their skills.

So we had board meetings once a year. Someone once wrote a delightful summation of a board meeting: "Malcolm and the four bozos got together and said they were all wonderful."

Clapperstick was a complete shambles. If a bill came due, I'd go to whichever account—Heyday or Clapperstick—had the money and pay them. I didn't see what the problem was. In the end, when I'd have to go to the accountant and sort out the taxes, it got really convoluted.

By this time I realized that the organization was functioning, in reality, as a nonprofit. So first I merged Clapperstick Institute with Heyday Books and created the nonprofit Heyday Institute around 2003, with a full board. Eventually we named the entity simply "Heyday." Kate Brumage, who worked for us for a while, did some branding. Lorraine Rath, our spectacular art director, created three acorns as our logo.

This was for me and for Heyday a major transformation. The previous Clapperstick board was no more than a legal necessity. But as time passed, I found myself coming around to the idea that we would benefit from an active board. I also came to understand that if I wanted to attract people who would take on responsibility, I'd have to give them the power that comes with responsibility. So I ceded my power as designator of the board, creating instead an independent board that would elect new members and

Art director Lorraine Rath decorating a wall in the Koerber Building on the occasion of Heyday's move to the sixth floor. (HEYDAY ARCHIVES)

would have the power—if they wanted to exercise it—to fire me or tell me what to do. By then I had just turned sixty. I found, to my surprise, that I was growing older, and I started to think about succession. What would happen if I were to retire or die? I felt a strong board would be a necessary part of that future.

I'm crafty rather than strategic or systematic. I'm really good at small schemes, at putting things together. When Heyday was small, I knew where all that money was going. I'd sit around and say, "It's the end of March. The rent and payroll are due on the first. Ingram owes us $3,000. Baker and Taylor owes us $2,000. And we ought to get another $6,000 from Amazon. I'll be able to pay the rent and meet the payroll." But by the year 2000, so many strands of income were coming in and going out that I couldn't keep track of it all. It needed a different level of accounting and oversight.

The board I recruited has been a wonderful asset. They raise money for us and give us stability. They do things for us. Sometimes it's painful, but I've needed them. We're too big to be managed by somebody who has no discipline, who is so emotional that he can't keep his act together for more than two hours without weeping, who has deep friendships and strong loyalties that often determine publishing priorities, and who is almost psychotically optimistic, who only sees how things can work and has no sense of a safety net. It means that other controls are difficult but necessary to impose.

So though I brought in a board as a *legal* necessity, over the years, the board has taken on a crucial function of support and guidance. We've currently got a great board of directors, the most skilled and talented people you could ask for. There's Guy Lampard, the president, who's a financial advisor. He's been so generous. Every time he gives us money and I thank him, he says he gets much more than he gives. Guy brought Rick Baum onto the board. He was the deputy insurance commissioner under Garamendi. He knows money, and he loves poetry. Then there's Marty Krasney, a wonderment! One of the smartest people I've ever met. He runs the Dalai Lama Fellows. He knows everyone in the Bay Area. He works hard; he's at ease with money. He also brings a freshness of insight.

This group of people knows how big structures work. They bring a core of expertise. Mike Traynor is a lawyer. He was active in the Bar and in civil liberties. His father was a California Supreme Court justice. Lisa Van Cleef is a marketing person with the Nature Conservancy. Of course, Patricia Wakida is a phenomenon. Sonia Torres is into fundraising and development. Nik Dehejia works for the Oakland Zoo, and Barbara Boucke was head of the fundraising effort for the de Young Museum when they did their expansion. I met her on the Yosemite Association board. And there's Theresa Harlan and Steve Costa, Katharine Livingston—each of them adds something special.

They come from such different places, so they cast a fresh eye on it all. Guy has pulled the board together into a strong force. They come to the board meetings with respect for me as a person and for what we're doing. There's such a tenderness to it all. I feel I'm bringing the car in to them for a tune-up and, every so often, for an overhaul. They don't go out riding in the car, but they really like the car! And they love that the car is going on such interesting trips. They live vicariously through the stories.

When Heyday finally became a successful nonprofit, I felt it had found its proper form. I don't care that much about money. I don't have that instinct for maximizing profit. I love what we do as a *cultural* enterprise. I love the effect that we've had. I love watching new manuscripts come in, how they're shaped and, in turn, how they shape the people that work on them. Then these books and publications go out and affect the way California thinks about itself. I just love what we do. Money is something that we need, and we've got to pay attention to it. But it's secondary. It's not at the top of my mind.

So Heyday functions well as a nonprofit educational institution. I feel much more comfortable in the nonprofit world than I do in the for-profit world. The whole business of business—I'm not good at it, and I don't care about it as much. I used to hang around publishers a whole lot, but I haven't seen one in a while. I hang around Indians; I hang around artists, writers, and ecologists. I can talk about literature and values, beauty and truth, and all that other stuff.

I love the events at the California Historical Society. Anthea Hartig is the director there now. She's alive, bright, fun to be with. We just hit it off. She amplifies. It's such a wonderful thing in this world to say something and instead of your statement being halved and coming back at you without arms and legs, it returns with so many arms and legs that it looks like a Hindu divinity. Anthea adds arms and legs to things! Since she took over the CHS, it's just been a party. We practically took over their store, we're cooperating on books. We have a contest now, the CHS Book Award, for a manuscript that deepens public understanding of some aspect of California history, and we publish it together. These are great prospects.

We have regular events over there, like when we celebrated the launch of the book we did with the San Francisco Arts Commission, called *San Francisco: Arts for the City, Civic Art and Urban Change, 1932–2012*. Putting together the book and the event involved a nonprofit historical society, a government agency, a couple of foundations, and a cast of writers, designers, photographers, and others, all serving the public, all together at the reception. Tom Layton was there from the Gerbode Foundation, Tere Romo from the San Francisco Foundation. Artists and photographers were circulating. I feel so at home with civic art. Someone made a wonderful statement that the purpose of art is to lessen the distance between people. If you're going to have a rich culture, having civic art is an absolute necessity, with arts and

Deborah Miranda with her book Bad Indians *at the Heyday Harvest celebration, California Historical Society, San Francisco, 2012.* (PHOTO BY YULIYA GOLDSHTEYN, HEYDAY ARCHIVES)

Joanne Campbell, blessing the Heyday Harvest celebration in her Coast Miwok language, and Malcolm Margolin, California Historical Society, San Francisco, 2012. (PHOTO BY YULIYA GOLDSHTEYN, HEYDAY ARCHIVES)

artists in different ways lessening the distance between people. Otherwise you end up having warring camps that don't relate to one another.

Just being part of that enterprise that bridges cultures and people, gets texts from authors to readers, art from artists into people's hearts—*this* is where I live.

Another good partnership is with Sierra College. It's a community college in Rocklin, east of Sacramento, with satellite campuses in Nevada City and Tahoe. They have an eclectic museum on campus and a Center for Sierra Studies, which supports the Sierra College Press. The first book we did together was *The Illuminated Landscape,* an anthology of Sierra literature, and we've gone on to publish other books as well as work with the college on increasing the visibility of local Indian tribes.

You know, this place, Heyday, exists on the kindness of the world. It exists on people who give me money to produce books. It exists on people who give me manuscripts to turn into books. I keep saying that if this were a dog-eat-dog world, I would have been eaten a long time ago.

GEORGE YOUNG

A CO-CONSPIRATOR WITH MALCOLM in the small press world dating from the early 1980s, George Young is also a veteran of large publishing operations. As a friend, consultant, ex-Heyday board member, and sales expert extraordinaire, George has been invaluable to Malcolm and to Heyday for over twenty-five years. He shares here the wisdom he has imparted to Malcolm and to Heyday from his own diverse experiences in the publishing world.

I was one of those perpetual students. I started college in 1953, puttered at the University of San Francisco for one year, then took night classes for several years. Finally, in 1957, I got a job in magazine circulation with Dell Publishing Company, which had this new thing called "paperback books." Nobody then knew that this was the beginning of the paperback revolution! Anchor Books and Vintage Books started about then, and Penguin expanded its paperbacks. Soon you had the mass market paperback and the quality paperback, which we now call the trade paperback. At that time, some paperback books were original, but most were reprints of hardcover books. I was lucky that I walked into it. I got to locate books in odd places, like bus stations, drugstores, cigar stores, and supermarkets.

In the early 1960s, wonderful new bookstores had opened up and very different books were coming out. I remember when the *Whole Earth Catalog* focused a lot of people's energy in 1968. It was the bible of the different ways people were thinking at the time. There was the Tides Bookstore over in Sausalito, City Lights in San Francisco, Kepler's in Palo Alto. I got my education in all those stores. Fred Cody of Cody's in Berkeley handled a few hardcover books, but at his store the paperback reigned. Those bookstores provided the soil in which this revolution was planted in the 1960s and early '70s. Then in the '70s, publishing bloomed, with Shambhala, Ten Speed, Heyday. Even the computer presses started around here with Osborne, Sybex, and O'Reilly.

I later worked for a large book distributor called Kable News Company. One of the publishers they distributed was Ballantine Books. I did a great job placing orders for Ballantine. The first day that Ballantine shipped its new books, sixteen thousand invoices, of eighteen or nineteen thousand total, were from me. Very soon after that, I met a man named Ian Ballantine! That was the beginning of a thirty- or forty-year mentorship with him. I was lucky to hook up with one of the founders of the whole game at the start of my career.

I was always a scout for Ballantine Books. Ballantine had the idea of starting regional publishing companies in paperback, so in the early sixties I became the regional publisher in the West for something that eventually became Comstock Editions. When the editor-in-chief left, they asked me if I'd like to move to New York and take over. Would I like to? Of course!

The idea was that some books are more successful in different parts of the country, but not really good nationally. Three or four predominant regions, particularly the South and the West, could support regional publishing, mostly with fiction and some nonfiction about the area, a lot of focus on history and a few guidebooks. Other people were already in the guidebook game, and sometimes they're better at them. The Comstock region was the whole West, not just California. Actually, Heyday has reprinted a couple of books that were Comstock's.

That time was magical for me, the high point of the paperback revolution in the sixties and seventies. At Ballantine, we had the Tolkien books. I brought in *The Teachings of Don Juan*. I did forty environmental books. They did many science fiction books, which readers had so much interest in during that period. And great literature, too. I was one of half a dozen young editors in New York who had this incredible tool called the mass market book, where you could get fifty to a hundred thousand copies out on every newsstand in America. We were incredibly free to do things at that point. On a smaller scale, in Northern California, or even more specifically the Bay Area, we could do magical stuff!

For about five years, I was in New York. I kept coming back a couple of times a year. Friends from here would send me ideas. I was very aware of the culture that was building here. That was one of the reasons I wanted to come back; I knew I'd fit in somewhere. Then I came West when my mother had a heart attack. While I was here for a couple of days, I saw an ad in the paper. It turned out to be from a friend of mine looking to hire somebody in a publishing company here. I talked to my family back east, and we all returned around 1974 or '75.

The new publishing scene developing here at that time was exciting. For a year and a half or so, I ran a company called Celestial Arts that published New Age books before there was a New Age. Then I peeled off from there and started consulting with smaller groups that were expanding. Ten Speed was one of my first clients; Friends of the Earth was another, along with the *San Francisco Examiner* and a bunch of others. I soon realized I was so focused on Ten Speed that I didn't have anybody else. I told the publisher, "I'm here five days a week. I think I work here!" So he hired me. I became the vice president at Ten Speed for about ten years. Ten Speed developed based on its first book, *Anybody's Bike Book,* the first one about ten-speed bikes. After the bicycle books, they published cookbooks and how-to books. They started with the memorable books *The Moosewood Cookbook* and *What Color Is Your Parachute?*

At the time, Malcolm was interested in buying some bicycle trail guides from us that he could sell to bicycle shops where he was distributing other books through the Book Camel. Malcolm admired our craziness and our marketing prowess at getting books out. The first time we sat down together, we met up in a café. We each had a dozen things to do, but we decided to talk for a little while. Well, three or four hours later, we both looked up! We just had so much to talk about in relation to our experiences and questions, publishing, writing, authors, ideas. After that we had lunch from time to time, which were mostly about "How do you *do* that?" I always knew he was going to put together something worthwhile and good. We stayed in touch. Over time, as Ten Speed grew, so did Heyday. I think he was very much in the small press world then, but gradually moving over into something bigger.

Later, I became one of the first board members of his nonprofit arm Clapperstick, in 1997. During the first few years when I was on the board, in describing me in public, Malcolm would say, "George showed up to help us figure out how to do things in a large organization because he knows how. I don't have a clue." I've been a consultant for almost half of my publishing career. I've worked with about twenty-five smaller or medium-sized publishers, as well as three or four large ones, so I'm very familiar with the dynamics of a smaller organization, how to get them moving along and not get bogged down in the development process.

That was very important for Heyday. Get things in line so that the book you said you'd have in January, you'll actually have in January, which wasn't always the case. It wasn't unique to Heyday. Just about every smaller publisher I worked with had the same problem.

A lot of the process during those first years at Heyday was about making a transition from doing things free-form, where the attitude was "Maybe we'll make it, maybe we won't." No! If you're going to build an organization that's going to stick around for a while, you've *got* to do what you say you're going to do, when you say you're going to do it, and put the bells and whistles together so they all work in tandem. That took four or five years, part of a process of natural growth.

I always thought Heyday had the capacity to do more books. When I got here, Heyday was doing maybe eight or ten books a year, then gradually crept up to fifteen, and now we do about twenty-five. Eventually you find equilibrium between imagination, energy, and the right number of people. That's probably about where we're going to stay.

That was what the board focused on for the first five years. The last ten years have been about building and perfecting, improving and expanding, paddling harder. The problem is that everyone wants to grow, and that's natural, but then things get more complicated. You have more people, more to work out in a different ways, and sometimes you get bogged down in the management of things. So you have to develop processes that allow you to keep the old spirit while keeping solvent.

I still fill in wherever the need is. I'm older than Malcolm! I do this not because of the fabulous income as a volunteer but because I love it. They let me come and play, so I'll come and play as long as I can.

PATRICIA WAKIDA

ATRICIA WAKIDA STARTED to work at Heyday in 1999 and stayed until 2005, when she took on other roles as author and, eventually, Heyday board member. Here she explains how her own career trajectory intersected with Heyday as the company was transforming in the years of the shift to nonprofit status.

I'm from a Navy family, so we moved from San Diego to Honolulu and ended up in Fresno, where my father was based at the naval air station in Lemoore, an area where both my mom and dad grew up. I went to Mills from 1988 to 1992, including during the Mills student strike of 1992 to remain a single-sex college, which was really exciting for me. I think that's where I got the understanding that the strongest vote is going to come from wherever the money is.

After I graduated, I was put on the board of directors for the Mills College Alumnae Association. That was my first experience with boards and fundraising. After some short-term jobs, I went to Japan for four years. I did my whole roots thing there and studied Japanese. While there, I met Stephan Kohler, a German artist and papermaker, in the mountains of Gifu. He offered me a job, so I worked for him and made a ton of paper. It struck me one day when he told me that paper is really all water, and that water is very conducive to reflecting light. So when you're working with paper, what you're really seeing is the reflection of light. Ink is the shadow of the text that you're trying to lay down. That was the moment I realized it was time for me to come back to California!

I found a new apprenticeship with a bookbinder and letterpress printer called the Arts and Crafts Press in Berkeley. I was also volunteering at the San Francisco Center for the Book, a book arts program. So I was immersed in paper and books all around. I found the whole publishing world intriguing.

I was doing that work when I saw the job opening for Heyday in 1999. I interviewed with Malcolm and Amy Hunter, who was director of sales and marketing at the time. Amy and I discovered that she and I had both taught English in Japan. We had a really funny conversation at the interview. She told a story about how everybody around her neighborhood thought she was so weird because she was the white *gaijin* girl. She said,

"They always thought I was so stupid and clumsy because I'd do all these things wrong. One day I was in the bathroom—" A lot of homes in Japan still don't have flushing toilets; they're just pit toilets. Amy had somehow dropped the lid to her teapot into the toilet.

She said, "They must have thought, 'Oh, that crazy foreigner,' when they cleaned it out."

I'd just met this woman, but I said, "No, they probably thought, 'My god, what is she eating?!'" Malcolm laughed so hard. I hoped that the fact that I could make him laugh was a good sign.

So I got the job at Heyday, which was for accounting and development, but also to help run the California Poetry Series, a new collaboration that Heyday was starting with Joyce Jenkins of *Poetry Flash*. And we were experimenting with the nonprofit arm of Heyday, Clapperstick.

My experience was like that of a lot of people who've worked at Heyday: you charm your way in the door, then they adjust to what your *real* strengths are and figure out what you're really going to do. What's both challenging and interesting at Heyday is that Malcolm tends to hire young people who don't have a lot of experience or skill in a particular area, but he sees the potential and is willing to work with them. That means a burden falls on Malcolm to sustain the business with new learners and make it into a smoothly running machine. Usually it works.

As for me, I was not great at accounting. I sucked at it, actually. And while I was there, the business grew exponentially. As development grew and we were moving into nonprofit status, Malcolm needed more assistance in that area. Eventually we found a real accountant, Janice Woo, while Malcolm put me on development duty, which we hoped would pay for my salary—like, "Why am I still here?"

Eventually, we got a full-time CFO, which has been David Isaacson for a long time now. What's interesting is that before I took on the accounting, Malcolm's daughter, Sadie, was doing it. It was not exactly a super sophisticated system at that point. Sadie would come in once a week and go through the bills. She had an index card system in a box. I think I remember a drawing with clouds on it that said something like "This is where we look occasionally to see what the future might be, but we don't really know what the future will be." That was where our accounting system was stored!

Anyhow, the project management I was good at. It was challenging to pull together the poetry series from the ground up. The idea was that you would subscribe to the California Poetry Series, and you'd get a book every six months or something. I think we did six books total before the money ran out. Working with Joyce was fantastic. It plunged me into poetry, which Heyday does not get to do regularly, then or now.

The development position got more interesting over time. I was officially an employee of Clapperstick Institute, and everyone else worked for Heyday. It was named "Clapperstick" after the traditional Native American percussive instrument made of a split elderberry branch and used by California Indians to make music and keep the rhythm at dances and ceremonies. The name was symbolic because the clapperstick sets the pace of the dance and contributes to the unity of the participants.

By 2000, we decided that we should build a full board, not just the four "Friends of Malcolm." We were writing grants, trying to figure out if we could create a membership. Eventually, we sought the creation of a whole new identity for Heyday, new ways to get worms for the birds that were forever hatching, as we would describe it.

With the complete change to nonprofit status, we were finally able to go for larger and larger grants. The new funds coming in helped us grow beyond the six of us or so in the office (besides Malcolm) when I first started, which was Amy Hunter, Janice Woo, the receptionist David (not David Isaacson, later our finances guy), Rebecca LeGates, who did design, and Jeannine Gendar, who was editing *News from Native California*. Rina came in sometimes to do proofreading and editing for *News* and for some books. And of course, there was George Young, our publishing guru! By the time I left in 2005, the office staff had grown to about twelve people.

So the grants allowed us to have this capaciousness of titles and to think on a bigger scale. For the first time we could do large-format color art books. Malcolm had done a few anthologies, but we really got into doing a lot more anthologies. We had a spurt of growth, from doing only small projects closer to home that were coming through the door, mostly from Malcolm's friends and associates, to the point where we were approaching museums, libraries, archives, and other organizations, along with new people—absolute strangers sometimes—who were walking in the door with really magnificent ideas.

A good example would be Tom Killion and Gary Snyder's book *The High Sierra of California*. Tom had done this book as a letterpress edition, completely hand-printed originally, and he wanted to reissue it through trade publishing. We joked that it was like taking the most gorgeous thing possible and making it uglier. But the fact that people were approaching Heyday at that point said a lot.

We were also able to have more space. We moved to the top floor of the Koerber Building from the fourth floor. We had a main room with four desks, and a little conference room to the side. Malcolm's separate office was right by the entrance. The accountant, Janice, and I had our backs to each other. I was always on the phone on development, so I'd say, "I'm sorry, Janice. I know I'm so loud!" I thought she was great for tolerating me.

A couple more small offices were off that room for Jeannine and Rebecca and Amy; they could shut the door if we were a pain in the ass. Before we got a real receptionist, we all took turns answering the phone when it rang. It was like chicken: Who's going to pick it up? Are you going to pick it up? Amy Hunter was the only one in the office who had email capacity on her computer, so when she went to lunch, we'd sneak into her room and check our email and then run away. We were pretty low-profile— and it wasn't that long ago! Malcolm was coming in at four or five in the morning and typing up these little notes. Whenever you came in, your box would be stuffed with them.

NOTES AND MEMOS FROM **MALCOLM**

PATRICIA WAKIDA INTRODUCED a topic that arises often among Heyday staff and friends: that is, the notes and letters that Malcolm has written over the years, his personal newsletters of ideas bursting nearly uncensored from his fertile imagination, notes of gratitude for gorgeous books produced, letters of thanks for gifts rendered to Heyday, memos working out the latest configuration of scheduling or a structural change.

1.

[No date, like most of Malcolm's memos for staff, but probably around 2001, when *Shades of California: The Hidden Beauty of Ordinary Life* came out]

To Patty/Kimi/Laura/Jeannine, cc. Dave Bullen

I came in this morning (Saturday, early) and found the finished copy of *Shades* waiting for me.

I have often talked about how I love the process of putting books together: watching a team develop, seeing problems solved, witnessing how beautiful people become as they rise to meet challenges and take advantage of opening doors. I love also the social aftermath: the reviews, readings, receptions, and social and emotional consequences of having done a good book. But I have little interest in the book itself. I think often of the quote from William James: "What really exists is not things made but things in the making. Once made, they are dead."

This is something of an overstatement. I do take interest and pride in the physical book. But in this particular case, it's not just an overstatement but an outright lie. I can't take my eyes off this book. I can't stop opening it and turning the pages. I put it down, try to get back to work, but within five minutes I'm thumbing through it again.

My congratulations to you all. This is a very great thing you did: warm-hearted, intelligent, moving, filled with quiet integrity and a very sweet kind of playfulness.

Thanks,

Mal

2.

[No date, around early 2005]

Everyone

This is a brief note of reflection and gratitude. We seem to be in an absolutely terrific place. I find myself coming to work with a sense of deep joy and pride in what we've done. I hope others do as well.

Mal

3.

[No date but probably mid-2005. This excerpt is from a longer memo, one containing a recurring theme found in the Heyday archives of Malcolm's communiqués with staff about the larger context of their work. After reporting on relevant facts and statistics in recent news, he adds his thoughts, which are indicative of his constant efforts to keep Heyday healthy.]

Thoughts on the State of the Publishing Industry

If the industry as a whole is ailing, and with little hope of recovery, we need to be wary of our dependence on it. In other words we have long questioned the viability of doing a book on speculation and putting it out into bookstores, promoting it in the conventional ways, and expecting a return sufficient to cover costs and show profit. I think our way of going about things with partners and programming and more unconventional sales and marketing is probably the only way to go. I also imagine that our nonprofit cultural institution with support from individuals and from foundations and other institutions will be increasingly necessary and beneficial in the future.

...If we remain relatively stable and robust while others around us falter, we can expect some extraordinary opportunities in the next few years. I don't look forward to this, by the way: I'd much rather be a lean predator among many in a healthy environment than a scavenger in a decaying environment. But I think we should be seeing some exceptional possibilities before long.

TOM LAYTON

TOM LAYTON IS president of the Wallace Alexander Gerbode Foundation in San Francisco, which helps fund organizations with visionary leaders working for conservation, civil rights, and the arts, among other concerns. As Malcolm indicated, Tom played a crucial role in helping Malcolm transform Heyday into a nonprofit organization, while protecting his emotional investment in the company he had so lovingly started. Tom's initial interest in Malcolm's work as a writer and publisher grew into his commitment to establishing a new vision of Heyday through Gerbode, as he said, "helping with the legal costs and strategies around the transition, and pulling people together to support Heyday."

I knew about Malcolm because I'd read *The Ohlone Way*, which made a big impression on me. I thought the book was terrific. I learned a lot about the history of this region and the indigenous people here. Then I continued to follow Heyday's publications. At some point I heard Malcolm speak. Probably like everybody else, I was completely captivated and remained captivated when I finally did meet him.

Malcolm is a force of nature: his presentation, his use of language, how he makes images and stories come alive. I've heard him speak many times now, and he's always fascinating. Some years ago I was involved in planning an environmental grant makers' conference in Asilomar down by Monterey Bay. We had two opening speakers, Alice Waters and Malcolm. Malcolm painted a visual picture with words of what the bay looked like before the Spaniards and the rest of us showed up. Everybody loved it. It was classic Malcolm; he was the perfect person to set the stage and to give us a sense of place.

We got involved with Heyday when we received an application from them, via their fiscal sponsor, regarding funds, first to start Clapperstick as a nonprofit arm in 1997, then again a few years later to make this transition from a for-profit to a nonprofit, around 2002 or so. We paid the legal costs. It was never a huge sum of money, but enough to get good advice.

It seemed to me that if Heyday were to raise substantial philanthropic dollars, it needed a vehicle and governance structure that were clear to everybody—unlike the connections to Clapperstick at the time. In the case of Clapperstick, being a "captive" fiscal sponsor that was related was just too unclear, as was the understanding of how funds moved back and forth. So that required turning Heyday into a nonprofit altogether. A number of publishers have done this, basically running nonprofits without nonprofit structures. They changed over when they couldn't bring in adequate funds through sales or through indirect donations.

As Malcolm and I talked, it seemed to us both that a simple, straightforward vehicle would be the best way to go. Of course, it involved some risk in Malcolm giving up some *de facto* and *de jure* control, trusting his "child" to a nonprofit board that he didn't control. I'm not sure he really felt he had a great choice. If he wanted to raise a substantial amount of capital, he needed a nonprofit which controlled the publishing entity. Foundation funders want to see control vested in a board of directors. They're uncomfortable moving funds from a nonprofit to a for-profit business, regardless of the public benefit.

I think Malcolm got good advice all the way through, including from his board. Of course, he picked them, but that doesn't mean that there's no other "risk."

The Gerbode Foundation is generally not in the business of supporting publications or publishers, but the reason why we supported Heyday was Malcolm. Malcolm seemed to us to be an artist and educator who was principally focusing on real issues and concerns, on histories and context and cultures, all of which interested us. So we didn't see it exactly as supporting a publishing venture; we saw it as supporting a very important public educator and public intellectual.

Malcolm has helped Heyday survive by personally making important collaborations happen. He inspires extraordinary confidence in everybody, including funders. It's his vision, his integrity, his charisma, his eye, his use of language. Malcolm is clearly the world's best letter writer. I know people who don't generally save letters, but they save *Malcolm's* letters. They're wonderful. With a few words, Malcolm can make a personal connection on a piece of paper unlike anybody I've ever known.

I wish that we could have done more for Malcolm than we have, in terms of more significant funds. Unfortunately, like many funders, I work within a set of guidelines and rules. I remember conversations with Malcolm about my being both a funder and a groupie. He's been one of the very few people I feel I've been able to talk with candidly about the frustrations that come with my job. Then he was worried about me! I was worried about Malcolm, and he was worried about me. That says so much.

MICHAEL MCCONE

IKE EXPLAINS HOW his friendship with Malcolm took off when he was the executive director of the California Historical Society. Later, at Malcolm's behest, Mike joined the full Heyday board when it began in 2003, chairing it for many years. In his vital role as board member and friend, Mike put his years of expertise with administration and fundraising into shaping Malcolm's thoughts about how this small organization could stay solvent and effective.

I started working for the California Historical Society in 1990. I got to know Malcolm in the early 1990s. He and someone else at Heyday came to the Historical Society with a suggestion to copublish a book about a young white boy whose family came to the Central Valley and left him with Indians, so the boy grew up in that milieu. It's called *Indian Summer*. I said that that partnership sounded pretty good. That book was followed by three or four others we did jointly.

When I met Malcolm, we immediately hit it off. I like to think that I'm a very open person, but Malcolm was not like anybody I'd ever known before! He reminded me of a Hasidic Jew that I'd seen on the streets or like John Muir with a really full beard. I liked him right away because he was so straightforward. I believed in Malcolm. I had an instantly positive reaction to him. Both fortunately and unfortunately, I make quick decisions about people. But with Malcolm it was just a positive visceral reaction to him, which a lot of people have when they meet him.

I also love books. I'm a history buff; I'm really an amateur, but I read a lot. I think world history in the 1920s and '30s is the most fascinating time to read about. Anyhow, talking about books and history, Malcolm and I got along fine, and we still do.

I picked up right away that Malcolm was *somebody* and that he produced a good product. I was also in a position to respond to him positively. So I would give him two or three or four thousand dollars from the Historical Society for a book, and then the society's name would be on the spine or inside. I thought that was a good deal because it got our name out there.

My own background was to be an itinerant administrator and a generalist with no known skills. I had spent most of my life in nonprofits as an administrator or trying to raise money. I graduated from Yale University in 1956, went into the Navy for two years, then worked on the waterfront for a stevedore company. When John Kennedy got elected, he touted public service: "Ask not what your country can do for you; ask what you can do

Mike McCone and Malcolm Margolin on University Avenue in Berkeley, 2012.
(HEYDAY ARCHIVES)

for your country." Like a lot of people, I said, "That's for me." I wanted to go into the Peace Corps. I had two kids by that time, so I applied for a staff job. For two years I was in Freetown, Sierra Leone, where my youngest son was born in 1962.

The Peace Corps experience really turned me on to thinking of my life as an adventure. Of course, I never made very much money, but I've had a hell of a good time, and I've enjoyed serving people. Sargent Shriver, who was directing the Peace Corps at the time, was an incredible human being and was also my inspiration for thinking about a life of service, after listening to him talk about what service meant. In the Peace Corps, I made a lot of great friends and went all over the place: Malawi, Borneo, a year in Washington.

When I came back to San Francisco, I worked for Mayor Joseph Alioto, as his appointment secretary. After that stint, I became the head of the Model Cities program, a federal poverty program, working in Bayview–Hunter's Point and the Mission District. Then I got a call from a man named

William Matson Roth, who was on the board of the San Francisco Museum of Modern Art. He said, "What do you know about modern art?"

I thought for a minute and said, "I like it." I ended up as the deputy director, doing administration and fundraising for SFMOMA. After thirteen years, I did the same thing at Grace Cathedral, then John F. Kennedy University, and eventually the Historical Society. In 1990 a woman from a search firm found me and asked, "What do you think about putting your name forward to be the executive director of the California Historical Society?"

I said, "Well, I'll tell you right out that I'm neither a historian nor a scholar."

She said, "They don't want either of those."

"Okay then!" I replied. They *did* want an administrator and fundraiser because they were really on the skids. When I took over the Historical Society, it was struggling, and its reputation was down. I was hearing "What's happened to it? Is it still alive?" I said to the staff, "You're going to enjoy my benign neglect because I've got to get on my bicycle and pedal around and talk to people." When I did talk to people, they had a good opinion of the organization. The money came back in. By the time I left, they had about two hundred thousand dollars in the bank, which itself was historic.

I retired from the Historical Society in 1999 at age sixty-five. A couple of years after that, Malcolm said, "I'm putting together a board of directors so that Heyday can become a *real* nonprofit. I want you to be on the board." Not only did he talk me into being on the board, but he hoodwinked me into being the chair of the board for many years. In early 2011, I stepped down as chair, but I stayed on the board until my time limit ran out at the end of 2012.

When Malcolm asked me to be on the Heyday board, I thought it would be interesting because I know a lot about boards and what it takes to be a supportive board member. I remember saying to Malcolm, "One thing I'll really work on with you is to keep the board out of your hair."

But he said, "Wait a minute! I *want* more people communicating with me, helping with this."

When I came on board, I had a lot of experience, including having served on boards with Evelyn Haas, the Laskys, and other big hitters, so I

LETTER FROM MALCOLM TO MIKE

September 2, 2012

Dear Mike:

YOUR GENEROSITY, MIKE, has long outstripped my capacities to acknowledge. It's not so much a limitation of feeling, more a limitation of language. English offers just so many ways to say "thank you," and I seem to have run through them all. Yet your generosity continues. Your friendship, financial contributions, leadership, wisdom, and presence flow like a great river through the fields of Heyday, irrigating the crops and nourishing the inhabitants on a daily basis. I love sharing the joyful aspects of Heyday, and when things are rough I take great comfort in your presence.

You have been a friend and mentor, older by a few years and further along in our exploration of what lies ahead. Your grace in letting go while staying involved is for me a revelation. When my time comes, I feel I'll be able to walk onto the stage with a sense of what the role demands of me, and I only hope that I can play it with the deep wisdom, humor, and kindliness that you have shown.

Warmest regards,

Malcolm

---

suggested we get people that give credence to the enterprise. We recruited Lynne Withey, who was the executive director of UC Press and also a great friend of Malcolm's. Then there was Guy Lampard, a new friend of mine through his wife and my friend Charlene Harvey. Guy was a real go-getter, adept in the world of finance. He later became the Heyday board chair.

Anyplace I went, I watched the budget. If you run an organization and you come up with some crazy idea, you can probably sell it, but not if you're a nickel over. So I always found somebody who could both do the numbers on behalf of the board and work with whoever handled the accounts internally. In this case, I recruited a friend named Peter Dunckel, who worked for Zellerbach Paper Company. This was one of the best decisions I ever made for Heyday. Where we're really struggling with the future of a small publishing company, having such expertise has been tremendous.

LETTER FROM MALCOLM TO PETER AND JEANETTE DUNCKEL

Peter Dunckel served on the Heyday board as the treasurer.

June 19, 2010

Dear Peter and Jeanette:

I'M ONCE AGAIN truly touched and honored by your generosity—by the meaningful gift of money and the approval and applause that the gift suggests.

For years, I've managed Heyday by leaning on my secret companion who has faithfully stood at my side, leading me and advising me, governing my every action, responsible in large part for Heyday's growth. I think you've probably noticed him in the room with me at various times. It's my dear friend Captain Denial, a man of superhuman powers, capable of making problems disappear by refusing to see them, able to invent opportunity where there is none.

"Who's this guy Peter?" he asked suspiciously when he first met you.

"Don't worry about him, Captain," I replied. "He's a busy man, distractible. You can charm him the way you've been able to charm others."

But you weren't that easy, Peter, and I acknowledge the great generosity of spirit with which you rose up to do battle with Captain Denial.

The other day I conferred with Captain Denial, and the conversation turned to you. "You know, Malcolm," he said, "you're going to live forever, and that's why you need Peter in your life."

And so I do, dear friend, so I do.

Thanks for everything. I'm genuinely and deeply appreciative.

Guy started an executive committee, on which we put the then new Heyday development director, Marilee Enge, and Gayle Wattawa, the editorial director, who's been around several years and is made of pure gold. I have a story about Gayle. Two board members said to Malcolm, "You've got to have an executive editor who's able to make decisions. You've got to slide some of this stuff off, all this work you're doing."

Malcolm thought that was a good idea, so he made Gayle executive editor. We were always wondering how any shift in responsibilities was working out, so I asked him a couple of months later, "How's it going with Gayle?"

He said, "Well, I'll tell you a story. I got a manuscript in from a friend of mine. I sent it over to Gayle, and I said, 'Take a look at this. I think it's pretty good, and he's a friend of mine.' Gayle wrote back and said, 'I've read it, but I don't think it fits our deal.'"

So Malcolm wrote her back and said, "Well, take another look at it." Then she wrote back and said, "I'll take another look at it, but I'm not going to change my mind." Malcolm and I both laughed.

Malcolm is an extraordinary human being. It's fun to work with him. I remember one time we were going to meet someone from a Sacramento publishing family at the Bohemian Club in San Francisco. I told Malcolm that I thought he should wear a tie. If you know Malcolm, you know he never wears a tie, but he was open-minded. He said, "Okay."

We had the lunch, and then we walked out. It was kind of a cold day. Malcolm noted, "Mike, look, I wore the tie, but because it was cold, I wore a sweater, so between my beard and the sweater, nobody knew that I had a tie on." Those kinds of things endear him to people. He's funny.

He tells great, wonderful stories. I remember when he was accepting an award from the Bancroft Library. In his acceptance speech he said, "When I first came to California, I arrived in my Volkswagen bus with my wife. We stopped on a hill overlooking San Francisco Bay. I said to Rina, 'If we have children, and I hope we do, I want them to grow up here. And if we succeed, and I hope we do, I want to succeed right *here*.' We continued on our trip. Two days later I realized I was overlooking Vallejo."

I do not associate the word "retire" with Malcolm because this is his life. He loves his family—his wife, three wonderful children, and several grandchildren—but I'll call Saturday morning and here he is. Malcolm told me recently a story about a big payment that Heyday had to make. He'd said at a staff meeting that he was going to take his money out of his retirement account. Someone at the meeting said, "What is your wife going to say?"

He said, "I'll tell you a story about my wife, Rina. Not long ago, Heyday was having its usual financial crisis, and I came to her and said, 'Things are rough, money is tight, and we'll need to cut back. But things will get better in a few months, and we'll be all right.'"

Malcolm said, "She responded, 'There are two remarkable things about that statement. One is that you've been saying that for thirty years now. The other is that I still believe you.'"

LEE SWENSON

A S A FELLOW seeker in the realm of cultural exploration and social justice struggles, Lee Swenson became a close friend to Malcolm and the rest of the Margolin family. Lee was among the first people Malcolm asked to form a board in 1997 for the nonprofit Clapperstick Institute. Lee later joined the board of Heyday when it changed into a nonprofit altogether. Lee shares his insights into Heyday's development, as well as stories of his travels with Malcolm and family, both real and metaphoric.

I met Malcolm in 1982 through Peter Nabokov, an old friend doing California American Indian studies. We immediately became friends. Malcolm was so sweet and generous. He offered me whatever Heyday could do to help with the projects I was doing, public events and gatherings. We evolved into doing a tremendous amount together, including traveling. When he switched to a nonprofit, I was engaged in that dialogue and helped as part of the original tiny board. Now he has a fabulous board, one of the best I've seen. So it's been a total mix of friendship and travel and more together for years.

I grew up in El Sobrante, just over the hill from Berkeley, and joined a fabulous wild gang of mountaineering and early rock climbing folks in high school. I then wound up at Stanford. I'd already been reading a lot about nonviolence, anarchism, and socialism as a kid. In 1959 in Palo Alto I met a great nonviolent community through Roy Kepler, who had Kepler's Books. His memoir, *Radical Chapters*, is beautiful. The cover has a photo that shows Roy sitting in the streets of Oakland for a protest. I later went to jail with Roy. He was a wonderful guy.

After college, I taught at the Peninsula School, a superb old radical, anarchist, Jewish, but mainly Quaker place in Menlo Park, started by an amazing woman, Josephine Duveneck. I taught there for four years while I was doing draft resistance. Then I moved to East Palo Alto and directed daycare and preschool programs for three years, a young radical white kid in a tough black community. Later I decided to travel in South America, Europe, and Africa. But many people were going to prison for draft resistance. So I turned around and came home.

The first day I arrived, I got together with Joan Baez and David Harris, her husband, who was doing a big talk. They said, "Let's move the Institute for the Study of Nonviolence from Carmel Valley to Palo Alto." So we did. For the next seven to eight years, I was the director, during the time when a lot of young men were going to prison for draft and war tax resistance.

That organization closed up in 1975 at the end of the war. Then I became the editor of a Quaker newsletter called *Simple Living*. Next the Farallon Institute asked me to become their executive director, which I did from '78 to '81. Around then, I got involved with the philosopher Ivan Illich, and soon met my wife, Vijaya Nagarajan, here in Berkeley in '82 when Ivan came to do his gender lectures. I fell in love with Viji; we had a great courtship, and we've been together thirty years. That's when I finally moved to Berkeley.

I met Malcolm at that time because I was doing an American Indian art slide show, which I still present. When I'd been the director of the Farallon Institute, I'd travel a lot, and I began seeing all this wonderful art that people were doing, but few people knew much about it. So I slowly gathered up information. Through that process, I got close to Peter Nabokov. He's a genius. Then, when I walked into Malcolm's office, we also had a great time and immediately started doing things. I'd been interested in his work all along. I feel *The Ohlone Way* was a very important book and still is, especially for kids like me who grew up here in the Bay Area.

Viji had helped start the nonprofit Institute for the Study of Natural and Cultural Resources. Our main goal was to do community education with Illich and others. We also put on gatherings of people since there were all these great people in Berkeley we were getting to know but hadn't spent much time with. Viji had the idea of doing a luncheon every other

Wednesday. We invited Malcolm, Susan Griffin, Bob Hass, and Candace Falk from the Emma Goldman project, a great Berkeley gang. We jokingly called it the people we want to grow old with in Berkeley.

Malcolm was fabulous in those gatherings. He brought in Chick Callenbach and a lot of other old friends of his. He was helpful and catalytic as a friend coming to those events, which got us much more engaged with this group. He's a very good listener of other people and a really good storyteller.

I was often in dialogue with Malcolm about the nonprofit concept. He was always struggling, trying to keep the business together. Around 1996 or so, Vijaya and I were doing a lot of community support activities, and Malcolm would help get things printed. Alice Waters was a friend here in Berkeley. From time to time she'd give Vijaya and me a free luncheon for eight at her Chez Panisse café, to help our organizing activities. So we thought, "Let's do a meeting for Malcolm and talk about the nonprofit world." Tom Layton, a very smart guy from the Gerbode Foundation, came. So did Paul Hawken and another friend, Lexi Rome. I think we raised six thousand dollars at this luncheon to support Heyday.

Immediately, Heyday folks went out and bought new computers to have the newest design and communications elements. I'd focused on that because I could see the staff needed them when the Heyday folks did a little book I wrote called *Field of Stones*, about my own family history and the story of Norwegians and Swedes coming to Minnesota and then California. The Heyday staff had been using old computers with little screens, so it was just impossible to do layout and work well. Getting computers was a great use of the money we'd raised and a real boost for them thinking bigger. It also helped catalyze thinking about what a nonprofit could do with help from these kinds of people. Basically, they'd always been oriented toward book sales, which is fragile.

At the time, though, Malcolm was still scared about changing over. He'd heard horror stories of founders creating a business or nonprofit and getting a board of directors, only to watch the board take over and run its own show. A small slice of the nonprofit world may behave that way, so it's a little real but also a myth. Anyhow, Malcolm started small with the Clapperstick Institute as a separate arm. Then he saw how complicated that got. How do you sell books over here and get money for that over there?

We kept saying, "Malcolm, it's going to be okay. You'll survive." My whole world has been about working with nonprofits and fundraising, so I felt confident.

Money issues were especially painful for Malcolm. At least he had some strong financially oriented people to help him deal with it. Mike McCone came in with a lot of amazing professionalism. I remember those board meetings were very difficult for Malcolm. Afterwards, we'd go have a drink; he'd feel low, with people beating on him to shape up, that it was his responsibility to put the accounts together and make transparent what was going on. Everyone was looking critically at his budget and analysis. It was a sobering time for Malcolm.

Then along comes the stupid recession! Everyone on staff took a voluntary 10 percent pay reduction when they were already making little enough money. *That* was tough.

So Malcolm has had growth pains going from his own business and being responsible for himself to becoming this nonprofit. I remember meeting his mother and father once at Malcolm and Rina's small apartment, sitting around the kitchen table. His father was a businessman himself, and clearly Malcolm had gained a lot of business savvy from his father, but he ran a business his own way. He's built up a great staff of loyal people, like Jeannine Gendar and Rebecca LeGates. I remember when Rebecca didn't know how to do layout or design, but what she's grown to!

In fact, all of Heyday has grown and solidified. A kind of catalytic energy comes through Heyday. A tremendous amount of hands-on labor goes into nurturing each book, each hand-tailored. Then when they give birth to get the book into the world, they keep nurturing it. This is why Heyday and Malcolm are treasured.

One thing to add about Malcolm is the awards that he has gotten, like the Lannan Cultural Freedom Award in 2008. I think he'd just won a San Francisco Foundation award for $10,000. Then he got the Lannan Foundation Award right after that. They give these Lifetime Achievement

The Margolins at the San Francisco Foundation Community Leadership Awards, 2008. Left to right: Rina Margolin, Malcolm Margolin, Sadie Margolin Costello, Reuben Margolin, Josh Costello. (HEYDAY ARCHIVES)

Awards, $150,000—a great thing, enormous! It was the whole basis for Malcolm's retirement. He's never even bought a home for him and his family. He put Heyday first.

FRANCES PHILLIPS

FRANCES PHILLIPS IS the program director for the arts at the Walter and Elise Haas Fund, and director of the Creative Work Fund. Her friendship with Malcolm led Frances to help sponsor Heyday, first through the Intersection for the Arts, and more recently at the Haas Fund. Her perspectives on how Malcolm and Heyday are viewed in the foundation world shed light on the unique place that Heyday has as both publisher and cultural institution, itself a foundation for so many important creative projects.

In the mid-1990s, I was the executive director for the Intersection for the Arts. The late visual artist Ann Chamberlain approached Intersection about doing a project that would trace different communities' paths of immigration through San Francisco. Her idea was to create these maps with some oral history on them and post them as bus shelter posters located where the stories appropriately fit. We had a set of advisors for that project, an

African American artist, a Japanese American artist, a Chinese American artist. Ann also wanted to include the Native story, so she invited Malcolm. He and Ann had known each other for a number of years. He spoke at a group meeting for that project, at which he told—as he always does very eloquently—the story of what it must have been like at that moment of discovery, who was living in the area, the communication with the Spanish landing here. Malcolm is so articulate on that particular topic that, of course, it was great fun.

I also got to know him better when Intersection became a fiscal sponsor for a project related to Native California language preservation, identifying living speakers and connecting them with apprentices. It was supported by one major funder who was a descendant of the Rockefellers, Marion Weber. I remember Malcolm coming by one time with some papers for us to sign and checks that needed to be written. He had just been to the American Booksellers annual gathering. He told me this story about having a drink at the bar of the conference hotel. He said he was suddenly filled with a glow of happiness and well-being, and it wasn't just the alcohol! He realized he was surrounded by supermodels. One of the best-selling items of the year was a big coffee table book with images of supermodels, and he happened to land among them at the bar. I recall that as my first interaction with Malcolm's incredible sense of humor.

Another connection to him was when I was involved in the Bay Area Book Reviewers Association, later the Northern California Book Reviewers Association, and we honored Malcolm years later. He won the Fred Cody Award.

I've been at Haas for eighteen years. When I got here, I remember being interested in the question of the well-being of California tribes, with so many of them being so small at this point, and I continued to be interested in their language survival. I encouraged Malcolm to do a proposal to try to increase people's awareness of that particular issue of the languages. The Haas fund focuses on San Francisco and Alameda Counties, so it's always been a challenge here to support Heyday's work with Native Californians, because there aren't all that many in the two counties where we and Heyday work.

Eventually, the Haas Fund's guidelines changed. With more of a focus on cultural participation and cross-cultural understanding, it became more possible for me to fund Heyday. Also, Heyday completed its nonprofit incorporation, and it looked more like other nonprofits we were supporting. I always had to struggle a little with Heyday because they aren't like other organizations also supported here. They don't look like a dance company or a theater group, so translating how they fit is a bit of a stretch.

So it's been great in that more books have been produced as a result, and it's made a lot of terrific cultural and natural contributions.

That said, some things were really tricky about the transition. It was reasonable to sell the assets of the for-profit to the nonprofit, but the nonprofit was just getting off the ground, and that was tough, hard to saddle this brand-new entity with the old expenses. I'm concerned that Malcolm doesn't really have anything to retire on.

On a personal level, I've supported Heyday in many ways, like subscribing to *News from Native California*. That magazine is really important in pulling together connections and relationships around the state for a very abused and disenfranchised people. Heyday has formed a base for a lot of activity initiated by *News*, and organizations were certainly elevated by those connections, like the California Indian Basketweavers Association and the continuing language work.

One of my favorite Heyday experiences was a number of years ago, when we made a grant to them to produce a series about successful revivals of Native practices. They brought artists into the Heyday space to make presentations, most of them to small groups of people, about their traditions and what they had learned, how they were keeping their culture alive now. I went to one about bird songs, and another about Native language acquisition. While it was usually a small number of people, maybe twenty or so, it struck me how they were hungry for what was being said! The degree of rapt attention was profound. The speakers were not necessarily fabulous speakers, but every word was being relished. Those events were very moving. That relates also to *News* because they were creating a series of articles about these revival activities, so that the publication and the presentations fit together.

I also own a number of Heyday books that have a natural history bent to them. I really like them, like for knowing how to draw a bird better, or the little foldout guidebooks and books about the bay and its past. I'm just a lay reader, but don't underestimate the value of a lay reader! And the books are visually beautiful. They always have appeal as objects.

Another important thing about Heyday is that it's a resource for others to use, like for the University of Santa Clara's Legacy Series, the zoo, the California Historical Society, and so on. It's been a really important partner for these institutions that probably were not robust enough to have their own publishing entities. Heyday is filling an important need there in a partnering role.

I think it's great that Heyday is all about California, too. I moved to California when I was in second grade from Massachusetts, like Malcolm, though I'm not from Boston. This is a big, complicated state, and we can learn about its diversity through Heyday.

I treasure Malcolm's sense of humor. I was just attending a long-range planning meeting for the Alliance for California Traditional Arts. Malcolm is on their board. We were going around the room, and people were discussing their personal relationship to traditional arts. Malcolm said that he didn't really practice any traditional art forms, but that he'd been raised in a Jewish family where they practiced the traditional art of complaint. I've always remembered that remark.

I remember another of Malcolm's stories that always impressed me, though he can tell it much better. In 2007 I was the co-chair of the annual Grant Makers in the Arts Conference, held in Taos, New Mexico, that year. We decided to make it a retreat conference and put together a publication with a dozen papers in it with big-picture thinkers. There would be no panels, just papers and conversation. It worked pretty well. But we needed somebody to edit the papers, so I thought of working with Malcolm or someone on the Heyday staff. After a lot of interaction over the publication, we invited him to the conference since he was so central to it. And finally, we gave him and a few others an important role, to give summary remarks at the end of the conference about what they had heard and seen, and what the conference had made them think about.

Malcolm told a beautiful story—I'm sure he's told it before. It has to do with a Native culture building a roundhouse. They build it so that it falls apart every twenty years to give the next generation the opportunity to build it again. He conveyed how important that practice is. It's sort of ironic, now, thinking about Heyday: you have to allow people the experience of the making and the remaking. Just preserving for the sake of preserving is not enough. It was a beautiful story—the most wonderful capstone.

People hear "Heyday" and think of Malcolm. It's not the only cultural organization with a charismatic leader, but it *is* the kind of cultural organization where the presence of that charismatic founder is very strong. Since Heyday was a business with sole proprietorship, it made a lot of sense to change it into a nonprofit. Clearly, that gave Malcolm access to some working capital, so that was really wise. I love what they've done in terms of events and distribution. They've really made Heyday a cultural center. It's not just a technical producer of books but a whole cultural space. As something benefiting public life, it's been wonderful. I just hope it's been good for Malcolm and his family.

CHAPTER 7

HEYDAY'S CULTURAL
COMMUNITY EXTRAORDINAIRE

*"This place lives on this archipelago of projects that tie in with
one another and tie people together."* —MALCOLM MARGOLIN

ROM PUBLISHING A single book in 1974, Heyday has developed a broad mission
over the last forty years. It now relates the history, literature, and cultural expressions
of California's many diverse communities: Native people past and present; early
Spanish and Mexican settlers; later Yankee arrivals; Japanese and Italian Americans
in World War II California; African Americans leaving behind the segregated South;
Jews in turn-of-the-century San Francisco; Chinese and Armenians; Hmong immigrants
adopting a first-ever written language; and still others.

In its cornucopia of publishing about California and as a cultural institution,
Heyday both creates and feeds communities, not only in this state but nationally. For
this reason, in 2012 Malcolm was presented with a Chairman's Commendation from
the National Endowment for the Humanities in honor of Heyday's contribution to our
national cultural arena. Malcolm was only the second person to have received this
honor. Ralph Lewin, president and CEO of Cal Humanities, commented on Malcolm's
receiving the commendation:

> Malcolm Margolin deserves this national recognition for his extraordinary
> vision, commitment, and passion for deepening our awareness of what it
> means to be Californian, American, and, ultimately,...human. Margolin brings
> a serious and jubilant lifelong commitment to publishing that has shaped our
> fundamental understanding of the people and places that make up California.
> He is a national treasure and it is good to see him recognized as such.

In this chapter many cultural leaders—including Malcolm—reflect that jubila-
tion. These interviews explore Heyday's commitment to growing many cultures and

communities over the last twenty years in particular, from the literature of California that Heyday publishes to the organizations that Malcolm and Heyday have helped birth.

MALCOLM: "WHAT A TREASURE COMMUNITY IS"

MALCOLM HAS OFTEN been asked whether he wished he could have written another book instead of giving himself over so fully to creating others' books and organizations. In his "Publisher's Note" to Heyday's twentieth anniversary catalog (Fall 1994), Malcolm described the arrival of seven thousand copies of his first Heyday book, *The East Bay Out*, and he answered that very question with a focus on celebrating the greatest gift he has received from Heyday: community.

I had done the deed and was now a publisher....

What about selling, distributing, promoting, shipping, billing, collecting, depositing, and accounting? None of those mundane details struck me as a problem. A book as joyous and beautiful as this would simply sell itself....

It didn't take long for my ancient nemesis, "reality," to rear its ugly head. When I woke up in the morning and threw open the door, the books did not run out like chickens. In fact they showed no inclination to move....

So I did what had to be done. I introduced myself to distributors and booksellers, struggled to get the book reviewed, unpacked and repacked boxes, made out invoices, kept track of accounts receivable and accounts payable, collected bills, wrote out checks, filled out tax forms, told people that the check was in the mail, was told the same, and in short, started to run a business. What irony! Hadn't I become a writer precisely to escape such a destiny? I complained for years. I'm an artist, not a businessman. Isn't anyone listening?

During those years of hollering, however, an unexpected, even embarrassing awareness was sneaking up on me and taking root. Not only were these commercial aspects of publishing necessary, they were not entirely unrewarding. Could it be, I began to wonder, that one can run a business with something of the same creativity, playfulness, affection, and integrity that go into writing books? Could it be that I might actually be enjoying this activity more than I was willing to confess? Don't tell any of my writer friends—and most of all don't tell the writer in me who still likes to put on airs—but I think I've gotten to like many of these mundane tasks and necessary, nourishing contacts.

Publishing my own books would, I had hoped, set me free....I would be able to earn a living without having to work for "The Man."...Where has this quest led me twenty years later? I am at this moment completely dependent on others. I am dependent on the wonderful people who work at Heyday Books; on the printers who have so graciously allowed me to get into major debt; on a banker who periodically covers my bad checks; on sales reps who promote my books beyond any commercial justification; on wholesalers who tolerate missed deadlines; on booksellers by the hundred who stock the books we publish and display them so generously; on book reviewers and other media people who honor us with attention; on foundations who give grants; on a network of more than 200 friends who contribute yearly to our efforts; on my wife, Rina, who has edited every piece of my writing (including this) for the last twenty years; on authors who entrust their manuscripts to us; on the California Indian community who has welcomed our presence; and on tens of thousands of readers who buy our books and our magazine. In short my quest for freedom has led to complete and utter dependence on untold numbers of people.

The real irony, though, is not simply that the search for freedom has led to dependence. Rather, it is that I have come to love that dependency with my whole being. What a treasure community is, and how proud I am to be a member.

KEVIN STARR: HEYDAY'S IMAGINATIVE WORLDVIEW

ONE OF THE preeminent historians of California today, Kevin Starr wrote the multi-volume *Americans and the California Dream* series. He has also written several pieces that appear in Heyday books. In his role as the California State Librarian from 1994 to 2004, he collaborated in Heyday's efforts to produce books and events that provided opportunities for new voices to be heard. He provides historical perspective on the place of Heyday in the greater arena of California's cultural production.

A publishing house, like a great magazine or newspaper, both comes out of its time and place and offers further definition of that time and place. For example, *Sunset* magazine, which started in the 1920s, helped define the western lifestyle of its time through articles about gardening, construction, design, architecture, recipes, conservation, etc. Heyday has some parallel in its range and defining of California.

If you look at Heyday, you see the Berkeley that Heyday came out of. A certain flowering of the Berkeley left goes back to the 1890s as a city of choice for many of the Bay Area intelligentsia at the time. Then there were the developments in the late 1940s of KPFA and Pacifica Radio, and eventually the uprisings of the sixties and seventies. Malcolm has a generalized and gentle left-liberal orientation, not coming out of the violent orientation to all the problems that tore Berkeley apart in the late sixties during the Panther era and into the seventies. Heyday is not leftist, but there's a sensibility of elements that Malcolm has put together in his company. Look at Malcolm's interest in anthropology and Native American culture and life, the fact that he authored one of the great classics, *The Ohlone Way*. He provided a reconsolidated Berkeley sensibility, "a sensibility of place."

This reconsolidated sensibility takes into consideration the presence and the heritage of the university in Berkeley, so Heyday has an academic dimension to it as well. Malcolm himself is a very highly educated man, a graduate of Harvard University. At the same time, the development of Heyday's Berkeley sensibility was running parallel to the evolution of the University of California Press, a major branch of which is also located in Berkeley, but which had a wider responsibility to the academic world.

So Heyday came of age operating within a Golden Age of publishing at the University of California and moved parallel to that press by focusing, by its own act of definition, meaning that every book selected, every title brought to fruition, defines a space. Heyday's definition moves in an expansive, less academic way, but equally encompasses California, especially Northern California, in our era.

The Heyday list as a whole helps us map out an imaginative worldview of California. Establishing a list of books is usually dominated by the marketplace, what will sell, what the intrinsic merit of the book is, but it's important to look at Heyday's selections as this map of the *imaginative* universe of California. If you read through the Heyday list cumulatively, it's like you're filling in a mosaic on a wall, with title after title mapping its interests in flora and fauna, in Native Americans, in the gentler side of emergent minority family life. The Native list itself is overwhelming. It has helped define, map, and chronicle a kind of renaissance we're seeing in Native American California.

When I was State Librarian, I was able to help Malcolm with many of these topics by providing grants or suggestions or pictures. He's had a big interest in Japanese Americans in World War II, with which I also helped, giving grants when I was administering the related state funds for that program.

Malcolm and I were born the same year, in 1940, but we're very different people. When I met Malcolm, I was taken aback a little. I had to adjust to the eccentricity of his beard. It's a rabbinical beard. With Malcolm being Jewish, you can use "rabbinical" in terms of his moral imagination and his interest in the development of people and the state. Within a few meetings, I realized what a good entrepreneur he was. In an article that appeared once in the *Chronicle*, I described Malcolm as "hierophantic" based on two Greek words: *hieros*, meaning "sacred" and *phantic*, meaning to "appear." Malcolm has a demeanor like a clergyman. He emanates the sense of something larger.

In the future, Heyday will need someone as educated as Malcolm, with as fine a mind and with a similar polymathic range of interests and approach to the continuing development and definition of California culture. You want somebody who's participating in the culture. Malcolm doesn't just observe; he *participates* in the state's emergence and definition. None of us is indispensable. Changes will happen. But Malcolm has left a distinctive mark.

MAXINE HONG KINGSTON: HEYDAY AT THE HEART OF COMMUNITY

WORLD-RENOWNED AUTHOR AND social justice advocate Maxine Hong Kingston is another longtime acquaintance of Malcolm. Maxine's work appeared in Heyday's 2012 anthology *New California Writing*. She explains how a shared interest in literary work initiated her friendship with Malcolm and describes the subsequent ways she has come to appreciate the many cultural endeavors of Heyday.

I was putting together an anthology, *The Literature of California: Native American Beginnings to 1945* with my fellow editors. I was in charge of the early phase of California, working with the stories and songs of California tribes. The first thing I did was talk to Malcolm since he is *the* person that helped launch a gathering of such stories. What Malcolm said was so helpful! He made me promise not to write about the Indians as if they were of a past era, but I had to show that their literature and artists are *still* contributing to the literature of California, and they have been all along. Malcolm insisted my thinking be very clear that we are not talking about a dead civilization. Instead, an anthology of California literature had to reflect the ongoing contributions of the Indians. He truly helped us shape that book.

His mentorship on that project was long after I first met him. Our joke is that we've known each other since we were twins together, because we were born on the same day in the same year. Our mythic meeting was in our two mothers' wombs. That's part of our friendship. We're also both avidly in love with literature, and we care about writing and stories. We also care for the people who write stories and poems. Probably both of us are intensely private, which includes when he goes on his rambles and walks, and when I garden alone. At the same time we're both very social and politically active.

Being exactly the same age, it's interesting to have participated in the same history and events of our time. It's very good to have Malcolm's take on what we've been through. I remember when we were turning fifty, twenty-one years ago, there was a party with a lot of people turning fifty around that same time: Robert Hass, Richard Nelson, Lee Swenson, me, Malcolm. We were recalling how privileged we were in being exactly that age, born exactly at the right time, 1940, just as the country was going into World War II, but we were babies so we didn't have to go. We skipped the rest of the wars of our lifetime, too. They were all men born just before the draft age, so they were lucky not to go to the Vietnam War. Birth control arrived just in time, so there was more of that freedom. We talked about

*Grace Paley,
Maxine Hong
Kingston, and
Malcolm at
Lee Swenson's
home*
(COURTESY OF
LEE SWENSON)

buying houses before the housing crisis happened. We listed all those things that we were privileged to have. It was fascinating.

My impressions of Malcolm have always been that he's very articulate, able to speak with such a natural order. In each conversation he's very funny and so thoughtful. He's honest in his thinking and evaluations. I'm very impressed by his caring for authors, whether or not he's going to publish them. I've been at book parties at Heyday where I think we're supporting a Heyday author, but I find out that this person isn't even being published by Heyday. It's a young author of a book that Malcolm really likes and is impressed by, and he's just going to give this person a forum, whether or not Malcolm is that writer's publisher. He's so generous with his time and abilities and resources.

For example, when the writer Jade Snow Wong was alive, some people were collecting an oral history about her for a film. Malcolm gave them a meeting room at Heyday. They piled in all the equipment for this film, and Jade Snow Wong was there. Malcolm just made room.

I saw that same generosity with the writer James Houston. When Jim died, it was Malcolm's idea to publish his posthumous writing because Jim died when he was halfway through a novel about the Hawaiian Queen Lili'uokalani. Malcolm convinced Jim's wife, Jeanne Houston, that what Jim had written would be enough, that it could stand alone as a complete book.

He published *A Queen's Journey* posthumously and a little pamphlet with a biography of Jim. He also gave book parties in which he raised quantities for the James Houston Fund that he started, a yearly fellowship for Heyday to sponsor publishing a new young writer who's working in the same spirit as Jim Houston.

All of this shows how Malcolm supports writers, including discovering young writers and keeping old ones going. I also noticed that if you just drop by Heyday, there he'll be, and he'll talk to you. You don't even need an appointment. Or you call and he picks up the phone himself. And then he's at so many events all the time! He seems to take it easy, and he makes time for you, yet he accomplishes so much! I just don't see how he does it.

As for dealing with folks at Heyday, Malcolm has gathered such a bright, caring, skillful team of people. They're so socially capable. *They* know how to organize parties! I would not have wanted to give that huge birthday party for our seventieth if not for his whole team behind us. At an event for Andrew Lam I was talking to Lillian, who organizes the book parties. She said, "I love giving these parties. I think I like it better than publishing the books." It's incredible how successful they are at drawing a crowd for a small press—and at a time when big presses are cutting back. So Heyday is forming a literary community. It's not just the books. It's a community and culture, both in the Bay Area and up and down California.

JIM QUAY: "A MINIATURE HUMANITIES COUNCIL"

JIM QUAY AND Malcolm began collaborating on creative projects when Jim became the executive director of the California Council for the Humanities (now Cal Humanities). Their lasting friendship in the name of developing culture and community has clearly been the best collaboration of all.

I met Malcolm in 1982, when I was a humanities producer for California Public Radio. I interviewed him for a piece I was doing on California Native American summer solstice ceremonies. Among other people I was told to see, everyone kept saying, "You've got to talk to Malcolm Margolin."

I went over to his house on Berkeley Way. After the interview, he invited me to sit down with his family for lunch. I instantly felt this was not your normal interviewer-interviewee relationship. He'd invited me into his home and made me part of the meal. We've been friends ever since.

For years and years we've had lunch once a month. We'd meet and talk about the state of the world. Malcolm once alluded to it as playing badminton. It's just delightful. He's interested in everything, knows a lot about many things, and knows a profound amount about some things. I treasure those meals.

I remember one conversation that we had just after 9/11. We were both very concerned that this trauma would not be good for the *culture*. The tendency would be for the culture to get paranoid and small and then shrink. What could be done about that? Not that we could do anything about a reaction that large, but I remember the gravity of our fears. Eventually, the Heyday book *Wherever There's a Fight,* about civil liberties in California, became one kind of response to the aftermath of 9/11.

Heyday is like a miniature humanities council. When I joined the California Humanities Council in 1983, I emphasized the concept of *community*. Since Californians come from all over, pulling together a state this diverse is probably impossible. But what a great diversity of stories and history! I just love the state, and it's a love that Malcolm shares. Because Heyday publishes on every aspect of California, a community of readers and writers and activists has formed and continues to grow around Heyday. If you care about the state, you're going to be reading many books that Heyday has published.

My own sense is that a Californian is someone with a notion of hope, tied to the fact that immigrant experience is not very far away. Immigrants who come here have to have hope. To break those bonds with your particular place, you either have to be driven out or you might also have thought, "There's something better, and I can get it in California"—like Malcolm, coming from Dorchester so long ago. Everybody likes to tell the stories of their own group's experience in coming here. Some of the anthologies that Heyday has published and some of the programs that we've done have given people the experience of seeing, "Oh, that's like my grandmother's story." We're promoting hope in such stories.

I call Malcolm an advocate of hope. Part of what Malcolm is doing, not only with Native American cultures but with many cultures and in many ways, is leaving a legacy of history and natural history that people can draw on. Like Darryl Wilson's memoir *The Morning the Sun Went Down*: I found it a fascinating and valuable book that embodied Darryl's struggle to try to get through a difficult life and pull together the shards of his Pit River culture, a culture shattered by genocide. Darryl's doing his best to find what can be kept alive. Heyday facilitated that legacy.

Heyday has done so much with the California Council for the Humanities, including three anthologies, beginning with *Highway 99* in 1996. A big grant we got from the National Endowment for the Humanities included not only the creation of that book but also public events at libraries all along the Central Valley, the archetypal public program, bringing people together with intellectual content. Stan Yogi did the first edition. The reception was great. We discovered a kind of inferiority complex in the Central Valley since often it feels either colonized by the coast or ignored. Does the Valley have a culture? Here was testimony: yes! And that culture has a history and a future. *Highway 99* was a best-selling book in the Central Valley and in other places as well. The pride that book engendered was an unalloyed good.

Then there was the Gold Rush anthology that we did for the Sesquicentennial, the 150th anniversary of California statehood. That also had wonderful pieces in it, literature that needed to be retrieved, revived, and refreshed from the library stacks. It turned out to be a much livelier anthology than anyone expected. Now, was it a best seller? Would a normal mainstream press have published it? There probably wasn't enough money in it. Malcolm doesn't care about that. Should it be published? Yes! His attitude is: okay, then we're going to find a way.

The last was the 2003 *California Uncovered* anthology. The council's project was to get people together to tell stories of how they or somebody in their family came to California. We wanted to get Sikhs, Hmong, Chinese Americans, and Anglo Americans in the same room at the same time to hear one another's stories. It was a terrific anthology.

Every time a Heyday book comes out, another little community gets created. For example, Malcolm always attended events at the Center for California Studies in Sacramento. They had wonderfully stimulating activities, bringing together writers, politicians, and scholars from various fields.

Jim Quay (left) and Chick Callenbach at the launch party for California Uncovered, *2005.* (HEYDAY ARCHIVES)

A coterie of people for whom California makes the heart beat a little faster make up a community there, and Heyday was right at the center of that group. I've been with Malcolm in public gatherings and witnessed the consequences of his generosity. He can barely escape from a room without a dozen people coming up and pitching a book idea. How he says "no" gracefully is quite a diplomatic art. I've always felt that Malcolm was directly creating community. A group of supporters, admirers, and lovers of Malcolm leads them to say, "If he's going to do something, sign me up. I'll be there."

LETTER FROM MALCOLM TO JIM: WHAT A HEALTHY CULTURE WOULD LOOK LIKE

December 6, 2003

Dear Jim:

As I mentioned, I've been mulling over your wonderful question: What would a healthy culture look like? Here are a few things I came up with, not very systematic nor deeply thought out, not arranged in any particular order of importance. My suspicion is that these specifics probably are circling around a few core values, but I'm not sure what they are. Love of place, perhaps?

Sustainable relationship to the environment. In other words, the present generation isn't strip-mining soil, water, forest, minerals, etc. and leaving the future impoverished and the world around them degraded.

Few outcasts. A healthy culture will have relatively few outcasts, e.g., prisoners, homeless, unemployed, crazy, etc.

Either relative egalitarianism or if there is a hierarchical structure, a widespread acceptance of it and one's role in it. In other words, if there is an unequal distribution of wealth or power, those without the goodies accept their role and feel protected or rewarded in some other way for their lack.

Good health. People are strong, active, zesty.

Widespread sexual satisfaction, or at least lack of ongoing sexual frustration.

Good wine (or its cultural equivalent), easily available and well used.

Capacity for change if external circumstances demand it.

Moderation or controls on power.

Widespread engagement in the arts.

Care and education of children.

Lots of laughter.

Relative sense of security, social and material.

The essentials—food, shelter—readily available.

Love of place.

Common language.

Low rate of internal violence.

Mechanisms for release.

Low "crime" rate.

Minimal resentment toward what is called work.

Your turn—
Malcolm

TERRY BEERS: HEYDAY REVIVES CALIFORNIA'S LITERARY LEGACY

A PROFESSOR OF ENGLISH at Santa Clara University, Terry Beers is also the editor of many Heyday books. Starting in 2000, Terry directed a ten-year collaboration between the university and Heyday to produce a series of reprints of literature from California's earliest days, called the California Legacy Project. These forty-plus books exemplify how Heyday has preserved and promoted California's literary culture, from early Natives to the Spanish and Russian explorers, Mexican Californios, African Americans, women writers, miners, dissidents, and Depression-era muckrakers.

My first experience with Malcolm and Heyday was in 1999, when I was creating a literary anthology tied to state parks, so it would be a park guide and literary magnet. I wrote a proposal and sent it to Heyday because they're *Heyday*. Malcolm wrote back to me. He was very encouraging. We kept batting ideas back and forth for a while. When we went ahead with the project, it turned out to be the first California Legacy book. Based on that book, *Unfolding Beauty: Celebrating California's Landscapes*, Malcolm had the idea of coming out with a series of reprints of great California writing, work no longer in print at the time. He asked me if I wanted to work with him on that project. I took the concept back to folks at my university, Santa Clara, and we came up with the name of "California Legacy." Heyday and Santa Clara University had a partnership in creating the books for ten years.

I was very grateful that Malcolm brought me into it. The whole experience was both wonderful and a little intimidating. A lot of the people who wrote the forewords are stellar. Jim Houston did the foreword for *Eldorado*, one of our first books. Patricia Limerick did the foreword for *Death Valley in '49*. Ursula Le Guin did the introduction for *November Grass*. It was a thrill to meet people whose writing I knew and respected, so working with them in even a small way was fun.

Probably the most fun was kicking around ideas with Malcolm, Jeannine, Gayle, or any of the Heyday folks. "What are we going to do? What's next?" Malcolm was always surprising to me because he'd pull these great ideas out of the air. I don't know where he gets them from or how. I'd find myself listening, amazed, saying, "What did he just say?! Where are we going with this?"

Malcolm really pulls for other people to succeed and takes great joy in seeing them do well. Sometimes it's difficult to partner with organizations that have different missions and goals. But in working through it, he never conveys a sense that we have a problem. It's always "We'll figure it out."

Whenever you see Malcolm, he's always glad to see you. I imagine that's the same as working there, that he's glad to see the staff show up, and they're probably glad to see him. The staff all seem to really enjoy the work they do, and that comes out in the products. Goodwill and friendship thrive there. As for the Heyday staff, I could say the same as about Malcolm: they're smart, generous, professional people who really want to do a good job. Authors like me coming from an academic background may tell ourselves we're good writers, but most of us aren't "professionals" in terms of actually producing books. So working with Heyday was a great education for me, to see a little more about publishing, marketing, and making decisions about books, how they can be reproduced and presented.

Heyday is like a clearinghouse. All cultural endeavors in California cross Malcolm's desk in one way or another, in part because he knows so many people, in part because so many people want to know him. When Heyday remade itself from a publishing company into a cultural institution, working with Heyday became a way for people to get a lot of public attention for their projects, which they might not otherwise have been able to do. Through partnerships and social networks, Heyday supports a network of social institutions and people interested in California. There's no one else like them.

MALCOLM: NEW COMMUNITIES BORN

MALCOLM DISCUSSES TWO projects in which he invested significant time at their initiation, the Inlandia Institute in Southern California and the journal *Bay Nature*, both founded in the name of community building.

Inlandia Institute started in 2006 when we did this anthology, *Inlandia*, of literature from the Inland Empire of Southern California. It was the most wonderful thing, coming out of Riverside and San Bernardino, an absolute hit. Gayle put it together. We ultimately sold thousands of copies. Redlands College ended up buying one for every student. The anthology defined a literary area.

Its success indicates that they didn't understand what they had. All these little towns there had writers writing about their town, like about Covina or Ontario. The creative writing department of UC Riverside had a wonderful influence, people like Susan Straight and Chris Buckley. The literature was so good.

When we came out with the anthology, we had a reception at the Riverside Library. I said, "Hey, we can have this anthology, and people can read it, but it will all go away. What I'd really love to see is a permanent institute here and to work with you."

I'd just been on a panel in Washington for the National Endowment for the Arts, looking at applications from literary programs all over the country, like the Loft in Minneapolis, places that had centers for literature and residencies for writers. I said that this is what Riverside needs. Damned if they didn't take me up on it! Marion Mitchell-Wilson was working for the Riverside Library in development. When Marion heard this, she knew exactly what this was. Like a retriever seeing a duck for the first time, she just lined up! She became so streamlined and effective. We worked with her as partners for several years and ran programs with them. I was down there maybe six or seven times a year. We had manuscripts generated from it. I've pretty much dropped out, but it's still going.

Another organization that I helped start was a magazine called *Bay Nature*. Around 2000 David Loeb came to me with an idea of starting a magazine for the natural history of the Bay Area. I'd actually already had that idea, and I had some donated, leftover campaign funds offered by Mary Jefferds, who'd run for the East Bay Regional Park District board of directors. With those funds, I could create a plan and an appeal for starting a magazine on the nature of the Bay Area. But like many other ideas, I'd put it away. With such an abundance of ideas, I start some and then leave them behind.

So David and I planned *Bay Nature* and decided that we'd do the magazine under our nonprofit. I went to the Packard Foundation and got $200,000

Malcolm Margolin and California poet laureate Juan Felipe Herrera celebrating the publication of Inlandia, *Riverside, 2006.* (HEYDAY ARCHIVES)

from them to start this thing. I came back, and we had a small planning group, David, Marilyn Smulyan, and me.

I had *News from Native California* in mind, something fairly simple and artful that would create a community. I think you can create a community through a magazine much more than you can through books. There's a continuing readership; the writing is ongoing and current, with news and events. Books are grand islands, much more leisurely and aristocratic, *sui generis*. With a magazine you're always engaged in a continuity of writing and people. I figured we could create a wonderful community that way.

Heyday was involved in the first issues. I originally thought *Bay Nature* could get folded into Heyday well, but it had its own budget. I was in the role of publisher and David was editor. After a couple of years I really didn't have the time for it, so I ended up getting several friends to create a board of directors for David, and he moved from editor to publisher. For ten years now it's flourished with a community of people supporting it. It's been loved and done a lot of good in the world.

AMY KITCHENER: MALCOLM AS A STEWARD OF CAUSES

YET ANOTHER CULTURAL organization that Malcolm and Heyday have had a role in founding was the Alliance for California Traditional Arts, or ACTA. A folklorist by training, Amy Kitchener has devoted two decades to building support for traditional arts, first through the Fresno Arts Council and then through ACTA, founded in 1997 and also based in Fresno. Amy's story illustrates how small organizations with dedicated directors and staff foment important acts of cultural preservation.

People tend to identify Malcolm with his work in Native California; that was how I first became aware of Malcolm and Heyday, through *News from Native California*. If you wanted to get to know California Indians, you read that journal. I had a job at the L.A. Public Library in 1990, and that's when I first remember seeing *News* and hearing about Malcolm.

Later I got into public folklore, a field that got its start with the 1976 American Folklife Act, passed by Jimmy Carter, which created the American Folklife Center at the Library of Congress. It also designated that every state would have state folklore programs to conduct fieldwork and research, and to develop public programs on the folk history and expressions of the diverse people of each state.

After getting a graduate degree in folklore, I came to work in Fresno in 1993 to start a county-level public folklife program at the Fresno Arts Council, programs that would highlight and cultivate appreciation between and inside various communities living here. But state funding for a folklife program had ended in 1989, so there was a big gap. Only a few tiny local folklore programs were left, and we had no state support, just a few willing funders, like the National Endowment for the Arts and the Fund for Folk Culture. The larger public folklore field was saying, "Poor California doesn't have a state folklife program!" Some of us were starting to talk about how to bring back a state program.

Every year the California Arts Council had a huge conference at Asilomar, by Monterey, which is where we got our start. Josie Talamantez, a program director from the Arts Council, suggested we get together people to talk about how to build a stronger network in California. Of course we all said, "Malcolm!" A lot of his publications and *News* had had a really important effect in stimulating the traditional arts.

So at Asilomar in 1997 we got a conference room and were told, "Here, it's yours. Caucus." Nine of us were the crew there, including Malcolm and

Beth Lomax Hawes, the first director of the NEA Folk Arts Division and a really major figure in our field, also the sister of Alan Lomax. We also had Charlie Seeman, a folklorist and the program director at the Fund for Folk Culture, which had seeded the Fresno program.

One thing we decided at that meeting was that we needed to rebuild a state apprenticeship program for California, a model where master artists are supported with a three-thousand-dollar stipend to work with an apprentice from their cultural community, over the course of six months to a year. Ultimately, we accomplished that. And we named ourselves, too.

Then at the big plenary session, we announced that we wanted the California Arts Council to recognize us as the field leader and fund a new publication and an apprentice program. Malcolm was a key spokesperson.

So that was the spark of ACTA. Since 1998, 220 artists have been in our apprenticeship program. The masters and apprentices somehow find each other and apply as a pair. We've advertised in *News* or we speak at relevant conferences. ACTA has funded the Advocates for Indigenous California Language Survival several times for the Breath of Life Conference supported through our Living Cultures grant program, so we've created several Native language apprenticeship pairs that way.

One of the apprenticeships we were really proud to support was between the master Jon Meza Cuero and his apprentice Stanley Rodriguez, around 2000. They're Kumeyaay, from the southern border area. Jon Meza was one of the only singers who knew the repertoire of the Wildcat Song Cycle. The project was to teach it to Stanley. In the process, Stanley ended up learning the Kumeyaay language. They lived together, so they had a really intensive apprenticeship going on apart from the ACTA contract, which enhanced the work that could be accomplished. Jon is very advanced in age now, and Stanley is recognized as an elder, a master tradition bearer teaching other young singers. It was so wonderful to protect a cultural practice that was endangered in terms of the number of people that could maintain that cycle.

A lot of our work is based on what Malcolm would call "deep hanging out." Most of our staff has ethnographic training, and we invest time in getting to know people and protocols in different communities. We invited people to get to know us, too. A lot of the work is about relationships over time.

Malcolm is a champion of causes and a steward of the organizations that he really cares about. He served a mentoring role for me on the ACTA board. By 2001, I incorporated ACTA as its own entity and set about building a board, with Malcolm the first on my mind to be on the board. He's been a guiding force from the very beginning.

Malcolm has a lot of ability to convince others of his opinions, yet he's totally intolerant of unnecessary bureaucracy. A consultant did an organizational assessment, in part to find out how the staff was spending their time, so we did an elaborate analysis. The next board meeting was at Heyday, and we gave an official report with a PowerPoint presentation showing how we had tracked our time. Pretty soon, Malcolm holds up a little piece of paper and says, "I want to share how I spend my time with you all." The gist of it was: "Saying things I shouldn't have said: 15 percent of my time. Apologizing for things I shouldn't have said: 5 percent. Daydreaming: 30 percent…" It was a really lovely "Malcolm" thing, making fun of how ridiculous we were being and pointing out what's really important here.

DAVID KIPEN: "CONTAGIOUS LOVE FOR THE STATE"

WRITER DAVID KIPEN contributed an introduction for the second volume of *New California Writing* (2012) and has hosted Southern California book launch parties at Libros Schmibros, his nonprofit lending library and used bookstore in Boyle Heights, Los Angeles. A former book critic at the *San Francisco Chronicle*, David noted, "I was shamelessly in the tank for Heyday while I was there, but I wouldn't have given a great review to a lousy book, and Malcolm doesn't publish lousy books."

I grew up on the west side of L.A., went away to Yale, majored in literature, came home after graduating in '85, and did a bunch of temp jobs, one of which was in an L.A. law library. To avoid doing my actual job, shelving books, I took refuge in the break room. There I found a copy of the magazine *California History*, through which I learned about the upcoming

California Studies Conference in Sacramento. I'd never been particularly fascinated with California before. Like most Californians, I took the place for granted, but after going three thousand miles away, I realized I had a place I was homesick for. The conference ad let me know that other people felt the same way.

In order to have the funds to get there and back, I made a mixtape of twenty-six songs about California and sold it in the conference book room, which is probably where I met Malcolm. We became annual friends until I moved to San Francisco for my book reviewer job at the *Chronicle* in 1998.

I remember having my first meal with Malcolm at that conference and being completely besotted by him, by his contagious love for the state, for which he stood out even at a meeting of the California Studies Association. Like Malcolm, I'm crazy about every inch of California, including its great literary and publishing tradition—and Malcolm is one of few inheritors of that tradition left today. I was very determined from the minute I got to the *Chronicle* to educate myself and my readers on California literature, so I read and reviewed as much as possible. I created the *"Chronicle* Western 100," polling my readers on what they thought were the best one hundred books in fiction and nonfiction west of the Rockies. Sure enough, one of the nonfiction titles was *The Ohlone Way*.

I probably reviewed more Heyday books than anybody else. Everybody should have been paying attention to these attractively designed and invariably handsome books. Usually I love the inside *and* outside, everything about these books. I was sheepish about the attention I gave to books published by a friend of mine, but thankfully I never saw a Heyday book that I felt tempted to pan. If I had a reservation, it might have been about something like the excessive length of *Under the Fifth Sun*, but that anthology introduced me to California Chicano and Latino writers whom I'm very glad to know about. And classroom teachers up and down California now assign it—or should.

I used to marvel at how Malcolm could keep finding writers I never heard of, off-the-beaten-path people who could either write or be rewritten by Heyday's sainted staff, not just into readability but enjoyability. Malcolm has brought many California books back into print through the Legacy series. The anthologies are great, too; each is a kind of checklist and scavenger hunt. You read ten pages of an author and then you go off to find more. Since the New Deal's Works Progress Administration, few publishers besides Heyday have been willing to tell these stories, so I love Heyday's attention to current California writing *and* vintage California writing.

My work connected me with Heyday in others ways. I eventually went to Washington, DC, as the director of literature for the National Endowment for the Arts. While there, I got Malcolm on a panel or two as a juror on grant proposals so he'd have a better idea from the other side what the NEA looks for in an application. Eventually, the NEA did give him some grants. Also through the NEA, I participated in the Guadalajara Book Festival, the biggest book festival in the world after Frankfurt. In addition to sending writers, artists, and musicians, we brought down publishers, so Heyday joined the caravan from L.A. I hope it did him some good to find Mexican partners and meet L.A. writers who ended up collaborating with him.

I was thrilled to be at the 2012 National Endowment for the Humanities celebration of Malcolm. It may have been bittersweet for Malcolm that it took place down here rather than in the Bay Area, where he has so many more friends. But since this was *national* attention for the first time, maybe it helped him make new friends in Southern California. He's certainly got more friends than he knows what to do with in Northern California! He's gotten dozens of awards from Bay Area and California organizations, but this was the first national one, and from a prestigious organization at that. I think the ceremony meant a lot to him; he seemed genuinely moved. Malcolm doesn't have a narcissistic ego. He's proud of what he's done. He's not so proud of himself, but he's proud of Heyday, as well he should be. No one wanted to leave the room, how about that?

ADAM DAVID MILLER:
IMMEASURABLE CONTRIBUTIONS TO THE CULTURE

AT AGE EIGHTY-FIVE, Adam David Miller saw Heyday publish his memoir, *Ticket to Exile* (2007), about growing up in South Carolina under the weight of racial prejudice and segregation. Adam has become a revered Berkeley writer, poet, and teacher. Here he speaks of enjoying a long affiliation with Heyday and its cultural milieu.

I've been acquainted with Heyday and Malcolm for quite a while. My first contact with Malcolm's work was through *The Ohlone Way*. I actually used it in the introduction to my first book of poetry, and I credited him. His book was helpful as a source about the region. It impressed me that someone had this interest in the Natives because it was a field that few people engaged in intelligently. If you come from a Eurocentric point of view, you're likely to take a narrow attitude towards someone who is not European, to see them as essentially "Other." So I was happy to find someone who instead regarded the Natives as wonderful people to be lived with and loved, rather than exploited.

I continued to follow the press over the years. Heyday did an anthology on the Addison Street Poetry Walk, which was a product of the Berkeley Civic Arts Commission. I was on the commission at the time, as the liaison between the commission and Robert Hass, the anthologist. I followed the anthology through its publication. Poems from the anthology, including one of mine, were placed in the Walk on brass plaques, right into the sidewalk.

Then, if an interesting reading or other event was going on at Heyday, I'd attend. I later became an "associate," a supporter, one of the ways that the press has sought to gain financial support. I followed Heyday as it was finding itself.

When my memoir, *Ticket to Exile*, was coming along, my agent and I sent it to quite a number of places. Finally I said, "Why don't we see what Malcolm might do?" They liked it and wanted it. Apparently they got money from the BayTree Fund to do a series of memoirs just then.

I found the editing process incredible. Gayle was the text editor and Jeannine the line editor. I liked that they were exacting. They were clear about what they thought should change but willing to be convinced otherwise. The designer was also very astute. The cover design that Lorraine Rath created for *Ticket* won a silver medal. I was very pleased that it came out so nicely.

One of the most wonderful receptions that the book has had was in the Central Valley, from the Salinas Valley and down to Merced. Youngsters there feel the story's conflict with prejudice and have been very receptive to it.

Heyday's been fearless. They always do fine work, never badly researched or shallowly treated. That's just Heyday's standard. People spend years working on these books. So when you see a book, you know that's just the tip of the iceberg of the work that went into it, from the author to the staff.

Malcolm himself is a fine researcher and a very careful worker, a master wordsmith. His words are so well thought out and well placed. You won't find him pulling any cultural or social gaffes; it's not in his bones. Then he infuses that spirit in everybody that works for him. Wonderful people come to work there, or he finds them and brings them in. Heyday is probably not for every worker. He doesn't have a lot of money, so people are surely not paid anything like their comparable worth at a big, fancy publishing house. Yet everybody works so hard. Some people come and go, but the people who stay are solid.

ROBERT HASS: "TO CREATE A CULTURE OF THE PLACE WHERE WE LIVE"

ROBERT HASS WAS the celebrated poet laureate of the United States from 1995 to 1997. A common love of story, language, and the environment drew Bob and Malcolm into a friendship and to serving in one another's communities of interest. Bob's colleague Pamela Michael edited the Heyday book *River of Words: Images and Poetry in Praise of Water* (2003) with Bob's introduction. Another cultural gift from Hass and Heyday was the book *The Addison Street Anthology: Berkeley's Poetry Walk* (2004), about poems etched into brass plates located in a sidewalk of Berkeley's downtown Arts District.

When the first edition of *The East Bay Out* came out in 1974, I read it and thought, "I like this book about how to relate to the outdoors. Here's a companion spirit!" Then I read *The Ohlone Way* and got to know Malcolm after that because my brother-in-law, Bill Simmons, was working in the anthropology department at UC Berkeley. He'd invite Malcolm to give talks to his class, so I'd show up to hear Malcolm too, because he was a brilliant storyteller. By the late 1980s we got to be friends.

Malcolm is a guy who shows up. If you need someone who is going to put his shoulder to the wheel for some cultural project, he's the one to ask. It's clear that his enjoyment is connected to who he is, his curiosity about people and his acceptance of them, his power of observation. He finds the world vastly interesting and amusing, so he has a lot of reasons to show up.

Over the years, I've followed Heyday as all their books on California history and ecology came out. Everything about the way he helped conceive a book and put it together, the beautiful production quality of the books, was impressive to me. On a few occasions when he had the annual Heyday Harvest events, Malcolm would invite me to join in and give a reading, which I was very happy to do.

We also worked on projects together. One of them was the *River of Words* book. Pam Michael and I began the environmental education project for kids called River of Words, which was close to some of Malcolm's concerns, so we asked him to be on the board. He did serve on that board, which meant a night out at least every couple of months for him, overseeing the workings of our struggling nonprofit. He was very wise and very helpful in the early years of our starting River of Words.

After some ten years, we had enough really beautiful work by the children, art and poetry, to think about putting together a book, to give back to the community the work of the children, but also to mirror to the community what we were doing in the hope of generating more fundraising to support work with the children. Malcolm loved the idea and helped with the design of the book. I wrote an introduction, but it was mostly Pam and Malcolm working on it.

Then Malcolm and I were both on the same board to create a poetry walk on Addison Street for the Arts District as part of the regeneration of downtown. Mainly because of the landscape architect involved in the project, one idea that developed was putting the history of Berkeley and East Bay literary life on the street in the form of a series of poems. Malcolm then had the idea that it would be great to have a guidebook to go with it, so people could walk along the street and have some stories and the history of the area that accompanies the poetry. So we worked together on *The Addison Street Anthology*, which was Malcolm's brainchild and design. That was really fun to do together.

So that's the story of our collaborations. I think he's a wonder, an incomparable resource. Larry Ferlinghetti has had City Lights, and Jack Shoemaker had various versions of North Point and Counterpoint Press, but nobody else in the area has done anything with publishing ventures like what Malcolm's done, to half record and half invent or create a culture of the place where we live. That's why I'm a real fan of his work. Heyday and its many branches have been important for California and beyond.

Thinking about Heyday as a poem, certain kinds of poems have something interesting to say but aren't especially handsomely made. Other poems are beautifully made, have a high level of craft and skill, but don't have much content. Then there are poems that have both a high level of craft and art *and* something powerful to say, with a unique vision. Those are the amazing ones. That's what Heyday is.

CHAPTER 8

SUCH BEAUTIFUL BOOKS

STAN YOGI: *Everything Heyday does is exquisite, with beautiful images, the content rich and thought-provoking.*

ELAINE ELINSON: *Yes, even the catalogs are beautiful. Nothing is dashed off. A book never comes out of there that isn't absolutely exquisitely done."*

EYDAY'S FOUNDING MISSION is to publish books. A constant theme among Heyday aficionados—from its founder, Malcolm, to its staff, authors, and readers—is the joy taken in beauteous books. Heyday books are lovingly planned, with the author a key participant, from first discussing the project with Malcolm to celebratory events with book in hand.

Following Malcolm's interview on the significance of beauty in his own thinking, several authors and friends share their experiences with the crafting of aesthetically pleasing books at Heyday. Not to be overlooked is the pleasing process of having books created there—supportive, thoughtful, even fun. These stories amount to a testimony on the significance of maintaining beauty and integrity in our lives.

MALCOLM: THERE OUGHT TO BE A BOOK, A BEAUTIFUL BOOK

Why such a focus on creating beautiful books? You may as well ask why I breathe.

Part of it is shame. I'd be ashamed to do something that *wasn't* beautiful. Somebody puts years of work into a book; they've got all their aspirations, all their ego in it. They're putting it out into the world. They've given me the best piece of their work, and we're going to do a lousy-looking book? I'd be ashamed to face them. So it's partly pride in what we do. But I'd just cringe with embarrassment if something didn't turn out very well.

And then it's so puzzling: Why doesn't *everybody* make beautiful books? Why do a book if it's not beautiful? Why do something ugly? Ugliness has always puzzled me. I've never quite understood it.

Beauty is also puzzling. There's something about beauty—it's not prettiness. Beauty is something else. There's a ferocity to it, a power to it. There's a wonderful Rilke quote from the first of his *Duino Elegies* where he's wondering what beauty is. He says:

> Who, if I cried out, would hear me among the angels'
> hierarchies? And even if one of them pressed me
> suddenly against his heart: I would be consumed
> in that overwhelming existence. For beauty is nothing
> but the beginning of terror, which we still are just able to endure,
> and we are so awed because it serenely disdains
> to annihilate us. Every angel is terrifying.

I collect quotes about beauty. I think about beauty all the time. If a day passes where I haven't thought about beauty, just for what it is, in the abstract, it's probably an odd day.

I like going to this French restaurant in Berkeley called La Note that has a courtyard in the back. I just sit in the back of La Note and enjoy it. It's so simple. A few trees, a few tables, a brick wall, some plants, but it's so lovely out there. It's so easy to create beauty. Why isn't it everywhere? Why do people tolerate the ugliness of place or personality?

My wonderful friend Dashrath Patel was active in the politics of Gujarat. He used to talk about the need for a Ministry of Beauty. Tourism already had someone to speak for it, commerce had somebody to speak for it, and the environment had somebody to speak for it. But who would speak for beauty?

One of the scariest things that ever happened to me was when Tom Killion brought me the book he had done with Gary Snyder on the High Sierra of California, a big, beautiful limited edition of one hundred copies, and he wanted us to do a trade book. It had hand-set type, special papers, and original prints. It exemplified the highest standards in book craft—a

Malcolm Margolin and Gary Snyder, Berkeley, 2008. (HEYDAY ARCHIVES)

luxury liner of a book, deeply satisfying and utterly thrilling. I was simultaneously inspired and distressed. In doing a trade edition, I was going to
take something beautiful and make it uglier! That kept me up nights.

The focus on beauty happens to some extent at our meetings. In other
businesses they talk about the bottom line, profit, costs. We do, too, but it
doesn't have the same sway as in other places. The main question here is
how to make this thing beautiful. Beauty has a voice in our meetings. People
are rewarded, praised, for doing beautiful work. When somebody comes in
with something beautiful, I'm just so delighted by it. When a book comes
in under budget, that's great, and I'm full of compliments. When a designer
comes in and has done a beautiful cover, I'm gushing all over the place.

For example, we had a meeting recently about what to do with a book
of photographs Cris Benton made, flying a kite over the South Bay salt flats.
We talked about keeping it within budget, but that was so minor. The *real*
conversation was what it should look like. We spend a whole lot of time on
these books, thinking about what their soul is, what motivates the author,
what's in there. We visualize people reading the book; they enter into that

book, and when they come out of it, they're going to be a different person. How are they going to be changed? What are we going to do within that book to facilitate that change?

So it's all a matter of beauty. Why else would people work here? For the laughter, I suppose, and there's a lot of that. But the laughter would go away if these things were ugly. The whole thing would collapse. It's just a *sine qua non*.

What I do is hire people and give them the best of my feedback, the best of my thoughts, make certain that they've got enough time to do something wonderful. Frankly, I do a certain amount of protecting people's capacity to create beauty. I run interference when necessary. A couple of people have said something interesting about my taking blame. I hadn't been aware of what that meant for others, but it's true. When something goes wrong, I'll take the blame for it so they can do beautiful work.

There's that wonderful story about Moses Mendelssohn. He was the grandfather of Felix Mendelssohn, the composer and pianist. Moses Mendelssohn was famous as both a Talmudic scholar and an enlightenment philosopher. He straddled worlds. He was also deformed, a hunchback. When he was a young man, a marriage was arranged for him with a woman from a distant place. On the day of the marriage, the bride came and saw him for the first time. She said she couldn't go through with it. The relatives of the bride tried to talk to her, to tell her that beauty is skin deep, that he was the most capacious soul that the world had ever seen, kind and brilliant, and that she'd be happy with these internal qualities. But she just couldn't picture herself with a person like this.

Finally, the relatives came to Moses and told him, "Listen, here's what's happened. We're sorry. We're going to have to call the wedding off. We'll settle about the dowry."

He said, "Hey, I understand why she wouldn't want to marry me. But I ask for just a ten-minute conversation with her."

They agreed. She came in very reluctantly for this conversation. What he said was this: "There is an understanding that before we're born, we're in heaven with God. In heaven, we discuss Talmud and Torah with the angels.

We're in total bliss. We can even see what our lives are going to be. However, at birth, that prior knowledge is erased so we can begin our lives afresh.

"For some reason, that knowledge was not erased for me, so I remember when I was with God and the angels. When I asked to see who I would be in the next life, I was shown a perfectly formed, handsome young man who pleased me greatly. "And whom will I marry?" I asked. They brought before me a hunchbacked woman, gnarled and deformed. I said, "No, *she* must be beautiful. Let *me* have the hunchback.""

So there's something valuable about creating a place where other people can do beautiful work. I'm just amazed at the people that have written these books, that have designed these books, that have kept this thing going.

What I love about publishing is creating books. I've never been very good at long-term planning, mission statements, those kinds of summations. I've been good at stories. Behind each is some kind of value, courage, excellence, and generosity. It's a life of tapas rather than main courses.

People ask me why we keep publishing books about Indians and others at the social margins. The metaphor I often use is that they asked Willie Sutton why he robbed banks, and he said, "That's where the money is." I'm a publisher. I need stories that are passionate, something to believe in. So I find where the stories are. And they're great stories. But I keep returning to the question "Why aren't twenty-five Heydays mining these stories?" The stuff that slips through my fingers is daunting.

It's not always easy, but I tend to just live with things. There have been money problems for forty years, and there will always be money problems. Then there's catching up on emails, a flood of them. It's relentless. But here's one that begins, "Beloved Malcolm." So I can't complain! I'm completely disorganized. I have no idea how to put emails in files and folders. Stuff will stick in my mind that I'll respond to, and other stuff I'll forget and won't do. Sometimes I'll just shoot it over to an assistant. Sometimes I'll answer it briefly. Sometimes I'll say the truth: "Hey, listen, in a better world than this, I'd give it all the care and attention that it deserves, but I'm over my head, and I just can't do what you would like me to do and what *I* would like to do."

It can be overwhelming. I wish I could be more of what people want me to be. People have these genuine needs. One of the things I determined, though, was not to be a slave to the inbox. There's a part of me that's in a daydreamy world, so sometimes I just don't give a damn. At the same time, I just wish I could do more. So I do feel bad.

How do I cope with it? I get up at five in the morning. I work late, and I work weekends. But a whole lot of it is not all that laborious. Much of each day, I'm reading inspiring words, talking to people about their deepest thoughts and most intimate feelings. I go to several parties and receptions a week. I'm out in the world, active and engaged. If this is work, I can't help but wonder what play must be like.

LETTER FROM **MALCOLM**

B ELOW IS A letter that Malcolm wrote responding to someone seeking to publish with Heyday, reinforcing Malcolm's reputation for writing meaningful missives and highlighting his appreciation of both books and baskets.

Many things stand out from your letter, including the sentence "Some things I don't talk about because, once you let it out, it loses something."

I think I know what you mean. Perhaps it has something to do with the fact that words can't capture all the tones and nuances, shadows and depths of the past, and once you put it into words, the words tend to take over the memories. Is that what you mean? There are things that might be best not to talk about, and I thoroughly respect that.

But I'm a writer and a publisher. The books and magazines that we do are the baskets that I present to the world in the best way I know how. Like basket weavers everywhere, I keep my eyes out for beautiful raw material. I see it there in your stories and your memories, a way of capturing not just historic facts, but the very mood and soul of the area and those who rose out of it. I don't want to intrude but if you'd like, I'd be pleased to visit you and work with you for a day or two to weave a basket of words out of your wealth of memory.

JOHN MUIR LAWS

J OHN MUIR LAWS is as passionate about Heyday as he is about the flora and fauna that he draws and explains so well in his field guides and other books, including *The Laws Field Guide to the Sierra Nevada* (2007), *The Laws Pocket Guide Set to the San Francisco Bay Area* (2010), and most recently, *The Laws Guide to Drawing Birds* (2012). In the same careful way, Jack analyzes the ambience at Heyday and the significance of relationships there, from the welcome he receives at the office to the joy of celebrating the final product.

Even though my name is John Muir Laws, I'm not a descendant of John Muir. My mom and dad named me John Muir after a grandfather and a great-grandmother, but the whole time I was growing up, I thought I was related to John Muir. Even my grandmother was giving me John Muir books as presents. As it turned out, I was always interested in nature, natural history, and biology as a kid. I started making field notes by doing sketches of everything I saw. Over the years, that morphed into keeping detailed, illustrated notebooks. Anything you do a lot of, you start to get better at it.

When I was in college at UC Berkeley, I knew of Malcolm's work, and I thought to myself, "I really like the books he makes. I'd love to be an illustrator for one of them." I'd done some drawings for a little field guide for a Boy Scout camp where I was a nature counselor. I brought those over to Heyday and proudly showed them to him. The booklet wasn't very good, but he was gracious. He listened to me and asked what I was interested in. He explained this wasn't what he was looking for right now, but he encouraged me to keep doing what I was interested in and keep working on it. And I did.

I would regularly run into Malcolm at California Indian events and other places around Berkeley, so over the years I got to know him a little. Then after he started *Bay Nature* magazine, Marilyn Smulyan, who was working on it, approached me. She knew about my sketches and suggested I find out if *Bay Nature* would want to have a "page from a naturalist's sketchbook." I ran it by them, and now it's become a regular feature. So I ended up getting to illustrate in a magazine that Malcolm had started.

I was then working at the California Academy of Sciences as an environmental educator. I wanted to write a natural history of the Sierra Nevada that would be easy to use and filled with color illustrations, one lightweight book about birds, mammals, reptiles, amphibians, wildflowers, insects—everything *together*. I hoped someone else would write it, but nobody was doing it the way I envisioned.

In 2001, I went to Los Angeles to help take care of my grandmother while she was dying. I had a lot of time to think about my life. I realized if *I* were on that bed right now, I'd be thinking, "What I really should have done is...." I realized I wanted to make this book about the Sierra, and I wanted to raise a family. So my grandmother was my motivation to start doing both.

I came back to the Bay Area and entered the science illustration program at UC Santa Cruz, quit my job, and took off to the Sierra Nevada. I started painting wildflowers, drawing bugs, and sketching everything I could see. One way or another, I was going to make this book work. By 2002, I took drafts of pages to different publishers, asking, "Would you be interested in publishing something like this?"

Everyone said yes! I thought I'd go with UC Press because of the UC connection, but they had specific ideas for the book: "Tweak this and that so it feels like the imprint that we have."

I had imagined that while you're writing your book, publishers give you an advance of thousands of dollars, and you happily live off it. I discovered that that wasn't the case. The advances were a small loan against expected sales, and it wasn't that much. I knew this book would take years to make. How was I going to do it? I was struggling with writing grants on my own. My friend Marilyn Smulyan was a grant writer and had helped me tighten up some of my proposals. I was pleased about getting one grant for a few thousand dollars on my own. But I was amazed by the amount of work this was going to take.

Again Marilyn said, "I think you should talk to Malcolm. Even if you decide not to publish with him, he'll listen to you and give you good ideas."

So I finally went to show him what I'd been working on. When I'd talked to other publishers, they were very businesslike about the product and marketing, what the financial outlook was for something like this.

When I saw Malcolm, he welcomed me and led me over to show me a painting on his wall from Chiura Obata. Then we talked about the Sierra Nevada and exchanged stories. When I brought out the stuff that I had done, his response was totally different than what I had been encountering. He said, "Oh, this is—this is *gorgeous!*" He was holding onto that word. Then Malcolm brought in another staff person to show her. "Look at this work!"

He then asked me to tell the story of what I was thinking about doing, what my inspiration was. I think he sensed I was committed to doing this book. He seemed genuinely delighted, as if the whole idea was audacious and fun. He liked it and wanted to be a part of it. Instead of doing any hard sell, like "Here's what we do now. Here's a contract," he just asked questions: "What are your thoughts about making this work?"

I told him that I was mostly looking to him for ideas about fundraising. Then he said, "I think you're going to need a lot more money than I could offer you in advance for doing something like this. I know other publishers out there can give bigger advances than I can, but probably even those aren't going to be on the scale of what you need so that you can throw yourself into it and work nonstop on it."

He said, "I've never done something like this before, but in the course of our conversation, I've got an idea. Don't say anything about it or make a decision now, but take it home and chew on it, and see what you think." He was very modest about what he could offer, but he said, "If you decide to publish the book through Heyday, we have a good distribution network in California. I haven't done a lot in the field guide area; this would be new for us, so we have to explore how that will be.

"We could offer an advance of a few thousand dollars, but that's not going to get you very far. Or, instead of giving that money to you, we could give that money to the grant writer that works with us at Heyday, and pay her to get some bigger grants on the size and scale that you need. We could approach various foundations. I think we'd have a reasonably good shot with those.

"But doing that is not a guarantee. I can tell you we would do the utmost on our part to try to raise that money, but we don't know what would come through. So there's a risk. It could be that you agree to do this with us, and we don't get the money, and you also don't have your advance!" He concluded, "Take that home, ponder it, and see what you think."

I went home and thought about it. One thing really struck me about the offer: I felt Malcolm saw my vision of what this book could be, and he really listened to me. He took the time to understand what my book was. He wasn't turning it into *his* book. He knows a lot more about books than I do and of course could make suggestions and help me tweak things. But the vision that I had in my head of the look and feel of this book was something that Malcolm would support. He'd let me write *my* book.

Also, Malcolm had enough faith in me to make this offer. He knew I'd do everything on my end to make this book work. I felt that he was sincere in his hopes of being able to raise money to support me in doing this. He was willing to go out on a limb for me. It helped that Malcolm had remembered me from before. There was some history, including the connection with *Bay Nature*. I felt seen, respected, and valued. I just loved the feeling from that meeting, the flow of the conversation, the breadth and depth.

That evening I thought, "If I go with Heyday, one of the things that will happen is that I'll get a deeper relationship with Malcolm." At the end of the day, the relationships we have with people are at the heart of what being alive is about. And that's what I wanted to do.

So I started working with him. His team went to work. He pulled out all the stops to try to get me funding. They did an amazing job. Patricia Wakida was the grant writer. The funding came from the Richard and Rhoda Goldman Fund. He brought me to their office with him. We put all the stuff out on the table in front of them. He said, "Look, this is good!" He helped frame it as a moral imperative to make this book happen and support this kid who's out on the mountain with his granola bars and his watercolor kit. "This book needs to be made, and we need to support it." He gave it everything that he had to support me—and the foundation did, in return.

I thought it would take six or seven years to finish, but I worked hard, and it took four. The book actually came out in 2007, ahead of time. They were surprised when it came in as quickly as it did. Malcolm said, "This may be the first time that a book has come in before it was scheduled to!"

Malcolm really sets that tone there. Everyone in that building is invested in the mission. They see why it's important. He makes the work joyful. My impression from the outside is that Malcolm respects the people there. He's hired quality people and lets them do their work. He helps set tone and direction, then gets out of the way. Then they all celebrate it together. It's not him taking the bow for their work.

I have an example. We'd finally sent off to the printer the last version of my most recent book, on drawing birds. When we got a few books in our hands, I decided that I'd like to take the principal people involved in this project out to lunch together to celebrate. So I sent Malcolm an email that I'd like to do this and asked, "Who should I invite?"

I didn't get an email right back. I was going to talk to him the next day anyhow, so I called him up, and he said, "I'm sorry I haven't responded to that email. I've been thinking about it. My problem is that almost everybody here has been involved and connected with the book, doing little things to move it along and support it." He wasn't just thinking about the major editor but everybody in that building. How did that book get done? He couldn't single out just this person and that one. He was valuing the work and input of *everybody*. Once he mentioned it to me, I thought, "Of course that's right!"

So I got some Indian food and brought it to Heyday. We all sat down together in the conference room and had a feast. It was totally fun and appropriate, celebrating everybody there. He was really aware of how collectively that team had pushed the project forward.

Also, when I've gone to the office to show Malcolm something, if he thinks it's beautiful and wonderful, he just has to go out and share it. He'll hurry into the next room and grab the first person he sees away from her computer. "You just have to look at this!"

I've heard him say that his metaphor for his job is that he's sitting by a river of beauty, and every once in a while, he takes his ladle and scoops some out. He helps form it a little and then brings it into the world. I think when he sees beauty, he wants to share it. Goethe said, "A joy shared is a joy doubled." That's Malcolm, thinking that seeing this beauty will make you a better person. If you're not moved by it, he can help guide you that way. He'll show you why it's beautiful. And it *does* make you a better person.

Talking about sharing beauty, I remember at one point I was coming by and had my baby daughter Amelia in the car, so I brought her in. What does Malcolm do? He doesn't settle for just saying, "Oh, what a beautiful child." The first thing he does is get down on the floor with her where she's crawling around. He gets into the zone of *her* focus and starts talking to her, goofing around with her.

A woman on the staff walked by and looked in. He called, "Oh, you have to come see this baby." She comes over, and she's looking at Amelia, saying, "What a sweet baby."

But Malcolm says, "You can't appreciate her fully from up there! Come down here." So the next thing you know, we're all lying on our bellies, at face level with Amelia! The way he lives is an invitation to experience the world more richly, perhaps to see beauty in places that you otherwise wouldn't.

I have a story about when I knew I had done something good with my own book. The rangers and naturalists at the park have fully adopted this guide. When someone is new to the service, they say, "Here's your hat, and here's your field guide." I felt I'd really made it at Yosemite when a ranger sent me some photos of a group of rangers pointing things out to visitors. Some pictures showed an older gentleman with white hair and a strong-looking face. You look carefully, and you see he's got my field guide in his hands or it's peeking out of his jacket pocket as he's walking around. It was E. O. Wilson, the eminent naturalist. I thought, "If E. O. Wilson has *my* guide in his pocket, I've done something right!"

On a regular basis, I get emails from people, like about how their kids can use the guide and connect with it. Their little daughter loves using it, too, and is able to identify all these plants and flowers and bugs now. It seems to be really functional and demystifies the struggles of identifying what you're seeing. That makes me really happy to know!

In Malcolm, we see how you don't have to lose your soul as your business grows. There's real value in figuring out what it is you really love, how

Malcolm and Jack Laws about to board the Alma *during "Year of the Bay" festivities, 2012.*
(HEYDAY ARCHIVES)

you throw yourself into it, while staying true to your original values and motivations. Good things will come out of that process. We can trust that that will happen. As writers, we can see that what emerges is authentic, joyful, a reflection of the best a book can be, as opposed to doing a lot of work and getting crushed by the process of trying to get it published or going through negotiations with the publisher—when something that was all love turns sour. I actually know somebody who got a book published but the process put him off so much that there's not a lot of happiness about or connection to the book. In the process of all the haggling, negotiation, pressure, and changes, their relationship with the book got turned around. Imagine resenting your own book!

Heyday is a place of integrity. They're doing things for the right reasons. They connect with people who have a lot of love. As a writer, you work on something that you love, but the writer's share is only part of what makes a book. You have this thing that you've toiled over, and then you hand it over to somebody else. If it's somebody you deeply respect, someone you love, then the work that *they* put into it has a different feeling about it. The edits from the folks at Heyday changed a bunch of things, and now it's much better. So the whole process felt very collaborative and fun. It allows a book to emerge into the world, both skillfully done in a technical way, but also treated with the right energy, prayers, ceremonies, practices.

When you're looking over something with Malcolm, he's another writer, so he appreciates and understands your journey to get to that point. He doesn't take it lightly that you're handing it off to him. It's a big responsibility. He wants to do his utmost to help that succeed.

FRED SETTERBERG

AFTER SEEING THREE books published elsewhere, Fred Setterberg has since had four books published by Heyday, including *Under the Dragon: California's New Culture* (2007), written with Lonny Shavelson, a book that captures in photos and text the multicultural nature of the Bay Area in often surprising ways. Heyday also published Fred's faux-memoir, *Lunch Bucket Paradise: A True-Life Novel* (2011). Fred's enthusiasm for working with Heyday points out how even the process can be beautiful.

I got involved with Heyday through Lonny Shavelson, my coauthor on the book *Under the Dragon*. It was still very unformed when we took it to Heyday. In our meeting with Malcolm, he had a spark of openness to the idea. "Tell me more. Those are great photos! Yes, the shape of the new California culture as a majority of minorities is an important issue. Yes, go into the project not from the conventional lines of speaking to experts, but rather do the reporting on the ground." We talked about it a number of times, and we always found excitement there.

One of the Heyday successes is great collaboration. I find it rare that people want to make things happen, much less to work with others in doing so. But that energy runs pervasively through Heyday, a tone set by Malcolm. People lock fingers and make a web that becomes the ground upon which you can build whatever the project is.

With our first book, *Under the Dragon*, I watched how Heyday dealt with problems that came up. At times it seemed like all we had was a bunch of unrelated junk that would never adhere into anything practical. One evening at Heyday, Lonny put up a projector and showed some of the photos. A bunch of people from Heyday and Heyday friends were there. Heyday does this well, bringing out a still embryonic work, inviting people to see it from their own positions of experience and expertise, and then talking about where it might go. That presentation gave us an opportunity to develop what we were seeing and thinking.

Lonny and I eventually presented the photos to the Oakland Museum board and staff for an exhibit. They immediately said, "Fantastic! Let's have a show here. We'll be copublishers. It'll be great." Two months later, the museum director left, so the museum moved into a netherworld for nearly two years until they hired someone new. Finally, we asked Malcolm to step in. He is both authentic and wise about resolving problems. Always foremost in his mind is getting a positive result. It's astounding how he makes it all work out and ends up with so many of these collaborative relationships.

I remember the first time I saw Malcolm. I was working at the East Bay Center for the Performing Arts in the 1970s. We had a summer children's theater program in downtown Richmond, a very poor part of Richmond. One or two of Malcolm's kids were in the program, along with other kids from Berkeley; he'd pick them up sometimes. I remember looking out the window one day in my office and seeing this long-haired guy in a VW bus piling the kids in, and watching some of the black kids in the neighborhood throw rocks as the white interlopers were driving away. I thought, "Oh, yeah, that's Malcolm Margolin. He wrote that book about the Indians."

I didn't meet him until we were talking about *Under the Dragon*. When we met, I was amazed by all the activity at Heyday. I thought, "Wow, people are making a bunch of cool stuff happen here!" Not in a frenetic way like at a newspaper with daily deadlines. Nor is there the typical ethos of living on crisis to get work done. Instead, everyone at Heyday is steadily doing a lot of work. It's a geological accretion. At the end you have a mountain of that season's output of new books.

As for *Lunch Bucket Paradise: A True-Life Novel*, I'm very pleased with it. I told Malcolm about this book I'd been toiling on for eight years, writing various versions that failed to work. He was interested, so I showed him what I'd rewritten thus far. Though Heyday doesn't do a lot of fiction, the content matter *is* Heyday territory, about California history, the founding of 1950s working-class suburbia in San Leandro. So he said, "Yes, we're interested. Proceed."

Everybody did a beautiful job with it. Jeannine, my editor, was really great, a perfect combination of critical insight and an attitude of letting the author finally decide. Such careful suggestions: "Might you phrase it this way?"

If I felt otherwise, I'd just say, "No, this is my preference." And that was that. More often than not, though, Jeannine was correct. Heyday folks convey the sense of "We're aiming to get it right for the book and for you." My experience with every book there is that editing has always improved the books.

That's *not* always been true in my experience with other publishers. In one project with a large press, I met with the editor after he had about half the manuscript. His questions indicated that either he hadn't read it or he hadn't understood it. It wasn't exactly difficult material. He communicated very strongly that this project was on the fringes of their overall program and not terribly important. That's never the case at Heyday.

In his essay "Why I Write," George Orwell talks about the four motivations of every writer, which include political purpose, a desire to effect change, a desire to be remembered, and aesthetics. He essentially says, "For any piece of writing beyond a train schedule, some aesthetic consideration should be involved." Those considerations are paramount at Heyday in the care that they take with the layout. Each book is regarded in an old-fashioned sense, venerable sense, of an art and a craft. At a big press, that approach wouldn't be paramount for them, not when they're disgorging five hundred books a year or more and the bottom line is always lurking.

Heyday has an elusive quality. It exists in the hard world of production, of dollars and cents, but it lives in a kind of dream world, too, artfully weaving between those things.

I don't have any complaints besides the fact that Heyday has failed to enrich me materially.

SUSAN SNYDER

⌠USAN SNYDER IS the head of Public Services at the Bancroft Library at the
⌡ University of California, Berkeley, and a four-time Heyday author. The Bancroft
Library, initiated by Hubert Howe Bancroft, was founded on his 1905 collection
of sixty thousand images, pamphlets, newspapers, diaries, oral histories, and other
works, now the foundation for a stellar research library of over sixty-eight million
items. Susan's story of her work with Heyday in conjunction with the Bancroft Library
illustrates both how Malcolm nurtures new talent and how he finds organizational
support for Heyday's work.

I never intended to be a Heyday writer. It was all in Malcolm's head!

We had been friends for a while. I adored him. He was a big fan of the Bancroft Library and came to a lot of library events. As a publisher of California history and culture, he saw the library as a great cache of treasures, and he very much wanted access to and interpretation of those resources.

I'd been asked by the Berkeley chancellor to find an image for the chancellor's holiday card. I came upon a lot of iconic images of bears on fruit-crate labels from the 1910s and 1920s. Something rang a bell for me: What's going on with these mythologized animals? I'm a Californian; why don't I know about this? After I made the chancellor happy, I kept looking through our holdings for grizzly bears. They were all over the place.

Malcolm came to the library for our annual holiday party and asked me what was going on in my life. I said, "Grizzly bears!" I showed him some of the items I'd found, including an original poster for a bull-and-bear fight. It was thrilling to me that we had that. He got very excited about all of it, too. He immediately said, "We have to do a book." He didn't know anything about me as a writer, yet he already envisioned a book! "You *will* do one, right? Can you have it ready by next August?"

This was in December. I just said, "Yeah, I guess!"

Before that, I'd always been a diarist, and I'd written a lot of detailed letters throughout my life and a number of articles. I thought about writing a book, particularly about my years living in Japan. I thought I *could* do a book but hadn't been able to make it happen. I was very naïve in agreeing to the bear book right off the bat. But I *did* get the manuscript to Heyday—by the following January, not August. Then it turned out that there would be an exhibit as well, so I was also working on the exhibit.

I was very motivated by the topic because I'd grown up in California, so this was "my" bear, but I knew nothing about it, which was kind of horrifying to me. As a child in Yosemite, I'd watch the black bears in the garbage pits, but I never thought about the grizzly. I've always been involved in wildlife issues, so I wanted to know more about this wonderful grizzly bear. I was also interested because this material had never seen the light of day before. It was exciting that the Bancroft Library had grizzly bear ephemera that could be found nowhere else.

Malcolm was excited, and that's one of the things about him: he gets so enthusiastic about people's projects, which is very encouraging and inspiring. If not for that, I might have been horrified that I'd just committed to writing a book with no experience. But Malcolm made me feel confident.

The resources of the library astonished me. Every morning I opened the library at seven o'clock and chose one whole shelf to go through before my workday started. I got really good at looking for those double z's. It was a wonderful time, and I caught the bug for doing that research. I told Malcolm that it was fortunate that he chose the grizzly bears as a first project for me, because it was a piece of cake in a way. Everybody wrote about grizzly bears in the nineteenth century; everyone had some kind of altercation or interaction, some story to tell about them. So it was like picking up a windfall of apples.

I didn't really communicate with Heyday much while I was writing. Not knowing how publishing works, I just felt I had to do *my* job first, and then I'd turn over the manuscript to them. Once I did, I worked with a couple of editors, including Jeannine Gendar, and then with Dave Bullen, the designer, who asked various questions. I got to see multiple proofs. It was a complex job for him because there was the text, then images with captions, and also my comments on those captions. I thought he did a great job. But it wasn't until I saw the printer's proof that I was blown away.

I didn't like the cover at first. One thing I'd been trying to do in the book is defend the grizzly from this idea of it being a red-eyed monster, which is what we have on the cover. I was horrified. I told Malcolm right away that I didn't like it. He just laughed! He said, "What would you rather have?"

I said, "Something that doesn't make the bear look like a ravening beast."

He said, "Susan, you didn't write a biological summary of the grizzly bear. You wrote a cultural history. Isn't this an appropriate image for that? And don't you think that if someone sees it on the shelf, they're going to buy it? It's a fantastic cover. Live with it." He convinced me, and he was right.

The book was beautiful! A magnificent, gorgeous thing, chock-full of so many great images. I thought it did a good job of saying what I wanted to say about the grizzly bear without beating people over the head with my environmentalist philosophy. I didn't want to turn people away from the book because I was a sob sister. I wanted them to read it and make those determinations themselves.

The grizzly bears just sell themselves. The book has paid for itself. It's an enormously popular topic that crosses generations and lifestyles. Everyone has a bear story and wants to hear one. I did a lot of talks for *Bear in Mind:* public libraries, historical societies, the Rotary Club, museums, all over the state. Heyday did a great job with publicity.

Over the years, one of my personal missions has become getting the Bancroft Library back into the hands of the people. I feel that's what H. H. Bancroft himself intended. In his interviews and collecting, he didn't limit himself to privileged, well-educated, and high-status people. He collected from all spectra. So through these books, I delight in getting exposure for the library in the general community, rather than just in academia.

After that book was done, Malcolm immediately said, "Let's do another! What do you want to do it on?" I came up with twenty-five topics I thought I could write a book about, using Bancroft Library resources. The Heyday folks weighed in on my list. Camping won out, which was fine with me.

I'd put it at the top of the list. That became *Past Tents*. It sold very well in national parks and state parks.

The next book was *Beyond Words*, taking selections of illustrated diaries we have at the library. Early on I'd given Malcolm the complete transcript of one of my favorite diaries at the Bancroft Library, by Isaac Baker. I wanted him to publish it, but he felt it didn't say anything strong enough. I learned that Malcolm is not interested in an event that's *isolated* in history. It's got to have resonance with the present, inform who we are now. The bears were perfect. There's an environmental message: Look at this animal that we lost. As for camping, people love camping, and they relate to it.

So now I thought that since Malcolm had rejected *one* diary before, I hoped that if he could see the whole collection of excerpts and images, he'd like it. I started out not telling anybody, just going through the stacks. The Bancroft Library has an *incredible* collection of diaries. H. H. Bancroft, bless his heart, catalogued all his diaries together, which is not how it's done nowadays. So I could go shelf by shelf and look at hundreds of diaries all at once. I didn't know what I'd find at first, but I set very clear parameters: They had to be illustrated. They had to be diaries, not memoirs. They couldn't be sketchbooks. The pages had to be dated. I had a spreadsheet, and I rated them as I read them.

Then I sent the diaries to the lab for scanning. After I had some pages mocked up, I showed it to the library director at the time, Charles Faulhaber. It knocked his socks off. He wanted to use it for a Bancroft Library Keepsake.

Finally, I trundled down to Heyday with my pages and—they loved it! It would have to be a rather lavish book with full color and large format in order for the diaries to be legible. I knew Heyday was not always doing well financially, so they might not be *able* to publish such a lavish book. But Malcolm liked it very much. He wouldn't give me my mockup back because he kept showing it around.

Jeannine told me right off the bat, "*I* am editing this because I love this." I was glad. I love working with Jeannine. It's comfortable with her, and she's very good at what she does. She's strict. When she makes a suggestion, she'll say, "This is an awkward sentence. How about if you do this instead?" and she's always right. Why didn't I think of that? Jeannine is very demanding, but I trust her. She's just brilliant. She knows everything about everything, when a passage is wrong or needs more clarifying, yet she doesn't try to change the way I'm saying things, to change me, and that's important.

The production on *Beyond Words* was easy and so much fun. The designer was fantastic, Jami Spittler, in Nevada City. She had just done the design for another gorgeous Heyday book, *A State of Change*, which blew me away. I actually got to work closely with her, even though I never met her. She would run things by me, stylistic details and color. At first I didn't like the way the diaries were placed on pages, such that sometimes you didn't know whose diary was whose, but she ran them all by me and took my feedback. I felt so fortunate to be included in that process. It was an added pleasure.

The end result was *beautiful!* I had wanted the diaries big enough so they were legible, which they were. Then the titles and scripts—she did a masterful job. *Beyond Words* got a mention by Oprah as her "Book of the Week." That's also thanks to Heyday pushing it.

It's interesting that Malcolm had no training in publishing; he was just flying by the seat of his pants. But he felt someone had to publish some of the books they did. In the same way, Heyday gives opportunities to people who wouldn't have had them otherwise. They also publish people who have lots of opportunities elsewhere; for example, Tom Killion and Gary Snyder chose Heyday. I think that's in part because of Heyday's focus on California history and culture *and* the quality of publications that they turn out, really extraordinary books.

I admire Heyday's stick-to-it-iveness: "I can do this no matter what anybody says." Kind of like Hubert Howe Bancroft and his collecting and history writing: "I'm just going to do it." It's astonishing that Heyday has survived, but there's a brazenness and confidence about Malcolm and Heyday. On the other hand, he's very modest and humble and lives from hand to mouth.

I *will* complain about the fact that Malcolm threw out all his papers when they moved out of the Koerber Building. That was not something we archivists wanted to hear.

It's extraordinary that Malcolm never seems to be in it for the money. He's got other objectives: exposing the Bancroft collections, celebrating young writers with the James Houston Award, or finding new California writing. Their choices are so vigorous and meaningful. Take *Wherever There's a Fight*—there's such zest in what they do! "Joyous" is Malcolm's word. His personality is to believe in people, and that comes out in the publications that Heyday produces. I've talked to other Heyday authors who've had the same experience. To have someone like Malcolm believe in you is pretty special.

STAN YOGI AND ELAINE ELINSON

STAN YOGI AND Elaine Elinson are the coauthors of *Wherever There's a Fight: How Runaway Slaves, Suffragists, Immigrants, Strikers, and Poets Shaped Civil Liberties in California*, published by Heyday in 2009. It won a Gold Medal in the 2010 California Books Awards. Stan was the editor of *Highway 99*, first published by Heyday in 1996. Stan also served as a Heyday board member. In his job at the American Civil Liberties Union, he worked closely with his fellow employee Elaine and so invited her to write *Wherever There's a Fight* with him.

STAN YOGI: I moved from Southern California to Berkeley in 1986 to start a Ph.D. program in English, but I decided quickly that an academic life was not for me. I was hired at a private foundation in San Francisco, where I got to know about grant making. Later I got a job at the California Humanities Council. When I first started, Jim Quay at the council gave me a list of people I should meet, including Malcolm. That's how our friendship developed.

I didn't have much knowledge of Heyday books before starting at the Humanities Council. Heyday was publishing far fewer books back then. But I was aware of their book *The Harvest Gypsies* by Steinbeck and another they published, *Photographing the Second Gold Rush*, photographs of East Bay locales during the Second World War. The *Highway 99* project was one

Stan Yogi and Elaine Elinson pose with the manuscript for Wherever There's a Fight, *2007.*

that the Humanities Council sponsored through an NEH grant. I ended up leaving the council soon after we got the grant, but I was able to edit the book on a contractual basis, so I continued to work with Malcolm.

Wherever There's a Fight got started when I was meeting with Malcolm and Patricia Wakida in January 2003, and Malcolm had a vision. It was his idea for this book. At first, our conversation was about the terrible political situation after 9/11, and then we talked about historical events when people fought back against the kind of oppressive forces and policies we were seeing rise up in the aftermath of 9/11. Malcolm said, "Wouldn't it be wonderful if there was a book about this history, so people would know that there's a precedent for this kind of social action in California?" I thought that was a great idea, and I thought Elaine would be a great partner for this project.

ELAINE ELINSON: I was introduced to Heyday through Stan when we worked together at the ACLU of Northern California, where I was the communications director for twenty years. The last ten of those years, Stan was on the development staff. Like Stan said, *Wherever There's a Fight* was really in response to Malcolm's great anguish about what was happening to civil liberties in this country post-9/11. He wanted to look at the history of people fighting against egregious civil liberties violations. Stan was very interested in doing that and invited me along for the ride.

We had a wonderful initial meeting with Malcolm and Jeannine Gendar at a crepe place in San Francisco and batted around ideas for this book. I immediately felt a closeness with Malcolm. He has such a warm and generous spirit, so maybe everyone feels that. But for me it was also based on our shared origins in *Yiddishkeit*—I could joke with him in Yiddish. He was like a very familiar cousin, even though we had never met before.

We were all anxious about the impact of the Patriot Act, the roundup of Middle Eastern, Muslim, and South Asian men—fearful of where the Bush Administration was taking this. We saw the value of doing a book on civil liberties, to put this event into historical perspective. Over my years at the ACLU, I'd done a lot of work around the history of the ACLU and its battles. The ACLU of Northern California actually has a unique and proud history in that it fought against the internment of Japanese during World War II when the national ACLU did not. In fact, we uncovered correspondence in which the national ACLU explicitly told the executive director of the Northern California ACLU *not* to take the Korematsu case to the U.S. Supreme Court. (Fred Korematsu became a fugitive when the United States ordered Japanese Americans to leave their homes and businesses; many were forced to live in internment camps. His case was taken up by the Supreme Court, and eventually he was vindicated, his original conviction overturned.) But the ACLU of Northern California defied that and our then executive director, Ernest Besig, basically said, "We're pursuing this. We made a promise to do this."

So Stan and I started looking at other topics related to the ACLU, which include so many of the issues we're now involved with post-9/11: national security, criminal justice, censorship, surveillance of political activity of dissidents. We came up with the chapter ideas, and that's how the book evolved.

When I went to Heyday for the first time and saw their books on their shelves, I realized they produced so many of the books I had on my shelf—*At Work*, about how the arts displayed labor; the Richard Bermack book about the Spanish Civil War vets; the Wallace Stegner collection; Upton Sinclair books. It seemed that everything I liked reading had been published by Heyday. It was a really good fit.

I'd been a journalist in the Philippines and actually wrote a book called *Development Debacle: The World Bank and the Philippines*. It was banned by the Marcos regime, which was a wonderful achievement! But despite being a writer, I wasn't familiar with the publishing world at all, the different niches in publishing or what a nonprofit publisher would be.

We thought it would take two years to do this book, but it took six. Jeannine became our wonderful editor. Malcolm was the most incredible cheerleader. Every six months or so, we'd check in with them. We felt like we were never going to finish this, but he'd say, "This chapter is so great!" or "I'm so glad you got an interview with that person." He really kept our spirits up.

I kept this note from Malcolm taped above my desk:

Dear Elaine,

It was a wonderful meeting indeed. Jeannine and I genuinely feel privileged to be working with you on a project of such depth, integrity, social and intellectual value. What a splendidly complex orchestration of skills and talents, dedication and perspectives, strategy and deep-thoughtfulness. What we are doing has left adequate behind in the dust and is heading straight for greatness.

This was 2006, so we were halfway through. In a few lines, you get all that generous spirit of Malcolm and his willingness to believe in us. I just love Malcolm.

STAN: I don't think any other publisher would have been as patient with us, with *Wherever There's a Fight*, given that initially we thought it would take us two years or so to complete and instead it took six.

Heyday is also remarkable in that with *Wherever There's a Fight*, we might not have been able to find another publisher or had the carte blanche to make it into the book we wanted it to be. Heyday publishes books that need to exist in the world—to share different ideas, to uncover and reveal hidden histories that otherwise would be lost, to share the incredible beauty of California and the western states. Whenever I look at the catalog and see the new books, I think, "Oh my gosh, I can't believe that this wonderful book is going to be in the world." I would never have imagined that there was someone who got married at fourteen in California in recent decades or that a home-health-care worker had these amazing stories to tell about her life or the experiences of Japanese immigrant workers in the early twentieth century whose stories would be lost if it weren't for Heyday.

ELAINE: When we started our formal research, we obviously looked at other histories of California. In many of those books, we certainly found valuable information, but we also realized that so many voices were marginalized, left out, or stifled: the voices of women, of people of color and left-wing dissidents. *Those* are the people that we admire so much and we wanted to make sure that their voices were heard.

The experience of traveling with *Wherever There's a Fight* has been a real community event. First Heyday organized book readings, and then Cal Humanities organized a traveling exhibit, so we traveled around the state a lot. At least one person always came up to us and said, "My neighbor was interned during World War II," or "My mother was a Rosie the Riveter," or "I was a teacher who taught this book that was censored." We usually inscribe their book, "Thank *you* for fighting against censorship," or "Thank *you* for educating our kids about the real history of what went on in this country." *Wherever There's a Fight* resonates with people because they see themselves in this book, which they can't do in a lot of other books. They see their family's struggle or community's struggle, or something they've been through. So the book has been doing really well. It's in its third printing now. Not that we're getting rich, but we're just happy that it's still circulating so widely.

I remember seeing Malcolm after that at a party. I told him that he's such an incredible writer and that *he* should be writing. But he spends so much time being a publisher. In a recent interview after he got the award from the NEH, Malcolm said it was his job to scrape the gum off the bottom of the seats so that other people could enjoy the movie.

CHAPTER 9

CREATING BEAUTY: HOW HEYDAY BOOKS GET MADE

MALCOLM MARGOLIN: *The place works on laughter, on people taking and having power. I don't interfere with your life at all. You just do what you do.*

LILLIAN FLEER: *There's no micromanaging.*

MALCOLM: *No. There's no macromanaging either.*

LILLIAN: *(Laughs) There's no management.*

MALCOLM: *It's how this dispersed, fragmented, chaotic vision actually works in the world.*

PICK UP A Heyday book and find yourself lingering over the cover's intricate design. You open to captivating images, or to voices rarely heard among mainstream publications, or to a lost story that once circulated, now returned. How did that book come into existence? In this chapter, as Heyday staff members explain what goes into making a book, they also speak of being inspired by the community they work with—from fellow staff to writers. Their experiences reveal the nature of a positive work environment, fueled by trust, flexibility, and friendship.

EDITING

GAYLE WATTAWA

GAYLE WATTAWA STARTED working at Heyday in January 2004 and is now the acquisitions and editorial director.

I went to Cal, and I majored in English and math. In English classes, I'd say I was also a math major, and they'd say with admiration, "Oh my goodness.

You must be a genius!" But when one of my math professors found out I was also an English major, oh my god, the derision! "Gayle can write us a sonnet about this theorem!" The difference in attitudes was pretty funny.

I wanted to avoid the English major, but I took a class and was a goner: reading all these fantastic works, listening to really intelligent people talk about them, and getting to explore them yourself through your papers. I also find math beautiful, a deeply aesthetic experience. I contend that math and English aren't that different on some level. The analysis and algorithmic way of thinking in math are completely helpful in editing. You have different styles of proving theorems, and you want the most elegant way possible. So much of math is logic, which is eminently applicable to writing and narrative, especially in nonfiction, where you're trying to be persuasive and build a logical argument.

In my last semester at Cal, I applied to be a part-time assistant for Malcolm. When I interviewed here, it was amazing. Malcolm's so good at interacting with young people. I cringe when I think how green I was. He asked lots of questions, like "Why are you interested in this job?" I raved about how much I love books; he chuckled. I heard later that he told his assistant at the time, "She comes across as bubbly, but a real intelligence comes through." He told me at the end of the interview, "Unless Madeleine Albright walks through the door, you've got this job."

I loved his style. Malcolm doesn't impose his own personality on the world. He absorbs, watches. He's genuinely interested in people, and they can feel that immediately. He gets people to open up in unusual ways. Who really asks you deep questions and seems so interested in your answers? That's rare.

I was his assistant for two years part-time, then went to full-time after I graduated from college. I lacked a clear idea of what I'd do after graduating. I just had a lifelong, fanatic love of reading. So I thought, "Why not try publishing?"

At first it was an administrative job. For a long time Malcolm didn't check his own email, so I'd do that, manage his scheduling, send out books with letters. Then—I've watched Malcolm do this with all his assistants, sussing out their interests—I started getting more research and editorially themed projects.

He'd tell me periodically, "I really need an assistant who just comes in with her hands on her hips and says, 'I'm going to take work away from you!'" But that's hard for a young person to do. I've gotten better and better at it. Even now, if Malcolm says, "I'll write to such-and-such person," I'll insist, "No, *I'll* write that letter."

When I went full-time and had been at it for two years, Malcolm and I rarely crossed paths. But one day I was at my desk, doing a crossword puzzle, and he saw me. We sat down together and talked about it. He said, "I'm not paying you to do crossword puzzles at your desk."

I said, "Yeah, I know, I'm sorry."

He took it a step further. "I can see you're bored; you're not being challenged." That's amazing to me. Most bosses would say, "You're bad; you're wrong." Instead, he saw *why* I was doing that.

Shortly after, the *Inlandia* project started. He'd gotten a grant from the Irvine Foundation to do an Inland Empire literary anthology based on writers in Southern California east of Los Angeles. The first thing he did was give it to me to research what was out there. Then I just kept working on it. I ended up editing that anthology. I told Malcolm years later, "You were nuts giving me that project! We got seventy-five thousand dollars from Irvine, and you were giving it to a twenty-four-year-old."

He said, "What's the worst that could have happened? A mediocre book? They happen."

Then the previous acquisitions editor left Heyday, someone who had gone from assistant to acquisitions. Based on my work on *Inlandia*, Malcolm said, "Why don't you step into this job?"

I said, "Oh, I don't think I'd be good at that."

But Malcolm insisted, "Yeah you would." So I was really pushed into it.

In fact, I loved it. He knew me, my organizational skills. I've always been very good with authors, persuading them or calming people down. I think Malcolm also felt confident that I could see quality writing, a huge part of doing acquisitions. Part of Malcolm's management style is about having faith and navigating by luck. It's not completely haphazard, but that openness to possibility has done him and Heyday well.

When a manuscript first comes in, we consider the quality, how much editing it's going to need, whether it fits with our mission and with our ability to market it well, to do well by it in the world. Just reading the manuscript, we're thinking about what the issues are, whether or not they're solvable. The writer's responsibility is to bring us a publishable manuscript. We're polishing, not rewriting. If someone is a poor writer, it's hard to bring the book up to a good level. But maybe it's a matter of organization, some crafting not beyond the abilities of an editor.

Sometimes developmental or concept editing happens before we commit to a book, because we're trying to see whether or not we can get parts of it up to the standard and then feel good about it. *Now* we can commit to this book with the understanding that all of it will come up to this level.

So Malcolm might have established a connection, and then the newly acquired book gets handed off to me. I'll guide an author through the process. Sometimes a project is four years in the making. I'll get chapters periodically. I do almost all the developmental or concept editing, helping authors craft their manuscripts. With the concept editing, you're looking at the overall arc and style. You're not correcting grammar at this stage. You're also questioning, "Is this something that's going to need images? Maps? Or can it live without that?" Thinking about the format is involved in a lot of the acquisitions editing, too.

One of the huge lessons in publishing is understanding what a book has gone through. You hold this beautiful book in your hands, and it appears to be such a contained universe, with a start and a finish. But books can go in all kinds of directions, with all sorts of ways you might organize material. That's what you're deciding on during developmental editing. I might say, "A huge portion of the manuscript is tangential to what I think is actually going to make a strong book, so you might consider trimming all that and refocusing around this theme." Or, "I really like what you've done, but I think that if you combined the chapters on this theme with the early chapters on this theme, you'd get a stronger argument altogether."

I've always enjoyed watching Malcolm's style—and every now and then I need to be reminded of it: you start from the strengths. You find the place that *worked* in the manuscript, and then build everything around that. Everything is focused on what the person did *right*. "Let's have everything be this wonderful!"

It's also amazing to me how present is the tendency to nag. I now know to write my letter and sit on it for a while, then read it again with the eyes of a writer who has put herself out there in the way that writers do with their work. How would I feel about somebody critiquing me in this way? Is this the most effective way to get what I want from this author? What I want is a good manuscript.

Jeannine's very good at sussing out the strongest theme, the main point, how to arrange things hierarchically around that. When you're a novice editor, the temptation is to be overwhelmingly critical. "You did this wrong and that wrong." You can overwhelm an author and sour a relationship fast.

Conflicts with authors never blow up, though; that's not my personality. A lot of it is explaining your viewpoint, explaining your expertise or the staff's expertise. "You can trust us. This is *why* we think it should be done this way." And we listen when somebody thinks it should be done a different way. It's negotiating and compromising. Being persuasive. Begging and pleading. Somewhat strong-arming, maybe a tad manipulative now and then. You have to know what style is going to work with which author. Some authors will send you a draft, and you'll say, "It's great," and they'll feel suspicious because you're not saying specifics. Others will say, "Okay, cool!" Some want more attention. It's interesting and challenging figuring out what they want, dealing with personalities and styles.

You have to pick your battles. What's essential for this first round of editing, and what's the priority for the next? Discussing everything at once is not effective. An early story leaps to my mind. We got in a wonderful memoir that was very episodic, exploring many different themes. The writing was lovely, but the manuscript was disorganized and had no arc. So I really went in deep. I'd give her feedback, but I'd get back something that wasn't what I wanted. I reorganized chapters. It was challenging to think about the book in a very global way.

Jeannine had read the manuscript early on and said it was not something in a state that we could take on. Then she was the one that eventually copyedited it. By that time, she said, "This is great. You've done wonders with it." To get that kind of a compliment from an editor like Jeannine is amazing. The author was really happy with it, too. It was a very rewarding experience.

There was another beautiful book by a woman enthralled with her subject. Her passion and enthusiasm came through, but the manuscript was sprawling, dense, and quote-heavy. She didn't always allow readers to make their own conclusions. But a lot of good was in there as well. In that case, my job involved brutal trimming. I sent the author back a manuscript reduced by two thirds! She was shocked. We did a lot of talking. It was hard for her that I was so invasive. *I* would mind. In the end, though, her book was really strong, and it got great reviews. The author was very grateful for the restructuring and whittling down to the core. That was very rewarding, too. And that book did really well for us.

It's definitely hard work. I don't think I ever just leave it at the door. Sometimes I wish I could.

When I'm done with developmental editing, I hand it off to a different copy editor. We have both in-house and freelance copy editors and proofreaders. By the time it gets to the line, or copyediting, stage, we're just polishing what's there, not moving around major parts of the text or trimming significant amounts. The copy editor uses the "Track Changes" feature in Microsoft Word. Then we print out the Word document so that all the changes are visible as comment bubbles in the margin. The author then goes through it, accepts and rejects, makes additional changes. The copy editor cleans up the files.

Next, editors communicate with the designer, explaining what we'd envisioned for the book. The designer puts together a design sample showing how she intends to handle things like font, captions, page numbers, every major aspect of the design. It is always subject to our in-house approval, but sometimes it goes out for the author's approval as well, especially if it's a graphic-intensive book, like a photography or art book. Once that's approved, a designer does a full "first pass" layout, which goes to the author. We're done at that stage with big changes, so you have to send it out with caveats: "At this point we can accept these kinds of changes. No moving chapters around!"

Then the proofreader catches the last little grammatical and typo problems, like hyphenation, making sure that the line breaks aren't bad. We try to make for easier reading and be sure that the design's consistent.

The proofreader folds in the author's comments and presents an entire corrected first pass back to the designer. The designer makes all the corrections and returns a second pass, along with the corrected first pass. The proofreader checks these against each other to make sure all the changes were made. It just goes back and forth until there's a final pass that the proofreader signs off on. The production director, Diane, makes sure that everything looks good, and it's ready to go to the printer. So that's the process.

Working with Malcolm, I learn things daily. I watch how he'll handle an author, how he'll persuade people, go between a good cop/bad cop thing. Sometimes in working with the author, you develop a relationship, then feel very protective of the author. I'll show Malcolm some of the work, and he may say, "No. This really isn't up to par yet," whereas I might feel enthusiastic.

One day, it was opposite. Malcolm had been working with an author and felt strongly about the history in his book, especially as Malcolm related to that history and saw its importance. So he asked me to read a chapter. I read a couple of pages and said, "I don't like it."

He asked, "What are you seeing?"

I said, "There's passive voice everywhere. He keeps saying that this stuff happened to workers, or workers did this, but I don't know *why*. He doesn't explain who employed these people; I don't understand the economics of this. I just keep having all these questions, and it makes me suspicious."

He said, "Oh, I see how the passive voice is muffling the power structure." It was cool how he really listened to my reaction. He had wanted me just to say, "Yeah, great." But it was frustrating to read, and I don't want to be the editor spending a hundred hours on that project, reading a book five times that's not up to our standards, may not get good reviews, and won't be something I'll be proud of in the end.

Tons of work goes into our books, everyone working together. I like the intimacy, the scale of Heyday. We all know each other on the staff. We're on good terms with our authors. It's just a really cool community.

Thinking about writing is challenging. When I get a new book, I often anxiously wonder, "Will this be the one that I won't know how to bring up to par or not do right by?" At the same time, this work is rewarding. It bends my brain in ways that not everybody gets to enjoy. I also like the emotional aspect of working for Heyday. Malcolm always talks about being an "emotion junkie." I'm on that page, too. All this beautiful stuff is incredibly inspiring. I'm always sitting at my desk, laughing or crying while reading manuscripts. Who can say that about what they do on the job? I feel like I'm doing good in the world by being a mediator between these writers with their incredible stories and their cultures revealed, and then getting these books out to their own community and to a larger reading public. It's important work.

JEANNINE GENDAR

JEANNINE GENDAR HAS had a long career of editing at Heyday, beginning in 1989 with working on *News from Native California*. She then took on a variety of roles, from acquisitions to developing manuscripts to copyediting.

I came to Heyday to work on *News from Native California*, and the editing required a lot of sensitivity. The question always comes up of when you edit to make something "proper" versus when you let things go so that the person submitting the article sounds like himself or herself. When do you let ambiguities slide because the author wants it that way? At least check with the person about it. That was a good education in not taking too many liberties as an editor.

I had a ton to learn. People spell tribal names three or four different ways. Sometimes you let that go, hopefully not within the same issue of the magazine, but sometimes there might be strong political reasons for some of those differences, including even one letter in the spelling of a tribal name.

Since books are a more permanent medium, they require even pickier editing. I've learned that most authors are so happy to have attention paid to their manuscripts that they hardly mind when you get into ridiculous levels of pickiness about their punctuation. There are two ways of spelling "descendant"; both are okay, but stick to one within the book. Most authors like that somebody else is dealing with those kinds of details. Also, they're appreciative when you point out a clumsy sentence or if you do some fact-checking that they never got around to. So that's been really good.

I'm just grateful we've been able to do that kind of close editing, which is getting a little uncommon in publishing. It's economic. But a lot of publishers work with people who are writers by profession, and we often work with people who are experts in their fields but not writers per se, so it's appropriate for us to work closely with the editing, trying to make things as readable as possible.

Those are important things that I've learned. Another lesson was about not being afraid to edit. I remember when I first started working full-time on books; we got a piece from a pretty well-known writer. I was so awed by working on that person's writing that I went really light on it at first. At that point Malcolm was looking at most of the things that I had worked on—that didn't last very long. He pointed out that this piece of writing could be made clearer, and maybe I should look at certain other things. I did, and the person who wrote the piece was very appreciative about it. So I got over my awe of well-known writers and went on to wonderful relationships with a lot of people.

DESIGN AND PRODUCTION

REBECCA LEGATES

A PART-TIME AND WELL-LIKED designer, Rebecca LeGates originally started at Heyday as a sales and marketing assistant in January of 1997.

My interest in publishing actually started in high school in Vancouver, BC. For a volunteer service project, two friends and I worked on publishing a children's book. We came up with a budget and received a grant for fifteen thousand dollars from the provincial government. We did workshops with children's authors and talked with a press in Vancouver to find out what went into making a book. It was more of the mechanical side of publishing, as opposed to marketing or editorial, but I was hooked.

Then in my senior year of college, when I was thinking about what I wanted to do with the rest of my life, that book project was at the top of my mind. My degree from UC Santa Cruz is in world literature, cultural studies, and women's studies, not related to design at all! But I researched local, small publishing companies, and publishing, and it sounded like a great first career. Although my main interest was design, I learned that marketing jobs were the easiest to get without prior experience. So I wrote letters to small presses in the Bay Area, asking about internships. I interned at Kelsey Street Press for a year, a one-woman poetry press that did about two books a year, very small but very interesting.

After that experience and later work in bookstores, I looked for a job in publishing again and got a sales and marketing position at Heyday. I was still relatively new to the Bay Area and hadn't really heard of Heyday. It was even smaller back then. I'd heard Malcolm's name; he was just as much known in the community then as he is today. I remember him being very friendly and nice, laughing and talking about the company. I left thinking it would be fun and exciting to work here.

At first I was assisting Amy Hunter, the sales and marketing manager and a wonderful mentor, very enthusiastic and interesting. I didn't work directly with Malcolm. I remember being told that Malcolm liked to know what people were working on, so he'd check out what was on top of your desk when you weren't there, to see what you were doing, with a sense of curiosity rather than snooping.

Making my transition from marketing into design was accidental. I took an evening class in PageMaker, the design program everyone used back then. I also worked on designing a student art and literary magazine. With that one skill, I was able to help with press releases and other marketing materials. Amy would say, "Here, take this one and make it look pretty." I enjoyed doing that.

Malcolm wandered by my desk one day, saw what I was working on, and said, "Hey, you want to try a book?"

I said, "Oh, my gosh, really?" So I did. I don't think the first one looked so great, but they published it anyway. Being given the opportunity was one of the best things that happened to me. One of the benefits of working at Heyday is that, because it's small, you get exposed to a little bit of everything, so there's freedom to do something more interesting to you and to get training on the job.

Design is very creative, but I don't call myself an artist because design is more about taking materials that other people have created, like artwork or photographs, using them with other elements, and laying things out in a way that looks beautiful, as opposed to drawing an image myself.

New projects can pose new challenges. The coffee table book called *Room to Breathe*, about regional open space preserves, was very challenging because it's a varied collection of photographs, art, poems, and quotations. Often with coffee table or art books, the editorial folks determine the general order in which elements should appear for the flow of the book. With this book, that task was left to me, so I felt, "Great, I have a lot of freedom. I can do what I want." But it was also difficult because of the huge amount of material to work with, the different media, art, text, and all. Each park presented has a different style and landscape, so the material reflected the huge diversity of spaces. It was a wonderful opportunity to use all my skills to create a narrative and put it all together. I think it came out to be a lovely book and a great celebration of wilderness. The people we worked with from the Midpeninsula Regional Open Space District really liked it. It's always gratifying when authors we're doing the book with are enthusiastic.

A fun book to work on was a photography book called *Cityscapes* on San Francisco, by John King, that had architectural themes and information on the buildings. It was fun to work on because the photos were really good, and I could take a modern approach with the type and the look.

As to the timing for working on a book, it depends on what type of book it is. Every project is different, of course, but there's the design and then layout. In design, it may take a couple of weeks to come up with sample pages; then it gets approved. Layout involves pouring all the text and images in and applying design styles to the pages. There's less thinking involved at that stage and more just doing the work. But with *Room to Breathe*, the entire layout process was also a design process. Each spread was different and had to be treated differently, while keeping continuity from page to page. I actually printed up thumbnails of all the work for that book and laid them out on my living room floor in little piles to figure out the order in which to put pages together. It took about a month to do the initial design; for another month it went back and forth between the editor and author. There may be delays as we're waiting for approval for this or working out corrections and other changes.

The specific process begins when the material is handed over to me in a Word document. All the text has been written, edited, and copyedited, but it will still be proofread multiple times. Some things might change, too, once it goes into layout. We hope the majority of errors have been caught. I may also get art—photographs or images—as digital files. Sometimes the editors have already been involved in prepping the art, or I may be asked to check for resolution, color mode, format, and so on. I may also get captions and "specs," information on how big the book will be, how many pages it should be, any other ideas that editorial staff has for the designer. Sometimes we get that information at a launch meeting.

When I start the design, I learn about what the book deals with and try to understand what the tone and look are, the feel we're aiming for, especially for the cover if I'm doing the cover design. I'll create a few sample pages, play around with fonts. If it's a text-driven book, I'll do a chapter with samples of different styles, some of the front matter and other elements that will come up frequently, like decorative breaks between passages or poems. I'll show what those look like in the design.

When I have the design approval, I'll start on layout, pour in the text and put in the art. I have to pay attention to specs, how many words per page and per chapter. Some books are more complicated, have more elements, and take much longer. Others are simple—narrative-driven without images—and go quickly.

Once I have everything in place, I'll make another PDF (a portable document format) and send that to Diane. We call that the "first pass." Diane will pass it back to whoever is editing it. If there are any major problems—something that needs to be moved around—that's the opportunity to do so. Also, with the first pass, the editor and maybe the author will do the proofreading and find any missing elements, like captions.

The first pass comes back to me with editorial marks. I'll go through and make all the changes. Then I produce the second pass, and we go through it all over again, continuing to polish. Diane and Gayle then make the final checklist; they double-check for specific things, like page numbers in relation to the table of contents, and that titles match on the cover and on the title page.

When it all checks out, I'll create a final PDF that's labeled "To Print." Diane sends that version off to the printer. We try to schedule a standard three-month production time between when the editorial staff is done with a book and when it goes to print. As for delivery, that is Diane's area of expertise, but a full-color book usually takes about three months overseas and another month to ship to the port here. If it's black-and-white text, it's usually a shorter turnaround, maybe six weeks, depending on many factors.

I like what I do. And it's because of Malcolm and Heyday that I've had the career that I've had. Malcolm's influence on my life has been tremendous because of his being willing to let me "try a book" when I had no design training whatsoever and didn't really know what I was doing. I appreciate his willingness to work with me. He's often hired people just starting out in their careers, and he gives them the opportunity to learn, to grow with Heyday. He sees their potential; even if they haven't had a lot of formal training, he lets them learn on the job. I've benefitted from that, basically having my whole career at Heyday. He's been a very strong, guiding figure with Heyday. It's been a real privilege to work with him over the years.

LORRAINE RATH

ORRAINE RATH, Heyday's former art director, earned a glowing reputation for creating beautiful covers for books and catalogs, along with interior book designs.

Having worked at Heyday from 2005 to 2013, Lorraine shared some of her own lessons in working with authors to create the most pleasing books possible.

I grew up on a farm in southern Oregon and moved here after college. I've been in the Bay Area for twenty-three years. My dad used to ask me, "You were always a country girl. Why are you moving to the big city?" I explained that I have more access to public lands and nature here than I ever did in the part of Oregon where we lived. Everything there is private or BLM land. If you don't want to be staring down the barrel of a gun—and that's very literal—you don't leave your plot of land. So I actually get more varied nature here. I *am* doing what a country girl would do! That's part of why I loved being involved with Heyday: the respect for nature there and throughout the Bay Area.

My education is in journalism and art. I'd been working as a freelance designer and art director, mostly in the corporate sector. Work was a little slow. For a while, you couldn't throw an empty beer bottle and not hit an out-of-work designer. To keep myself active, I thought I could broaden the net. I responded to a volunteer ad to update the *Bay Nature* calendar. I love nature, and I liked the idea of meeting new people outside the corporate sector.

One thing led to another. Eventually I got a part-time production assistant job with Heyday. They started utilizing more of what I really had a background in, and I went from designer to art director. I really liked the people there, too, and I thought it was a chance to become involved in something a little less soul sucking than some of the corporations I'd been working with. The end product coming out of a lot of those places didn't seem to have any intrinsic importance to it, and I dealt with subjects I was not necessarily interested in. At Heyday, I could branch out and feel like I was doing something important.

Even though I have my own personal style in working on illustrations for, say, band covers or band art, I really tried not to impose a style on the books that came in. With a book, I try to figure out what its personality is, what it needs. That could be something very modern and clean with a photographic image, or a whimsical illustration painted on an old board, which I've done before. I just try to envision what the book's cover *already* is.

Covers can be tricky, so often we kept the covers in house. I also enjoyed doing them. When an author turns over their baby to Heyday, they may already have a lot of preconceived notions of what the cover is in their head, but maybe not the visual tools to actually do it or even to communicate that idea to us. Everyone has an opinion with visuals. People with no design experience imagine themselves as designers. It seems to be an issue unique to visual art. No one would come in and say they didn't like the ending of a book and ask if we could rewrite it a few times. There's a respect for the privacy of the writing process, but the visual aspect of an image somehow seems easily malleable to the public.

It's also very emotional. In particular, the cover is the first thing you see. It has to work with the title. It's like meeting someone for the first time. You make a lot of first impression judgments based on the cover. So a lot is invested emotionally in what people are expecting to see.

The most important part is to talk to an author in depth early on and get an idea of what their vision is for the book, the feel and the personality of the book. Sometimes they have more specific input. Let's say they're very adamant about using a particular photograph or something. Unless there's a reason not to, we tried to accommodate.

That accommodation is modeled at the top: Malcolm really wants authors to *love* what they're putting out in the world. Then they help us to love it and to support the community that's going to receive the book. So it's important to everyone at Heyday that the author really likes the book cover. However, we do use our judgment, our professionalism, and our experience to guide that process so that we get a successful cover. That means it tells the story it needs to tell *visually* on the shelf so people are compelled to read it.

The editorial department helped a lot in guiding those early discussions. Once the author and editorial had a good idea about the book, we'd have an internal launch meeting. That's when we'd discuss what the cover should be. Usually that discussion was vague because the people would trust me and liked to give me creative room to interpret ideas, which I really appreciated.

When I create a cover, I tend to come up with only one or two designs at first, not because we're forcing anything on the author, but it's a problem when some designers provide twenty slightly different choices, thinking, "More is better." If you put them all out on the table, a salad bar of graphic design, it gets confusing. You'll hear, "Well, I like *this* color with *that* font. Can you switch them around?" With good design, you can't just pull one element and expect the rest to hold. Also, a lot of options might simply be hiding a lack of a strong concept. So I like to present as few choices as possible and have an author tell me if I've missed the mark. If that's the case, then, because they don't have a million other things to point to, they're forced to articulate what leads them emotionally not to respond to my cover idea or what it is they want. Ultimately this approach is much more efficient.

Knowing how the editor works with the author to pull together a manuscript is invaluable for knowing what I'm expected to create. The more I know what goes on behind the scenes before a manuscript hits production, the more I have to work with. Also, the longer you work in this field, the more you develop a language that becomes honed over time, more concise, a language that works with editorial staff and with authors.

You have a lot of interaction in a small company. Everything runs by Malcolm eventually, a cover or a design sample for an interior. He'd talk to me directly and tell me if there was a problem or if he loved it. He'd leave me little memos; I loved getting the little hand-typed memos in the inbox. I think I kept almost all of them, all the good ones.

When I started working here, I liked Malcolm right away. At first I was terrified I was going to say something wrong. It's funny because for someone who doesn't like to impose authority at all, Malcolm can't help but present an imposing, authoritative air, as if everything he's saying is coming from the mountaintop. But as I got to know him, of course, that went away.

At Heyday you work with super-creative people. The authors are all so intensely invested in what they're doing, and that energy rubs off. Maybe I'm reflecting my own enthusiasm toward what they do, but I'd say they're more intense there because no Heyday author is under any illusion that they'll make a lot of money or this is the next best seller. Their only motive is the love they have for the subject matter.

I did over a hundred covers. In the work I did, sometimes I struggled to solve problems that aren't necessarily apparent when you glance at the finished book. For *Lunch Bucket Paradise*, getting the feel of the 1950s was really important to Fred Setterberg, the author, and to us—to be able to glance at the cover and capture the imagery of the time, even if it's subliminal. It takes a second to recognize that it's a fin of a car. That color scheme is also very much of that era.

I also liked the cover of *Fup*. I painted the duck on a piece of an old raised-flowerbed wood that we found in the parking lot of Heyday. David helped me break the bed apart for the board. We brought it in, and I started with the blue background paint. Then I felt something weird, looked at my hand, and saw that a whole nest of baby spiders had hatched while I'd been painting and were now crawling all over my hand! It's a good thing I don't have arachnophobia. Those are the things we do to get a good cover sometimes! Anyhow, it was interesting to create a new interpretation, since there have been at least six covers since *Fup* was first published.

A more elegant book was *Ticket to Exile*, which won an award. It was another tough one, with a loaded topic, racism in the segregated South. You want to treat every book with the utmost respect, not be glib about anything. We didn't have any photos to work with, unless we put the author's face on it, which we try to avoid with most of the books because that doesn't tell a story. I found a historical image from the Library of Congress that shows a young black man around the same time period as the book's story, the 1940s. I loved the way that the background was obscured, and he seems to be between two worlds. It works well with the title, with the word "exile." It's very important to me that the title work with the image. The crumpled paper represents the note the author, Adam David Miller, handed the girl. Little things like that you don't need to know until you read it. I like the idea that people are reading a book, and then they flip back to the cover and they go, "Oh, okay!"

Doing *Making Home from War*, about the Japanese internment camps, was memorable in that it afforded creative freedom and a challenge. We were riding an interesting line with the authors, with the intention and emotion they wanted to show in the cover. Usually only a limited number of images stand out as appropriate for a cover, telling the story concisely. What the authors wanted to convey was very contradictory. They didn't want the situation to seem disparaging, hopeless, or sad, or to portray victimization. They wanted to reflect a hope for the future, at the same time honoring the gravitas, sadness, and horror of what happened to these people. So there was great concern with showing them as too happy or too sad. It was a really fine line.

I liked that this cover was nebulous. They were smiling, but obviously things weren't good. There seemed to be more of a background story to this one. I treated it by layering. I used Japanese print from old wallpaper and some line textures to create an almost static image, to obscure the woman's smile a little, to tell you there was more to the story than someone smiling for the camera. I wanted there to be that mystery to it. Her smile was just enough. The authors loved the cover. It had the feeling they wanted.

What became obvious from working at Heyday is that Heyday has integrity in giving voice to communities whose books wouldn't necessarily be published otherwise and may not be best sellers but that are really important, like *Ticket* and *Making Home*. Such stories need to be told; people should hear them. And no other California-centric publishers do what Heyday does.

DIANE LEE

DIANE LEE ORIGINALLY started as the operations manager at Heyday in 2003, taking all the orders from Heyday's customers. Now the production director, Diane is deeply involved with the physical aspects of Heyday's books, from assigning designers to arranging print bids.

I had a couple of big changes in college. I first went to California College of Arts and Crafts. I thought I'd be a graphic designer. Then I ended up at the Academy of Art in San Francisco and went into illustration. But I realized with art that you're never really done; you can always make it better. It's open-ended; there's never a vacation. I saw other people go to work, come home, and have a life. I realized I needed something with a little more structure so I'm not always feeling, "I could do better!"

I've had a lot of different jobs over the years: at an art store, then as a merchandizing assistant. Among other jobs, I worked at the *Monthly* magazine in Berkeley as the assistant to Karen Klaber, who ran it. They all fed into my work here in various ways.

In college I also went through another change, where I wondered about doing something more significant with my life. So I worked for Greenpeace Action, doing fundraising and outreach, and went to demonstrations. That was an important part of my life. I'm still always trying to figure out the meaning of life. I ask everybody, "What is the meaning of life?" I often get back, "I never thought about it," or "It's to have a good time." That's not very satisfying to hear. I'm still not sure what it is, but I thought if I could help change the world and make the world more what I think it *should* be, maybe that's the meaning of life. I want to do something more with my life than just make money and live day to day.

That's one reason I love working here. I love seeing these artists and photographers have their dreams become books. Everybody has a dream book. I *love* that I get to be a part of their dreams.

People always say, "If you had all the time and money in the world, what would you do?" I'd travel and did! Before I came to Heyday, I was still searching for the meaning of life, so I sold my house and traveled for two years. I followed the sun around the world because I love the sun and the water. As it got colder, I kept going south. I started in Europe and ended up in Australia, New Zealand, and Fiji.

I also wanted to learn how to fly. I went skydiving twice before I left on my trip, just to confirm, "Oh my god, this is insane! But if I can do this, I can do anything." Later in Switzerland I did paragliding. I fell in love with it. When I got to New Zealand, I took lessons and became a certified paraglider. I also wanted to scuba dive, but I was afraid of sharks because I grew up in Monterey. So in Thailand I spent some time getting certified and then went to the Great Barrier Reef to spend a week diving off a boat.

When I came back to the Bay Area, I wanted to work at something I could love. But it was post-9/11, and the economy was down. It was hard to find a job and a place to live. I sent out five résumés a week. Eventually I interviewed here with David. Then I met Malcolm. They hired me, and it was just perfect. I actually asked David about why they hired me, and he said that of all the people they interviewed, they were interested in the fact that I took off for two years of adventure. They were very interested in that story! "Who *are* you? Who *does* that?!" David said that I seemed to be passionate about things and have confidence in what I do.

Once I got this position, I just stayed on. I realized, "Wow, I could stay here for a while, learn a lot, enjoy myself, and see what this publishing world is all about." I can't believe I'm in my ninth year here. Before this, jobs lasted one or two years for me. I'd learn what I needed to learn and move on.

My first impression of Heyday was that it was a hippie kind of place, but I could see that the workers were very committed. What drew me was that it felt like a small family of people who really loved what they were doing. And Malcolm—I saw him as a crazy hippie character! I remember thinking, "If I'm going to make money for somebody, he's the guy I'd feel good about making money for." Unlike in big corporations where the money goes to stockholders, and your boss makes five hundred times more than you make, I felt that if I worked here, I'd be making money for *this* guy. We were a for-profit at the time. I thought, "Let me make money for someone who's doing good in the world."

I knew nothing about Heyday. The funny thing is that the month before I applied, I was looking at *Sierra* magazine, and it had an article about Tom Killion's book. I fell in love with it. I never pull stuff out of magazines, but I actually tore out the images. When I interviewed at Heyday, I saw that book here. So I knew it was something that had to happen.

Also, when I was at art school, at the Academy of Art, my English teacher was Michael McClure, and he made us read *Indian Tales* by Jaime de Angulo. I tried to drop out of his class because on the first day he got us all in a circle, and our homework was to think about our ten favorite childhood books. I thought, "I'm in college! I can't believe I have to do this! And we're going to read a kids' book? Are you kidding me?!" But I was unable to get out of his class. In the end, I *thoroughly* enjoyed it. It was one of my favorites ever. Then when I started here, one of the first books I put on the shelves was *Indian Tales*. Again, I just feel like I was destined to be here in some ways.

My initial job was to take all the orders for the books and be the liaison to the warehouse. Sometimes people would call and ask things like "You printed this book way back when. I have a dog-eared copy, and I wonder if I can replace it."

I'd have to say, "It's out of print, but let me see if we have an extra in the archives that I can send to you." They were really appreciative. I liked that one-on-one interaction with strangers.

I had that job for two or three years. Then, when Rebecca LeGates got pregnant and was taking maternity leave, I said, "I want to try that position," doing production.

There's a lot of internal movement here, which I think is really good. I've done a little of Lillian's job with *News*, processing donations and sub-scription renewals. Lorraine used to be Rebecca's assistant, doing some of what I do now, printing bids. Anna took my job. Gayle used to have Mariko's job. Rebecca started out in sales. So we all have a healthy respect for one another because we know what the other person does. When we switch jobs, we can understand what we're asking someone else to do, how much time or research it will truly take. Also, we can cover for one another. We're a small company, so if you go on vacation, it's nice to have somebody who can understand your process a little.

I didn't really know too much about what I was going to get into as the production director, but I shadowed Rebecca before she went on leave. I got whatever I could from her. Rebecca is self-taught, too. I also contacted a cou-ple of our printers and asked them to dump their brains on me, including Ken at Global Interprint—he was amazing. He told me as much as he could about printing, what to watch out for, how to do my bids. I'm very grate-ful. I still ask my printers for advice. I know my portion of the job, which is buying the print job, choosing the right paper and all, but I like guidance from printers and brokers to tell me if I'm making the right decisions or if they recommend something else.

I also subscribe to a bunch of online feeds about production, and I'm part of book publishing sites that have forums for questions. I feel like I have a whole group of people out there waiting for me if I want to use the forums. So I don't feel alone in this at all.

As for the larger process, the editorial department figures out how big the book is, what the look is. Gayle handles the front end of the development, all the words. We may consult early on, if they ask, "Is this going to look good?" The art director and I might have suggestions on changing things.

When we do the art management and it comes to any images in the book, I'll field those questions and either do the art management myself— such as color profiles—or I'll have our printer do it. It depends on the budget and the scope. We also prep the images, making sure they're not low-resolution images. If I have a hundred images from different sources, I need to make sure the color profiles are correct, that the colors look good and the resolution is right for the size we're planning on.

That's the art management before it goes to a designer. Once a designer has it, we're now looking at the layout of the book. I usually choose the designer, based on everyone's capabilities and the timeline. I also hire and manage the interaction with freelance designers. Every book is very different. With Susan Snyder's book *Beyond Words*, which was mostly images from diaries, the images were already picked during the editorial process. I hired Jami Spittler, a free-lancer who I thought would do a really great job, as designer. She was able to take all the elements and put them together into a beautiful arrangement.

Once the layout is done and we have a PDF proof, I also do proofing with authors. We look for typos and corrections before we go to print, of course. With a photo book, we do the layout several times with feedback from the authors. Then we do a checklist to make sure everything is as it should be.

Off it goes to the printer. They send us full-color proofs of the book as it will appear. We check to make sure the colors are "registered" as expected and that no anomalies show up in the printed piece that we couldn't see on the PDF. That's our last time to see what the book will look like and to make any changes or corrections, like remaining typos. The farther along we are, the more expensive it gets to change. Those are decisions that I make, with feedback from others.

I arrange all the print jobs for everything we publish: our books, reprints, and the Heyday catalog. Over the years we've established relationships with various printers with different capabilities; they bid on each job. Like Heyday's a family, some of our printers are an extension of Heyday. We've worked with them a very long time, so our relationship with them is solid. Establishing a one-on-one relationship is good because I may have a lot of favors to ask, like last-minute rushes or trying to lower the cost.

Also, that commitment I had to Greenpeace back in college I brought to Heyday, because we joined the Green Press Initiative when I first took over this position. I've tried my best to be as green as possible within our financial limits. I followed their guidelines, picking printers that were certified "green." For example, many of our text-oriented books had been printed on virgin paper. Now we're using 30 percent post-consumer recycled paper, and I'm trying to get most of them 100 percent recycled. Our favorite printer now is Thomson-Shore, which is worker-owned and Forest Stewardship Council certified. So those are my own subversive things that I'm doing!

When we print overseas, the books go to China, Hong Kong, Singapore, Korea. I worry about the conditions of workers, so I talk to people who do press checks because I want to be sure we aren't using child labor or something like that. At some point I want to go to Korea and see my aunt and uncle there and at the same time talk to the printer in Korea. If I can time it when I have a book there, I can tour the factory myself.

It's hard to quantify some of the press impacts. Is it cheaper and better for the planet to send the books overseas via a giant freight boat that has tons of other cargo? We're near a port, so that helps. Or is it better for us to print domestically? Then it's coming from the Midwest because that's where the paper mills are. But now we're driving it on a relatively little truck across the United States. I choose a lot of post-consumer recycled Glatfelter paper that comes from Ohio. If we mostly print in Wisconsin and Michigan for our domestic books, it's a relatively short truck ride. With so many factors, you see the dilemma of trying to figure out which method leaves a greener carbon footprint. So I think it comes to people doing their best and getting the conversation going.

A great thing about working at Heyday is the flexibility of my time. Sometimes the demands on me are huge and immediate. I may have forty-eight hours to turn around proofs, and it may be the weekend. I make sure the book's not going to be late on *my* account! Also, there's a time difference with Asia. I might need to arrive early to get answers that help with scheduling. I want to do my job to the best of my ability. I love that some days I can come in really early and leave early because of traffic. Or I'll come in later and stay later. At times I work at home to minimize distractions. As long as the work gets done, I'm not forced to sit here and watch the clock run out. So being able to manage my time is great.

Of course, there are two sides to the coin. This freedom is also difficult because I might expect people to be here at a certain time, and they're working at home. That can throw my schedule off, too. But we're all so connected electronically these days that it usually works out.

I'm still learning new stuff all the time here. I've always been more of a techie girl, so I also do tech support here for anybody who needs it. I know a lot about Macs. But I no longer fix the whole network, because it's gotten way out of control for me. We need to upgrade all of our computers. At some point we'll need new server software, but that's beyond my scope.

I also head our electronic books project. Something is always developing in that area. I'm really happy about that since I can learn while still doing my current job. With the trajectory of e-books, tablets will soon be in more people's hands, and we want to have *our* books in their tablets. That involves the sustainability issue, too. Some books translate well to e-books. Why have warehouses full of dead-tree books? Not that electronic books don't have their own environmental carbon footprint issue; transferring information takes electricity and other costs. But it would help with Heyday's inventory problems. Paper gets old, and storage of physical books costs money. Some books we're not going to reprint because it's cost-prohibitive, so it'd be great to have them available on electronic backlists.

Also, I don't like how someone can spend their whole life writing a book or put so much love and energy into it, and we print only two thousand copies. That's all there is in the world? That just breaks my heart! I feel like the books should be out there. Some books have valuable information and should live forever, books written by people who are experts in their area, especially a lot of the Native American stories. *Medicine Trails* should live on! The two thousand physical copies are eventually going to wear out and die, but the electronic books will live forever, and so will the authors' voices. That's my motivation.

SALES, MARKETING, PUBLICITY, AND EVENTS

NATALIE MULFORD

FORMER MARKETING AND publicity director Natalie Mulford came to the job with an unusual working background, like other Heyday mavericks. She explained the nature of marketing books at Heyday.

I studied writing and psychology at Hampshire College and did all kinds of artsy things. Eventually I got a master's degree in education at Lesley University in Cambridge and worked as a special education teacher in Massachusetts for eight years. I finally moved out here and helped start a film festival in San Francisco in 2007 called the Frozen Film Festival, based on the famous Mark Twain quote about the coldest winter he ever spent being a summer in San Francisco. Then I met a previous intern at Heyday who introduced me to Lillian, who does events. To be behind the scenes in a literary organization was a dream job for me. When I was living in Boston, I'd applied many times to publishing jobs, but I'd had no publishing experience, so it was hard for someone to take me seriously.

Lillian told me that this job was opening up. When I met with David, I explained my interest in publishing, in the arts, and in California, and that I write memoir and poetry. David said, "I took a weird path myself. I think you have more in common with people at Heyday than with people who come from big publishing houses and see things on the straight and narrow." I think he saw my work in education and with nonprofits and arts organizations as a plus, and he gave me a chance.

When I met with Malcolm, he was instantly engaged in our conversation, intrigued by my own personal history. I remember talking about my parents, who were originally from the Midwest. He asked, "Are they part of the great Iowa migration to Los Angeles?" He seemed truly curious about who I was and what I thought about things. I see that in other situations where I watch him meeting people for the first time, asking where they're from, what their unique story is.

He also asked, "What about this social media thing? How do you feel about that?"

I said, "Like it or not, we gotta do it. Whether we see any value in it ourselves, it's where things are headed. To get attention, it's the way to go." I'm thirty-five and of the iPhone-Facebook-Twitter generation. Malcolm let me run with it as much as I wanted to. We discussed strategies to reach people of a particular attention span, how to maintain our artistic and literary integrity.

A great example of someone using the new media to get his work out there is Fred Setterberg. He's done an incredible job as a tireless social media promoter, branching out into different communities. It's hard for authors sometimes to keep up those online relationships, but otherwise people forget about you and think you're just promoting your own thing, and they're not interested in hearing about the book itself very much anymore. You can beat people over the head with your own project. But Fred's been able to create some community around *Lunch Bucket Paradise*.

Two main pieces intersect in the marketing and publicity job at Heyday. On the marketing side, it's creating content for the website and catalog, as well as little marketing pieces, like postcards and flyers, "collateral" publicity. The job also involves moving things online, such as creating digital versions of Heyday materials, like e-books, or moving the whole sales catalog online so booksellers across the country or the world can access Heyday titles. You ultimately want to get electronic copies of galleys to reviewers, librarians, and booksellers.

I also created back-cover copy, getting blurbs from people, and creating little sales tools called "blads," mockups of books that include the front and back covers and sample pages. At the other end of the production process, I worked on maintaining relationships with members of the press and book reviewers, getting interviews for authors, and getting book reviews and articles written about Heyday books.

Another part of the job is working with the development team to raise money for Heyday. That involves thinking about how people process information, what inspires them or gets them excited, how to motivate people to give money or buy a book or come to an event or "like" us on Facebook.

Then there's maintaining the internship program, which is essential to Heyday's operation. Lillian and I would split up responsibility for interns that came in and give them projects. We usually had three to four sales and marketing interns a season. That means getting the word out, managing résumés, interviewing people, and, later, writing recommendations. One person works on Indian titles one day a week. Another works on literary California, the James D. Houston award winner, and *New California Writing* editions, while another works on a specific book. Last summer we had a full-time intern every single day, which was incredible. She was here nine to five, and people said, "Thank god you're here!"

The best thing, I would say, about working at Heyday was that an incredible amount of flexibility and creativity was encouraged. You get to work with a hugely talented, smart, fun group of people. The biggest frustration was needing more staff people and more help—and a bigger budget to hire people—to do all the incredible things we wanted to do. The world of books is changing so much that it's hard to keep up with all the print and digital demands. I always wished I could do still more for every book that came across my desk, for every idea and event. There's no end to the number of books you could sell. In that way it's hard to feel satisfied. I know that Malcolm feels that each one of these books is a gift to the world, a piece of him, a precious thing. Similarly, certain books I just loved, but I couldn't give as much attention to them as I wanted to. A book of poems is just not going to sell all that well, even if you love the author and the book and do everything to get it out there.

For example, Stephen Meadows is a Native poet, and his book *Releasing the Days* came out last year. It's so beautiful. I was practically crying over every poem. He's the nicest person you've ever met in the universe, sweet and humble. I sent out so many copies of his book, and I tried to get reviews from various places. I got a couple of different things. The same with events: Lillian helped set up a couple of events. He came to our Heyday Harvest last year, which was great, and that helped. But we both wished we could do more for him. We maybe sold four hundred copies of his book, and the print run was seven hundred.

Some books have a lot more clout behind them. We did Ken and Melanie Light's *Valley of Shadows and Dreams*. They're both extremely well connected. They have a photography agent in New York, so they have a whole New York connection with the photography world out there. Ken teaches at UC Berkeley, so they have that university connection. They had exhibits opening both in New York and in the Oakland Museum. We were able to get a lot of media attention, including a spread in the *New York Times*. So there was a lot of support behind that book.

Jack Laws's new book, *The Laws Guide to Drawing Birds,* is still going great. It became one of our best-selling titles of 2012 after it was out for only a month and a half. Talk about a magical person! Just listening to him talk is inspiring. It helps to have an author behind a book, like Fred, someone actively out there publicizing, doing events. And it's not just for a couple of months but continually. Jack has a great website and is very focused on education. He's an incredible advocate for his own work. That makes a huge difference, not only having spectacular content, but being able to promote it. Lillian always says that the author is the best advocate, the best person to talk about their own work, better than anyone else—well, except Malcolm, because he's good at that.

LILLIAN FLEER

NOW THE EVENTS and outreach director, Lillian Fleer started at Heyday at the end of 2005. Lillian has been lionized by authors and colleagues for her organizing ability, from a book talk for an audience of ten people in a rural library to a major celebration with a cast of ten and an audience of hundreds.

I moved to Berkeley pretty much right out of college and applied for a bunch of jobs. I really liked the vibe at Heyday. I didn't even meet Malcolm the first time I came in. I just talked to David and Diane because I was going to be doing administrative stuff, but they laid out this great environment. I liked that Heyday was casual, that you don't have to dress up for work. I especially liked that I could talk to them; they seemed like real people. I didn't even know what a publisher did. I was super out of the loop! I don't know why they gave me the job. I just remember feeling comfortable in the interview, which said to me, "I don't know what I'm doing, but at least I'm going to like doing it."

I started as the receptionist, answering phones and ordering office supplies. Six months into it, the events person went on maternity leave and didn't return. Malcolm said, "Why don't you do the events?"

I said, "Are you kidding?! I don't know how to do that. I'm just the receptionist. I'm just trying to get by."

But he said, "I think you can handle it."

I said, "Really? Okay. I'll do it." So I've been doing events ever since.

I went to college at Macalester, a small liberal arts place in Minnesota. I had a wonderful experience. My major was linguistics and anthropology— the play between language and culture. In my senior thesis group project, we analyzed a speaker of Somali. We couldn't use any outside resources; we just talked to this man all semester. We got all the sounds of his language, the vocabulary, the syntax and other stuff. It was a very social project, and I liked getting to know people. When I graduated with linguistics and anthropology, people said, "What the heck are you going to do?"

I'd say, "I don't know!" But the study of people is kind of what I'm doing here. I'm interacting all the time. The editors are holed up, reading their books, but I'm out there talking to people a lot. In talking to the authors, you have to get a sense of where they're at, what they're going to be comfortable doing. Do they like small gatherings? Do they want to talk to a big lecture hall of people? Do they have a huge network? Or are they going to need a lot of publicity to help people get to their events? Some are more experienced than others. So feeling out the author is a focus of my job. I rely on the authors a lot to make up their own chores. I don't just make up every single event that we do, or I'd be dead! I help them along. But really I take energy from the author, and I put it to work.

You can see it in book sales and attendance at events. The authors that are doing a lot of work to promote their book get lots of people at their events and sell a lot of books. Some people are gung-ho about events and can even be a little pushy. Then there are the sweet, quiet ones whose books aren't selling. Sometimes those authors find their public groove, figure out what kind of events and marketing work for them, and they make it. That's the most exciting.

We had one author who was a pretty quiet person. She'd done events, but she was a little nervous. I watched her do one, and I thought she could use some help. Malcolm said, "Why don't we have her come in, and we'll do a critique of her presentation with the whole staff there." So she did her presentation with us. When she was trying to do a "fly by," it was a little dry, but we saw that once she started getting into her work in some detail, she was amazing. She just lit up and really engaged the audience. So we focused on that. Since then, she's been doing great presentations and became a huge hit.

I've heard Gayle say this about how Malcolm deals with editing, and it's the same process for us. He doesn't say, "This is wrong." He says, "This is right. Let's work more on this." I think that's a good underlying process that goes on here, focusing on the positive stuff and ignoring the negative.

When I met Malcolm after my initial interview, we just clicked. He was familiar to me. My parents moved to Vermont as hippie back-to-landers. They bought property with a shack on it and lived there for eight years without running water or electricity. When they got pregnant with me, they built a real house with electricity and a flush toilet, but this hippie river always ran through our world. So when I met Malcolm, I thought, "You're just like my parents!" It was sort of comforting because when you're three thousand miles away from your folks, you want family. He was very familiar and familial.

Very early on, I got to go to events with him. One of the first was up in Tuolumne. He said, "I'll pick you up at five a.m.; we'll probably get back home around eleven o'clock." I said, "Okay!" But I was thinking, "What is going on?!"

We had this huge, long car trip in his old 1981 Volvo. It was very noisy, so you had to talk really loud the whole time. There was no heat or air conditioning, and I remember we needed both because it was very cold in the morning, and then it got really hot by the time we got there. We just talked the entire way. He told a bazillion stories, and I told him about who I was.

I loved listening to his stories. I'm not a very good storyteller, so I'm always in awe that he can remember all of them. I find myself retelling some of his stories, never as well. When he's telling all these stories, I think Malcolm is reliving wonderful adventures. Even if the story is not about him, in telling it he gets to have a fun or sad experience. He transports himself into these beautiful situations. Beauty can be heartbreaking, also. He's very good with words, so he creates vivid images in his stories. He can put them right in front of you, bring these worlds to life or back to life, make people come alive. Then they stay in your brain. And his stories always relate to the context of the conversation. Every single one has some connection, almost like a fable. "There was this guy…" or "My good friend.…"

Because he's such a good people person, that helps make Heyday work. He can focus in on somebody that's very interesting, and then our books are often by those people he interacts with. Malcolm is well loved for good reasons. He listens when you talk to him. He doesn't try to teach you. He doesn't come across as a person who says, "Let me tell you about this." He just listens and then pipes in with a story. That makes him lovable, and people trust him with their lives. All these books are very personal. Writers don't want to hand over their life to somebody they don't trust.

He's very good at homing in on people's strengths and pushing them to do what they can do with that strength. I'm not a writer, so he doesn't ask me to write amazing copy. I focus on getting people together. What

I like to do is make conversation happen. I'd say his style is to accentuate the positive.

Malcolm is very loose in his management style, which is good for me. I might get frustrated or discouraged if there was a lot of commentary, like "You should have done this at the event. You should have had that." Instead, he knows how to compliment you in order to help you do what you need to do. "Oh, you were so good at this! Why don't we do another one like that?"

"Oh thanks!" Wait, what did I just say yes to?!

He doesn't do a lot of micromanagement. He lets us grow to our potential. He's not trying to tell us, "Try to do this over here, and that over there." His attitude is more like "Oh, she's doing this. Let's see how far she can go with it."

So without the micromanaging, we all find what we're really good at doing, and we do that to our potential. It doesn't work for some people who need more structure, but those people usually don't stay here. We get a lot done because we don't want to spend lots of time in a meeting. Not a lot of flow charts and protocols here. We appreciate the flexibility and freedom we get in our jobs.

When authors come to meet with sales and marketing staff, we have a meeting that involves three of us: the publicist; our sales guru, George; and me on events. Malcolm often comes to those meetings with the author. We run through ideas for how to pump up sales and get books out there. The authors are always so happy by the time they get to us, saying, "Heyday's amazing!" We can almost do no wrong. I love that about my team.

The whole process at Heyday is about taking care of the book and the author. The editorial process is in-depth. We edit more than most publishers do. We spend a lot of time and attention on the author and their manuscript to make it better. Then they go on to the designer, who goes back and forth with an author on the cover—how it fits with the feel of the book—reading the book and figuring out what would work visually, listening to what the author says. Then we work very closely with authors to create a marketing and events plan. If they want us to throw them a party, we'll throw them a party and invite all their friends. I think that attention to the author is important. In this writing community, we have a good reputation because of how well we treat people, not only our authors, but everybody that comes along.

As for specific events, my job is easy because I deal with amazing people, and somebody else has done all the hard work. For example, when we do the events for the *New California Writing* anthologies at the California Historical Society, I give kudos to Gayle for putting together such a wonderful book.

My planning for a big event like that starts by emailing every single contributor to the book, saying, "I want to throw some parties for this book, one in San Francisco and one in L.A. Let me know who's interested." Even without specific dates yet, I first want to get a feel for who will be excited to be part of this party.

I get some emails back, saying, "I'd love to, depending on my schedule," whatever. Some people don't write back. Some are just too big for us. For this anthology, I send a personal email to someone like Maxine Hong Kingston, saying, "I know you're kind of a big deal, but I'd love it if you were there."

Malcolm is a really good sport. He loves events. Usually I plan them for when he's free, and then he's good at blocking them off in his calendar. He knows what to expect; he's got it down. So I can say, five minutes before, "Oh, yeah, you're giving a talk!" And he'll come up with something wonderful.

Anyhow, people write back and say if they can do the event or not. Then I check in with the venue. The California Historical Society is great; it's free space. They also paid for all the wine and half the food for the last event. I appreciate that! Next I let the contributors know we've scheduled a specific date. If I get a dismal response back for the date, I just change it. It's a lot of emailing, but I don't stress out about it too much. I've found it's better not to ask people when they can do it, but just throw out a date. The democratic process of getting ten people to pick a date doesn't work. That also really cuts down the emails.

Once I have a date and a lot of people, I just start promoting it. The good thing with the anthologies is that if you have ten contributors showing up, you have ten people to promote it. And if they each brought two people, then that's a lot of people already. So I tell the contributors to send the word to their friends. With the Historical Society, they send it out to their list. We send it out to our list and sometimes other related lists. We can get a good crowd.

I love the anthology presentations like I love tapas or a field of wildflowers—a lot of little, different things. So this is my favorite kind of event. Obviously we don't do them most of the time. Usually we have an author giving an hour presentation. But I love when you get a burst from everybody. And if you want to hear more, you read more of their work.

It's fun for me to get to help design an event. Sometimes, I pair up with an organization that has a specific idea of what they want the author to talk about. "We want to get this idea across." In that case, I'm just the logistical person—we'll get books here by this time and get the word out. I let the cohosting organization work on the program, which works well because they know their audience more than I do.

About three weeks before the event, I send out a confirmation email to everybody, saying, "This is what's going to happen. This is what time I want you to show up." In the case of the anthology presentations, everybody has four minutes to talk. I even said, "You have only four minutes. Don't be the jerk that goes over." That usually works because nobody wants to be a jerk, right? Once I get everybody's final confirmation, I can stop worrying that it's going to be a disaster.

Little details usually get hammered out in the couple of weeks before, like the food and drinks. The day of the event I make sure I have help with the food. Then at the event itself, you just try to make everybody feel welcomed.

That practice of welcoming people starts with Malcolm, and we just follow suit. He leads by example. He's never told us, "You have to be really nice to people. You can't just shove them off." No matter who comes into the office, he's going to sit down with them and give them his time. That's important. No matter who it is, you're interested in them, and you respect them. We do the same thing with our members and fans: whoever wants to come by, we'll talk to them.

ADMINISTRATION AND DEVELOPMENT

DAVID ISAACSON

SINCE 2001, David Isaacson has been the administrative director at Heyday. David's keen sense of humor insures that Heyday is a playful place to work, especially since David is in charge of hiring others into the fold. His vigilance with Heyday's financial well-being has sustained the organization.

My job is primarily to do the finances—all the bookkeeping and account-ing—and to make sure things are running smoothly on a day-to-day basis, but I wear many hats: I'm also the human resources contact and the office manager, and I manage facilities, from taking out the garbage to whatever needs to be done around here. Any problems people have, I see what we can do to solve them. I've been here a little over eleven years, so I'm still a rookie compared to Rebecca, who's been here for fifteen years, or Jeannine, who's been here for over twenty years. But I'm moving up the food chain.

It's a fun, comfortable place to work. We all enjoy coming to work for the most part. It's a fairly small, close-knit group of people. I've worked in large corporations, in all different kinds of work environments, but I like working in a small company. This is probably the longest job I've ever had in terms of staying with it. It's the personalities here. We all get along for the most part. We know each other's foibles. The people make a big difference. Fighting with coworkers all the time can be problematic. Also, the work that we do is interesting; there's always something new going on and a lot of activity in the office, people coming in and out all the time.

I moved to California from Detroit a long time ago. I was going to Wayne State University, in inner-city Detroit, and working at restaurants to help pay for college. I went for almost two years and then dropped out. Working full-time, going to school full-time, and trying to have a life as a twenty-year-old full-time didn't really mix! Back then, a college education was a good thing to have, but it wasn't a necessity. Growing up in working-class Detroit, there were always the factories to go to, GM, Ford, and Chrysler. My father had a job working for General Motors as a security guard.

In the mid-eighties, when I was in my mid-twenties, I decided to drive out to California and had a blast. When I got here, I asked myself, "Why am I living in Detroit?" By the early eighties there was mass migration out of Detroit, a lot of factories were closing down, the jobs were gone, and people were following them elsewhere. The economy of Detroit was radically changing.

I moved to San Francisco and changed my career path. I'd spent most of my free time in Detroit at the movies or at B. Dalton, really the only bookstore in Detroit. So I got an entry-level job at B. Dalton. Within six months I got promoted to assistant manager. Six months after that, I got my own store. I'd had managing experience at the restaurants, so that background helped. I spent about five years with Dalton. Eventually I found a job managing an independent bookstore called Minerva's Owl in San Francisco for a few years, then had my own bookstore, but it wasn't capitalized as well as it should have been. I learned a lot from that experience. I finally ended up at UC Press to get more into the publishing side of the business. When I saw the ad for Heyday, I remembered selling Heyday books when I was a bookstore manager and owner, so I decided that it would be a good company to work for.

UC Press and Heyday are wildly different companies to work for. In smaller companies, there's so much more variety and opportunity and a lot less bureaucracy. Getting things done is much easier. If you want to get it done today, just do it today! In a large company, it takes three months to go through committees, and a year later they decide, no, we're not going to implement that change. I remember at UC Press I was recording information in their MS-DOS system. By then Excel spreadsheets were all the rage. I told my boss, "I can convert this document in a couple of hours, and it will be much easier to use."

"Oh, no, we can't convert that. That'll mess up our system." Or, "We've been doing it this way for the last twelve years."

I got the sense that change is not a good thing. I'd think, "But you can do it better!" No. There was little incentive to make things better in larger organizations. So it wasn't a good fit for me. Instead, I've loved working with Heyday for the last eleven years.

As soon as I walked in for the interview, I felt a much different vibe about the place. Back then, Heyday was at 2054 University, on the fourth floor; it was a funky old building. There was a hippie sensibility about the office, like "Hey, everything's cool. So the carpet's a little frayed; we can work with that. The chairs don't match. That's not important." For me it was a "Welcome to Hippie World" after coming from Corporate World. The UC Press office was only two blocks away, but it was a world of difference. Still, it felt more comfortable to me, a good place to be.

I liked Malcolm right away. I remember in the interview he said, "Hey, come work for this company. We don't have any money!"

I thought, "He's kidding, right? He must have *some* money!"

But when I started working for him and first looked at the accounting, I realized he didn't fudge it during the interview: they *were* broke! I thought, "He's really doing this on a shoestring *and* on a wing and a prayer." I remember walking into his office and saying, "I just got a chance to look at the books, and you can't afford me!"

He looked at me like I was crazy. "But we just hired you. You want the job, right?"

"Yeah, I want the job, but it's going to be a struggle here."

I realized we were going to have to figure out a way to make the business run. I look back on it now, amazed that I stuck around the first couple of months, because it was a confusing and unstable muddle. But I had to provide my livelihood, even though I took a pay cut to come here. I'd just left a job, so I couldn't leave a job again so soon. Also, I knew I didn't want to go back to a bureaucratic environment. I was extremely motivated to try something new, to get into an environment like Heyday, which I thought was a company I could grow with.

Heyday also had an eclectic mix of stuff that attracted me. They weren't like your typical publishers that just published one kind of thing. At the time I joined Heyday, the quarterly magazine *Bay Nature* had just started, which was intriguing to work on. Heyday also had a nonprofit arm called the Clapperstick Institute when I joined. Both *Bay Nature* and *News from Native California* were handled by Clapperstick primarily. Malcolm had just started getting grants a few years before, so Clapperstick helped provide a nonprofit venue for Heyday, as well as for the magazines. Then there were the Heyday books. The bookkeeping was a nightmare! It took years to get it all untangled.

Malcolm then and now likes to stay on top of things. Back then he was more of a micromanager. He worked fifteen hours a day and knew everything that was going on, but after a while that takes a toll. He's gotten better over the years because we've expanded so fast that he can't stay on top of everything. He had to give up some things, focus his energies, and be more productive.

Over time I took on more responsibilities, doing the human resources component, too. We have benefits for employees, so I do the insurance and all that. As people either left or as we made changes in the organization, I took on more of the day-to-day operational aspect of things. I enjoy it. Each day is different. Parts of my job I don't like so much, but every job has that. I'm not crazy about doing insurance forms. Doing the taxes is not the most glamorous. But I enjoy the accounting and overseeing things. I have a chance to have input in areas I wouldn't if I worked for a large corporation.

When it comes to hiring, we look for people with a sense of humor, people who can laugh at things. I don't want to work with people that are really serious or boring or uptight. I guess I look for those aspects unconsciously when I'm interviewing people, to see if they do have a sense of humor *and* the ability to get along. It's hard to explain Heyday's culture. We all laugh and get along very well. We have a lot of smart people working here. Actually, sometimes I think we're too smart for ourselves. If you get too many smart people in a room and you ask a question, you're going to get eighty-five different opinions. That can be frustrating. But I look for people with a sense of humor and intelligence. They don't need to have direct experience. It's nice if they have certain skills; some of our jobs require a little experience in certain areas, but for the most part you're looking for *people*, not job descriptions.

I hired Diane, for example, to be the operations person, which meant sitting in front of a computer, taking orders on the phone, talking with a warehouse, creating invoices—a lot of data input, which Anna does now. Probably both Diane and I realized when I hired her that she wouldn't stick around more than a couple of years in *that* position. She'd want to do something else. In her interview, Diane talked about selling her house and spending the previous two years traveling around the world, having fun. I knew she was the kind of person that could get bored easily and required challenges, while the operations job requires enjoying a day-to-day routine.

Also during the interview I found out that Diane had gone to the California Academy of Art and had an art background. In the back of my mind, I thought that if she got bored with this job, she could do other things at Heyday. So when Rebecca was going out on maternity leave and we needed someone with both technical expertise and a creative background to fill her position, we had Diane step in. Diane's also a likeable person, very outgoing. I seek that kind of person for Heyday, someone who can fit in with the environment. If you're going to be at work for eight or ten hours a day, you want people you enjoy being around. No grumpy folks! You look for people who actually want to be here. We all have our bad days, but for the most part, we're pretty much in a good mood.

ANNA PRITT

ANNA PRITT HAS been the operations manager at Heyday since October 2006. On the morning of the interview, author Adam David Miller had brought Anna roses from his home because he appreciates her so much.

I grew up outside Philadelphia in Swarthmore, went to college at Middlebury College in Vermont, and was an English major. I love books, reading books, writing about books. When I finished college, I moved to the San Francisco area, and I've been in Berkeley for about eight years.

I was the clerk at a video store and enjoyed that, but I wanted something a little different. A friend of a friend, Kim Hogeland, used to work at Heyday. She still does a lot of work with *News*. They were interviewing for a receptionist position. I interviewed and did *not* get that job, but I'd met David and Lillian. In the interview David mentioned that another job might open up in a couple of months. When Rebecca was going on maternity leave, Diane moved from operations into Rebecca's role. So I called David and said, "Hey, what about that other position?" David remembered me and told me to come by and talk about it. They hired me on the spot.

My job deals with day-to-day operations. I process all the orders from individuals, wholesalers, bookstores, and Amazon. Every day I send a little packet of info to our warehouse in San Leandro, called Fulfillco, telling them what to ship to whom. When the warehouse gets our returns, I process that paperwork, too. Another part of the job is billing people and other customer service. I do the accounts for printers, office supplies, deposits, and all that. The computer system we use, Acumen, tracks stock, royalties, bills, all kinds of customer information. So I do a lot of different things. I work closely with David; he does the bill paying, getting money *to* people, while I'm getting money *from* people.

My previous work experiences were some preparation. Clerking at the video store had given me familiarity with databases. And in college I'd worked at the video library, so I was familiar with the point-of-sales system, money handling, and database management, inputting information consistently so it can be pulled out efficiently. As David says, "Garbage in, garbage out!" Diane trained me, and it was great to have that overlap. For a while I would bring an order to her. She'd look through it and clarify problems. After a week or two of that, she said, "Now you're on your own."

My position also requires sharing a small office with David, so when he was hiring, I'm sure he was thinking, "Who do I want to spend eight hours a day with five days a week?" Our working closely together means getting along personality-wise, especially being able to joke back and forth. He puns a lot. I think I'm an easygoing person, and he could probably tell that we'd get along. Six years later, I think we do! When he goes on vacation, I feel really lonely.

Malcolm was not part of the interview process; I met him later. Before I met him, I knew about the beard. When I did meet him, I found him soft-spoken, but everything he said, he *meant*. It had a reason. He didn't just talk to talk. I had a sense that he wasn't super hands-on every day, but he was definitely the guiding force behind Heyday. It's his baby. Once I got to know Malcolm, it became obvious he enjoys being involved in all parts of Heyday but in an advisory role, the man behind the curtain.

He still looks at the little packet of orders I put out every day. When I first started, sometimes he'd send it back with little notes like "Are you sure they wanted that book and not this book?" "Are you sure this is the right discount?" It was interesting that somebody who had so many other responsibilities took the time to look at what I was doing. Sometimes in the beginning I did make some mistakes. I'd be mortified when he'd catch one but also very grateful because then I could correct it. He'd write a nonchalant little note that I'd find in my box. I'd just think, "Oh, okay." It was usually easy to fix. I'm not sure how closely he looks at the info these days. I can't say I make zero mistakes now, but they're rare.

I've been able to try different things here. I like to learn new things, like seeing what's new in the monthly sales reports, how it changed from last year, or designing new reports for analyzing data, which we review in our sales meetings. Once a month in our sales meetings, we talk about which titles are moving, which aren't, and why not, what we can do to promote our books better. We might ask, "Why is Barnes and Noble moving half of our books but not the other half? Should we call up the buyer?" We talk about e-books, how the sales are going, which books will soon be in e-book format. We look at books that will be coming out a year from now, and which books will be reissued with a new cover, a new version.

I love the flexibility here, in that Heyday trusts me to make my own schedule. I come in when I want; I take lunch when I want. I don't punch a clock. Because I deal with a lot of the customer service stuff, I need to be here a lot of the time to get the calls and faxes, to make sure that when somebody has a question, it gets addressed. But when I had a relative visiting, I could say, "This week I'm doing half-days; I'll come in each morning, get my essential work done, and then go spend time with my family." You have a lot of autonomy as long as everything gets done and you're not putting your work off onto someone else. We have meetings, but other than that, there's flexibility and trust.

On the other hand, I know Malcolm notices if I'm not here. One time I was sick, but I was able to come in and do the morning work and then go home. He wrote me a note acknowledging it, something like "I know how sick you were, but you still came in." I got the sense that he really appreciated how I took care of my duties. Another time, I was on vacation. He had printed out a painting of a person feeding chickens. He knows I have backyard chickens. He wrote a little note on it, saying, "We're all anxiously awaiting your return." I liked the analogy he was drawing. I think he missed me feeding *him* with the daily orders—who's buying what, which books are moving. It seemed like when I went on vacation, I cut off his supply. He said, "I'm so glad you're back!" and the flow resumed.

The budget problems are the big frustration. I prepare the deposit of all the checks that come in. That number matters a lot for us to get by. Sometimes it feels like if we don't get a big check, if a grant doesn't come through, we'll be out of money in a month! I guess company security is my big worry. Still, I know our paychecks won't bounce because David keeps such a tight eye on the finances. When I first started here, it was exactly like this. The organization has also been like this for almost forty years! At a certain point, it becomes your "new normal," so even if I should be worried about it, it's easier not to.

We've had a couple of consultants coming in. They've all said, "You need to reduce your overhead, increase your revenues." It all sounds very plausible, and everybody's on board, but then the situation keeps going like it's been going. David has an analogy for it: Heyday is riding a bicycle, and as long as we're getting new projects, and things are moving along, we keep moving. But what's really happening is we're riding up a hill, and the hill keeps getting steeper, so we have to peddle harder and harder to go forward. What will happen when it gets too steep and we fall off? I know Malcolm cares about that, and he doesn't want us all dumped out on the street with no jobs suddenly. But it's hard.

I'm not sure what I can do from my position to prevent that from happening, but at least I do my job as well as I can, like providing great customer service and getting a little more involved in the sales, trying to drum up new sales. When I think a customer might like a book, I'll send them a free copy with a note, try to touch base with them, get them to order some. I manage our Amazon account to make sure it looks good and is accurate and that books get shipped in a timely manner.

Most of our customers and our warehouse are in California. I try to be responsive and friendly. When a lot of our customers call me in the morning, they'll have the book either the next day or within two days. A lot of our customers rely on that. Some smaller wholesalers know that when they call me, they can deliver that book to their customer the next day, while East Coast distributors take a week or two if they're not on top of their orders and because shipping takes a longer time.

I *do* hear the feedback that people love to work with us. "You're so easy to work with. We know we're going to get what we ordered." I just heard feedback from a customer about how great it is that we have books about California and the West that other publishers don't. Customers come to Heyday to get all sorts of information about California, books that are well produced, informative, and entertaining. They can be used as textbooks or pleasure reading, so they appeal to a wide range of people.

For example, one person who bought Malcolm's *The Way We Lived* off our website was having it sent to a friend in Virginia. On the website you can write a little comment to include with the book. The comment that she wrote was, "I picked up this book and read it almost in one sitting. It's got some light, funny parts as well as the unavoidable sad parts, but both parts are well worth reading, especially for anyone who calls California home." I was moved by the comment.

Another important aspect of what we do here is cultivating authors. For example, Jack Laws—every time he does a new book, we're all excited. We know it's going to sell, and we love to sell it. Matt Ritter's *A Californian's Guide to the Trees among Us* has also sold really well for us. So I'd love for Matt to do another book. It's great when we have an author that aligns with what we love about Heyday, and they do a book that people love to buy. Then when you think about Jack Laws, you think about Heyday because we carry his books. It'd be good to have such authors do more books. It strengthens our backlist, and we become more of a "go-to" company. "Do you want a field guide? Well, we've got those."

I love the environment at Heyday and working with David. In such close quarters as we are in our little office, it's good we get along. I feel like everybody who works here is bright and interested in what they're doing every day and wants to be here. We have great conversations about work, books, and life. Another thing is everyone's always laughing. We find so much to joke about. They're laughing often enough that I can distinguish among fifteen people. "That's Gayle. That's Diane." I love that. It's fun, not just drudgery. Even little interactions are really positive. Even if we're talking about a problem or something that's gone wrong, it's done in a positive way, with the sense that we're all tackling it together.

MARILEE ENGE

A MORE RECENT HEYDAY arrival, Marilee Enge was hired in September 2011 as the director of development and publishing partnerships. Helping keep Heyday afloat financially is a huge responsibility, one that Marilee clearly takes to heart. Like others at Heyday, she brought a strong set of skills but found Heyday helps her grow in new ways, as she seeks to help Heyday grow.

I'm from Alaska. I came here to college at San Francisco State, then returned for my first real job back in Alaska as a journalist. I was a newspaper reporter at the *Anchorage Daily News* for ten years. Then I returned to California and was at the *San Jose Mercury News*.

In Alaska, Native affairs was one of the things I reported on, and I was really passionate about it in my writing career. In Alaska, the Native presence is much more mainstream. Native people are in commerce and government and part of the everyday life there. It was certainly a major beat at the *Anchorage Daily News*. We had someone who covered Native affairs. And then everybody wrote about it to some extent because it's such a rich subject area there.

So when I came to California, I often sought out stories about Native California, but it just didn't rise to the level of interest of a major metropolitan newspaper. I'd bought *The Ohlone Way*, read it, read about Malcolm, and became aware of other Heyday books and *News from Native California*. I loved the idea that Malcolm was writing about and continuing to publish stories about Native California, especially since it was not such an obvious subject to publish about or part of everyday discourse in the Bay Area newspapers, so I was intrigued that someone out there was as interested as I was in the Native world. Heyday seemed like a great organization. I always thought it would be really wonderful to work here.

When I started to work on the cultural desk at the *Mercury News*, I'd see Heyday review copies come through all the time. I was fascinated that Heyday was branching out and doing all these anthologies and things that were broader than I was even aware of. I live in Berkeley, so I was also intrigued that there was a small publisher right here.

I finally left the *Mercury News* in 2007 amidst a big set of layoffs and buyouts. I went to Audubon California as a grant writer, which was a big career switch, the first time out of newspapers in my adult life. In my four years at Audubon, we worked with Heyday some, publishing four small Laws habitat guides to the Bay Area. So I was aware of Heyday's work in natural history.

I eventually met Malcolm at a big National Audubon Society gala, and he said, "Come over and visit sometime! Come tour the place." I was too shy to follow up on that then. The second time I saw him was at a donor cultivation event. Malcolm was there telling stories since he's a good story-teller, and he's a good friend of Graham Chisholm, the executive director of Audubon at the time. We connected again, and Malcolm said, "Come by! Visit anytime." I still didn't follow up on that.

A third time I met him at an Indian event, and he said, "Come over." So I did! I made an appointment to visit, and we started talking. I could tell it would be fun to work with him. I said, "I'd love to work for you if there were ever an opportunity, if there's an opening."

He said, "Unfortunately, we don't pay much, and we don't have any openings now; we rarely do." But the next time I dropped by, he said, "You know what? We have an opening for a development director. What do you think?" So we moved forward, and before too long, I was working here!

Probably like everyone else, I found Malcolm funny and charming. I remember that we had a conversation at a philanthropy lunch at the Yocha Dehe Indian tribe up in the Capay Valley. He was warm and witty, joking about how Heyday should set up a casino because, like the tribe, we're in the fundraising business. He said, "Let's get some tribal land and have a

Left to right: Jeff Lustig, George Young, and Leanne Hinton at the Heyday Harvest fundraiser, Berkeley, 2008. (HEYDAY ARCHIVES)

casino." Little did I know that that was a running joke with him. Not long after, he launched the Berkeley Roundhouse! So the idea of there being a roundhouse—a virtual one, anyway—here in Berkeley became a reality.

My journalism background was helpful because I know a lot about many different things in California, and Heyday covers a lot of subjects related to California. I'd been an environmental writer at the *Mercury News*, so I knew about the Bay Area environmental world. My secondary title is "director of publishing partnerships." The idea was to help with the projects we develop with institutions, like Audubon, Santa Clara University, and the Bancroft Library, all those important partners. So my job is a crossover between fundraising and project development because the funding comes with the projects.

As a nonprofit, Heyday gets about half of its budget from the sale of books and the rest from contributed revenue. Heyday enjoys different kinds of philanthropic support. Some comes from partners who contribute money to help with the publication of a book. We love those kinds of funding sources because we can work with another nonprofit to create a book that then has an institutional foothold—perhaps through sales or a course adoption.

The rest comes from traditional foundations, such as the Irvine Foundation, which was a very generous supporter of our work in the Central Valley and in the Inland Empire for ten years. The S. D. Bechtel, Jr. Foundation has been another longtime, generous supporter that has funded specific book projects and broader operating support.

Many of the grants go back to relationships that Malcolm formed, perhaps with the executive director of an organization. Eventually, he was invited to submit a proposal. Then the grant writer shapes a proposal around a conversation that Malcolm had with that person. Many of the past grants to Heyday have been for specific book projects. Malcolm will meet a funder interested in the natural world of California, for example, and say, "We'd like to do a book on drawing birds. Would you like to support this book?"

With more information, the funder might say, "Yes, we'd love to make a grant to support that."

So those conversations that Malcolm has had eventually evolve into formal requests. I often sit in on those conversations. We also try to make sure they are focused on projects we want to do anyway.

The other piece of our support comes from individuals. That's 10 to 15 percent of our budget. We get many substantial gifts from generous funders who give through their own personal or family foundations or their annual giving to Heyday at the $1,000 to $5,000 range. We have the Publishers Club, so we send letters to people annually asking them to renew their support. A lot of those gifts come in the $25 to $100 range, which is great, too. Of course, we do annual appeals to everyone on our list who has ever given. And we also do events, like the annual fall fundraiser, the Heyday Harvest, that raise money. That helps.

Grant writing itself is always about telling a story. The first step is finding a funder or foundation that supports what you do, because if they don't support publications, no matter how great a story you tell, they're not going to give you money. So it has to be a fit with the foundation's guidelines. Nine times out of ten, there has to be a relationship there before you write a grant proposal. Then you tell a compelling story about why their money will make a difference for the organization. Usually there's also a good background of the organization, what it has accomplished over the years, how it's continued to stay relevant, how their support will be valuable to the community by supporting Heyday.

You put together a budget that's very clear and shows where that money will fit into the organization's spending plan and how it will help. Also, most funders don't want to be alone; they want to see that you have a broad base of support, that other organizations are also contributing.

I've been trying to move Heyday to request more general funding for our core operating costs since that's the hardest thing for any organization to support. Supporting rent and salaries is a harder sell, but it also leads to much healthier finances if we can just get people to support core operations. And we can still talk about the many books we can publish with that core support. So far, I've moved several foundations from giving project-specific support to operating support.

On the other hand, a compromise is finding funders who will give us a grant for a *group* of titles, like our nature titles, or for an imprint of a series, so we aren't tied into using it for just one title, but can spread it over a group of books.

We've been doing a lot of proposals for the Berkeley Roundhouse. That's an area we're having a lot of success in fundraising for because there are funders that will give specifically for Native California art and cultural projects. And no one else is publishing books about California Indians. Plus we've expanded it into more programming and participating with Native cultural events, so that's working out really well.

One thing we try to do is reach out to individuals interested in a subject—like natural history or emerging authors or California Indians—and connect them to the books, make sure they're familiar with related books we've done, and we invite them to events where we're celebrating those books and the authors. Once you show them what the work is, how lively and exciting it is, the place sells itself. Larger donors require a lot of groundwork—phone calls and proposal writing—to get the right proposals in front of the right funders. Malcolm is usually key. If we can get people to talk to Malcolm, they'll easily fall in love with the place because his enthusiasm is infectious. So the best strategy is often to get people to come take a look around, peek into the computers of the editors and designers, and see how the books come to life. I sometimes wonder why this publisher has survived when others didn't. Partly it's Malcolm's force and personality. He has such a wide, voracious appetite for ideas and people and cultures. He's been nimble, too, able to look at things with fresh eyes.

He's also not paid any attention to finances, and the accounts will attest to that! He's never let the fact that a book wasn't likely to sell many copies stop him from publishing, or the fact that he didn't have any subsidy going into it. He just loves these ideas and the people who come in with them—like the kite photography of Cris Benton, who has the quirky hobby of photographing salt ponds from the air. Malcolm's enthusiasm and passion for a project will make it come to life. He feeds off other people who have these passions and extraordinary perspectives to share with the world. They come to Heyday and are given a very enthusiastic, open-armed audience with Malcolm and the rest of the staff and whoever happens to be here at the time. Can you imagine that first meeting between Jack Laws and Malcolm, the two most enthusiastic people on the planet?! That's fun to be part of.

It's also a challenge. I've learned so much since I came here. I was a grant writer at Audubon, but since I've been here I've done a lot more. I led a development planning session with the board of directors. I've organized a staff retreat, launched a strategic plan, and hired a consultant to talk about capacity building. I never knew how to do some of these things before I came to Heyday. Malcolm gave me the chance.

I've never worked at a place where I felt so comfortable with my boss, so supported, like anything I did was okay. It's an unusual workplace in that you don't feel you're being critiqued or evaluated. You just feel supported. It's subtle. Malcolm has never gone to a management training workshop. He's never had a human resources officer tell him how to talk to employees. There's something about being drawn in every morning with his amazement at something he's seen. Then we have a conversation about regular business. Everything's always fine with him. I can't even think of an example when he's said, "That's a terrible idea." He's just been incredibly supportive.

For example, this funder said, "We really need to see what Heyday is doing about planning for the future. We're not going to give you money until we know you have some strategic planning in place."

So I went to Malcolm and said, "I think we need to have a staff retreat and get everybody together to talk about the future for our strategic plan."

Having a staff retreat might once have been seen as too conventional, but Malcolm said, "That's a great idea. Let's do that." I knew it wasn't quite in his comfort zone, but he supported the idea. Ultimately, it was a really good exercise to get everyone together to talk about what they value about Heyday and want to preserve as we move into the future.

Malcolm has a constant sense of optimism that everything will work out, and everything is possible. On one level it drives the board crazy because every year when it comes to the budget, they say, "This is terrible. You can't continue like this."

And Malcolm always says, "Oh, don't worry. It will work out." And it does.

Heyday is such a world unto itself. I just love it when Malcolm calls me in to the round table at his office and says, "Would you look at these crazy photographs of salt ponds taken from a kite five hundred feet up in the air!" Or the parade of wonderful people that come to visit. The authors are in and out of the office, so they're part of the family, too. I love the possibility that you can have an idea, take it to Malcolm and Gayle and other people, talk about it, and think, "Wouldn't that be a great book?" And eventually it does become a book! That's pretty exciting.

Or when a brand-new crate full of these *beautiful* books arrives fresh from the warehouse, books crafted with such love by our editors and designers—they're like little jewels. I love being part of all that! As a book lover, it's a treat to put your hands on one of those books the minute they come in the door.

MARIKO CONNER

ARIKO CONNER WAS the assistant to the publisher and a development associate at Heyday at the time of this interview and has since moved into Heyday's marketing department. She is a relatively new person on staff, having started in the fall of 2012.

My original job description said that about half the time I assist Malcolm in various capacities, whether arranging his schedule or doing research for projects that he has a special interest in. The other half of the time, I work in development, fundraising, a whole different bucket of fish: cultivating new individual donors and writing grant proposals and reports for institutional funding. And if something pops up, I'll join in with other activities, like marketing; that's kind of the Heyday way. Like at the California Historical Society, we had a launch party for a book, and I ran the food table there, a power that I was pretty excited at wielding.

As for running Malcolm's calendar, that's like trying to jump on a horse and get the bridle and reins on it while it's already running. I do my best! One of the most useful things I can do is let the rest of the staff know where Malcolm is, a question that's often up in the air. Usually Malcolm will announce he's going somewhere—or he won't announce, but his black book will announce it, so it's my job to put out the fires when he's double-booked. It's only happened once or twice, and only once was it really bad.

I think that kind of disorganization comes from his being a leader and being more of an ideas person, more of a conceptual thinker. With that leadership comes the spirit of expansion, the spirit of adventure, seeking things out, initiating projects. It's useful for me to serve as an assistant because I'm more the kind of person to say, "Okay, let's do the logistics. Let's figure out how to implement the groundwork you laid out." It's good for a leader to have visions, to see what's not there but what *could* be. Sometimes that means little details get lost along the way. I'd say that Malcolm is pretty detail-oriented for being such a big-picture guy. He initiates so many different meetings and travels a lot, but that's part of what Heyday is all about. It's a statewide project, not just people in an office sitting around.

For example, Malcolm has been working with several different boards and funders on a book about the Sacramento Valley that ranges widely from the natural to the cultural, like the arts scene to whatever other aspects they decide are relevant and illuminating about the Sacramento Valley. He hired a researcher, Fred Setterberg, to pull some ideas together. My role was to make a database online, indexing all those notes and making them easily searchable. It was cool when I showed it to Malcolm the first time. He said, "If I weren't your boss, I'd say that's fucking terrific."

I was basically your standard liberal arts grad, with no idea what I was going to do with my degree in this recession. I graduated in 2011 from Carleton in Northfield, Minnesota, where I majored in English and concentrated in environmental studies. I'm still trying to figure out what I want to do eventually, but all the career tests I did pointed to publishing as one path since I majored in English. I'd taken a work-study job at my college in the development office. I figured the skills I gained there could parlay into a nine-to-five office job after college. It was either that or work in the cafeteria again. Once you've washed dishes for a football team, you're completely sour on the entire idea.

Then after college I returned to Berkeley, where my parents live. I applied for and got a one-year fellowship at the Berkeley Repertory Theatre in the development and events department. I worked there for a year, learned a lot, stressed out a lot. After my fellowship ended, I was drifting for a couple of months. It was a little terrifying and a little boring. Then I saw a job-posting board for nonprofits, and I saw "California books." It made me happy to see the info about Heyday, because I'm starting to figure out that I value having a mission that's in line with my goals and values. I also value having a day-to-day job where I'm good at the things that I like and I'm expected to do. Sometimes it can be hard to remember that you're trying to save the world when you get caught up in accounting, but I like Excel, so it's fun.

Actually, I think that if you set yourself up for saving the world, you're going to be completely burned out and disappointed. You're mistaking this huge goal for the progress that you really can make and the things that you really can do that are valuable and will improve society. I think Heyday has done great work to increase the visibility of California Indians and to educate people about all kinds of things in ways that are accessible and interesting and delightful. I don't know if we're changing the whole world, but we're changing a good corner of it for the better.

When I applied here, I had two interviews, the first with Marilee and David. David called later that day and said, "We really liked you. Why don't you come in tomorrow and interview with Malcolm? If he likes you, you've got the job." That idea was both exciting and terrifying! It meant that the interview wasn't going to be "Let's talk about your skills," but "Are you a likeable person?" Rejection from that would be way harder.

I went in to meet Malcolm, and of course, he was still meeting with someone—Fred Setterberg, actually—at the same time. Malcolm asked me to sit in on the meeting. I politely listened. I cracked some jokes which were probably all terrible, but Malcolm laughed. Offhandedly, he said, "You've got the job, by the way." Then he kept talking to Fred! So that was my first impression, which was generally very favorable. I felt very much at ease when I met him.

The thing about working at Heyday for me is that I kind of kicked my foot into the door and stopped them from closing it with my good looks and charm, obviously, and I told them what I thought I was good at. Since then, it's been a dance of finding out what I'm *actually* good at, what else I can do, skills that weren't necessarily on my résumé. There's a lot of great flexibility here. The last two development offices I worked for had big annual budgets, thirteen million dollars at the Rep and hundreds of millions at the college. With all that money come very regimented roles. At Heyday you can say, "I want to run an event for my friend who wrote a book. I think Heyday's audience would really like it, and I'm going to do that *now*." People here would say, "Go for it!"

I love seeing how people interact here, their argument styles, their agreement styles, what people are interested in. With only twelve people who are all more or less on the same level as each other, it can be tricky to navigate sometimes. It's fascinating, a completely different dynamic than anything I've ever seen. I might be one of the few people in the world who really enjoys going to meetings, probably because I have comparably little at stake. I'm not the head of a department, and I'm the most junior member, so I don't have to carry the brunt of the outcomes. I just contribute every once in a while, usually pertaining to Malcolm's calendar or whatever. But I see so many different spins on everything, people coming from very different perspectives—like the sales folks having a different point of view than someone from editorial. I've never been in a workplace where people can be so invested and passionate about things. It's very interesting to me.

In a professional sense, it's really fun to work for Malcolm. I'm sure everyone has talked about the memos we get in our boxes sometimes. "Can you give me a few pages about this incredibly obscure topic?" The other day he had me researching the history of Logan Heights, a neighborhood in San Diego. Barrio Logan next door has Chicano Park with a history much like People's Park in Berkeley. It was fascinating to find out about. It's enlightening to work on things I've never even heard about before.

On a personal note, before I got hired here, I'd become cynical and stressed out about graduating into a horrible recession and finding out that everything I'd studied in school was not valued in the workplace—unless you're like my friends who went into lucrative positions in technology and business with the same big fat degree as I have. Last year, I learned a ton from my Berkeley Rep fellowship, but I had some resentment about being put in the position as a lowly apprentice after doing everything that the system told me was right. It was easy to become jaded about that.

Ever since I started working here, I have a sunnier outlook, due in no small part to Malcolm. He's so willing to look for the good, which is not my natural predisposition. It's just great to be around him, to have that attitude channeled by osmosis into the rest of the people here.

I have this post-it I saved. It was maybe my second week on the job, and I drafted some letter for Malcolm. It was a forty-word thing, not that big a deal at all, but I slaved away on it and stressed out about it. I put the letter in his box. It came back with this note that says, "Perfect."

One time, he was saying, "If I don't choke up at least three times a day, I consider it a wasted day." That's so special—to go out into the world and find something to be *emotional* about, something to care about, and have a strong reaction to. It's very inspiring to be around, a good path to be on.

CHAPTER 10

THE JOURNEY AHEAD

"I love the laughter in the other room. Do you hear it? This is work!
Isn't that wonderful? The place works on laughter, on people
taking and having power." —MALCOLM

THE LAST CHAPTER of the Heyday story actually inaugurates a new beginning as Heyday, at age forty in 2014, faces its future with several changes, challenges, and opportunities ahead. For one, the shipbuilder and captain will naturally retire from the helm one day. Many staff and friends noted in interviews that replacing the charismatic leader of a self-made organization is often difficult, yet Malcolm confronts the question forthrightly here. He also sums up his managerial style and philosophy, a valuable blueprint not only for Heyday but also for other publishers and organizations.

MALCOLM ON HOW TO SUCCEED IN PUBLISHING

I keep coming back to the idea that I've been lucky. People have bailed me out; projects came along at the right time. So I've been lucky. Sometimes you're lucky and you end up attributing your luck to your wisdom, but it's really just luck.

I have no regrets at all. I *have* wondered in the abstract what I would have explored, what else I would have done, what I might have written. I suspect I had the talent to become a first-rung American writer. It's something I wistfully would like to do. But it hasn't been very strong or immediate. It was kind of like wondering what it would be like to be rich or to be something else. It's not a deep desire, just a curiosity: what would have happened to me if I hadn't gotten into publishing?

Malcolm by Reuben Margolin

But I think I've been tremendously creative and tremendously helpful in what I've done. I love what I do! I'm proud of what I've done. I can't imagine having done any better or being any more content or more proud or more at home with what I've done. I can't imagine finding something that better fits all the phases of my personality. There's no way you're going to phrase this as a life of sacrifice. I haven't sacrificed a damn thing.

You have the luxury of being yourself at Heyday. It's so interesting watching people come to work here and bring in a kind of professional demeanor, then watch them lose it and take on their own voice, instead of having to pretend to be someone else. I see them begin to speak from a core of their personality, where their true power lies. You're not just playing a role; your work becomes a vehicle for self-expression. There's tremendous force when people get to be who they are.

Being yourself is essential, but it is not sufficient. You have to be your best self. You have to strive, dream big dreams, risk failure. You have to understand that it's permissible to fail, but you also have to understand that it's a hell of a lot better to succeed.

My advice to anyone wanting to start such a thing as Heyday is to learn to be entertaining. Learn to tell good stories. Also, create a level of honesty to the place. There's not much hidden. You're not dealing with secret cabals and power structures. It's just assumed that people are going to do their best work because they'd disappoint the people around them if they didn't. And we do tremendously valuable, worthwhile things. The work is valued by people that work here.

Also, I feel that people have genuine power here. I'm not all that competent at certain things, so people come in and rescue me. I'm happy to be rescued, and they relish their role. I don't think I've stolen all the juice, all the power. I genuinely appreciate what people do. I'm just astounded when people do something I'm incapable of. The other day I was watching Gayle do something on the computer with images and text. It was so astonishing, just a thrill to see. Someone brings in some amazing images, and I'll invite other people in to witness. The other day a friend came in and was telling me stories. It was so damn wonderful that I started feeling guilty that I had it all to myself, so I invited other people in.

I feel that the place is fairly expandable, full of opportunity. There's a relative egalitarianism among the people that work here at Heyday. The jobs are not too tightly defined. The jobs are built around people; people aren't built around the jobs.

On the other hand, I'm clearly at the top. There can be a feeling that everybody's dependent upon my own goodwill. There are no performance evaluations, none of the ordinary protections. We don't have an organizational chart, though people claim that we should be more organized, that it would be a lot better if people knew exactly what they were responsible for. I suppose it would look smoother if Heyday were better organized. In some ways it's a game of chicken.

I was reading about the history of cities recently. In the early days, in the city's center, craftsmen, like silversmiths or printers—people with a particular craft—would take apprentices into their shops. They worked closely with their apprentices, teaching the skills involved. Then when the factory system got developed in the 1830s and 1840s, labor was degraded into routine work, with foremen supervising the workers. The owner now became a planner or finance minister.

This place is still in that craftsman stage, with an apprenticeship system going on. That's not true elsewhere. I wasn't conscious of making it an apprenticeship model, or any model. But that's what it is.

Some people have talked about my capacity to choose good people. They said that in the job interviews, I never asked anyone if they could type, but instead I wanted to know who the hell they were. *That's* the big question!

When we were hiring someone for the Berkeley Roundhouse, to run the Indian publishing program, one of our board members asked if we had a scoring system for hiring somebody. I said, "Scoring?! We never did that." But I *did* have a list of what I was seeking for that position. The list included laughter, a positive outlook, being funny, and a whole bunch of other qualities that make for a good person. That approach may have something to do with the harmony of the place.

This thing about being mythologized at this stage in my life, becoming a "cultural treasure" before I'm even dead: there's the image of somebody who has clear goals and fulfills clear expectations, sets out to do something in this world. I never did! I just did what was in front of me.

I remember when Amy Hunter was working here, for a while she was having a really rough time. I said, "Come on, we're gonna take care of it."

We took a walk and went off to a bowling alley. I took her bowling. She beat me. And she was happy.

I don't make plans and never have, much. I can't use computers very well. I'm completely inept at systems, and I don't have organizational charts. The assumption that I know what I'm doing is vastly overrated. When I interview people for a job here and I want to know who they are, it's not that I have a theory about it. It's the only question that I know how to ask.

Some people become part of Heyday by riding in on our sea of friendships, our shared passions. There's Graham Chisholm, for example. I met him when he was head of California's Nature Conservancy, then he moved over to the Audubon Society. We worked on projects together, like with the Cosumnes River Preserve. Graham had an intelligence and a social grace but also a playfulness that I really understood. At the same time as he could be playful, he knew everybody in California related to the environment and politics.

When he left the Audubon, he was out in the world, so I just suggested he have a desk here at Heyday. "You need a phone, you need people to be around, just take a desk." Then he ended up giving us some advice and helping with some of his foundation contacts and with our strategic plan. He's run a couple of large organizations, so he has a sense of how they run. He talks to the board. He attends our finance committee meetings because he understands finance. He understands a lot of things I don't understand. But like other developments here, it's unplotted. He's not on the payroll, but he uses a desk, and we work together collegially. He's an extraordinary friend.

I had lunch recently with Tony Platt. He wrote a book, *Grave Matters,* that we published. He had just retired from Sacramento State University and was talking about how harsh the university is, how people claw their way to the top, and once they're at the top they keep clawing. I don't want people like that around me. People that work here aren't like that at all.

Yet when you run an enterprise, you think you have to hire ambitious people who are trying to get ahead and willing to screw over others. I don't think that's necessary. I think you should hire people that are kind, smart, and fun to be with. Smart and funny are two important things. Funny is really important to me. There's a wonderful saying: "The world's best surfer is the one who's having the most fun." It's about keeping the social culture strong, working among friends. My first rule of publishing is to deal only with people you like. And the second rule of publishing is that anything that gets you out of the office is good. But it's really dealing with people you like—*and* being loyal to them.

When I introduce people around here, I say that this is someone who works *with* me, not someone who works for me. I'm very clear about that. If they were all to walk out on me, I'd just walk out with them. I'd join them. If they were carrying picket signs, I'd go out and carry a picket sign with them.

There has been a filtration, though. Some people don't last. When my last assistant found out who she was, she left; she wanted to write. Or projects don't work out. I've had people that I haven't liked. But I find that if I ignore them, they eventually go away. Some people who worked here were not at the top of their professional form, but they were all friends, and they did good work. Of course, if someone becomes damaging, you have to do something. I do fire people. That's been really hard. I do not enjoy it. As a matter of fact, it's been traumatic for the whole damn office whenever I fired anybody. It calls attention to the fact that there's no conventional structure here, no formal evaluation process.

Another thing about Heyday that keeps people engaged is that it's not specialized and narrow, so you end up having crosscurrents of intellectual work, enough to keep people's interests stirring. You have Native American, Japanese, natural history, poetry, art, social justice—all kinds of topics. You're not just burrowing into one particular area. That also makes for a positive environment.

People generally think good work and enterprise mean one has to be self-sacrificing. According to that concept, for me to do good would mean I'm leading a life of denial, but that's just not the case. There's a tremendous amount of self-indulgence in my life.

For me, work has been always important—even for someone who almost never had a job in his whole life except for publishing and writing. It helps me that I was functionally unemployable. Would I make a good employee? Only at Heyday. And how many places like Heyday are there? I'm lucky here. I tend to get my way. It's lucky that my way is a way that doesn't put other people down or exploit them. So I can just go ahead and do stuff that is completely self-defined and unconventional.

We were doing a book on the history of the federal courts, and a bunch of lawyers we were working with wanted a contract. So I wrote up a contract with a clause like this: "Both parties understand that this agreement is entered into with a spirit of celebration, adventure, and a sincere desire to bring valuable knowledge to the public. Both parties pledge their best efforts toward making a worthy book and toward a rewarding, humane, and joyous experience in the collaboration of its making." It put them completely on tilt because they'd never seen a contract like this. The contracts they're used to are based on opposition. And they loved it.

BRIDGING DUALITIES

I have tried to set a tone here. The first thing I tell people about a manuscript that comes in is that before you criticize it, before you start correcting it, make sure you understand what's right about it, where the power is. Look for what's good in it. That becomes the kernel, the core. Make sure you work on bringing the power out in something rather than shaping something to your image of it. I look at the people in these books, these little furnaces of passion and integrity, and I'm realizing what is beautiful in them, relating to that.

I grew up in a culture of criticism, and we know how damaging that is. So I avoid that. When I do criticize, I hope it's in helpful ways. If there's a trick that I know when it comes to conflict, it's to embrace rather than to push away. To grow bigger than something. It's a kind of aikido. When you're in conflict with somebody, you don't push against them. You use their own strength to find another way in. It's not my will against your will. You accommodate the other person's will and use it. There's something in that process that I think I'm pretty good at. It's seeing what somebody has to offer that nobody else could offer, and then expanding upon that. Get the vision big enough. Peter Nabokov commented on my use of the word "capacious." That's what it is. It's enlarging and embracing, not either/or. It's big enough to include all things.

I don't really have much anger in me. Maybe that's part of if. Other people walk around with all this anger and look for places to dump it. I'm not too angry about anything.

Maybe it's an avoidance of conflict. Or I just pick my battles, and in the few battles I pick, I play to win. Let me tell a story about Bart Abbott, and it's even relevant, too. We did this book called *Jack London's Daughter* by Joan London, one of Jack London's daughters. She couldn't get it published, and then she died. Joan's son, Bart Abbott, brought it to me. I thought it was a wonderful story, and I decided to publish it.

It was the story of Joan and her sister, Becky, who were from the first wife, before Jack ran off with Charmian. For them their father was this distant figure who'd disappeared. As he grew more and more famous, he grew more and more distant. So it was the story of this young girl worshipping her father, craving some kind of approval or association, something she badly needed. In the end, Joan writes him a letter asking him for some small sum of money for school. He writes her back, saying:

> Let me tell you a little something about myself....When I grow tired or disinterested in anything, I experience a disgust which settles for me that thing forever. I turn the page down there and then....[U]nfortunately, I have turned the page down, and I shall be no longer interested in...you....
>
> Unless I should accidentally meet you on the street, I doubt if I shall ever see you again. If you should be dying, and should ask for me at your bedside, I should surely come; on the other hand, if I were dying, I should not care to have you at my bedside.

It was such a cruel letter! Such a cruel, soul-crushing letter.

Milo Shepherd, London's cousin, had the Jack London estate, so he had the rights to decide on uses of the archive. I wrote to Milo, saying I'd like to use that letter. Milo replied, "You can't. I'm not going to let anybody reprint that letter."

So I wrote him back, saying, "If you don't let me reprint it, I'm going to paraphrase it and then comment on it. And by the time I'm through paraphrasing it and commenting on it, you'll wish I'd just used the original." I went up there, and we had a good talk. I got the letter from him after all. And we published the book.

How do we hold all of the tragedy—and all the joy—around us? This is one of the great stories that I've heard and experienced in my lifetime: Mahatma Gandhi's grandson Ramchandra Gandhi comes into town. I'm showing him around and setting up readings for him and various things. One day we're up at the office in the Koerber Building and he says, "I would like to know more about your Jewish background. I would like to meet your rabbi."

I said, "You're thirty years too late. I've dropped out of that world. But there's a Jewish museum in town, the Magnes Museum. Let's go there. We'll look at some of the displays, I'll talk about how I grew up, and we'll discuss what it meant to be a Jew."

He said, "That would be very good."

So I call up Seymour Fromer, who was the head of the Magnes Museum. I tell him, "Listen, Seymour, I've got Mahatma Gandhi's grandson Ramchandra Gandhi here. We're going to be over there in fifteen minutes. Can you give him the royal treatment? This is a world-class man. Let's treat him well."

Fifteen minutes later, I arrive with Ramchandra Gandhi, and Seymour already has the newsletter editor, a photographer, and the chairman of his board assembled. Seymour knew how the world ran.

We're looking around. Everything is just so wonderful, so polite. We're looking at images of a wonderful old synagogue at Cochin in Kerala. I actually visited there once. It was created after the destruction of the Second Temple in Jerusalem. The Jews fled to India centuries ago. It served until the fifties and sixties, when everyone went back to Israel. When I saw that temple, a couple of old men were hanging around. It reminded me of some of the California Indian communities I had seen, where people described what once had been. And this was my own culture. I was so touched by it.

Then we looked around at some other exhibits and talked. We're walking around, and it's utterly pleasant. We get up to the third floor, the Holocaust room. The place is gloomy, the photographs chilling. The artifacts are dusty and gray, and there's the stench of death up there.

Seymour picks this moment to attack Ramchandra. "Have you heard of Hitler?" he says.

Gandhi says, "Of course."

He asks, "Have you heard of the Holocaust?"

Gandhi replies, "Of course."

Seymour angrily says, "This is where we have absolutely no use for people like your grandfather. There are some things for which you cannot be a pacifist. Some things *must* be fought. Some things can *never* be forgiven."

I'm thinking, "This just went to hell in a hurry." We stumble around, make some polite sounds, and walk out.

I was shaken by this encounter. I say, "Listen, Ramu, I'm sorry about what happened, but I don't know what to think. It seems that some things happen that are so horrendous that you can't just forget and forgive. On the other hand, if you dwell on it, it poisons you. No matter what you do, you're screwed. There's no way out of this one."

He said the most astonishing thing. "You know, some things have happened in this world that are so momentous that no *one* of us is big enough to have the full response. Some people like my grandfather will forgive. Some people like Seymour will be full of hatred and anger. Some people like you will be confused. And we need all of us to work out the right response."

It was so capacious, so inclusive. It was the Hindu practice of *advaita*, of bridging the dualities. When you see things in opposition, you rise above them to see what the commonalities are. I saw Ramchandra take this attitude again and again. It was the most instructive and wonderful approach. It gets you beyond a world of right and wrong—for me to be right, you have to wrong. Instead, we can just see the world as a complicated place, and we each have our own ways of going about things.

In the California Indian world I see how white people have gone out and done ridiculous things—folly and stupidity. The crimes were so momentous.

And I see such different responses in the Indian community: some people become Christian, some become old believers, some go in a modern direction. I don't take sides on this. Somehow or other, all of us are working out the solution.

It's become my job as a publisher to embrace all that.

ANXIETY DEFICIT DISORDER

I think of David Risling, who came from a confluence of Hoopa, Karuk, and Yurok tribes. His father was the richest man on the Klamath River. It was religious wealth, the wealth of dance regalia, like red woodpecker scalp and white deerskin. The regalia was brought out for the ten-day dances that were needed to rebalance the earth. Although it may have been an exaggeration, I have heard it said that David's father could outfit everyone for a Jump Dance for all ten days, with different dances every day, and all these different riggings for all the dances.

I remember my friend Julian Lang talking about an old lady up there who fervently wished to see one more dance when the regalia would come out, because the regalia were gods who had turned themselves into regalia so that you could see the beauty of the other world.

Anyhow, David taught at UC Davis. In the sixties all these intertribal organizations were created: California Indian Legal Services, the California Indian Education Association, D-Q University, the Native American Rights Fund. David founded all of them. I once asked him, "How did you do it? How do you found something that lasts? It's hard anywhere, and in Indian country it's almost impossible. Nobody does this kind of thing. How did you do it?"

He said, "The story goes that I created California Indian Legal Services in 1969 in a Chinese restaurant. Actually, I created it several years before. I started by planting seeds."

"Look at who's sitting at the table," he said. "When I set up California Indian Legal Services, I brought in So-and-So, So-and-So. I thought deeply about what an organization needed. I thought that it needed moral governance; it needed money; it needed executive ability, and somebody that understood the law. I looked at everything that it needed, and I made certain that everyone necessary was sitting at that table when it was founded. People think that they have an idea and the money will come, or they have money, so an executive director will come. You have to have it all there at the beginning. If you do, then the organization has a chance of lasting." He had this wonderful kindness and wisdom.

I said, "I've been planting seeds all my life, and I don't get permanent institutions."

He says, "No, Malcolm, you throw seeds around! I plant them." I thought that was pretty good.

I don't know how it is that, on the one hand, this place is an extension of me, but at the same time I have a sense of detachment about it. It's not that I feel it's unimportant. It's just out of my control. I can't control *myself*, let alone control my kids or anybody else! I'm forever making resolutions to be a better person and failing at them. So if I can't control myself, what hope is there that I can control the future of Heyday? It's not like driving a car; it's like sailing a boat. You have winds and currents. You tack and reset the rudder. You put up the sail and take it down. You're forever screwing around. You hope you have a destination, and you hope you don't sink. Sometimes the wind dies, in which case you'd better hope you have a chessboard.

When someone takes over, it'll change. I've created a place that's wrapped around my own personality, my strengths and weaknesses. I was not only a publisher; I was also a writer. I had an entrée into different worlds as an intellectual, as a writer, as somebody who's made a contribution to history, to natural history, to the community of Indians, to ethnic stuff.

You're not going to get the same personality walking in. It's going to need a different structure. It'll be somebody that's not going to work all the time, somebody who has keener talents in some areas, maybe less in other areas. I have a tremendous amount of power as the person that created Heyday and is identified with it. No one else is going to have that same power. No one else is going to get away with the stuff that I've gotten away with. It'll change.

My Parkinson's is the elephant in the room in terms of succession planning. I've tried to camouflage the elephant as if it were a sofa, but it's not fooling anybody. It seems wrong not to mention it, but I don't like having people feel sorry for me. I don't like people helping me. So I don't focus on it. It's something that I have, but it doesn't have me. It's the kind of thing that can stamp your identity, but I don't feel it's my identity. I suppose I haven't come to terms with it yet. It's something that's there, off in a corner somewhere, and I keep it off in the corner. Every so often it growls and comes out and causes difficulties. I push it back into the corner. I'm planning to pay absolutely no attention to it until it kills me. I have absolutely no plans to surrender. I'll wait to be conquered.

I'm pushing it, though: I keep going from six in the morning until late at night, and I'm getting closer to the edge. I know that. I just deal with it the best I can. This disease is contemptible. I don't find it very interesting. In fact, I act like maybe if we don't pay any attention to it, it'll go away. I'm still making appointments to give keynote speeches next year. I assume that at some point it won't work. But for now, I keep going.

I have Anxiety Deficit Disorder, too—I simply don't get anxious—and that predominates. Besides, there are so many other wonderful things going on around here to focus on!

I was hiking last summer in Yosemite on a trail back of the Wawona that goes up to some falls. I've been up it many times, hiking this trail for years. It's four miles up to the falls, with a 2,500 foot elevation, so it's fairly steep. I'm hiking up this thing, and I come upon a family of five sitting there, all pooped out, drinking water. They look at me and ask, "Do you know this trail?"

I say, "Yeah, I know it really well."

They ask, "How far are we from the summit?"

I look around. "Oh, just another fifteen minutes or so."

They said, "Oh, good." So they took off. I paused. I hiked for another half-hour and then came upon them on the trail. They said, "Geez, we thought you said it was only another fifteen minutes."

I said, "It's just right around that bend."

So then I hiked ahead of them. An hour later I came to the summit. I realized that I wasn't lying, I have an optimism problem! Truth and beauty are always just ten minutes away.

I don't want there to be problems. I want everything to be easy. And what does it matter how long it took? You get there, and it's just so beautiful. There's this pool of water in the granite, water coming over a rock cliff and breaking into little falls that move around the cliff and come down. The water is cool; the rocks are warm. Azaleas are flourishing out there. Such a beautiful trip into the high country, falling in love with ordinary flowers. Those little phloxes, so simple; they look like a kid drew them. And miniaturized mountain penstemons. They've got a growing season of about three weeks, so they just do what they can. They hang in there. They don't grow very big or colorful. They don't have much time for anything with their fragile little lives. They get pollinated, and then they're buried again. Just so lovely!

So my approach is like on that trail: everything is fifteen minutes away. I think I live in a world of abundance.

The board periodically feels panicked about money and wants to manage things; everybody seems to get into worrying about money. So I talk to the staff or board about what I'm going to do to get us the hell out of the problems, out of that *mentality*. There's just something wrong with it. I tend to live with things. There have been money problems for forty years, and there will always be money problems.

We've done so much here that whether Heyday, as an organization, exists or not, it's still going to have a future, from what other people have carried away from it and with the other institutions that have been created and involved.

I want Heyday to succeed, of course, but I don't feel a possessiveness for it, any more than I feel that my family is "mine." I don't feel that the house is my house. I don't feel that Heyday is my company. People are taking more and more control and authority, and I have absolutely no problem letting them do that. I'm missing that gene. I take great pride in what's here, but not because it's *mine*. I don't know. Maybe I'm conning myself.

There's a strong structure to Heyday; it has a backlist and assets. A publishing company is not a cash cow, it's a cash pig; you have to feed it, and then at the end, you kill it, and you get the benefit of it. With publishing companies, as long as you're producing, you're always in trouble. As long as you're putting out more things, you're always in hot water. Once you stop, you sell out the backlist; you have your inventory, titles that continue to sell. You create something smaller and more stable, as long as it doesn't do anything. That's an economic possibility. I'm not too interested in it, but that's a possibility.

In some ways I'm more worried about the state of publishing in general than I am about Heyday. I'd much rather be a small fish in a healthy pond than a big fish in a pond that's drying up. We depend upon public interest, a quality of intelligence that excites people about a subject area. The more that publishing and the world of the book shrink, the less hold they have on the public imagination. The more the physical book world shrinks, the more you end up losing the infrastructure: the sales reps that put books in bookstores, the bookstores themselves, the skilled printers, the editors and designers. That entire infrastructure begins to wither.

What is the basic work of a publisher? You're fighting for space in people's imagination. And you just have to approach that space through any avenue that you can. The amount of noise from the dominant culture is just so spectacular, so deafening, that the place for a subtle and quiet idea, a deep quiet truth, is very difficult to find. When that noise goes into the mind, it's like something gone bad in the refrigerator, spreading the odor of greed, of anger, of getting ahead, the subtleties of racism, the cruelty of it all—tainting everything. It's hard to get something into the public sphere in a positive form. There's really a fight on for the human imagination.

One time I was at a conference in Berkeley devoted to urban ecology, about creating new cities, making the city ecologically sound. It was very technologically oriented. David Brower was there and others. I was sitting next to Edgar Mitchell, the astronaut. This was a guy who'd been on the moon! So I said, "Hey, you've come a long way to be here."

He said, "Yes, I flew in from Seattle."

I said, "That's not quite what I meant." He had little sense of humor, but I enjoyed talking to him.

It got to be 10:30 at night. I came back to the office, and Julian Lang was waiting for me. We then drove up to the Klamath River in time for a ceremony in the early morning. I was thinking what an amazing world we live in. In the same ten hours you can be talking to somebody who walked on the moon and you can be hearing songs and stories and ceremonies that have existed from the beginning of time in California. It seemed to me unique; this time is not going to last forever. How to hold on to what we can?

And the future? One of the most wonderful metaphors that I keep coming back to is that when the first Polynesians settled Hawai'i from the Polynesian islands, they couldn't pack too much on an outrigger, but they packed twenty-four things with them: breadfruit and taro; the leaves in which you wrap things; pineapple.

As Heyday heads to the future, what do we pack onto the ship? What would we like to bring with us? We have no idea what the future is going to bring; we don't know where we're heading. Which of our assets do we want to put on the ship to send into the future? What needs to be left behind?

I remember something that Diane Lee said, thinking about Heyday's future: "I believe we'll make the appropriate changes as things come up, and it will all fall into place, one small step at a time, as things need to happen. I'm just going to see what unfolds. It could be more amazing than I could have ever imagined."

I like the idea that the Heyday of the future could actually be better than that of the past.

ABOUT THE AUTHOR

KATE BLACK

KIM BANCROFT is a longtime teacher turned editor and writer. She earned a B.A. in English from Stanford, an M.A. in English and a teaching credential from San Francisco State University, and a Ph.D. in education from UC Berkeley. She has taught at various high schools and community colleges in the Bay Area, at the Universidad de Guanajuato in Mexico, and at Sacramento State University. Her classrooms were lively with discussions about culture, society, and identity. Kim has edited several memoirs, including *Ariel: A Memoir,* by Ariel Parkinson (Ariel Imago Publishing, 2012); *The Morning the Sun Went Down,* by Darryl Babe Wilson (Heyday, 1998); and *Ruth's Journey: A Survivor's Memoir,* by Ruth Glasberg Gold (University Press of Florida, 1996). Most recently she edited *Literary Industries*, the 1890 memoir of her great-great-grandfather Hubert Howe Bancroft, historian and founder of the Bancroft Library at the University of California, Berkeley (Heyday, 2013).

HEYDAY

ABOUT HEYDAY

HEYDAY IS AN independent, nonprofit publisher and unique cultural institution. We promote widespread awareness and celebration of California's many cultures, landscapes, and boundary-breaking ideas. Through our well-crafted books, public events, and innovative outreach programs we are building a vibrant community of readers, writers, and thinkers.

THANK YOU

It takes the collective effort of many to create a thriving literary culture. We are thankful to all the thoughtful people we have the privilege to engage with. Cheers to our writers, artists, editors, storytellers, designers, printers, bookstores, critics, cultural organizations, readers, and book lovers everywhere!

We are especially grateful for the generous funding we've received for our publications and programs during the past year from foundations and hundreds of individual donors. Major supporters include:

Anonymous (6); Alliance for California Traditional Arts; Arkay Foundation; Judy Avery; Paul Bancroft III; Richard and Rickie Ann Baum; BayTree Fund; S. D. Bechtel, Jr. Foundation; Jean and Fred Berensmeier; Berkeley Civic Arts Program and Civic Arts Commission; Joan Berman; Nancy Bertelsen; Beatrice Bowles, in memory of Susan S. Lake; John Briscoe; Lewis and Sheana Butler; Cahill Contractors, Inc.; California Civil Liberties Public Education Program; Cal Humanities; California Indian Heritage Center Foundation; California State Parks Foundation; Keith Campbell Foundation; Candelaria Fund; John and Nancy Cassidy Family Foundation, through Silicon Valley Community Foundation; Charles Edwin Chase; Graham Chisholm; The Christensen Fund; Jon Christensen; Community Futures Collective; Compton Foundation; Creative Work Fund; Lawrence Crooks; Nik Dehejia; Chris Desser and Kirk Marckwald;

GETTING INVOLVED
To learn more about our publications, events, membership club, and other ways you can participate, please visit www.heydaybooks.com.